Published by The Rebel Publishing House GmbH

That Art Thou

Bhagwan Shree Rajneesh

Fifty-one discourses given by Bhagwan Shree Rajneesh
in January, March and October of 1972
at Meditation Camps in Mt. Abu and Matheran
on the
Sarvasar Upanishad
Kaivalya Upanishad
Adhyatma Upanishad

Editing by Ma Dhyan Sagar, B.A.
Typing by Ma Dharma Pratito, Ma Anand Shahida, M.A.
Design by Ma Dhyan Amiyo
Production by Swami Prem Visarjan, Swami Prem Ramarshi, M.A.(Cantab)

Published by The Rebel Publishing House GmbH
Venloer Strasse 5-7, 5000 Cologne 1, West Germany
Copyright © Neo-Sannyas International
First Edition:
Printing by Mohndruck, Guetersloh, West Germany

Distributed in the United States by Chidvilas Foundation, Inc., Boulder, Colorado
Distributed in Europe by Neo-Sannyas International, Zurich, Switzerland

ISBN 3-89338-006-X HB
ISBN 3-89338-011-6 PB

PART ONE

Mt. Abu

Sarvasar Upanishad

One . . . . January 8, 1972 . . . . 7:00 P.M.
Two . . . . January 9, 1972 . . . . 8:00 A.M.
Three . . . . January 9, 1972 . . . . 7:00 P.M.
Four . . . . January 10, 1972 . . . . 8:00 A.M.
Five . . . . January 10, 1972 . . . . 7:00 P.M.
Six . . . . January 11, 1972 . . . . 8:00 A.M.
Seven . . . . January 11, 1972 . . . . 7:00 P.M.
Eight . . . . January 12, 1972 . . . . 8:00 A.M.
Nine . . . . January 12, 1972 . . . . 7:00 P.M.
Ten . . . . January 13, 1972 . . . . 8:00 A.M.
Eleven . . . . January 13, 1972 . . . . 7:00 P.M.
Twelve . . . . January 14, 1972 . . . . 8:00 A.M.
Thirteen . . . . January 14, 1972 . . . . 7:00 P.M.
Fourteen . . . . January 15, 1972 . . . . 8:00 A.M.
Fifteen . . . . January 15, 1972 . . . . 7:00 P.M.
Sixteen . . . . January 16, 1972 . . . . 8:00 A.M.
Seventeen . . . . January 16, 1972 . . . . 7:00 P.M.

PART TWO

Mt. Abu

Kaivalya Upanishad

Eighteen . . . . March 25, 1972 . . . . 7:00 P.M.

Nineteen . . . . March 26, 1972 . . . . 8:00 A.M.

Twenty . . . . March 26, 1972 . . . . 7:00 P.M.

Twenty-One . . . . March 27, 1972 . . . . 8:00 A.M.

Twenty-Two . . . . March 27, 1972 . . . . 7:00 P.M.

Twenty-Three . . . . . . March 28, 1972 . . . . 8:00 A.M.

Twenty-Four . . . . March 28, 1972 . . . . 7:00 P.M.

Twenty-Five . . . . March 29, 1972 . . . . 8:00 A.M.

Twenty-Six . . . . March 29, 1972 . . . . 7:00 P.M.

Twenty-Seven . . . . March 30, 1972 . . . . 8:00 A.M.

Twenty-Eight . . . . March 30, 1972 . . . . 7:00 P.M.

Twenty-Nine . . . . March 31, 1972 . . . . 8:00 A.M.

Thirty . . . . March 31, 1972 . . . . 7:00 P.M.

Thirty-One . . . . April 1, 1972 . . . . 8:00 A.M.

Thirty-Two . . . . April 1, 1972 . . . . 7:00 P.M.

Thirty-Three . . . . April 2, 1972 . . . . 8:00 A.M.

Thirty-Four . . . . April 2, 1972 . . . . 7:00 P.M.

PART THREE

Mt. Abu

Adhyatma Upanishad

Thirty-Five . . . . October 13, 1972 . . . . 7:00 P.M.
Thirty-Six . . . . October 14, 1972 . . . . 8:00 A.M.
Thirty-Seven . . . . October 14, 1972 . . . . 7:00 P.M.
Thirty-Eight . . . . October 15, 1972 . . . . 8:00 A.M.
Thirty-Nine . . . . October 15, 1972 . . . . 7:00 P.M.
Forty . . . . October 16, 1972 . . . . 8:00 A.M.
Forty-One . . . . October 16, 1972 . . . . 7:00 P.M.
Forty-Two . . . . October 17, 1972 . . . . 8:00 A.M.
Forty-Three . . . . October 17, 1972 . . . . 7:00 P.M.
Forty-Four . . . . October 18, 1972 . . . . 8:00 A.M.
Forty-Five . . . . October 18, 1972 . . . . 7:00 P.M.
Forty-Six . . . . October 19, 1972 . . . . 8:00 A.M.
Forty-Seve . . . . October 19, 1972 . . . . 7:00 P.M.
Forty-Eight . . . . October 20, 1972 . . . . 8:00 A.M.
Forty-Nine . . . . October 20, 1972 . . . . 7:00 P.M.
Fifty . . . . October 21, 1972 . . . . 8:00 A.M.
Fifty-One . . . . October 21, 1972 . . . . 7:00 P.M.

INTRODUCTION

When I was asked to help out with the Sanskrit text which appears in this book, I had no idea that I was being invited to set out on a journey....

Perhaps it was the serene, unearthly atmosphere of the Lao Tzu garden, charged by Bhagwan's presence; the stately, meditative trees, friendly ducks waddling through the walkways, which made these timeless upanishadic times come alive.

As I started listening to the audio cassettes one by one, Ma Yoga Taru's raw, enchanting voice singing those ageless chants of the Upanishads reversed the time track and once again I was transported into the early seventies, when Bhagwan actually conducted these meditation camps.

These camps were a love affair! All the people who had gathered were Bhagwan's lovers and beloveds, who did not care much for growth or spirituality. In the sixties Bhagwan used to travel extensively throughout India, always staying with people who invited him. He would chit-chat with them, listen to their woes, and shower love on their hearts thirsty for love. Every member of the family would feel, that Acharya-ji – as he was called in those days – was one of them, their very own. So for all the people who attended the camps, it was a case of their beloved turned God! The camps were conducted in a very informal and friendly manner.

Bhagwan would choose to speak on one Upanishad, which is the most precious treasure of ancient Indian wisdom. First he used to speak in Hindi, and later in English for westerners, who had just started to appear in the meditation camps.

There were three sessions of meditations each day. The morning session would begin by his discourse, followed by dynamic meditation. These discourses happened on the open grounds of one of the hill stations like Mt. Abu or Matheran. These were the first days of his most dangerous and bold dynamic meditation, which he courageously introduced to the repressed, traditional Indian audience. So he would sit through the entire meditation now persuading, now provoking people to shed their age-old conditionings. He was even heard shouting "Hoo! Hoo!" to encourage the participants. People painfully threw out their unconscious garbage, and the compassionate sky above would absorb all the poison that human civilization had imposed on human beings.

The meditation would end after forty minutes, but the devils let loose out of the Pandora's box would be active even after that. The hills reverberated with the mad shrieks and "Hoos" throughout the day!

A kirtan meditation was conducted at 3:30 p.m. in the afternoon. This meditation was very popular with the Indians. Bhagwan would again come for this session exactly at 3:30p.m. Dressed in a spotlessly white lungi and a shawl casually thrown over his shoulder, he would sit on an ordinary cane chair, covered with a bed sheet. And that chair would become a throne! He would sit there majestically, watching the people sing and dance around him with great love. They had never seen God, but they would shower all their bottled-up emotions on one god that was sitting before them. After one hour, he would leave the premises as quietly as he had come.

As the dusk descended on the hills, preparations for the evening sessions would begin. Every session would be preceded by some devotional singing. The organizers would request someone from the audience to sing, and he or she would oblige. It was often out of rhythm, out of tune, but who cared? Their hearts were already tuned with their beloved. The day's work had made their hearts sensitive and vulnerable, and as the darkness deepened, Bhagwan's seductive voice would delve deeper and deeper into the mysteries of Upanishads.

The last night of meditation, called tratak dhyan was absolutely out of this world! Bhagwan would stand on the platform, his arms spread out like wings, looking like an angel just descended from the sky. He would ask people to look at him without blinking their eyes, while jumping and shouting "hoo hoo" at the same time. There was such a magic in the air with Bhagwan standing against the black sky! The two flames burning in his unblinking, magnetic eyes would encourage people to shout and jump more and more vigorously. When the whole thought process stopped, the mass of their energy rose to a crescendo, and then he would invoke the divine energy to come down to meet this peak. And a great uproar used to explode into the electrified atmosphere.

And he would slip away quietly into the night.

He has been doing this for years: bringing new methods of meditation to fit the modern man; creating the thirst of higher values of life.

Then, and then only, you turn inwards and set out on a new journey, till you yourself arrive at a point when you dissolve in Him. And you experience what the Upanishads have been saying:

That Art Thou!

Ma Amrit Sadhana
Poona, July 1987

PHOTOGRAPHS

taken at
the meditation camps

I.   Bhagwan arriving at the meditation ground at Mt. Abu.
II.   Bhagwan giving His morning discourse.
III.   Listening to Bhagwan's discourse at the meditation camp.
IV.   Preparing for dynamic meditation.
V.   The last stage of dynamic meditation.
VI.   Bhagwan encouraging people to put their whole energy into the meditation.
VII.   Bhagwan leaving after the meditation.
VIII.   Bhagwan resting between sessions.
IX.   The Kirtan meditation
X.   Bhagwan watching the kirtan meditation.
XI.   Bhagwan watching people meditating.
XII.   Bhagwan unravelling the mysteries of the Upanishad.
XIII.   Stage of *Tratak* meditation.
XIV.   Stage of *Tratak* meditation.
XV.   Stage of *Tratak* meditation.
XVI.   Bhagwan in samadhi.

I.

II.

III.

IV.

V.

VI.

VII.

VIII.

IX.

X.

XI.

XII.

XIII.

XIV.

XV.

XVI.

PART ONE

Mt. Abu

Sarvasar Upanishad

January 8th - 16th, 1972

AUM, Supreme One, guard us
(master and disciple) *together.*
Nourish us together.
Let both of us strive together.
Let our learning shine brightly.
Let us not hate anyone.
AUM, shanti, shanti, shanti (peace).

To know and to be are one and the same. To be is the only way to know. And there are two dimensions of growth: one of knowledge and one of being.

You can know more and more and more, and still remain the same. *Be* more. The being must grow; not knowledge, not accumulation, not information – but being. Not knowledge, but consciousness, must grow. And only that growth which is of consciousness is spiritual. All else that just adds to your knowledge is nothing but a burden.

It is always dangerous to play with truths, because they will destroy you as you are. They will give you a rebirth. We are just pregnant for centuries and centuries, and lives and lives, and the birth has not happened. We are just pregnant, just a seed, because no one is ready to pay the price. And before one comes to that bliss which is our seeking, one has to pass through a deep suffering. That deep suffering is a must. That is the birth pain – you cannot escape it.

Why this prayer?

The relationship of the master and the disciple is the most intimate relationship possible, because bodies are not related, but spirits. All relationships are bodily, even that of the mother and son – it is just a physical relationship. The relationship of lover and the beloved is still something earthly. The only relationship on the earth which is unearthly is that of a master and the disciple. So if the disciple is lost, the master is lost.

One is never safe with the ego. The ego is the source of all errors. So, to feel that one is saved already, means that one is still prone, one is still tending to fall back down. Rather the more we know it, the more unknown it becomes. The other shore means the unknown – not only the unknown but the unknowable. This is the mystery; this is what makes this type of knowledge esoteric. This is what mystery means: one knows and still remains ignorant.

Money continues to circulate, just like blood in the body. Knowledge cannot be circulated like money; this knowledge cannot be transferred. Then what to do? What should the master do with the disciple? The master only prays, "Give us strength. We should endeavor together, we should make an effort together" – but we endeavor *together*. The family of the master – a member of the family, because they are not teachers.

To be a buddha is one thing, but to be a master is something plus.

To know truth is not as difficult as to communicate it. Communication is a greater difficulty, because the other comes in. In knowing, you are alone, but in communication the other comes in. And when you are trying to communicate, the other has to be considered. It becomes difficult. So there are many enlightened persons, but not so many masters. What has happened? The thing has happened, the explosion has happened, but even the person is not able to grasp the totality of it. What has happened?

Buddha remained silent for seven days after his enlightenment. Why? One of the reasons, amongst many, is this: for seven days he tried to comprehend "What has happened? To whom has this happened? What has happened and to whom has this happened?"

Knowing is just riverlike.

It goes on and on and on, and there is no end to it.

CHAPTER TWO

What is bondage? What is freedom?
What is vidya *right learning and* avidya, *false one?*
What are these four states:
waking, dreaming, sleeping and turiya, *the fourth?*
What are these five koshas – *bodies:*
sheaths of food, breath, mind, knowing and bliss?
What is the meaning of the doer, living being,
panchvarga *five groups,* kshetragya *knower of the field,*
sakshi *witness,* kutastha *the supreme and* antaryami *the imminent?*
The same way what are these three:
self, supreme self and maya, *the world of appearances?*

Right enquiry begins with prayer; otherwise, the enquiry is not right. Without prayer, doubt is just a disease. With a prayerful mood, with a prayerful heart, doubt becomes just a methodology to enquiry, and to enquire.

Doubt is healthy if inside there is faith. A faithful doubt is a good sign. The end remains faith; doubting is just a means. The doubt must not be the end. If doubt is the end, then it is an infinite regress: you can go on doubting and doubting and doubting, and there is no end to it. You go on falling, with doubt, into more indecisiveness. To reach somewhere, doubt must not be the end. Use it as a means – it is helpful – but remain centered in faith, because that opens your mind; doubt closes it.

Doubt is a closing – you are closed. So doubt is a self-destructive process; it is suicidal, because you ask and you are not open to receive. You ask but you are not ready for the answer. You go on asking, and preventing the answer from reaching you.

Prayer means receptivity, festivity – you are open. Be open and ask, be open and enquire. This *Upanishad* begins with prayer to the divine force for help, then the enquiry, and then the questioning. With prayer questioning is not just curiosity. With prayer it becomes a sincere quest.

The first thing towards freedom is to know that you are not free. The first step, the basic, is to know that you are in bondage. Then comes the longing, then is created the desire; then one begins to dream about freedom. But one must be aware that one is not free, one is just a slave. So the enquiry begins with the question: What is bondage?

Bondage doesn't mean knowledge. *Vidya* is not knowledge. Vidya means the methods, the techniques. "What is wisdom?" It doesn't mean, "What is knowledge?" it means, "What is the methodology? How to achieve it; how to be free? Tell me about the highest, the supreme-most truth – because the supreme-most truth is not to be born at all."

The primary truth, the foundational truth, the best, the highest the supreme-most is not to be born at all. And the second is to die as soon as possible after you are born.

False doors, false keys, pseudo-methods are there. *Avidya* means pseudo-methods.

Dreaming is not just a dreaming; it is substantial, it is significant. You cannot dream without causes. Even a dream has a causality. It is relevant, it shows something about you. Rather, it shows more about you than anything you are doing and showing when you are awake, because one can deceive oneself and others when one is awake, but one cannot deceive in dreams. Dreams are more innocent because we have not yet found any technology to polish dreaming, to use masks in dreaming. Dreams are still naked real, authentic; they show the real face more sincerely than any face you use when you are awake.

So this paradoxical thing happens: a dream becomes more real than all that you think is real, because you cannot maneuver it, you cannot manage – you are just helpless. A dream happens; you cannot do anything in it. You are not the doer, you can just be an observer. In a subtle way, you are totally helpless. Because of that helplessness, a dream becomes more real, more authentic, and shows many things about your mind. Dreaming is worth knowing, worth enquiring about.

So the *Upanishad* asks, "What is this awake state of the mind? What is dreaming? What is non-dreaming sleep? And what is *turiya*?"

This word "turiya" only means "the fourth." So what are these three states – being awake, dreaming, being deeply asleep – and what is the fourth which transcends all these three? The fourth has not been given any name; it has only been known as "the fourth," the turyia, because really that is not a state of the mind but one's being, one's nature.

These three are states.... When you are awake, this is a state, a mode, a form, a shape of your being. This is not your being. This is a state – it can change. In the night you will be dreaming. Dreaming is still a state, because it can change. Then you will be deep in sleep, dreamless sleep – that too is a state. By "state" is meant something which you can take and change. The fourth, the turiya, is not a state, it is your being. You cannot change it, you are *it*. So the fourth goes on in all the three states, and transcends them. But the fourth is not a state, it is your being. So what are these four?

All sociological interpretations of religion are just nonsense, sheer nonsense, because they cannot conceive that religion is born in a consciousness. They can only conceive that out of fear every god is born. No, never out of fear is any god born – out of love, out of prayer, out of a deep glimpse into the nature of existence. But this glimpse is bound to be individual. When others begin to follow, they are just following a dead ritual.

The sun can become divine in a moment of opening, in a moment of deep exposure, when there is a deep opening in all of your five bodies and the innermost becomes one with the outermost – even for a single moment. In that exposure, everything is just divine. *Everything*! In that exposure nothing remains material; in that exposure everything becomes just a benediction, a bliss, a blessing. Matter just dissolves; everything becomes alive.

Divisions fall, barriers are not, oneness is felt.

Out of this oneness, out of this love, religion is born.

So all sociological theories about religion are absurd. They just miss the point! But that is natural, because for one who has not known love, fear is the only thing in life, the only experience. These are the basic experiences: either you know love or fear; if your life is not oriented in love, then it is bound to be oriented in fear. So, man's mind can have only two conceptions about the universe: either fear-oriented or love-oriented. If it is love-oriented it becomes religion; if it is fear-oriented it becomes just a material science. If you are in fear, then you begin to fight.

Science is a fight, a conquering of nature, a conquest, a struggle – nature becomes the enemy. If life is love-oriented – and that is what is meant by a religious life – then it is not a fight. Then it is a communion, then it is a reverence; you are not an enemy and nature is not your enemy. Then there is a deep friendliness; then you become one.

So, if one has not felt deep love, love towards each and everything, then there is only one interpretation possible – one can only interpret through fear.

The self or soul is both God and living being.
But the body, which is not the soul,
gets infected with a sense of ego,
and that is what is called living being's bondage.
The cessation of this ego is what is called freedom.
That which gives rise to the ego
is called avidya *false learning.*
And that which leads to the cessation of the ego
is called vidya *(right learning).*

Ône is to analyze a thing, to divide it into its parts, but parts are not the whole. They constitute the whole, but they are not equivalent to the whole. The whole cannot be created without the parts. But still the whole is something plus, something more than all the parts combined. That something plus is the mystery.

Science divides, and the knowledge achieved is through analysis. Religion is quite the opposite dimension. Religion believes, not in division, but in synthesis. Religion goes on adding, totaling. And when everything is totaled – nothing remains outside, everything is included; and this whole, taken as a whole, is looked at – the divine appears. That's why science can never say that there is a god – that is impossible. So no one should hope that any day science can say there is a god, because the very process of scientific analysis cannot lead to the total. The very process leads to the part, the minutest part – never to the whole – because it depends on division.

Science can never come to any divineness in the universe, in existence, because divineness is something like a perfume that comes out of the whole. It is not mathematical; it is organic. It is not mechanical; it is alive. You can divide me into parts; then put back all those parts, but I will not be found there. You have put everything again in its place; but I am not a mechanical device, I am not just parts accumulated and arranged. Something more is there, more than all the parts – that something is lost.

Life can never be known by analysis.

Analysis can only know the material, never the spiritual. These are the two dimensions of knowing. So if someone concludes that there is nothing except matter, that only means that he has used the analytical method – nothing else. When someone says there is no matter, but only consciousness, it only shows that he has used the method of synthesis – not analysis.

Freud used analysis as a methodology; then he couldn't conceive that there is any soul, any divine element in man. But another psychologist, Assagioli, is now using synthesis as a method, and he says: There is no body, only the spirit, only the consciousness. Whenever someone asserts matter or consciousness, it means a particular method for the search has been used.

Logic is analysis – love is synthesis.

That's why religion has always been illogical, and science has always been loveless.

To be identified with something which you are not, is the formation of the ego. Ego means to be identified with something you are not.

Whatsoever one is needs no identification.

You need not be identified with it: You are already it.

So whenever there is any identification, it means *with* something else – that you are not. One can be identified with the body, with the mind. But the moment one is identified, one is lost to oneself. This is what ego means. This is how ego is formed and becomes crystallized.

Whenever you assert "I," there is identification with something – with some name, with some form, with some body, with some past; with mind, with thoughts, with memories. There is some deep identification: only then you can assert "I." If you are not identified with anything else and can remain with yourself, then you cannot say "I"; the "I" just drops.

"I" means identity.

Identity is the basis of all slavery:

Be identified and you will be in a prison.

The very identity will become your prison. Be non-identified, remain totally yourself, and then there is freedom. So this is what bondage is: Ego is the bondage, and egolessness is freedom. And this ego is nothing but to be identified with something that you are not. For example, everyone is identified with his name; and everyone is born without any name. Then the name becomes so significant that one can die for his name's sake.

What is a name? But the moment you are identified, it becomes very meaningful. And everyone is born without any name – nameless. Or, you take form; everyone is identified with one's own form. Every day you are standing before your mirror. What are you seeing? – Yourself? No. No mirror can mirror *you*, just the form you are identified with. But such is the stupidity of the human mind that every day the form is changing constantly, but you are never disillusioned.

When you were a child, what was your form? When you were in your mother's womb, what was your form? When you were in your parents' seed, what was your form? Can you recognize – if a picture is produced for you – the egg in your mother's womb? Will you be able to recognize and say, "this is 'I'"? No, but you must have been identified with this egg somewhere back.... You were born – and if the first scream can be reproduced for you, will you be able to recognize it and say, "this is *my* scream"? No, but it *was* yours, and you must have been identified with that.

If an album can be produced before a dying man.... A constant changing form – there is a continuity but still every moment a change.... The body is changing every seven years, completely, totally; nothing remains the same, not a single cell. Still, still we think, "this is my form, this is me." And consciousness is formless. The form is just something outside that goes on changing and changing and changing – just like clothes.

This identification is ego. If you are not identified with anything – with name or with form or anything – then where is the ego? Then you are, and still you are not. Then you are in your absolute purity, but with no ego. That's why Buddha called the self, no-self; he called it *anatta, anatma*. He said, "There is no ego, so you cannot call yourself *atma* even. You cannot call yourself 'I'; there is no 'I.' There is pure existence." This pure existence is freedom.

This term *avidya* really cannot be translated. It is not synonymous with ignorance; it is not ignorance...because ignorance is just negative. You don't know something, you are ignorant. But this avidya is not something negative, it is very positive. It is not that you don't know something; it is rather, on the contrary, that you know something which is not. This avidya is, rather, a positive projection of something which is not.

The "I" is not – the ego is the most non-existential thing in the world.

It looks very substantial, and is absolutely empty.

Avidya means the projective source in you of this ego, of this identified image of yourself. Avidya is a projective force within you. It is not just ignorance, it is not that you don't know something; it is that you can create something which is not. You can dream something which is not, you can project something which is not. When the mind is projecting something which is not, it is avidya.

When this mind destroys all projections, all identifications, remains without any projective activity, then this method of destroying all projections, all that is not, but appears to be – is called vidya. Vidya is not knowledge; again, vidya is a positive force to destroy all that which avidya creates. Vidya is untranslatable. Vidya means a positive force in you which can destroy ego formation. Both are positive: avidya creates that which is not, and vidya destroys that which is not. So vidya means yoga, vidya mean the science of religion.

THE NIGHT MEDITATION

This night meditation is going to be a constant staring at me for thirty minutes, without blinking the eyes. Just go on staring at me for thirty minutes. Feel your eyes just as doors, and from those doors your consciousness is coming towards me. Go on feeling that your consciousness is coming towards me, and don't blink your eyes – go on constantly staring for thirty minutes. This constant staring creates a very deep mutation of the bio-energy, of the kundalini, of the coiled energy, the serpent power.

For thirty minutes go on jumping. Your hands will be raised towards the sky as if you are just about to fly towards the divine. So your hands will be raised, your eyes will be staring at me, and you will have to jump and go on using a mantra, the mantra of "hoo." This "hoo" is not a word, mm? – this is a meaningless sound. This "hoo" is to be used just as a hammering inside on the coiled energy, so that it uncoils and the serpent within begins to move upwards. You will begin to feel a subtle flow of energy in your spine; the energy will be going up and up. You will become weightless.

For thirty minutes constantly using the mantra, "hoo! hoo! hoo!" forcefully, jumping, staring at me . . . . Then after thirty minutes I will tell you to stop and just lie down, dead, for ten minutes. This is the night experiment.

Tomorrow morning we will do a new meditation. Whatsoever we did this morning, today, that meditation will be done in the afternoon. Kirtan meditation will be done in the afternoon instead of silent meditation. And in the morning we will be doing a meditation of four steps. The first step, ten minutes fast breathing – so fast that your body becomes just oxidized energy. Then for ten minutes, a catharsis. Whatsoever happens inside you, just throw it out. Go on dancing, crying, making noise, laughing, weeping – whatsoever. Whatsoever you feel, just be free to express it. And then in the third step, for ten minutes the mantra "hoo" will be used. And then in the fourth step, for thirty minutes totally rest, as if you have died.

So this will be the morning meditation tomorrow. And today's morning meditation will be used in the afternoon meditation from four to five. And in the night, this meditation which we are going to do now, will be continued for the whole time of the camp.

So now we will begin the night meditation . . .

The state in which the soul, with the help of
the energies of the sun and other gods, and through
the instrumentality of these fourteen: mind,
intellect, mind stuff, ego, and the ten sense organs
– becomes sensitive to sound, touch and such
other gross objects, is called the waking state.
When the living being, on account of the
unfulfilled desires of the waking state, becomes
sensitive to sound, touch and such other gross objects
– even in the absence of the latter –
it is called the dreaming state of the self or soul.

The Eastern mind divides conscious-
ness into four states: one is when we are awake, or the first; the second is
dreaming; the third is deep sleep, dreamless; and the fourth is beyond all
the three, the *turiya*, the fourth.

What is this which we call the awake state of consciousness? Knowledge, knowing is possible in two ways: mediate and immediate. Mediate
knowledge means knowledge through some means, not direct – indirect.
Senses are the means, the windows through which we know the extension
beyond us. But the knowledge gained is indirect; it is not a face-to-face
encounter, the mediator is in between. The senses are mediators, and when
senses inform us of something, it is not a simple information, it is an interpretation also. The senses are not just passive receptors; they are positive
interpreters also; they impose something, they add something to the information.

So whenever anything is reported by the senses to the consciousness, it
is not a passive receptivity; the senses have added something to it, they
have interpreted it, they have imposed something on it. This imposition
creates an illusory world around every consciousness, and everyone begins
to live in a world of his own. This world, the Eastern esoteric mind says, is
the *maya*, the illusion. It is not the real, the objective, that-which-is: it is
something that you have created.

Everyone is within his own world, and there are as many worlds as there
are minds. So whenever two persons are near, two worlds are in collision.
And otherwise is not possible, because you have not known the objective
as it is.

The second dimension, the alternative dimension to know the world as it is, is not through senses, but through transcendence of the senses. And human consciousness can be in a direct encounter: the senses are just dropped; and still, knowing happens. That knowing is about the truth, because there has been no mediator. Now you have known directly. To know the truth through the senses is maya; to know the truth immediately, directly, face to face, is *brahman.* That which we know remains the same, but the *knower* changes. If he is using senses, then he creates an illusory perception; if he is not using the senses, then he is face to face with the reality.

Meditation is the path of how to drop the senses, how to drop the windows and just to be in reality without anyone in between. The *rishi* says that this contact with the world through the senses is the first state of consciousness, the awake state of mind, *jagrut.* When you are in contact with the world through the senses, this is jagrut – the awake state of the mind.

Dreaming is the second state, deeper than the state we call the awake. Dreaming is a substitute state, secondary, but deeper. Whatsoever has been left unfulfilled in the state when you were awake, has to be completed. Mind has a tendency to complete things. If you leave something incomplete, then you will create a dream to complete it. The mind tends to complete a thing. You must complete it; otherwise, there is something restless inside.

You have seen a beautiful figure, but you couldn't look at it as you liked, as much you liked. Now a lingering incompletion will continue inside. You can suppress it when you are awake – you are occupied in many other things, and the suppression is possible – but when you go to sleep, the incomplete link unfolds a dream and completes the thing.

This state of dreaming, the rishi says, means without the instrumentality of your senses. The senses are closed – they are not aware of the world beyond you; now you are within your cells, within your body, but still you can create you own worlds. This creation of your own worlds in dreams becomes possible because your mind is a conditioning of everything you have known, you have felt; everything has been accumulated in it. It is an accumulation, not only of this life, but of all the lives one has lived; and not only of human lives, of animal lives also; and not only of animal lives, but of vegetable lives also.

So in a dream you can become a tree; in a dream you can become a lion. Sometime you have been a tree: that memory is still there – it can unfold. This unfolding of past memories, of past lives, means only that you have never lived totally – always partially. You have not loved totally, you have not been angry totally, you have not been *anything* totally. Everything is incomplete. So many things incomplete inside, create the situation in which dreaming happens. The moment one begins to live totally, every-thing is completed, dreaming ceases.

A christ, a buddha, will not dream, because he has not left anything in-complete. A Jesus says this moment is enough – live it totally. Do not think of the other moment that is to come; do not think of the other moment that has gone. That which has gone is no more, and that which has not come yet, has not come yet. Both are non-existential.

This moment, this very moment, this passive moment is the only exis-tential time. Live in it! And leave all else aside. Be totally in it, then there will be no dreaming, then everything is complete. And by the night, when you are dropping into sleep, nothing is incomplete and needs to be com-pleted. And when dreaming ceases, mind becomes more aware.

This is the second state: dreaming. When dreaming ceases you become more awake; and when there is no dreaming in the night, in the morning when you are awake, you have more innocent eyes, more fresh, more alive. In your eyes there is no dust, there is no smoke; the flame is clear without the smoke. Dreaming creates a smoke around your eyes.

And one who has been dreaming in the night, really goes on dreaming in the day also. Deep down there is always a continuous dream film. You are hearing me: just close your eyes and look inside and there is a dream unfolding.

You are too occupied outside, that's why you cannot become attentive to your inside dreaming; but the dreaming continues.

Look at the sky; there are no stars now. Where have they gone? They cannot go anywhere; they are where they have been in the night, but only because of the sun, we cannot see them. Our eyes are so occupied with the sun, they cannot penetrate through to them. They are still there. If you can go down into a deep well, even in the day, you can look at the stars, because then there is a gap of darkness and again stars appear.

Just like this, you are continuously dreaming. But when you are occupied in the outside world, the dreaming continues inside without your being attentive to it. The moment you are not occupied, relaxed, you become again aware of the dreaming. This is a constant state – in fact, continuous. And this dreaming is more indicative about your mind than whatsoever we call being awake, because it is less inhibited, less suppressed, more naked and therefore more true.

So, if your dreaming can be known, if your dream can be known, much is known about you. You cannot deceive – in dreams, at least. They are still not a part of your will, they are not voluntary. You are not the controller; that's why they are so wild, so animal-like. This second stage must be penetrated, must be transcended. Only then we can come to the third – still deeper, the deep sleep, the dreamless sleep.

The more you go deep inside, the nearer you are to existence. The deeper you go to the center, the nearer you are to the center of the universe. These three are concentric circles around the center: awake, dreaming and deep sleep. These are three concentric circles. If you transcend all these three, then suddenly you are face to face with your own center. Then you are centered in it. That centering is all.

That centering is to achieve the deathless.

That centering is to be deep inside the heart of the universe.

That centering is divine realization.

Dreaming has to cease, one must cease dreaming. Dreaming has to be transcended – dreaming is the barrier. A dreaming mind can never know the truth; a dreaming mind is bound to live in illusory worlds. Dreaming is the problem, and if dreaming stops.... And it stops when ambition stops, it stops when desiring stops, it stops when one begins to live moment to moment, just here and now. If you can remember two words, "here" and "now," dreaming stops. Be here and now, and there can be no dreaming, because dreaming is always from the past and for the future. It originates in the past; it spreads into the future.

Dreaming can never be in the present. To be in the present and to be in a dream is impossible; they never meet. So if one is awake, aware, attentive of the time that is just here and now, dreaming stops. And when dreaming withers away, you can become aware, really aware; you can really become awake. And when you are awake, this awareness can penetrate the third state of consciousness: dreamless sleep. Really, in no language other than Hindi, is there a word for it – *sushupti*. In no language is there a word for it – sushupti.

Sleep is not sushupti – that's why we have to add *dreamless* sleep. It is not just sleep, it is non-dreaming sleep – without any ripple of the dream, with no waves of the dream. The ocean is totally silent, not even a dream is there to disturb. Then you are in sushupti – the third state, dreamless sleep, the non-dreaming sleep. But you can never become aware of it unless dreaming ceases.

The waves must cease; only then can you become aware of the ocean; otherwise, you are always aware of the waves. Waves are on the surface, so when you see, you see the waves, not the ocean. The waves must stop totally. Only then, for the first time, do you become aware of the ocean, the waveless ocean – the dreamless sleep. And if one can become aware of dreamless sleep, one transcends sleep. One transcends sleep only when one becomes aware of it. And then you are *turiya*, the fourth; then you have passed all the three.

This fourth is the being; this fourth is the search. For this fourth effort is needed. And one may go on continuously dreaming and dreaming and dreaming – one can never acheive this fourth state through dreaming. That's why there is so much insistence on non-desiring, non-ambition. The buddhas go on saying, "Do not desire," because if you desire then dreaming cannot cease. The buddhas go on saying, "Do not be attached," because if you are attached the dreaming cannot cease. Do not be ambitious, do not long for any becoming, do not think in terms of the future;

otherwise, dreaming cannot cease. And unless dreaming ceases you will never *be*. You *can* never be! You will always be a becoming, just a becoming: "a" changing into "b," "b" changing into "c," "c" changing into "d" – and always the longing for the far off. And then you go on running, and you never reach; then you go on becoming this and that and you are never a *being*.

The being is here and now.

Drop dreaming and you are *there* where you have really been always, but you were never aware.

All meditation techniques are just antidream efforts, just dream-negating devices.

THE NEW MORNING MEDITATION-DYNAMIC MEDITATION.

Three steps are to be followed. They should be followed as vigorously as possible. One has to put everything at stake, totally – nothing less will do.

The first step is fast breathing. Breathe as fast as possible, because we are using breathing as a hammer. It is to be a hammering inside for the coiled energy to be uncoiled. So use it as a hammer for the inner serpent, to awaken it.

So do not withhold; give in completely. For ten minutes I will go on encouraging you to make any effort possible. Whatsoever you can do, do it at your peak, your climax.

In the second step you have to be in a catharsis. Dance, jump, cry, laugh – whatsoever happens to you, but do something. Movement is necessary – whatsoever is inside must be thrown outside. This catharsis leads to a purity, to a very deep cleansing.

In the third step you have to use "hoo!" So go on crying, "hoo! hoo! hoo!" – this too is to be used as a hammer. This mantra, "hoo," goes deep down to the *muladhar*, to the sex center, and hammers the energy to rise upwards.

After thirty minutes, the fourth step – we will be lying, just as if dead, and waiting for the divine to descend.

Make a space around you so you can be just totally mad. Make space around you. Don't be in a group, don't be in a crowd – just spread out.

Now close your eyes with the blindfold.

Make space. Look around and see, because you will be jumping and dancing and going completely mad.

Now we should begin. Close your eyes....

The sleeping state is one
in which all the fourteen organs are still and tranquil,
and when – for lack of real knowledge – the self or soul
is insensitive to sound, touch and such other objects.
And the one which is aware of the creation and dissolution
of these three states – waking dreaming and sleeping – but which
is itself beyond creation and dissolution,
is known as turiya – the fourth state of consciousness,
the state of turiya.

Consciousness in itself is nothing. One is always conscious *about* something; so the "about" is important. Consciousness is always objective: you are conscious of something. If there is nothing in front of you, consciousness will drop - you will not be conscious.

This state, the oriental religious perception says, is the *sushupti*; this is the third state. When there is no object to be known, the knower is lost. When then is no object in the outside world to be aware of, and when there is no object in the mind, dream object, when all objects have dropped - *outside* all are dream objects - then consciousness drops. Then you are not conscious; then you are unconscious. This unconsciousness is sushupti, the third stage.

But this is amazing: it means that we are not conscious really, we are only objectively conscious. We have not known ourselves, we have known only objects and things. Our consciousness is other-oriented; it is not self centered. I can be conscious only when something else is present. When nothing is present I will go to sleep. I have not known any subjective consciousness which can exist without the object. That's why in the third state, consciousness equals unconsciousness - it becomes unconscious. When there is no object as a challenge, one becomes unconscious.

So this consciousness, this so-called consciousness, is just a struggle, just a challenge, just a constant stimulus-response; it is not anything in itself. You are not the master of it; you are not really *conscious*: you are only being forced to be conscious constantly. Everything is forcing you to be conscious; otherwise, to go to sleep will be the spontaneous act - one will just drop into a coma. So can we call it consciousness? It is not. This state is not the state of self consciousness, it is just a constant tension between you and the world, between you and the thoughts. If there are no objects and no thoughts, you drop...and be unconscious. This is the third state, sushupti. And unless one transcends it, one cannot be called conscious.

Gurdjieff used to say that man has no soul. He used to say that you have got no self, because self means self consciousness; otherwise, how can you be said to have a self? If you are not conscious, how can you be a self? How can you be an individual? So Gurdjieff's teaching doesn't believe that every man has got a soul. He says, "Every man has got a potentiality he can develop, he may not develop."

If you become self conscious, then you develop the individual; then you become the individual. If you are not self conscious then you are just one object among other objects, and there is nothing more. Gurdjieff's teaching makes this central point the supreme point. He says, "Try to remember yourself without any object. Try to remember yourself without any object, without any relation to anything else. Remember yourself directly, simply." It is very arduous; in a way it seems impossible. You cannot remember yourself without in any way relating to something else – Can you?

Can you remember yourself?

Can you feel yourself?

Whenever you feel, you feel in relation to: someone's son, someone's daughter, someone's husband, being rich or poor, belonging to this country or that, being healthy or ill – but this is all in relation to something else. Can you remember yourself without any relation? – unrelated? without any context? just you? It becomes inconceivable. Really, we have not known ourselves, we have known only in relation. And this is the miracle: you know yourself in relation to someone, who knows himself in relation to you. See the absurdity of it! Everyone knows themselves because of others – and the others know themselves because of him.

Everyone is ignorant, but by being related with other ignorant people, you become wise. You know yourself because you know your name, you know your house, your address, your city, your country – and not for a single moment have you known who you are. This sushupti, this third state of unconsciousness must be broken apart, must be penetrated beyond. One must become aware of oneself without being related to anything else – this is self knowledge. This fourth is known as the *turiya*.

We must make a distinction between the being and the states. Any state, whether it is awake, or dreaming, or nondreaming sleep, cannot be synonymous with the being, because the being is that upon which these states happen. The being is one who goes through all these three states. He cannot be identified with any; otherwise, he cannot move.

You cannot be awake if you are identified with dreaming: if you are dreaming, then you cannot be awake. If you are awake, then you cannot go into sleep. But you move – just as one moves into one's house and out of one's house, you come in and you go out; so you cannot be identified with the inside of your house or the outside of your house. You move: you can come in, you can go out; so you become the third. You move from dreaming to non-dreaming; you move from sleep to dream, from dream to wakefulness.

So this mover must be something else, more than all the three – this is the fourth; hence, it is called "the fourth." And therefore no name is given to it... because from the fourth it can never move. From the fourth it can never move. When I say this, a question must come into your mind: "But this fourth goes into sleep, goes into dreaming and other states?"

This is something very subtle to be understood. No, this fourth never goes anywhere; those states come upon it and pass – this fourth remains in itself constantly. Dreaming comes over it just like clouds coming over the sun. The sun remains, then there are clouds, then the clouds have gone. This fourth is the non-moving center within you. Dreams come, then objects are seen, then thoughts are seen; then objects drop, and thoughts drop, and you are engulfed in a dark sleep; but the fourth remains its center – it has never moved. That's why no name has been given to it; no name is needed – it remains the nameless. One has to penetrate to this fourth.

This is not a state really; when we talk we have to call it the fourth state, but it is not a state. All the three are states; this fourth is beyond these states. This fourth is the being – this fourth is the very nature of one's self. Unless one goes to this fourth, unless one becomes aware of this non-moving center, unless one is centered in it, there is no freedom and there is no bliss. Really, there is nothing except dreaming, many many dreamings, many types of dreamings; but nothing else – just bubbles in the air.

This fourth.... How to achieve this fourth? How to reach this fourth? How to penetrate this deep sleep? How to destroy this darkness within? What to do?

The one basic thing is to be aware first: in the first state when you are awake, be aware. Be aware whatsoever you are doing. Walking on the street, then be aware that you are walking. Let your awareness be double-arrowed: one arrow conscious of the act of walking, another arrow going deep inside and aware of the walker. Listening to me, be aware, double-arrowed: one arrow of your consciousness going outside listening attentively, another going inside constantly aware of the listener.

Mahavira has a very beautiful word. He used "listener" *shravak*, with a very original meaning, and he has given a very new shape, a new nuance to it. He says if you can be simply a right listener, nothing else is needed. This much will do: if you can be a right listener – *samyak shravak*. If you can listen attentively with double-arrowed attention, then this much is enough, you will be awakened. No other discipline is needed.

Buddha has used the word, "mindfulness" – *samyak smriti*, right mindfulness. He says whatsoever you are doing, do it mindfully; don't do it in sleep, do it mindfully – whatsoever you are doing. Do it consciously, then consciousness begins to crystallize in the first state, wakefulness. When you have become conscious, when you are awake, the your consciousness can penetrate the second state, dreaming. It is not difficult then. Then you can become conscious of your dreams; and the moment you become conscious of you dreams, dreams disappear. The moment dreams disappear you become conscious of your dreamless sleep, and the arrow goes on. Now be aware that you are asleep, and by and by the arrow penetrates – and suddenly you are in the fourth.

Religion cannot be a belief.
Religion cannot be a tradition.
Religion cannot be an accepted dogma.
Religion is totally individual:
One has to discover it again and again.
One has to know it for oneself, *for oneself.*
Unless *you* know there is no knowledge.

All knowledge gathered from others is just false, it is pseudo, it is deceptive. One has to encounter the reality oneself. This is just like love – you know if you love. If you have not loved you may know everything about love, but love will not be known, because love is not really a knowledge, it is a realization, it is an experience...rather, not even experience, but experiencing. Experience means something which you have experienced and now it is dead. Experience means something which has finished, which is finished with a full stop. Experiencing means a process, a continuous process. You have to go on discovering, discovering – and there is no end to it.

Religion is like love:
There is a beginning to it but no end.

You have to begin it but you never reach it – you go on reaching. You go on reaching, but it is never of the past. It is not that there comes a full stop and you can say, "I have reached." No, never. That's why we call the religious search, the ultimate search. By "ultimate" we mean that which begins, which never ends. Rather, on the contrary, a moment comes when you are lost but the end has not been achieved. But *this*, this seeker being lost is the explosion.

So unless you know, never believe. Unless you know, never feel at ease with words, doctrines, scriptures. Unless you know, remember continuously that you have to seek and find, that you have to go on a far, faraway journey. And that's why religion really is the only adventure; all else is just childish. That which can be found is just childish; that which can be found is not really the adventure; that which is possible needs no courage. Only the impossible needs courage, only that which cannot be found. If you go on the search for it, you have gone on an adventure.

But the moment one is ready for the impossible, the impossible become possible. The moment one is ready to take the jump, the miracle happens. You are not in a way, in the jump – you are lost. And still, for the first time, you are – you have found yourself.

The states are lost, the identities are lost, the names and forms are lost. There only remains the original source of all This rishi says: These are the states; these three are the states. The fourth is the knower of all these states. These three states come out of the fourth, again are dissolved in the fourth, and the fourth never comes out of anything and is never dissolved in anything else.

The fourth is the eternal principle, the eternal life, the eternal aliveness.

A collection of sheaths composed of nourishing food
in the form of the physical body
is called the annamaya kosh, *or the food body.*
The fourteen kinds of winds, like the vital energy, et cetera,
circulating through the food body,
are called the pranamaya kosh, *or the vital body.*

Now, we have to go into an enquiry about the bodies. Man is not one body, man has many bodies – layers of bodies. The body we know is only the outermost; inside it there is another, and inside that, another. Rishis have divided these layers into five.

The first is known as the food body, the physical body. Ordinarily, we remain attached to this body. We are in a deep illusion and are identified with the physical one. This attachment to the physical body will not allow you to move inside. But why this attachment? – because we don't know that there is another; we have never become aware that inside this body there is another. This body is so solid, so non-transparent, you cannot have any glimpse within. This solidity of the body means that we have been using foods which make it solid. This body can be made transparent also – just like a glass body in which you can have a glimpse inside.

The change of food is bound to change the qualities of your physical body. Food is not just energy, it is also a qualitative thing. Food is not just a fuel, it contributes more than fuel – it gives you either transparency, or non-transparency. The insight into this phenomenon can mutate, and you can have altogether a different type of body. And it is not so difficult to change this body, because the body is a flux, every moment changing itself; it is a process, it is not a static thing. The moment you came here, you had another body; now the body has changed. It is changing constantly, every moment; it is riverlike, moving and changing – it is not a static thing.

If you change direction, the body takes a jump; only the direction has to be changed. One should become aware, that whatsoever one is eating must be such that it doesn't make one's body heavy. This heaviness is not concerned with weight: sometimes you feel that you are weightless, as if you can fly. So the food that can give you the feeling of weightlessness is the right food. The food that gives you the feeling of being burdened is not the right food. All non-vegetarian foods make you more rooted in the earth; you cannot fly. Vegetarian foods give you wings; you have an inner feeling that you can just levitate, you can just go out of gravitation.

Food is right if it is non-gravitational. If you can feel non-physical in it, it is good. Really, the body is felt only when it is heavy; when you have the feeling of heaviness inside, only then you feel the body. When the body is not heavy with wrong foods, you are bodiless. That's why when the body is diseased, when the body is ill, you feel it; when it is healthy, you don't feel it. You feel your head only when there is a headache; when there is no headache, there is no head.

So to define health positively, there is only one way: A person who is not feeling his body, is healthy. The more you feel your body, the more ill you are, because when the body is really healthy, there is no need to feel it. Only pain is felt. And if you even feel pleasure, it must be a sort of pain. Pleasure is never felt, because only a disturbance is felt. Silence is never felt really, only noise is felt. And if you begin to feel silence....

Real, authentic silence is not felt. Really, when you are not feeling any noise, it is silence. When you are not feeling your body, it means you are not feeling any disturbances; you are healthy. So the feeling of bodilessness is healthy. Any food that gives you a feeling of bodilessness is good, is right food. So be discriminative; be consciously discriminative. Don't eat anything which makes you more embodied, which makes you more of a body. Go on eliminating all that gives you a bodiness, and then you will begin to transform your body towards a transparency.

This may look paradoxical, but this is true. When you are really healthy, you are desireless – illness and unhealthiness create desires. This is one of the basic distinctions between Eastern and Western thinking. They say, in the West, that to be filled with desire means you are healthy. But their understanding is very superficial, because desire is a disturbance. Something is still incomplete, that's why the desire. Something is incomplete, so there is the urge to fulfill it. But when you are really healthy you are so fulfilled, you are so complete – the circle is so complete – that there is no desire.

Desire means you are incomplete. Somewhere, something is still lacking; somewhere, something is absent; somewhere, you are feeling a vacuum.

This is what illness means: a vacuum. Health means: so much fulfilled, so much filled there is no more space. When there is no inner space, there is no desire; so a really healthy person is desireless, and a really healthy person is bodiless. These both are associated: To be a body is to be in desire; to be in desire is to be heavy with the body.

Make the body as if it is not. The more absent, the better; the more present, the more you are falling downwards. You can just become a stone, and many are that – just stones. They only feel awake when the body demands something; otherwise, they are asleep. When the body demands, they feel awake; then the demand is fulfilled – they again fall deep into sleep.

One should create a body which has needs but not demands. Needs are natural; demands become crazy and obsessions. Demands mean you are addicted; the body is the master. All the austerities were not meant as suicidal methods, they were not masochist – they were really an inner transformation, they were really a change of power.

When a buddha is fasting, it is not to destroy the body; it is to destroy the demands. Understand it very clearly: when a buddha is fasting, he is not destroying his body, but he is changing the seat of power, who the master is. The body must not be the master; otherwise, you cannot go inwards. The master is outside. How can you go inwards? You are just a slave, and you have to be around the master. The power seat must be transformed; the body must become a slave. A slave has needs, but no demands; a slave has needs, but no commandments. The commanding must remain with the master, and the master must be inside, not outside. The deeper the master, the more is your freedom.

So when a buddha is on a fast, it is to change the seat of power. He is saying to his body, "Now I will fulfill your needs, but not your demands." The body will struggle – no one can lose the power, the master, the sovereignty, so easily. And you have lived with the body as the master for millennia. The body was never challenged, so the mastery has become natural; it has become such an old habit that the body even cannot conceive it, "What nonsense are you talking? You are the master? You have always been the slave. Always! Have you gone crazy? The orders have already been issued by *me*! – you have always followed."

Austerity means, *tapascharya* means, *tapas* means, that now you are not ready to continue this status quo, this state of affairs. The body will struggle: the fight is really not from the inside, the fight is from the outside. But the body is a very subtle and miraculous mechanism; it adjusts to anything if you have the will – the greater the will, the sooner the body is adjusted again. It begins to feel, "Now the mastery is lost." And really, when the mastery is lost, the body becomes more healthy, because now it is natural.

The mastery by the body is really unnatural; it is not healthful – even to the body – because the body has no consciousness, and goes on demanding; the body has no discrimination and goes on demanding. It goes on doing things which are not even good for it. Consciousness becomes the slave; and the material desires, the mechanical ones, becomes the master.

This is the deepest accident, the deepest misery that has happened to humankind. But in a way, it had to, because we have developed from an animal existence. We have developed from animal existence. There is no need for a Darwin to prove this – we have know it always. Because an animal has no consciousness, the body has to be the master. There is no one other to claim the mastery – the body has to be the master. But when consciousness grows inside, the body goes on, just as old habit.

You have to change it. Now you are not in the animal world; now you are not animals. Austerity means that now we declare we have passed the state of animalhood. The suffering that one goes through in austerity is just a birth pain – nothing else. And that suffering is good and healthy, because out of that suffering is transformation.

But it should not be done as a masochist – that's altogether a different matter, a very diseased thing. You can make your body suffer and enjoy it. If you are enjoying it, then you are suicidal: then it is not austerity. Then it is not austerity; then you are really a very impotent, violent mind. You cannot do violence to others, so you are doing violence to yourself. So you can fast as a masochist, as a person who enjoys suffering. This is not austerity; this is very abnormal, this is really a mental case.

Out of one hundred, ninety-nine percent of the people who go on austerities are masochists, but they can deceive; they can deceive others and themselves also. To deceive others is irrelevant, but to deceive oneself is very dangerous. You *can* deceive yourself. The point to understand is that one must not enjoy suffering; one must take it as a necessary measure – that's another thing. One must go through it as a cleansing; one must go through it as a purity, as a catharsis, as a change, as a mutation. One must accept it, but not *enjoy* it. That is the thing: If you are enjoying it, then this is not austerity at all; this is madness.

This is the point to be remembered: never enjoy suffering because that is abnormal. To suffer suffering is normal, but to accept it as a necessity, as an inevitability, is another thing. Accept it, go through it; don't enjoy it. You have to do it, because as you have an animal heritage, one day you have to assert your humanity. Against the animal heritage you have to assert yourself. You have to make your body know exactly, *now*, that the body is not the master. And once the body has know it, the body is adjusted. And really the body is freed from a responsibility it cannot carry. It *cannot* be the master because it has no consciousness; it has no awareness. It is an automaton, it is a mechanical device.

The body is an automatic device, so it goes on working. If you make it the master it goes on demanding without any consciousness, without any discrimination, without any intelligence. It has a mechanical intelligence just like a computer: it goes on demanding . . . it goes on demanding. It has a built-in process of how to demand, but without any consciousness: without any consciousness it tells you when you are hungry, it tells you what to eat, it tells you what to do.

But this whole arrangement is just mechanical – it goes on repeating.

That's why a person who lives with the body feels life as a boredom, because the body can only repeat; it can only repeat continuously. So we are just repeating every day the same thing. It is a circle, a closed circle: the same things, the same demands, the same desires, the same lusts – the body goes on repeating and repeating, and in the end one feels just bored, but still one cannot do anything. Even if you feel bored, again the second day, the body will demand the same thing; and you will have to supply, because you have never been in command.

This physical layer is the first, is the primary layer – the outermost. If you can be aware that you are unnecessarily the slave and need not be, then change your body habits consciously. By and by, change. Change the seat of power; be more in control. And give to the body all that is needed by it, but never fulfill any addictions. It will be painful in the beginning, but it is a bliss when you have reached beyond the body and have become the master. And when you are on the throne, it is one of the deepest blisses possible.

Matter and energy are not two things.

Matter is just energy, energy is just matter –

Two states of one thing.

The second body is the vital. The vital body is the energy body, the electricity body, or whatsoever name we like to use for it – the bio-energy body. One thing is certain, it is not material, it is energy. But energy can be transformed into matter, and matter can be transformed into energy.

Energy means not static, moving.

Energy means vibrant, waves.

Energy means alive.

Instead of just a physical body, a tree has two bodies, the physical and the vital. Some energy current is running, and sometimes a tree is more alive and sometimes less alive. Now, even scientists are ready to agree that when someone is near a tree who loves it, the tree is more alive. And when someone is near the tree who doesn't love it, the tree is sad and less alive.

When the gardener comes in, the whole garden is happy. And it is not just a poetry; now, it is a scientific fact. It has been a poetry always, but not it is not a poetry at all; it is a scientific fact. When a person who loves a tree is nearby, the tree is different; and now that difference can be detected by machines. It is more alive; it feels something more – love is flowing. It is vice versa also. If you can love trees when you are under them, you are more, because it is reciprocal. When you are near a flower, you are not just the same. If you have love, then you have an opening, and the flower and you become deeply related in a communion.

This vital body can be purified, and when it is purified it becomes transparent, and then you can look beyond. How is it purified? it is purified by *pranayama*. It is purified if you can have a deep breathing system. Less carbon dioxide inside your lungs, and more oxygen inside you – the more vitality you will create. The vital body can also be purified by pure vibrations. In a crowd you are creating many impurities for your vital body. That's why, whenever one comes back from a crowd, one feels a bit less, less than oneself. Going out of the crowd, far away from man into the nature, one becomes more alive, because up to now there are no sinner trees, no sinner oceans, no sinner sky.

But man has divisions, so in a crowd you are sucked. Your energy has been sucked. You fall down to a lower level. But there are some people – a few, very few – with whom you can feel that you have been refilled; you have been filled, you have been vitalized. To be in the company, in communion, and communication with someone with whom your vital body is charged, recharged, is what is meant by *satsang* – is what is meant to be near a master. There need not be any verbal communication; there need not be any communication at all outwardly. Just to be near and intimate …just to be open and near, and your vital body increases; it begins to be more – it begins to be richer and purified.

So seek company where your vital body becomes transparent. And sometimes it happens that even a dead master can help; even the place, the bodhi tree, can help. Buddhists have tried to save this tree continually for twenty-five centuries – that same tree. It is not just infatuation; it is not just superstition; it is not just a memorial. There are subtle reasons, more significant reasons to save this tree; Buddha has been near it once, and the tree has absorbed something of Buddha. The tree has been in a very deep relation with Buddha; the tree has a subtle buddhahood itself. Now, it vibrates with a different vibration. No other tree on this earth vibrates like that, cannot.

It is a rare tree; it had a rare opportunity: Buddha has walked around it for days and for nights. Buddha has been lying, sleeping, sitting....And Buddha could not help loving; and Buddha could not help being compassionate. And the tree was a constant companion; and the tree has imbibed the very spirit. And still today *this* tree is totally different. When you are around it, and if you are receptive, in a subtle way you are again in the intimacy of Buddha himself.

So shrines can help, temples can help, mosques can help, *samadhis* can help. It is better not to be in the company where you are sucked vitally, even the person is alive. It is better to be in the company of a dead one, if you can feel vitally recharged.

So remember this, remember this continuously: avoid all that which destroys your vital body. And much *is* destructive. In a cinema hall it is not only the film which destroys you; rather, deeply, the film is relevant, but the whole crowd destroys you more. And it is a particular crowd – it is not just a crowd, it is a particular crowd – with a particular type of mind, with particular stone bodies. They destroy you more. It is not the film really, the film cannot destroy you so much, but the crowd around you....And continuously for three hours, they are in a very rapt attentive mood – it is very dangerous because you become vulnerable. For three hours continuously, without blinking the eyes you are vulnerable! Anything can penetrate you, and all around, just bad vibrations – they go inside.

When you are out of a cinema hall, you have a very much lessened vital body; coming out from a temple, you have something plus. So be aware, not only of the physical body and its purification, be aware of the second, vital body also.

About the third body, we will discuss tonight....

When the self – living inside the food body –
and the vital body thinks through the instrumentality of
the fourteen organs like mind, et cetera, about
objects like sound, smell, touch, et cetera it is
called the manomaya kosh *or the mental body.*
When the self, united with these three bodies,
knows through intelligence, it is called the
vigyanmaya kosh *or the knowing body.*
When the self, in union with these four bodies –
food body, vital body, mental body and the knowing
body – dwells in its primeval and causative ignorance
it is called the anandamaya kosh *or the bliss body.*

In the morning we discussed two bodies: the physical, and the vital. The third is known as the mental body, as the mind-body. This third is constituted of thoughts. But the science of yoga believes that thoughts are not only thoughts, they are things, they are substantial; they *are*. They have an existence of their own – a very subtle existence, but there is existence. So whenever a thought goes into you, you are changing your mind-body; you are giving food to it.

And we are so unaware about this phenomenon, that the mind is being fed every moment, and we are giving it anything, without any choice – it is just a confusion.

Whatsoever we go on giving to the mind, we are only concerned that it must remain occupied; that's all. Occupation in itself becomes an aim. One should not be unoccupied, so go on reading anything, go on listening to anything, go on seeing anything, go on...do something with the mind! So whatsoever is around, we are vulnerable to it. This is fatal, because then you create a very confused mind-body, very confused – with contradictions, with infinite contradictions. And that's the reason there is so much anguish, so much tension, and so much misery inside. That's the reason the mind is just mad.

Now psychologists say that really no one is normal, and there are only two types of abnormalities: one, normal abnormality – another, abnormal abnormality. So there are two types of insane people: one, who are insane in a socially accepted way – another, who are insane in their individual whims.

But everyone seems to be insane. And it is because we have never thought that our mind-body requires an inner harmony, an inner music. Thoughts should not be in contradiction; thoughts must be in a certain harmony, in a certain inner balance; otherwise, you become just a crowd – you are a crowd! C.G. Jung came to realize that no one has *a* mind: everyone is *many* minds; everyone is polypsychic. We go on talking about "my mind" – never talk about it again! You are just a crowd, not even a group, but a crowd; and not even a crowd, but a warring crowd – each thought fighting with someone else.

Gurdjieff used to say that man is just like a palace where there are so many slaves, but the master has gone out. And he has been out for such a long time that the slaves have now completely forgotten that there was a master. Now, whenever someone passes by the palace...and it is such a beautiful palace that everyone wants to enquire to whom it belongs. So any slave who happens to be on the door says, "It belongs to me. I am the master." But another time, the same person passes by; someone else is on the door, and he asks, "To whom does this palace belong?" He says, "It belongs to me, I am the master." So the whole city is confused, "Who is the master?" Everyone says, "I am the master" – every slave.

Gurdjieff used to say, "Such is the condition of man. Every thought that passes, even on your surface mind, becomes the master; and the master is either asleep or has gone for a long journey and has not come back. And it has been so long...."

That's why we have no will. We cannot have a will if we are just a crowd. You decide to do something, and the second moment you decide not to do it. And the third moment, neither you are decisive to do it, nor even not to do it – you are simply indecisive. You decide that you are going to be awake in the morning at four o'clock; and then at four o'clock you yourself say, "There is no need." Another slave is on the surface of your mind, not you – the same one is not here who decided. In the morning when you are awake at eight o'clock, you begin to repent, "Why, when I had decided, why couldn't I get up? Why?" This is the third. And these three will never meet; they have no dialogue – they are just atomic thoughts. And any atomic thought on the surface becomes the master. You cannot have the will; really, you cannot have any soul. You are not an individual.

You must know the meaning of the word "individual." It means indivisible, that which cannot be divided. But we exist in division, so we cannot be said to be individuals. We are just a divided crowd.

Yoga is the science of individuation. It is how to create the individual, how to crystallize this crowd into one, how to create a center which can be the master always, and how to put every slave in its place.

Then you will need a purification of your mind; you will need a catharsis – a deep catharsis is needed then. You have to throw out all that is just contradictory; you have to create a harmony in your thoughts. And don't allow any thought to come in, because to allow it to be in is easy, but then to displace it from there is very difficult.

So the first thing is don't allow inside, thoughts which are not going to help create a harmony, and then go on searching for, and observing what contradictory thoughts you have. Be the chooser. Emphasize the thoughts which can create an inner peace and inner silence – then you have a purified mental body. And with this body-transparent you can look beyond, and you can go to another body.

Beyond the mind-body is the fourth, the fourth body. The fourth body is known as the consciousness-body – *vigyan maykos*. It will be difficult, a bit difficult, to distinguish between the mental body and the conscious body, because we don't know any consciousness except the mind. But if the mind is purified, then you become simply aware that something else is still behind the mind, and the mind becomes a door. But we can understand....

You have thoughts – that's one thing – but you can be aware of your thoughts; and this awareness is not a thought at all. You have anger – this is a thought, a thought process. You can be aware of it: "Now in me is running a thought process, a combination of thoughts which is known as anger, or jealousy, or love." You can be aware. You can stand out of it and be aware that this is anger. You can be aware, "This is a thought." This awareness that, "this is a thought," this observation, this possibility to observe the thought process, creates the fourth body. So everyone doesn't have the fourth body really developed, but only as a potentiality, only as a possibility.

When you become aware of your mind, only then you have the fourth body, and then there is a growth. Sometimes we have glimpses, sometimes we become aware. In moments of sudden danger, in accidents, in encountering a situation we have not faced before – we become aware, because for the first time, the mind in the shock of the accident or of a dangerous situation – in that shock the mind stops.

For example: If someone suddenly throws a dagger into you, the mind will stop, because there is nothing to do now or to think. Thought will stop. And when thought stops, you become aware. You become aware that thought has stopped, but still there is consciousness: "I am conscious."

This is the fourth body, the consciousness body, our conscious body. We have it but in a very undeveloped form. To develop it is arduous, because it needs much effort to remain conscious of every thought that passes through your mind, of every thought that has become an accumulation in your mind – a part of your mind, all the conditionings of the mind – to become aware of them is arduous. It is difficult, but not impossible; and only when this becomes possible, you have the dignity of being called a human being; otherwise, not. Because an unconscious human being means nothing. Then you are just being thrown from here and there by impressions and influences from the outside. When you become conscious then you cannot be influenced. For the first time you become the chooser.

Buddha was passing a village and many people came to him with great abuse; they were condemning him, abusing him, throwing stones at him, and he was just standing there. Then someone asked, "Now what are you going to do?"

Buddha said, "Nothing, because now I have become the chooser. You cannot manipulate me; you can abuse me – that is up to you – but you cannot create the reaction. You cannot manipulate me. If you abuse me and I react – and the reaction can be predicted by you – then it is just a manipulation. I am nowhere in it. You push the button and the anger is there."

Reaction means that you have no conscious body developed, so you go on reacting. Really, when you go on reacting, those reactions cannot be said to be actions, because actions come only with a conscious body, developed and mature. Then you *act*; otherwise, you go on reacting. Someone says this, so you say that; someone does this, so you react in that way, and everything is predictable.

We know when the husband comes back home in the evening, he knows what is going to happen. The whole scene is predictable: what the wife is going to ask…he knows the question already, and now he is preparing answers. And the wife knows already what answers he is going to give. The whole game is predictable, and daily it is repeated. What are we doing? The husband knows very well that whatsoever he says, whatsoever he may say, it is not going to be believed; and still, he will answer in the same way. And the wife knows that whatsoever and howsoever she may ask, he is going to give the deceptive answer, but still she goes on asking.

Is there a dialogue? Impossible. There is just a deceptive game that both are playing. And this continues for their whole lives. People go on reacting in the same old routine way. Why? If I know that if I ask *this* question, *that* answer is to be given; and if I am conscious, there is no need to ask. The whole thing is just absurd; there is no need to ask. And I have asked many times, and many times I have been frustrated – and – and again the same thing. Really, we are not conscious.

The moment the husband enters the house, the question comes out – it is not the wife who is asking it – it is just mechanical. The question comes out, and the moment there is a question, the answer is manipulated.

Have you ever done anything as a conscious agent, as a conscious action? No. If you have done, then you must have become aware of a different thing than the mind. The awareness of mind, the consciousness of the thought process, this standing outside the mind – beyond, just as an onlooker, an observer – is the fourth body. The third body is constituted of thoughts; the fourth body is constituted of consciousness.

The fifth body is known as the bliss body. This is the last, the innermost body – but still the body. When the fourth body is purified, when the fourth body becomes just a transparency, the fifth is realized, because the fourth becomes so transparent then the fifth is felt directly. That's why, when you are in deep meditation you don't feel meditation, you feel bliss. When you are deep in meditation, when you are deep in awareness, you don't feel awareness, you feel bliss.

When you begin to feel bliss, that means now you have begun to be aware.

Awareness creates the situation in which bliss is felt.

Awareness creates the transparency of the fourth body, and the fifth is seen. The fourth becomes so transparent, that not only you can *see* through it, you can *pass* through it without any resistance – it is just a door, it is just an opening. This fifth body is the bliss body. This bliss is already there. It is not to be found somewhere else, it is not to be achieved; it is there only to be discovered. And you discover it by purifying the fourth body.

But this, too, is just a body and has to be transcended; bliss also has to be transcended. One has to go beyond, because if you cannot go beyond bliss, you are still off the center. Because bliss is still an experience, and the experiencer is still beyond.

So whatsoever you can feel will belong to some body, this or that. All experiences belong to these five bodies.

And when there is no experience, only the experiencer remains. When there is no known object, only the knower remains.

When there is nothing to be witnessed, but only the witness is, then you are centered in yourself – then you *are*; otherwise, you belong to this body or that.

This is not a body.

This is the original nature.

This is the existential source of all being.

Two or three things more. When you transcend the blissbody, you transcend individuality also. When you transcend the blissbody, you transcend life and death also, because life and death are phenomena which exist only in the bodies, and in relation to the bodies. Where there is no body, you cannot die and you cannot be reborn. So once one becomes aware of the no-body existence of the center, then there is no death and no life – then you are existence itself. Then there is no individuality, then you are not, simply the being is. All form and all name is lost.

Meditation is the method to purify the fourth. Then what to do with the fifth . . . how to transcend it? How to transcend bliss itself? It is difficult to understand because we don't know bliss at all, so how to transcend it is irrelevant. First one has to know, and the moment you know you will know the key to transcend it.

The key is known very easily because this is the last body. With every body it is difficult, because again you face another body. So you transcend one body, but again you are rooted in another. When you reach the bliss body, the next behind, then behind the bliss body – for the first time – there is no body now. Now you are near the very center of existence. And it has a gravitation of its own: that gravitation is known as grace.

You throw something, and gravitation pulls it down, mm? – the earth pulls it down. But beyond two hundred miles above the earth, around earth, gravitation cannot work. So the moment a spaceship passes the two-hundred-miles barrier, the earth cannot pull it down. This is the boundary of earth's pull – two hundred miles.

The bliss body is just the boundary of the no-body existence. And when you are in the bliss body, you are in the pull. Now a new gravitation begins to work; that gravitation is known as grace. That's why those who achieve the state beyond all bodies say, "This is not by our effort that we have reached it; it is by God and His grace."

Really, with the fifth, nothing is to be done anyway. You have only to reach to the fifth – that reaching itself is the doing.

Reach the fifth, and you will be pulled.

The reaching itself is anyway transcendence.

In the context of pleasure and pain,
the desire for pleasurable things is called the sense of
pleasure, and aversion to painful things is called
the sense of pain. And because of what one does to
gain pleasure and shun pain, one is called a doer.
Sound, touch, form, taste, and smell –
these five objects are causes of pleasure and pain.
When the self, in pursuit of virtuous and sinful acts,
identifies itself with the body, which it is not,
then it is called the diseased being.

Why does consciousness become so involved with the body – not only involved, but identified? Why do we begin to feel that we are the bodies? – not that we are *in* the bodies, but we *are* the bodies?

This is really a miracle, because the knower can never be the known; the observer, the source of consciousness, can never be identified with the object. This body we know as an object; this hand I know, I feel, as an object. I never feel... I *can* never feel it as me. It is always something outside – an object. It hurts, I know; it doesn't hurt, I know – but I remain the knower.

But why does it happen that the knower becomes the known? How? How does the subject become the object? It cannot become really – that is impossible; becoming is impossible. The subject can never become the object – but it appears, it appears that it has become the object. We have become the bodies, and we go on living as if we are bodies.

One philosopher has written a very strange book. The book is called *The Philosophy of As-if.* Really, this is our whole life. We behave as if we are bodies; we behave as if we are material. We behave always not as we are, but *as if* – the "as if" is always there. How does this happen? – this which is impossible – how does this impossibility happen? What is the key? What is the clue?

The clue is very simple. The logic in the trick is very simple. You begin to be identified with anything which is pleasurable, because if you feel identified with the pleasure, you can feel more pleasure. If you do not feel identified with pleasure, then you cannot feel the pleasure at all, really. So the lover begins to feel identified with the beloved, the friend with the friend, the father with his son, the mother with her son; they begin to feel identified. The mother feels as if she is living in the son, and that if the son succeeds, the mother succeeds. If the son achieves, the father achieves. Then the son becomes just an extended part of the father's ego.

With whatsoever we feel as pleasure, we begin to be identified. The moment the son becomes rebellious or becomes a criminal, the father tries to destroy the identification. He says, "Now, no more. You don't belong to me at all." Why? Why does the son belong at all?

I have a friend – he is an old man, an old politician, with many ambitions unfulfilled, obviously. A politician can never feel fulfilled, that is intrinsically impossible. He is now seventy-five. His son died; he was only forty, but he was a minister in a state.

The son was a minister; this old man could never be a minister, he had tried in every way. And now he says, "There were many chances but I just escaped; I never wanted to be in any post." He had tried everything possible, but now he says that he is beyond. But his son was a minister...he had two sons – one was just ordinary; the second was extraordinary. The old man has never felt identified with the first son – never. His identity was with the second one, who was a minister. Then the second son died, and this old man began to feel that he could not live anymore.

He came to me and asked, "What to do? I think of committing suicide, I cannot live anymore. My son has died; my young son has died, and I am old and I am still.... It is not good – the father should die first."

I asked him, "Had your son been a criminal, bad, evil, unsuccessful, would you have felt the same?" He pondered over it and said, "No." Then I told him, "It is not the death of the son which has become so significant to you, really – it is your death, your ambition's death."

I asked him, "If your other son dies, will you commit suicide?" He said, "I have never loved him at all. He is just ordinary." He has loved his ambition, not the son. The other son is as much a son, but there has been no communication between the two, never. They have not even talked. He said, "No, if he had not been up to *my* conceptions I would not have felt like this."

The ego begins to be identified with something which is pleasurable. And this is the logic of our minds, the logic of this whole illusion, that we feel that our body is the source of pleasure. Of course there are pains and there are sufferings, but we always transfer pains and sufferings to others. Suffering is always created by someone else.

Jean-Paul Sartre has said – and said a very beautiful thing, but of course absolutely nonsense. He has said, "The other is hell." The *other* is hell, always the other is hell. Oneself? – it is heaven, the very heaven. The *other* is the hell – this is the division, the bifurcation.

We continue to be identified with the body because we feel this is the source of pleasure. Whenever someone else's body becomes the source of pleasure, we begin to be identified with that also. But always, pain comes from someone else; suffering comes from someone else. With this trick, this deep involvement in identification becomes possible.

The truth, the fact, is quite different: the body is both *or* neither. Either it is both the source of pain and pleasure.... Remember this; it is both, because it cannot be one or the other. Pleasure and pain are *one*. Your body is the source of *both*. If you can feel this and realize this, then they both negate each other; the pain and the pleasure both negate each other and the body becomes neutral. Or, feel that pleasure and pain both come from outside, both are devices. They both come from outside; don't divide, take them as a whole. Then also there is no identification with the body; the body is neutral.

And if the body is neutral, this rishi says you become a soul; otherwise, you are a conditioned soul. And this conditioned soul is the bondage; this conditioning is the bondage. And the rishi says this is the only disease, the spiritual disease: to be conditioned so much, identified so much with the body that one begins to feel as if one is the body.

This "as if" must be broken.

But it begins to be difficult. One feels to break it, but it looks impossible, because we have investments in it. We can break it if someone can make us confident that "if you break this body-consciousness, you will be very happy and blissful" – then we can break it. But again the old fallacy goes on, the old longing goes on. So I am not saying that if you want happiness, then break this conditioning and identification with the body, because you cannot break it. Rather, be aware of the fact that happiness or misery both will always remain side by side; you cannot leave one and choose the other. That is not possible. They are just like negative and positive poles of electricity; they are two parts of one phenomenon.

So be aware of this, that they are two parts of one phenomenon. Then you can just drop them without any further longing.

You cannot drop anything if there is a desire to gain something else; then that desire is again desire for happiness, pleasure. Be aware of the fact that both are one; pleasure and pain are one. Your interpretation differs, but the thing is always the same. This awareness of the fact becomes the dropping, the turning. And the soul, for the first time, realizes that it has never been identified with any object at all; it is the subjectivity.

Kierkegaard has said, "To know the subjectivity as the subjectivity is the realization. To know the subjectivity as an object is the bondage."

Why this bondage with the body and bodies? What is the secret? How are we in it, and why do we continue to be in it? Why is it such a struggle to go beyond? If bliss is inwards, and outwardly we cannot achieve anything other than anguish, then why this absurdity of living outward and outward? Why not go inward? Who is preventing you?

You are the prisoner.

And you are the imprisoned.

No one else is involved in it –

No one except you, yourself.

Then why not take the jump?

There must be something which hinders you, which prevents you, which becomes a barrier to you. What is that? This rishi says that the longing for pleasure, the fear of misery, and the fear of pain are the root causes – the longing for pleasure and the effort to avoid any pain, any suffering, any *dukkha*. And the illusion is created because pleasure and pain, happiness and misery, are not two things, are not two opposites; they are two polarities of one phenomenon, two ends of one phenomenon.

They are joined and one. That's why pleasure turns into misery; they are convertible. Anything that you feel as pleasurable this moment may become unpleasurable the next. So pleasure and pain are not qualities of a thing, because the thing remains the same. I love you and feel happy; you remain the same. And the next moment, I hate you and feel miserable. But happiness and misery are not qualities of *you*, you remain the same. They must belong to *my* mind, to *my* attitude; they must belong to *me*.

That's why the same thing can be a source of deep happiness to one, and a deep source of misery to someone else. The same thing can be a source of happiness to you this moment, and the next moment a source of your very hell. Pleasure and pain, happiness and suffering are not qualities of things as we presume; they are not. They are your attitudes – they belong to you.

So try an experiment: You are feeling happy in some situation – then be in that situation and begin to feel unhappy. And soon, soon you will begin to feel unhappy – it depends on your choice. Your beloved is nearby; you are feeling happy – now begin to feel unhappy, and soon you will be able to create unhappiness. Begin to feel happy, and soon you will change the whole situation – it depends on you.

Once you know the secret, the whole clinging drops – with pleasure or with fear of pain, the whole clinging just drops. The moment you know you are the master – whether to feel happy or to feel miserable depends on you – you become free of all dependence on others. But one has to know, one has to experience.

Things are just neutral; they don't give you anything. It is you who contributes the feeling – not the thing. Really, you determine the whole thing *unconsciously;* that is why there is clinging. Determine it *consciously.*

Try an experiment. You are feeling very pained, suffering, you are ill. Then accept the illness; don't fight it, remain in it, be a companion to it – don't try to escape. Accept it totally, be with it, and soon a moment comes when you explode into a new dimension. The illness may be there still, but now it belongs only to the body, not to you. It is just on the periphery somewhere, as if it belongs to someone else – you have transcended.

Once the consciousness begins to feel that there is no bondage from the outside, then the longing for pleasure drops, because it is your projection. Then the fear of suffering drops, because it is your projection. In a very subtle way you become the master, the converter. You can convert anything into anything, because it is only your choice, your decision, your mind. Whatsoever you put into things you can get back – it is really just an echo.

You fall in love with someone, and if I ask you why, you will say, "Because the face is beautiful, the person is beautiful." But really the thing is quite the reverse. It is not that the person is beautiful and so you have fallen in love; rather, because you have fallen in love the person looks beautiful. Your falling in love is primary, and the second thing is just a projection, because the same person can become ugly the next day – he remains the same with the same face, but everything has changed. This happens so often but still we are unaware. You say, "I cannot live without you!" And soon a moment comes when you cannot live *with* him. Why? – because you have not taken things in the right order.

You fall in love – that means you begin to project; love is a hypnosis. Love is a very delicate state of mind in which you can project anything – anything! So the beloved is not really there outside, it is here inside. It is a projection, and the person is just a screen. And you have projected much, you have contributed much. The moment you withdraw your contribution, the person is just ordinary. There is no halo around, no aura; everything has just dropped. The person is just ordinary, even more ordinary than ordinary, because now, it is so without luster. Now dreams have dropped, and dreams were the thing the whole stuff was made of.

Remember this fact: It is your mind which begins to feel happy or miserable – it depends on you. And once you know the secret, you have become really the master. Now you know the alchemy; you are the alchemist now, you can change any base metal into the higher. Now, you have the secret to turn anything into gold – now you can convert. And once you begin to convert base metals into higher metals, nothing is higher and nothing base. Now you know it is just you and your projection – your mind is doing the whole trick.

But one has to do much to be aware of this fact; one has to go deep into the facticity, into the very phenomenon of desiring, of avoiding, of longing for this and trying to escape that – one has to go deep into it. And it is not a doctrine – whatsoever the rishi is saying is not a doctrine – it is not a conception really; it is the facticity. It is how the mechanism of the mind works; it is just a fact. It is not a philosophy; it is a science in the sense that it is how the mind works. You project first, then you begin to believe. Then any moment you can withdraw your projection and the idol is lost, the temple is destroyed, and there is nothing left. But again you will do the same thing, and you will go on doing the same thing: projecting, then feeling miserable or happy, and never being aware that you are creating – that you are the creator.

Everyone is a magician – *everyone* is a magician, and everyone goes on doing tricks with himself. Then these tricks become habits, mechanical habits; you can repeat them ad infinitum. And we have repeated them ad infinitum – lives and lives and lives. We have been repeating them always.

Buddha and Mahavira both tried a very novel experiment with the human mind. Whenever someone would come to them, seeking, they would tell the seeker, "First, try to remember your past lives. First, go deep into past lives." But the seeker would say, "There is no need. I am concerned with the future; I am concerned with how to know the truth, how to realize the divine, how to be liberated, how to get to nirvana. What is the need of going into past lives?"

And Buddha would say, Mahavira would say, "There is a deep need. Unless you know your past, you will never be able to see that you have been playing tricks with yourself, continually, repeatedly. In each life you have done the same. It is a repetition: the same love – the falling in love and then frustration; riches, and then the feeling of inner poverty; prestige and power, and yet the helplessness. And the same!"

But we forget. Every life we drop all memories and we forget, and we begin anew. Esoteric science says that this forgetfulness is intentional. It is intentional that you have forgotten your past lives, because you wanted to forget. Psychologists say that you forget all that you want to forget. Sometimes you say, "I know your name, but I wonder why I have forgotten it." Really, you wanted to forget. You are playing tricks with yourself; you wanted to forget; you never wanted to remember the name – that's why you have forgotten.

We go on forgetting things. For example: Everyone remembers childhood as the very heaven, but it has never been so. Ask any child – he is in a hell. He is trying to grow up rapidly, trying to be a young man soon, because he feels very helpless. Everyone is more powerful than him, and everyone is suppressing him; everyone is just trying to destroy him. Everyone is just ordering him to do this and that; everyone is trying to discipline him. He is not at all free, he is feeling he is in prison and trying to get away soon from all this – trying to be a grown-up. But when he is grown-up he says, "What bliss it was to be a child."

And when he is old, he is remembering childhood, painting about it, making poetries about it, dreaming about it. What has happened? – the trick of the mind. He has forgotten all that was not good to remember; now, he remembers only the good things, and all else has been just dropped. Now he remembers the love; now he remembers the freedom from all responsibilities; now he remembers...it was never a fact!

Whatsoever he felt as total helplessness, now he feels as freedom from responsibility. Whatsoever he has really felt in the past as a very bothersome burden of the parents, now he feels as love. He has dropped all that was not good, not ego strengthening, not creating a beautiful image – he has dropped it all.

Bring that man into deep hypnosis and ask him, "How was your childhood?" And he will begin to say that it was just hell. Awake, out of hypnosis, he says, "It was a heaven; I am longing again and again to go back." Put him into hypnosis, then ask, and he will say, "It was just hell. There was nothing in my childhood."

Psychologists have come to know now that all the misery, all the diseases, all the schizophrenia, all the insanity that develops later in life, is just a by-product of your childhood. So how was it a heaven? They say all that happens later on is just a by-product of your childhood. In your childhood, seeds are put into you which will develop into insanities, into abnormal perversions.

But the poets have always been talking about the innocence of childhood, the beauty of it, the benediction, the blessedness.

Psychoanalysts know more, and better. Whenever someone is ill, they have to bring out this very seed that has been planted in childhood. Unless that seed is destroyed – that seed is traumatic – unless it is destroyed you can never be really well. So psychoanalysis goes on trying to make you free from your childhood and all its impressions, all that childhood has done with you. If you are free from it, only then you can grow positively; otherwise, positive growth is impossible.

Buddha and Mahavira will say, "First go deep" – and there are methods. There are methods which can bring you back all the memories of your past lives. And once you know and go back on this time track, once you know that you have done the same nonsense every time, and you have longed for the same things, and always received quite the opposite.... This has been a wheel constantly turning and turning and turning, and always forgetting and forgetting, and doing the same thing again and again. If one becomes aware of it, the very awareness becomes transforming.

The very awareness is transformation.

It is an inner revolution.

But leave aside past lives; even this life is enough – if you can go back in this very life and can find out that whatsoever was happiness one day became misery the other, that whatsoever you longed for, when you achieved it, was totally frustrating.... One of the greatest miseries of human life is to get that which you long for. If you never get it you are still happy, happy in the hope, happy in the possibility. But when you get it, even hope is lost. Now there is no future – you have got it.

Every achievement is frustrating. They say, "Nothing succeeds like success." But I say, "Nothing fails like success."

Nothing fails like success.

The moment you succeed, you know nothing has been achieved. It was just a dream, and now you are disillusioned.

So go back in this life, even this life is enough; go back and feel. Really we always go to the future, never to the past; we always go for the tomorrow, never for the yesterday. Go back and feel, go back. You have lived with the same desires, with the same longing, with the same dreams. Now take account of your past – what have you achieved? What have you gained? Was any hope ever fulfilled, or has every hope just proved hopeless? – go back. Don't always move into the future, because in the future you will be doing the same – repeating the past. Go back. Realize your whole past; feel what has been wrong with it and don't continue that wrong again. Drop it. Drop it consciously because it has become a habit now, it has become a mechanical routine. Drop it consciously!

Don't repeat the past in the future, and you will be a new man.

This is what I mean by sannyas, by renunciation – to be a new man. This is what I mean by "breaking with the past," discontinuity with the past. Remember what you have done with yourself in the past, and then drop it! Don't drop it in steps, because you can never drop anything in steps – drop it totally, suddenly. Only then there is a discontinuity; otherwise, if you drop it in steps, there is a continuity.

Drop it suddenly.

This is what is meant by sannyas:

Dropping the past as useless for the future.

This is a reorientation of all your attitudes, a reorientation of your total consciousness. Once this reorientation is there, you begin a new journey, and that journey is inwards. Then you can pass all the five bodies and come to the one which is embodied, but is not a body itself.

*Grouping of mind, vital breath, desire,
essence and virtue with the associates is
called* panchvarga, *or the five groups.
A living being identified with the nature
of the* panchvarga *cannot be free of them
without knowledge or knowing.
The disease arising out of the subtle
elements like the mind and the rest of it seems
to be covering the self, and it is called the seed body;
it is also known as the knot, or complex of the heart.
And the consciousness dwelling inside it is called
the* kshetragya, *or the knower of the field.*

Now the rishi is discussing the complexities of the mind, complexities of the consciousness. Why are we just a complexity? Why is there no innocence and no simplicity? Why is everything just a knot, just a confusion, just insanity inside?

If we can open a mind, then we will see just anarchy there, chaos. We go on somehow managing ourselves, but inside there is nothing which can be said to be a cosmos. Inside there is chaos, simple chaos. This is a miracle that we can manage ourselves; it seems impossible. How are these complexes built? How are they formed? How do we help them form? And how many complexes are there?

There are five divisions of all the complexes. The first complex is the mind. Eastern mysticism has always looked at mind as the disease, as the basic disease. It is just the opposite from the Western attitude towards life. The Greek mind, which is the originator of all Western thinking, always looked towards the mind as the supreme-most thing. Mind is the peak according to the Greek attitude, Greek thinking.

For Aristotle, mind is the peak, mind is the most evolved energy. But to the Eastern mind, mind has been a disease. That's why the East couldn't develop science, because if mind is diseased then you cannot develop science really, because science has to be developed with the mind.

The Greek mind could give the impetus to the Western mental evolution, so they could create a very complex structure of science and scientific knowledge. The structure has arrived; the structure is there now, but the consciousness, the human being itself, is lost. It has been at a very big cost. Machines have evolved, but the creator itself is just feeling empty and meaningless. Technology has developed, and now we can create with this technology a very different world – but the very interest to create a different world is no more there.

Sartre or Camus or others – they all feel that there is no sense in existing at all, there is no meaning. Sartre says we are condemned to be alive; there is no need, there is no purpose, nothing is going to come out of all this effort, it is just futile. So Camus asserts that the only philosophical problem, the only metaphysical problem now is suicide. The only possibility for us in which we can be free and active, seems to be suicide; all else is just meaningless.

This has to happen, because with mind, ultimately there can be only madness and suicide. With mind, ultimately there can be only meaninglessness and an effort to forget it. So the whole of the West is now trying to forget – through chemicals, through alcohol, through so many methods, to forget themselves. Life is so meaningless that to be aware is to be in suffering. To know it – the misery all around, the suffering all around, and the meaninglessness of it – to be aware of it is too much; it creates anguish. So it is better to forget it somehow and drop into a world of dreaming.

Chemicals can help. You drop out of the world, and they say to you "turn on." Where do you turn on? You turn on really to a dream world; there you can find meaning, there you can find purpose. There you can find again the romance and poetry, but not when you are awake, aware, conscious. And they say these chemicals are helping the expansion of consciousness. This is absurd. They are not helping the expansion of consciousness, they are helping only the expansion of the dreaming process. They are only helping you to dream more beautifully, more deeply, to dream more intensely. They are not helping consciousness; they are helping unconsciousness. They are helping deep processes of *sushupti* – of sleep and dreaming.

This had to happen, because with the mind you cannot go beyond this point. With mind there is no meaning; there cannot be. With mind there is logic, but no meaning; with mind there is reason, but no life. With mind you can create the dead and mechanical, but you completely lose track of existence, of life, of being, of consciousness.

Mind, this rishi says, is the first disease, the basic disease in a way. Why is mind a disease? – because mind is just a disturbance. Mind is just a disturbance in consciousness. It is not your nature; it is just a disturbance. The moment there is no disturbance, there is no mind. And this state of no-mindedness is the state of consciousness – the expansion of consciousness. You drop into yourself: not into dreaming, not into projections, into yourself. Consciously, with full alertness, you come to your center the moment mind is not there.

Meditation means how to be not a mind.

How to be not a mind!

Meditation means how to create the state of no-mindedness.

It doesn't mean unconsciousness. It means conscious and still, without any disturbance in the consciousness; conscious with no ripples, with no waves, with no vibrations; conscious as a deep, calm, silent pool with no ripples on it, with no disturbances on the surface; just a calm silent pool with no breeze to disturb, just mirrorlike.

With mind one goes on being disturbed more and more, and then this whole process of disturbance is self-perpetuating. One disturbance creates ten more, and those ten create a hundred more. This is self- perpetuating, and then you are in a vicious circle. With this mind something can be done. That is, you can travel outwardly, you can go more into the world. But the more you go into the world the farther you are from yourself. And the farther you have gone, the more the track back is lost. Then you only remember that there is a home, but there is no way to get back. And we continue to remember there is a home; there is a homesickness always somewhere present. There is a home and one has to go back.

But there is no way, and we continually try to find the home with the mind itself, which has lead us astray. Then we go into scriptures, then we go into words, then we go into philosophies, metaphysical systems. And then we are lost even more in it, even more deeply, and the track is not found at all. The track can be found only if you begin to feel and understand that mind is the disease, so you cannot go back with the mind; the mind cannot be used as a vehicle, it cannot be used as a passage. It is not a door towards consciousness. It is a door towards the world, towards objects – not towards the subjectivity. That's why it is said to be a disease, a complex.

The second is *prana*, life itself; rather than life, the lust for life. There is a deep fear – fear of death – and there is a deep lust to continue anyhow, to live anyhow. Life itself seems to be the end.

Life cannot be the end itself; if life itself is the end, then one will have to exist on the periphery. Something must transcend life itself, something must be higher than life itself; otherwise, life can have no meaning. If you say that life itself is the end, then life is bound to be meaningless, because meaning comes from the beyond – always from the beyond. Something for which you exist gives the meaning – that's why we create many so-called meanings all around us.

Money becomes the meaning because you live for it; power becomes the meaning, prestige becomes the meaning. You create meanings, but those are just bogus meanings – because really, if life is at peril, you will be ready to lose power, money, everything. So you just deceive yourself, but those deceptions can never become the reality. Life remains above them; they are not beyond, they cannot be. That's why in the West, there are so many feelings of frustration and meaninglessness. That's an obvious corollary of life being taken as the end.

Life originates in something and then again dissolves into something. Life comes up and then goes down and is dissolved. So the original source of life must be beyond life. It comes out of it and then goes back, just as a wave raises itself and then falls down into the ocean; the ocean remains beyond the wave. The wave comes and goes; it is there this moment, and the next it is gone. The ocean is behind, beyond.

Life is just a wave. Existence is beyond life.

So one who begins to be too involved and too attached, too infatuated with life, loses the existential source of life itself.

Life is just the periphery:

The center is existence.

We have called that existence *God.*
We have called that existence *moksha.*
We have called that existence *nirvana.*

This is something very delicate to be understood. Really, we have never said that God exists. We have said, rather, *God is existence.* Those who say God exists don't know what they are saying. Man exists; God cannot exist in the same way. Trees exist, the earth exists, the sun exists, but not God. A tree may go out of existence, man may not exist, the sun may not exist, but God cannot be conceived as not existing. God is existence; God is *is-ness.* So really, to say God is, is to repeat oneself.

God *means* is; God means *is-ness.*

That is-ness is beyond life.

Life is just a wave on the ocean of is-ness. So we are separate as waves, but not as the ocean. We are separate on our peripheries, but not at the center. At the center we are one. So many waves on the ocean, but *in* the ocean they are one.

But no wave will be able to conceive it, because it seems so absurd. How can a wave conceive that all the waves around are one with it? – because when another wave is just rising up, one is just dying and falling down. If waves are one, then they must fall simultaneously, they must rise simultaneously. That's why we are the same. If we are all the same, then how is one rich and how is one poor? Then how is one young and how is one old? And how is one born and how is one dying? – we must be separate, obviously. Then how is one intelligent and one is not? And one is beautiful and one is not? – we must be different, we must be separate. But we are not. There are small waves and there are big waves; there are waves which go higher, there are waves which cannot go higher. But still they are the same – in the ocean they are the same.

If you are aware only of your wavelike life, then you cannot go inside; then this becomes a disease. And if you are aware that you are a wave, then you must be afraid – you are bound to be afraid of death, of dying, because every wave has to die. You can see that every wave is dying – coming up and down – so you are afraid. This fear comes because you have not known the oceanic existence which is yours; you have known only the wave existence which means life, which means *prana*.

So, the rishi says the second bondage, the second complexity, the second division of diseases, is lust for life. What does it mean?

It means if one is to go deeply into existence, one has to be ready to die. This readiness to die is the basic quality of a religious mind. This is what constitutes the very essential core of being religious: this readiness to die. This doesn't mean a suicidal tendency. This doesn't mean any suicidal tendency, because really all those who commit suicide, commit suicide because of lust for life. This may look paradoxical – but never has a buddha committed suicide, never! Why?

A person who is not in the least lusting for life, desiring life, why is he not committing suicide? Buddha would say, "I am so indifferent to life, I cannot be so infatuated with death. How can I be so infatuated with death? To me, they both mean the same. If life is – okay. If death is – okay." A buddha okays everything. He cannot choose.

Whenever someone commits suicide, really he is imposing conditions on life. He is saying life must be like this; otherwise, I commit suicide. "I must get this woman, I must get this post, I must get this and that. If I am not getting, I can live only with my conditions. Then if there is no fulfillment of my conditions, I am ready to die." Really this readiness to die is not readiness to die. He is asking too much. He is asking too much of life, and out of life; he is so filled with lust that he is even imposing conditions. This death is just a revenge, just a revenge towards life, because life could not fulfill his demands: "I will destroy life if life is not going to be what I desire it to be!" This is revenge, this is violence.

So when I say readiness for death, it means no lust for life, so that whatsoever comes, one is always in a welcoming attitude, in a receptivity. Whatsoever happens, one is ready – even death. Lust for life is the disease. This readiness, simple readiness to die, unties the lust for life.

The third complexity is that of desires. We don't live in existence, we live in desires. Really, we don't live in the world at all, we live in desires. Our life is not here and now, it is always somewhere else where the desire

97

is arrowed. It may be anywhere, but it is never here. Never here, because desire needs time – desire cannot be here.

Can you desire anything in the present moment? The moment you desire, you desire for the future; you cannot desire here and now. Here and now there is no desire, there is no possibility of desiring.

Desire needs space – that space is time.

Desire needs some point somewhere else from here – only then can desire exist. It exists as a bridge: a bridge needs two banks, a bridge cannot exist only on *this* bank. How can the bridge exist? There must be the other; the other bank must be there. Only then does the bridge become possible.

Desire is creating a bridge from here to there.

And the moment you have gone there and lost this moment, you will live always in an inner tension, inner anguish. And really you will never be existential; you will always be in desires, in desires, in desires – always longing for the other shore. Even if you can get to the other shore, you will be again longing for the other shore. No shore can be the fulfillment – desire is self-frustrating. We are nothing but desires. Can you find anything in you which is not a desire? Even when you are praying, it is desire; even when you are meditating, it is a desire; even when you are thinking of the divine, it is a desire. We convert everything into desire. This is the disease, that we cannot conceive of anything without desire.

Buddha used to say, "There is no God." And he was himself one of the most existential proofs of the divine. He was the perfect argument for the divine; his presence was divine. And he used to say there was no God. One day, Sariputta asked him, "Why do you continue to say there is no God? – because we all feel that when you are, God is. It seems contradictory, a person like you denying God. It seems contradictory because you are the proof, you are enough! We don't require any argument, but why do you deny it?"

Buddha said, "I deny it because I don't like God being made an object of desire. If I say God is, you will begin to desire: 'Then I must get, then I must reach.' And God is something which you cannot desire, and by desiring cannot get."

People would ask him, "Is there existence beyond death?" And he would say, "No, there is no existence beyond death." Why? – simply because if there is existence beyond death, you will begin to desire it.

They would ask, "Is there bliss? Is bliss possible?"

Buddha would say, "No. There is only the cessation of misery, no bliss."

He was one of the rarest geniuses to see the phenomenon of desiring, the tricks of desiring, and the cunningness of desiring. He would say, "No, there is no bliss at all; only cessation of suffering." Why? – because if bliss is positively asserted, one begins to desire it.

We convert everything into desiring. We have a mechanism for converting and transforming anything. Put anything into it, and it become as desire. We can even desire desirelessness. I have come across people who come and say, "How can I be desireless?" How to be desireless – they are asking for the supreme-most desire – how to be desire*less*! But we go on converting. This is the disease; really, this is the disease.

Look at the disease, look at the fact, and don't ask the "how." Look at the fact: this is the fact. Live with the fact. Be aware of your minds's mechanism, and how it transforms everything into desiring.

In that moment of awareness, desiring stops.

And when there is no desiring, you are just here – this very moment.

That moment becomes the door to the infinite.

That moment becomes the door to the divine – to nirvana.

That which is aware of the creation and dissolution of the knower,
the known and the knowable,
but is itself beyond creation and dissolution is called
the sakshi *or the witnessing self.*
That which dwells in the minds of all beings,
from Brahma (the creator) down to an ant,
and which lives everlastingly even after
the destruction of their gross and subtle bodies
is called the kutastha *or the crest-indweller.*
From among the kutastha and its different forms the self,
for the sake of the realization of its nature,
permeates the body like a thread threading a necklace,
and it is called antaryami or the imminent.

Now, three situational dimensions of the being: We discussed personalities; we discussed bodies; we discussed complexes of diseases. Now the enquiry into the being itself. What is the being? Behind all, beyond all, transcending all – what is the being itself? Three definitions have been given. One is called *sakshi*; sakshi means the witness. Another is called *kutastha*; kutastha means the eternal, the indestructible, the immortal. And the third is named *antaryami*: the innermost, the inner one. It is good and helpful for the seeker to understand these three definitions. They define the one and the same, but they define in different contexts.

First is the witness. This is the essential character, the essence, the very essence of the being. Whatsoever is named is never the knower; whatsoever is objectified is never the subject. The moment we know something, we are different form the known, from the object, because the knower cannot be the known, the observer cannot be the observed. A distance is created by knowledge, by knowing. Knowing is the bridge between the known and the knower.

The being is not, and never is the known; it is always the knower – always and *always* the knower. Whatsoever you know, remember one thing certainly – that you are not that. This much is certain, that whatsoever you have known and experienced, you are not that. That's why the *Upanishads* say, "Neti, neti – not this, not that." Whatsoever *you* say, the *Upanishads* say, "No, not this, not that – never!" This is the nature of the being; it always transcends objects. It is pure subjectivity, and this pure subjectivity can never be turned into any object. So in a way, you can never know yourself in the same way as you have known all else. So "self-knowledge" is in a way, a very contradictory word, because really the self cannot be made an object of knowledge. But still, self-knowledge exists. But that knowledge has to be defined and guarded, and defined in a specific way.

Self-knowledge means: where all knowledge stops. Self knowledge means: where there is no self. Self-knowledge means: the knower is not, the known is not, the knowledge is not. But when I say that you are never the known, then one thing must be understood: if you are not the known, how can you be the knower – because the knower is just in reference to the known. The knower is just in reference to the known. If you are never the object, how can you be called a subject? – because subject means in relation to object; it means the other end of the object. That's why the *Upanishads* say, "It is just a witness – not even a knower."

It witnesses all the three: the known, knowledge, the knower. They come up, they dissolve, and the witnesser remains. It will be better not to call it even a "witnesser," but a witnessing, because when we say "witnesser," a subtle crystallization comes into the world, a subtle feeling of the ego and "I." So it is better to say "witnessing." Then there is simply a process of knowledge without any ego, without any "I" crystallizing it.

And then in the world, there are not things, but processes. This is the difference between a materialist and a spiritualist. This: a materialist sees things in the world, and a spiritualist sees in the world events – not things. The difference is not whether matter is or not; the difference is not whether mind is or not. The difference is basically this: a spiritualist sees in the world energy, processes – energy processes, events, alive events – not dead things.

Now physicists are ready to accept this as far as matter is concerned. They say now, "There is no matter. Matter is dead; matter is not there – only energy waves, only quanta, only processes." Even a stone is just a process, it is not static; it is dynamic, it is moving. Not only is a river moving, the Himalayas also.

A Zen fakir, Bankei, has said, "I have not seen only rivers moving, I have seen bridges also moving. And once it happened that the river was not moving, and the bridge was moving." He means by this that there are not things – static, dead – but movement, continuous processes, waves and waves and waves; and each wave is turning into the other. This is what is meant by a spiritual attitude.

So matter is energy, waves. Inside also there is no knower as fixed, as "I," because the ego is a thing – dead. So it is better to call it not the witnesser, but witnessing – with no center really, just a process.

Buddha says, "There is rebirth, but you are not." So how can rebirth be? Ordinary logic will say, "How can rebirth be? If you are not, if there is no ego to be reborn, then how is rebirth possible?" Buddha says, it is just a process – a process just like a flamelike process. In the evening you see the flame: the lamp is burning and there is a flame. In the morning you blow it out. You say, "I am blowing out the same flame." Buddha says not, because the flame is constantly changing. It is a process, it is not a thing, so it cannot be the same. In the evening you saw one thing; this is something else – flame has been constantly changing and going into nothingness, and new flames are being replaced continuously.

It is continuity. The flame is not a thing, it is a continuity. Every moment the flame is changing, so whatsoever you are blowing out is not the same flame you saw in the night. It is the same continuity – a continuum.

Witnessing is there just like a flame.

It is a continuum.

This is the first situational definition. The rishi talks about it first, because it can be made a means; it can be used as a device; it can become a vehicle towards your being, your center.

The second is kutastha; it means: the eternal, the immortal, that which cannot be destroyed – indestructible. What can be destroyed really? What is destructible? – only the form and the name, *namrup*. Within these two words is the whole Eastern standpoint: namrup – name and form – can be destroyed, are destructible. Your name can be changed and your form – nothing else.

The ice is transforming itself into water, and the water is evaporating. What changes? – not the essence, but only the form and the name. Now it

is ice; now it is water; now it is vapor. What is changing? The essence remains the same, but the name and form change.

This whole world is just name and form. Everything is changing: the
child becoming the adult; the adult becoming the old man; life turning
into death; birth turning into death; health turning into disease; disease
turning into health – everything is changing. Even opposites are not really
opposites, because they can change into one another. The north becomes
the south, the south becomes the north. The east is also the west, and the
west is also the east. It depends. It depends on where you are looking.

Someone asked Mulla Nasruddin, "Where is your house on the road?
On the left or on the right?" he said, "It depends: sometimes it is on the
left, and sometimes it is on the right. It depends from where you are coming."

Life is a movement, but name and form change; the essence remains the
same. But when I say the essence remains the same, I don't mean it is a
static thing. I mean it is a dynamic force, but still the same. *Dynamic* and
the same must be remembered; otherwise, God becomes just a static phenomenon – dead, with no opening.

Kutastha doesn't mean a dead thing, it means a dynamic force, essen-
tially remaining the same, but changing its name and form all the time. Beyond name and form, the essential one is known as the kutastha. If you
destroy everything – every form and every name – the remaining is the kutastha. If all my five bodies are destroyed, if all my five diseases are destroyed, then the remaining will be the kutastha – that is the essential being
which cannot be destroyed. This always is.

This is the end definition; the first one was a means definition. If you
proceed by being a witness, you will reach the kutastha, the eternal, but
both are far away. Neither we are using witnessing, nor are we standing in
the eternal. Then it is, therefore, the third definition: it is called antaryami,
the innermost.

This definition belongs to us here and now, as we are. A link must exist
between the kutastha, the eternal, and us; otherwise, there can be no traveling towards it, no journey towards it. Somehow, we must be linked in all

these bodies, in all these diseases, in all these ignorances. Still the innermost being is here; it is just hidden. it is hidden just like the thread of the beads: the beads are apparent, but the thread is hidden. You cannot see directly, immediately; you have to make a gap between two beads, and then suddenly in the gap is the thread – the innermost running force, the innermost running energy.

So whenever one has to go deep into oneself, one has to make a gap between two diseases or between two bodies or between two thoughts. Wherever you can create a gap between two things inside you, suddenly you become aware of the thread.

For example, there are thoughts in the mind – continuously one thought is followed by another. Bring a gap between two thoughts. There *is* a gap, because two thoughts cannot exist without a gap: an interval is a basic necessity. One thought is followed by another, but there is a subtle gap. Be aware of the gap.

We are aware only of the thoughts. From one thought we jump to another, and the gap is lost. Remain in the gap, stand in the interval, slow down your thought process and you will feel a gap. One thought has gone, another has yet to come – there is a gap, a sudden silence. In this silence you will become aware of the thread; that thread is known as antaryami. It is here and now, and we cannot proceed; otherwise, we have to proceed from here and now.

So antaryami is the definition for us. Then sakshi, witnessing is the method; then kutastha, the eternal one is the end.

Now, two more diseases, two more complexes, two more illusions. We discussed three in the night: mind, lust for life, and desiring. Now the fourth is *sattva* – it means virtue. It means an inner accumulation of being good.

This feeling of being good is also a disease – for so many reasons. One is: you cannot feel you are good, unless you feel others are bad; that's impossible. You cannot feel you are good unless you feel others are bad, and the feeling that others are bad is a disease; the feeling of good is just a relative term. So a person who wants to feel good is bound to condemn others as bad; and the more you condemn others as bad, the more you can feel you are good. So these so-called good men go on condemning everyone.

Bertrand Russell has criticized Jesus for this reason. He says, "Everything is divine, everything looks holy, except one thing: why Jesus condemns the sinners so much – that they should be thrown into hell, and they should be condemned? Jesus cannot feel good unless he condemns." I don't think that Jesus ever condemned – a person like Jesus cannot condemn. The condemnation has come through the tradition; it is really St. Paul who speaks through Jesus, and he is one of the most deeply involved personalities who feels himself to be good. But whosoever it may be – whether Jesus says so, or St. Paul puts is in Jesus' mouth – the criticism is valid.

A good man can never be good if he is condemning others as bad, but you can never feel good unless you condemn. So a good man must be unaware of his goodness; only then it is not a disease. He must not be aware at all that he is good; only then is he not aware that others are bad. No religion other than Hinduism has condemned even goodness – even goodness becomes a sin, because it is ego-strengthening. It feeds your ego – of course with very pure food. But sometimes poisons can also be pure, so purity in itself is not something to be hailed. Poisons can also be pure, and when the ego becomes strengthened by purity, by virtue, by being good, it is pure poison – it is dangerous. That's why you can never feel at ease with any so-called good man. Around him there is always restlessness; no one can feel at ease. and unless you can feel at ease, the man is not good, not good at all.

So around mahatmas you cannot feel at ease – never. There is a very strained atmosphere, because their feeling of goodness can exist only if they create a very tense atmosphere around them. Everyone is bad, and they are on the high pedestal. Only they are good; everyone is bad. That's why two mahatmas condemn the other. They have always condemned. So only confirmed sinners, only persons who feel themselves inferior, who are suffering from an inferiority complex, can be around them. Two mahatmas cannot meet, because that is the meeting of two diseases, two strong egos – purified, poisonous. These are the pious sinners.

This disease must cease. Not that goodness is bad, but to feel good is bad, because to feel good is comparative; it is always in relation to someone else. And anything that is related to someone else is not of any worth for the inner journey. And man is so cunning and so deceptive that he can go on being cunning, he can go on being deceptive. He may change methods, he may change devices, but the basic disease remains the same.

For example, one can even boast of one's humility. This is the deceptiveness: one can boast even of one's humility, one can say, "There is no one more *humble* than me!" Now, through humility, ego is strengthened – I am again asserting my superiority in humility! But the contradiction is never seen. You can even say, "I am just a sinner," and feel good about it.

Tolstoy remembers that once he went to a church early in the morning. The streets were dark and there was no one in the church, only Tolstoy. Then the richest person of the city came. He didn't know that Tolstoy was there; Tolstoy was praying. This rich man began to pray and confess. He began to say, "I am one of the most fallen, deeply fallen, from the right path. I am a sinner. Forgive me" – and he began to relate his sins.

Tolstoy was just bewildered, because this man was known as one of the most virtuous. He listened silently; then the darkness withered away, and the rich man felt someone's presence. He looked around and he saw that Tolstoy was there. So he said, "Were you here when I was confessing?" Tolstoy said, "I was already here. When you came I was here; I was praying." So the man said, "Look, I must make you aware of the fact that I have confessed to God, not to you. So please forget whatsoever I have said! And don't talk about it in the city, because this was a dialogue between me and my God."

This is the deceptiveness of the mind. Really, he is confessing so as to feel good. He is not authentic – he is not feeling that he is a sinner. By confessing his sins he is now feeling a very holy man. This is a disease.

The fifth disease is *punya* – the feeling of holiness, the feeling of serving others, the feeling of doing good to others. And there is a difference: To be good is one thing, and to feel that one is doing good to others, is another. Punya means doing good to others. There are so many do-gooders. Really, the world would be less confused and in less conflict if there were less do-gooders, because their do-gooding just creates more mischievousness in the world. They are not concerned with good at all, really. They are concerned to be doers of good – so anyhow they must do good.

Kirkpatrick has written a book; a very strange statement is in it. He says, "If there will be no poverty, then how will we do service to others?" So poverty must remain, because when you cannot do service....And without service, these scriptures say, you cannot go to heaven. So if poverty is completely destroyed on the earth, then there is no bridge from the earth to the heaven. Kirkpatrick is a good man, and whatsoever he is saying, he means it. It is not just a statement, he means it. He feels it, that if there is no poverty, then how can you serve others? And service is such a necessary thing, that even poverty is needed for service to remain, it must remain.

This is a disease. Then service itself becomes the end, not the served one – he is irrelevant. There are social workers, servants of the people; and psychologists say, "It is their need really – not the need of the people. They cannot remain without doing good to someone else; they cannot remain without serving others. This is an occupation for them." What will happen to them if a society is really there which needs no service? This has happened so many times.

Revolutionaries are chronic revolutionaries. By "chronic" I mean, if they succeed and their revolution succeeds, they become anti-revolutionary. Stalin had to face these revolutionaries, and he killed all of them. The phenomenon was that those revolutionaries were just chronic revolutionaries. A Trotskyite is a chronic revolutionary; he cannot be without a revolution around him. The revolution must be there; otherwise, where will the revolutionary be?

So there are only two possibilities; whenever there is a revolution, a social revolution, there are two possiblities. If the revolution succeeds, then there are two possibilities: either the revolutionary has to turn traditionalist and orthodox and anti-revolution, or he has to continue his revolution. Stalin chose the first alternative; he became one of the most orthodox minds possible. Not even a czar was such as Stalin was – he became a czar.

Trotsky chose the other, or was forced to choose the other. He continued to be a revolutionary. And how then can you be a revolutionary? You have to go against your own revolution. Trotsky made endeavors for this revolution, and then he was against it. He was trying for a proletarian dictatorship, and then he was against it. And Stalin was doing the same. Stalin, in a way, is more consistent; but he himself turned anti-revolutionary. He was for the revolution he had started, but then he became anti-revolutionary, because no revolution could now be allowed. So Russia, after the great revolution, has been the country without revolutions. So the chronic revolutionaries had to escape and they continued *there*.

If really, there is a society where no one needs your help and your do-gooding, your service and your revolution and reformation, then all these do-gooders will be just mad, insane – they cannot do anything.

This fifth disease doesn't mean don't do good to others – it doesn't mean that – but don't be a do-gooder. Let it be just a spontaneous thing. Don't make it a plan, don't seek it, don't go for it; let it be just your spontaneous behavior. Whenever there is a situation, do whatsoever you feel; but don't plan it, don't make it a scheme. Don't sacrifice yourself, because persons who sacrifice themselves are very dangerous: when they sacrifice themselves they begin to sacrifice others. And they have a right because they can say, "We have sacrificed ourselves, so now we have the right to sacrifice others." They become violent. Persons who have been violent to themselves in doing good to others, ultimately turn to being violent to others. But now they have the credit of being good, and their violence can continue in the garb of being good. And when someone is good *and* violent, it is the most criminal, the deepest criminal combination.

If the father is good, then he can be a criminal to his son. If the mother is good, then she can be a criminal. This happens daily. Women are more good than men; not that there is any inner necessity, but they are more fearful of being bad, more suppressed. That's why wives become dictato-

109

rial, because the husband feels a bit inferior. He is bad in many ways: he smokes, he drinks, he looks all around at other beautiful faces.

Then the wife becomes dictatorial; she becomes a do-gooder. Now she can sacrifice her husband; now she can virtually kill. And because she is good, the husband is just helpless – he cannot argue. Smoking is bad – of course; and he is smoking, so he is bad. And really, to smoke is not so bad as to feel good on account of someone smoking. It is deeply criminal…it is *deeply* criminal; it is very violent. This is the disease.

Don't feel good on account of others, and don't try to be a do-gooder. Be good, simply naturally. That is completely different. If someone feels restless around you, know that you are not a good man, just a do-gooder.

I have read somewhere about a Tibetan mystic, Milarepa. It is written that Milarepa was a saint, because sinners could feel at ease with him – at ease, totally at ease. There was no condemnation in his eyes, in his words, in his behavior. Really, a saint means this: one with whom sinners can feel at ease, friendly; otherwise, the do-gooder is there. That is the ego, and the ego is always destructive of others. And you can destroy in such good ways that you may not even be aware what you are doing. A good mother can destroy the whole life of the child, just by being good – too good.

This, the rishi says, is the fifth disease. And if one is identified with these five diseases, there comes into existence a personality which is not your being. That personality is known a *lingasharir* – the subtle personality.

This word "personality" is very meaningful. It is a Greek word; it is derived from "persona." Persona means a mask. Actors use masks in Greek drama; that mask of the actors is known as persona. You are not *that*, but you use a mask and become that. You are not a lion, but you use a mask of a lion and you behave like a lion.

Personality is not your being, it is a mask. This mask is very subtle, and this mask is created by being identified with these five diseases. If you become totally identified, and feel that you are this – this disease of the mind, this disease of desiring, this disease of being good, this disease of being virtuous – if you begin to feel that you are a combination of all these five, these five classifications, then you create a persona, a personality. That personality is known as lingasharir – the subtle body. And behind this subtle body, lingasharir – behind this identification, behind this barrier – is the knower.

So to dissolve the personality, to withdraw yourself from the personality, to renounce the personality, is the essential renunciation. That is what is sannyas: to renounce…not the world, because how can you renounce the world? – it has never belonged to you. What nonsense, talking about renouncing the world. When? When are you master of it? – it has never belonged to you. Really, again the trick of the ego: one says, "I renounce the world," and feels very good that one has renounced the world. A beggar renouncing the empire, renouncing the throne, the palace – renouncing everything…. It has never belonged to him, so how can he renounce it?

So really, a sannyasin doesn't mean a person who renounces the world. A sannyasin means a person who renounces the personality. That belongs to you; you are the creator of it, so you can renounce it. Nothing else! You cannot renounce anything that doesn't belong to you. The personality belongs to you; you can renounce it, but you can renounce only when you begin to be aware that you are not the personality. This is known as *kshetragya*, the knower of the field. The field is personality, and the knower, the center which becomes aware of this personality. If you become aware of the center, of the knower, then there is not difficulty in renouncing the personality. It is just a clothing, *just* a clothing, and very dirty and very diseased.

When the self as consciousness, which is
truth, knowledge, infinity, and bliss,
devoid of all its attributes, shines like pure gold
freed from all its forms such as a bangle and a crown,
it is called twam *or thou.*
The brahman *is truth, infinity and knowledge.*
That which is indestructible is truth.
And that which does not perish even after the destruction of space,
time, et cetera, is called the avinashi, *the imperishable.*

There is a dialogue, a deep dialogue between my existence and existence itself, a constant dialogue, a continuity every moment: the incoming breath, the outgoing breath. I am constantly linked with the universe, with existence.

If we take two points, between these two points the dialogue continues. One point is "I," and the other point – the total – is "thou."

A non-religious mind, a material mind, will say that the dialogue is not between "I" and "thou," the dialogue is between "I" and "that," because the world is just a thing; it is not a person. And really, if the world is just a thing and it is not a person, then there can be no dialogue, there can be no intimacy. But if the whole world is just a thing, then myself – I myself cannot be a person; this "I" is also a thing. This is what is meant by a materialist conception of the world.

Of course there are relations – stimulus-response relations – but no dialogue, no intimacy. You cannot address existence as "thou," because there then is no poetry, and then there is no religion. Among *things* only science can exist; among *persons* religion grows.

The religious attitude towards existence is a personal attitude: the whole universe is taken as a person. The you can talk, then you can love, then you can be angry with the total; and your life becomes deeply rich, because life and richness develop only through deeper dialogues with the reality.

But still, even if a religious person thinks that the world is not just material, the world is personal, and existence has a personality – then too, "I" continues to be the center; "thou" is just the periphery, just the circumference. I remain at the center of the universe, and the whole universe just belongs to me as a periphery.

In this sutra, the rishi says that when the pure consciousness is known, when the witnessing consciousness is known, there is a mutation, a total change of emphasis. "Thou" becomes the center and "I" becomes the periphery. "Thou" becomes the center, and "I" just the periphery. This pure consciousness therefore is known as "thou" – *twama, tu.* It is not known as "I" because now I exists only as a periphery. It is really non-existential because periphery, in fact, is non-existential. It is just a line, a demarcation line and nothing else. It belongs to the center; it is just a projection of the center, an extension of the center.

When pure consciousness is known, pure consciousness is known as "thou." This has many implications. One, the moment we conceive pure consciousness as "thou," the whole universe, the whole of existence becomes a very different thing than we know it now. If you address the tree as "thou," the tree is not the same; it has become a person, and a new dimension opens – a new dimension. And when the tree has become thou, you also cannot remain the same, because with a new relationship, with a new dimension, you are also different.

But as we are, even a living person, even a human person, is not "thou" for us. We use the word, but not meaningfully. We behave with persons as if they are not persons. For example, you love someone and then you begin to possess him or possess her. A person can never be possessed; only a thing can be possessed. How can a person be possessed? And how can love be possessive? If love becomes possessive it means that you are transforming a person into a thing.

That's why a beloved may be a person, but a wife becomes just a thing, just a thing to be used. Why this possession? Because we just go on saying "thou," but we never mean it – we never mean it. If you are really saying "thou" to someone, it means you accept the other as a person and you cannot possess him. A person means a freedom; a person means: now you cannot be the master. So we turn even persons into things. But with this pure consciousness developing inside, things turn into persons, and the whole universe by and by takes a shape of "thou," of a great "thou" – everything becomes a person.

We live among things, mm? Even if we are living among persons, we live among things. And the more you live among things, the more you will be a thing yourself – that's bound to happen. So a person who tries to possess someone becomes himself a possession. The phenomenon is reciprocal – if I try to possess someone as *my* property, I am bound to become myself a thing, a property. So it is not that the husband possesses the wife; the wife also possesses the husband. They both are possessors and both are things.

The moment you begin to feel someone as a thing, you begin to expect. With a person there can be no expectation, because person means a freedom. You have loved me this evening, you have been loving towards me; if I expect that tomorrow also you must give me love, it means I am thinking of you as a thing. And if tomorrow you are not going to love me, then I will be angry, I will be frustrated, and I will take revenge. I will begin to feel that my possession is being lost. Why?

With a thing you can expect that it will behave the same tomorrow also – but not with a person. A person is a constant flux, the freedom to move. He may be something else tomorrow, who knows? He may be not love me at all. If I take you as a person, then I will never be frustrated with you, because the frustration comes when I take you as a thing.

But this pure consciousness begins to feel the whole universe as a "thou"; therefore this consciousness is never frustrated. Never! There is no reason to be frustrated at all. Whatsoever happens, happens. It is never against expectation, because there has been no expectation at all. If tomorrow the tree moves from my garden to somewhere else, even that will not frustrate me. I will just say, "Oh, so thou hast gone. So thou hast moved."

The truth, the infinite truth, the eternal consciousness, the formless is known as "thou," never as "I." Then you begin to live in a world of freedom, of non-possession. And when you behave in a non-possessive way, the whole world begins to behave non-possessively towards you. The whole universe becomes non-possessive of you.

This is what is meant by freedom: if you give freedom to the whole universe, you become free. But this freedom happens only when "I" is not at the center, but "thou." Really even "thou" is not exactly what the case is; even "thou" is a bit less than true, because "thou" cannot exist without a subtle feeling of "I." I cannot address someone as "thou" without myself being there, even indirectly, even in a very absent ways – even unconsciously. But the "I" must be there to address someone as "thou."

So this is just to express something in language which cannot be expressed. Really, when you are not in the center, not even the "thou" is the center. "I and thou" both dissolve into oneness. But that oneness is inexpressible, and still, the rishi tries to say something about it to the disciple, to the enquirer. So what to say? He says at least one thing is certain; it cannot be called "I," it is called "thou." And when the disciple is ready, the the inexpressible can also be indicated. But in the beginning, it is more than enough. "I" is not in the center, that consciousness is impure. And "I" *is* in the center, so consciousness *is* impure. That happens only when you know the formless. And if it is not happening and "I" is in the center, that means you are in the form, obsessed with the form, obsessed with the superficial. You have not gone deep, you have not gone to the innermost core of your being. You have just lived outside your house; you have not know it from the inside.

"I" in the center is symbolic, indicative that we have not known what we are. We have known only identities with the for. The body is form, the mind is form, thought is form – all that we know about ourselves is form. And these forms happen upon the ocean of the formless. With that formless coming into your awareness, the "I" becomes the periphery and "thou," the center.

Now the definition of truth. What is truth? Everyone is seeking, and everyone is trying to find it out, but what is it? How to define it? The materialist mind defines truth as the *fact*; whatsoever is objectively true, objectively factual, is truth. And personal experience which cannot be objectified will not be considered as truth. So if Jesus says, "I see my father in heaven," either he is a dreamer or just psychotic, neurotic, just mad – because no one else can see the father in heaven. So either he is just a poet, just an imaginary dreamer, or just mad, insane, abnormal...seeing things which are not.

This definition of truth as fact is dangerous in many ways. It is useful, it is utilitarian, it helps – particularly it helps the scientific research – but it is dangerous. Because even if there is no objective proof, even if all cannot see a particular thing, the thing can be. It is not necessarily that because all others are not seeing it, it is not there.

For example: there are color-blind people; out of ten one is color-blind. By being color-blind it is meant that he cannot see a particular color. For example, George Bernard Shaw was blind to yellow; he couldn't make any distinction between yellow and green. But for sixty years continuously he was not aware of it, because how could he be aware? It was just an accident that he became aware.

On one of his birthdays, someone presented a suit of a green color, but he forgot to send a green tie with it. So Bernard Shaw went to purchase a green tie, but he purchased a yellow one, because there was no distinction for him between yellow and green. His secretary said, "What are you doing? This will look very funny. This is yellow and the suit is green." For the first time after sixty years' living in this colorful world, he became aware that he was color-blind. He could not see any distinction between yellow and green – both were the same.

If ten persons are color-blind just like Bernard Shaw, and you can see yellow and ten cannot see yellow, what will be the truth? You will be either neurotic or just a dreamer.

There are personal faculties which may not have developed as a communal thing – the community may be lacking. There are personal faculties....But this definition of truth as fact will deny them. So sometimes even very intelligent people, very logical rational people, go on being superstitious in denying things which are, but which cannot be shown objectively. The whole psychic phenomenon has suffered only because of this. There are people who have faculties, but only individuals. So either they are deceivers – either they are playing tricks, deceiving others – or they are just claiming things which are not real.

There is one man, Peter Herkos. He can see things from very, very far off. Three hundred miles distance makes no difference to him. From here he can see three hundred miles away, a village on fire. No one would believe him, no one; but by and by, people became aware that yes, he was seeing things, and things proved objectively true.

There was a fire and someone died. He said from just *here* that someone had died in that village, and that very moment someone *had* died; but still scientists tried to disprove it. They thought somehow that he was maneuvering things – someone might have telephoned, some signal, something …something was there which they did not know about. But many many experiments were carried out, and still no deception was found. And the thing became more amazing because Herkos himself was a skeptic; he himself did not believe that such things could happen. How could they happen? So he said, "If this would have been the case with someone else, I myself would say that he is deceiving. But how can I say it now? I am not deceiving at all – I go on seeing things." But they are personal….

A buddha experiencing what he called *nirvana* – it is a personal experience. It is not a fact, but it is a truth. So it is not necessarily that truth should be a fact, and not vice versa also that a fact is bound to be a truth.

The rishi defines truth more deeply, more absolutely. He says truth means that which is always unchanging, which is always. If a fact changes, it is also not a truth. And if a dream remains continuously, eternally, it is true; it is truth. So by truth, the *Upanishads* mean: the absolutely eternal.

What is absolutely eternal in this world of movement and change? Only change seems to be eternal and nothing else. Everything changes except change. And change cannot be called the eternal truth, because the very definition is "the unchanging one," and change means "changing one." Where is the eternal? – we never see it, we never feel it, we never know it – nowhere; everywhere is form and movement and change, and everything is impermanence itself.

Buddha says, "Everything is impermanent, *everything* – even you yourself – just impermanent. Nothing is permanent here." So is there any truth, or not? Only one thing seems to be deeply eternal: the see-er, and nothing else – the witnessing soul, nothing else. Buddha says, "Nothing is permanent." But who has seen this? This "nothing is permanent" – who has seen this? Someone must have seen this impermanency. Someone must have felt this constant flux, change. And to feel the change, this constant change, to be aware of it, at least the awareness must be eternal. So that's why truth and the inner consciousness become synonymous.

For a philosophically minded person the enquiry into truth becomes a logical enquiry – metaphysical, philosophical. He goes on finding what is truth, logically, rationally. He may create a philosophy but he is not going to find the truth. For a religious mind, the enquiry begins to be a search for the eternal. And when a religious man says, "I am seeking the truth," he means "I am seeking that which is always, that which is eternal- -the eternity itself." Time ceases, space ceases, everything is dissolved, but that which is remains still.

This witnessing consciousness . . . . You are ill, then you are healthy; you are rich, then you are poor; you are respected, and then you are condemned; you are in hell, and you are in heaven – everything is changing. Only one who goes on knowing, "Now I am in hell, now I am in heaven; now they are respecting me, now they are condemning me; now I am ill, now I am healthy; now I am this, now I am that" – only one, and all else goes on moving, moving, moving. But this movement is known, and the knower is immovable, because only an immoving knower can know movements. Only an immovable knower can know movements. Only the eternal one can know change. If the inner one is also changing, then change cannot be felt. You know that once you were a child, now you are not. If the inner consciousness itself has changed, who will remember that you were a child? If you have completely changed, then there will be no continuity. Who will remember that once you were a child and now you are not? Something behind all change remains the same. That something remembers, "I was once a child, now I am young, now I am going to be old, now I am going to die."

This continuity, this consciousness, for the rishi of the *Upanishads*, is the truth. This truth is eternal, infinite, and the nature of it is just knowing, pure knowing. It is not love, it is not bliss; it is pure knowing, because even love has to be known, even bliss has to be known. So ultimately, love and bliss and all else become objects of knowledge. This remains to be always the knower, always the transcending knower, the transcendental one.

*Eternal consciousness, itself beyond creation
and destruction, is known as* knowledge.
*The consciousness that is whole and all- pervading,
and that permeates the entire cosmos like
clay permeating the articles made of clay,
and like gold permeating articles made of gold,
and like yarn permeating articles made of yarn,
is called the* infinity.
*That which is blissful consciousness, which is
an ocean of limitless bliss, and which is the very
nature of everlasting happiness is known as* bliss.

To define *brahma* as knowledge is to use a word which is very much contaminated. Our whole language is so much bound with our minds that whenever we have to express something beyond the mind, either it is impossible or we have to use a word which cannot be used. This knowledge is bound with the known; knowledge exists as a relationship with the known. It cannot exist in itself. As we know it, it cannot exist in itself. It is a relation between the subject and the object, between the knower and the known – just a relationship.

And relationship is not substantial. If one relater is not there the relationship just disappears. If the known is not there, then there is no knowledge. How can you have any knowledge if the known is not there? If you are in a vacuum and nothing is to be known, how can knowledge exist there? Only this much knowledge can exist: that there is a vacuum, because the vacuum is there. And even if there is no vacuum, not even a vacuum, this much knowledge also will not exist there. Knowledge just disappears; it is a relation.

So when we say that brahma – the supreme consciousness, the innermost consciousness, the eternal one – is knowledge, we are using a word with a very different meaning. Not only different – rather, a very contrary meaning, just the contrary.

Brahma is knowledge without the known and the knower – simply knowledge, simply knowing, simply consciousness. Why is this unrelated phenomenon to be insisted upon so much? There are reasons: if knowledge is dependent on the known, it is a slavery; it is not a freedom. And knowledge must be a freedom, only then it is knowledge.

Ignorance is a bondage; knowledge must be absolute freedom. If knowledge itself is a bondage, then what is the difference between ignorance and knowledge? Ignorance is always related: you are ignorant *of* something, you are not simply ignorant. You are ignorant of something – then you are knowledgeable; then you are the knower of something. Both are the same in a way, because both are related to the object; both are dependent on the object. Ignorance and knowledge – so-called ignorance and so-called knowledge – both are dependent. So what is the difference? The dependence remains the same.

And the search for truth, the search for the secret of secrets, the real knowledge, is the search for total independence. It is the search for absolute freedom. So even the presence of the known is a limitation; the presence of the knower is a limitation. These two limitations must be broken.

Knowledge must exist, not as a relationship between subject and object, but something self-oriented, something independent, something in itself. When we say brahma is knowledge, we mean this knowledge: absolute freedom from the known and the knower. How is this possible? It looks just impossible; it looks absurd. It is as absurd as to conceive love without the lover and the beloved. It is as inconceivable as to conceive experience without any object of experience, and without any experiencer. But it is not. If we go deep, it is not, but the depth must be found inside.

Leave objects: that's what we mean by silence. Remain conscious without any objects; then you are silent. Remain conscious without any thoughts; then the knower is there, but not the known. And when the known disappears, the knower disappears automatically, because it cannot exist without the known.

This is the secret: drop the known.

In meditation what are you doing?

Drop the known.

The known must cease for knowledge to be.

Drop the known, go on dropping, eliminate anything that is an object to your consciousness. Forget everything, go on forgetting, go on eliminating. Go on saying, "This is the object" – drop it.

Then there comes a moment when you are simply silent, conscious. The light is there but nothing is lighted; there is no object to it – simply light. You are, but the known has dropped. The moment the known drops, suddenly, simultaneously, the knower drops itself, because it is a relation. The knower cannot exist without the known – they both drop.

Begin with the known, and then this happens automatically – the knower is dropped. What remains? Now the remaining is called knowledge. *Now*, the remaining is called knowledge. It would be better to say, knowing; or even better, simple consciousness, alertness. Buddha called this enlightenment. This is the ecstasy of the mystics; this is the *samadhi* of yoga. This is *nirvikalp* samadhi of yoga-samadhi without any thoughts. This is known as *nirbeej*, seedless; because now there is no seed – no seed for any thought, any object to arise. You are now just a mirror, mirroring nothing.

In this mirrorlike consciousness, without mirroring anything, for the first time you know a different dimension of knowledge, of consciousness – not as a relationship, but as your spontaneous nature, as your being, as your is-ness, as your existence. *This* is the knowledge meant by the rishi when he defines brahma as knowledge, supreme consciouness as knowledge.

This consciousness is infinite, with no beginning and no end – with no boundaries. We have boundaries, limitations; we have bodies. Because of these bodies we have limitations – not because of the consciousness. The consciousness is infinite but embodied. The embodied form is not of consciousness it has been imposed by the matter around it.

You have a pot. Go to the sea and drop the pot into the sea. Then seawater will fill it. The seawater will be inside, and the seawater will be outside – the same, but only a mud wall, just an earthen wall will divide the two. And even that division is not so much, because the earthen wall is porous and the seawater is constantly coming in and going out. We are also porous; and every moment, life is coming in and going out. It is not only that you breathe from your nose, you are breathing from your whole body. So even if your nose is allowed to breathe, and all the pores of your body are covered, closed, you will die within a few minutes.

Every moment there is a constant communion between the infinite and you. In so many ways the communion is happening: through your breathing, through your food, through the rays of the sun, through water; through everything you are constantly moving into the infinite and the infinite is moving into you.

Where is the limit of my body? Really, where is the limit of my body? Why is this skin to be my limit? This skin cannot exist without the sun being there millions of miles away. And if this skin cannot exist without the sun, why not the sun be my limit? It is part of my body. I cannot exist without breathing for a single moment; so why should the nose be my limit? Why not the air? The airy ocean all around should be my limit, because I cannot exist without it; it is my existence. Every moment I have to be constantly changing energy with the air; every moment carbon dioxide has to be thrown out, and every moment oxygen has to be taken in. Constant communion – a single moment and the communion is lost, and I am dead. So why take the nose as my limit? Why not the whole ocean of the air around? – because without it I cannot exist, just as a fish cannot exist out of the ocean.

But the air cannot exist unless there is the sun. And those who know the system of the universe and the stars, say that this sun cannot exist if there are not greater suns, because this sun has to get energy constantly just as we have to get energy. So this is a great chain; no one seems to be independent – even the sun is just a small star. To us it is so big – thousands of times greater than the earth! In relation to our bodies it seems infinite. But this is just a very mediocre star in the whole universe – just a mediocre star. There are stars which are thousands of times bigger.

There is a constant chain...life moving around. So this limited feeling of embodiment, of these bodies, is just a fallacy; life is one. Life is one: the deeper we go, the deeper the oneness is uncovered. Life is one; the inner light is one; consciousness is one. When we say brahma is infinite, this is what we mean. It is just ignorance, a fallacious conception to feel oneself limited and finite; we are not. But this infinite cannot be known, cannot be understood by any argument, by any rational thinking, by any intellectual understanding.

You may be able to conceive that it seems that life is one, but that is not enough – intellectual understanding will not do. Rather, on the contrary, it may become a hindrance, because you may begin to understand that life is one and you will still behave as if life is not one. And there will be a sharp division inside; a very divided consciousness will be there. You will behave as if you are finite, and you will begin to believe that you are infinite; and there will be very deep restlessness inside.

So intellectual understanding will not do, one has to *feel* it; not *know* it, but feel it. And the feeling can come only when the known and the knower are dropped. Then suddenly you are one. Then it is not an argument; then it is not a philosophical concept; then it is not even a scientific explanation. Then it is a realization.

So really, the known and the knower are the two limitations. Deep within the known and the knower are the two boundaries. Drop these two boundaries, be just knowledge, and suddenly you have become one. William James calls this "the oceanic feeling." Now there are no barriers to life, to inner light, to inner consciousness – all barriers have dropped. Really, the universe has dropped, and now there is brahma.

We use two words: *brahman* for universe, for the embodied form, and *brahma* for the innermost center of consciousness. As long as we are feeling ourselves as bodies, we can never transcend brahman, the universe. The moment we become consciousness, the brahman drops; it becomes brahma. Then there is no universe, then there is just an infinite ocean of consciousness. This infinite ocean of consciousness…the moment it is realized, you are in bliss as never before – as never before.

We have known pleasures; we have known pains; we have known so-called happinesses and so-called sufferings – but never bliss. By bliss is meant a state of consciousness where happiness is not coming from out, but from within. We have known happiness always coming from the out, from without, from outside, from someone or something. It has always been something from without towards within – that has been the direction. Bliss means the total reversal of this direction: happiness coming from within, going without.

And really, the moment happiness is coming from the inner center and going out, it goes on expanding; and goes on expanding....It goes on expanding to the infinite, and the whole universe if filled – not only you, the whole universe is filled with bliss. Just as if you drop a stone in the river and there are ripples and the ripples go on spreading, spreading, spreading – they go on spreading just like this, just like this, this bliss happens.

In your innermost center, the moment there is no known and knower, this happening happens. There are ripples, ripples of bliss. And they go spreading, and they go on spreading, they go on...and there is no end to them then. And continuously, one lives in bliss.

Because now you are the source:

This bliss cannot be destroyed.

Because now you are the source:

This bliss cannot be taken back.

Whenever something else is the source, it can be taken back; it is bound to be taken back, it can only be momentary and temporal. It is not your being, it is just a happening outside – just a foreign something outside. Bliss is unrelated to anyone; bliss is not produced by any cause; it is not causal. It is not in a particular situation; it is not related at all to anything else other than you. Can you conceive yourself in happiness, in bliss, without anyone being the cause, or anything being the cause? We have known only causal happiness. And because of this causal happiness, misery comes as a shadow, always behind it, waiting for its moment.

When you begin to feel yourself enough unto yourself, if the whole universe just drops and goes into nonexistence, it will not make any difference – *then* it will not make any difference, because now you have an inner source of happiness, an infinite source of happiness. This is your being and cannot be taken from you and cannot be destroyed; and therefore, there can be no anti-state of your inner bliss.

This analysis is not meant as a philosophical doctrine – the *Upanishads* are not philosophical doctrines; they are not. They are not metaphysical;

really, they are not concerned with any doctrine at all. They are paths to follow; they are ways to live; they are methods for the inner search. If words are used, they are used only to convey – not a doctrine, not a principle, but a method. Remember this! – but *a method.*

The Indian consciousness has basically been concerned with method and not with principle. So a very wonderful phenomenon has happened in the East. The rishis say, "Use any principle – it makes no difference. Believe in God, or not believe in God – it makes no difference. Believe that there are reincarnations, rebirths, or don't believe – it makes no difference. Believe that there is a soul or not – it makes no difference. But use the method." The emphasis is on the method, because they say if the method is used you will realize whatsoever is the principle – the principle is meaningless. That's why in India, there have been nine systems, but the method has remained the same; the matter doesn't differ at all.

Mahavira says there is no God, but achieves the same; the matter is the same. Buddha even says there is no soul – no God, no soul; but the method remains the same and he achieves the same. Hindus say there is a God, there is soul; but the method remains the same and they achieve the same. Doctrines are just jumping boards, so what board you use is irrelevant.

Only *jump*! – that is relevant.

What board you use is irrelevant, because really we are concerned with the jump! If you can jump from a blue board, okay. If you can jump from a red board, okay. If you can jump from a black board, okay. We are not concerned with boards, jumping boards. We are concerned with jumping – Jump!

That's why yoga is the essence of the Eastern mind, not Vedant, not Buddhism, not Jainism, not Samkhya, not *Vaisheshik*, no – yoga is the essence. These are all doctrines, jumping boards. The jumping board is your choice, your liking.

And really, the wise ones have never argued about the jumping boards. They say, "Okay, it is your liking, so choose the color." You can be a Mohammedan, you can be a Christian, you can be a Hindu; or, you can even be an agnostic. And really, this is one of the wonderful things: even if you are an atheist, okay. Use the method, take the jump, and the thing will happen, because the thing is not dependent on doctrines. And the happening will be there because the happening is not dependent at all on what principle, what ideology, what *ism* you follow – the happening depends on the jumping!

Because of this emphasis, the Eastern consciousness has never tried to convert anyone. They say that the mosque is as good as the temple, as any church. They say that *The Bible* is as good as the *Veda*; the *Koran* is as good as the *Gita*. And one need not go to convert someone from a Mohammedan to a Hindu and from a Hindu to a Mohammedan – this is childish nonsense. There is no need to convert anyone.

Let him stand on his board; but let him not continue standing there – that is the thing. Let him jump! Let him jump from the Christian board; let him jump from the Mohammedan board, but let him jump – the jumping is essential. Remember this always. Only then can you go deep into the esoteric, oriental esotericism. Enough about the jumping boards – now the jumping....

These four (truth, knowledge, infinity and bliss) are the characteristics, and that which is changeless, in spite of symbolic objects like space, time, et cetera, is called Tat or that, which is the equivalent of paramatma or the supreme self.

That which is separate even from such definitive distinctions as "thou" and "that," and which is as subtle as the sky is called parabrahma or *ultimate beyond ultimate*.

I, the ego, is the center, as we exist. As we are, we exist around the crystallization of the ego. And ego is just a falsity, so the whole crystallization is just an appearance. There is nothing like "I," nothing substantial like "I" – it is just a shadow existence. Go deep into it and it just disappears. But escape from it and it becomes stronger and stronger. Try to destroy it, and you will not be able to, because a nothing cannot be destroyed. You can destroy something which is; you cannot destroy something which is not. You cannot fight with a shadow; and even if you fight...you can fight, but you can never win. On the contrary, you will be won over by the shadow.

This seems paradoxical, because how can a shadow which is not, win? But a shadow can win. It wins because you believe it *is*. It wins because you cannot destroy it, but in the very effort of destroying it, you are destroyed. You dissipate energy in the conflict; in the absurd conflict you just waste yourself.

Try sometime. Fight with your shadow. You will be exhausted and the shadow will be as fresh as ever. You cannot even touch it; how can you destroy it? And that which is not...that which is not becomes stronger because you go on dissipating your energy. And a moment comes when you just fall down defeated, destroyed. Of course, again you will think that the ego is very very strong, that's why you have been defeated. Of course, obviously this is how logic will work: if you couldn't win over the shadow, that means the shadow is stronger than you – so escape from it.

There are two alternatives: either fight with it, or escape from it. If you feel that you are not so strong to fight, then escape. But how can you escape a shadow if it is your own? And the ego is you own shadow. So go on running, and the faster you run, the faster comes the shadow behind you. Again you are defeated, again you feel there seems no way: "Howsoever I run, and wheresoever I go, the shadow follows me. I cannot dodge it, even." You dodge it, and it is there with you; it has dodged you. So ultimately, the fighter and the escapist both come to the conclusion that it is impossible to win over the ego – to destroy the ego. It is impossible!

This happens because you are fighting with an absence. Just like one is fighting darkness. So you may fight it, you may go on fighting it. You cannot decide, because darkness is not a positive something; it is just the absence of light.

Bring light and it will be no more. But don't fight it.

The "I" exists as absence: absence of your real nature, absence of your real self, or real no-self – whatsoever you like to call it. It exists because you are not. So it is a false shadow, an absence of something which can be and is not. It is needed, because the master is absent and someone must be there who works, behaves as the master; otherwise, life will be very difficult.

A child is born, not with an ego, really – without the ego. Then we begin to cultivate the ego: society needs it, survival needs it. So we begin to create the ego through education, through competition, through comparison. We begin to create, because without the ego we cannot conceive how the child will fight for existence, for survival. How will he be able to move even? So there must be created a strong ego. Our whole culture, education... all training is just to create a strong ego in the child so that he can fight, so that he can move, so that he can compete, so that he can survive. This ego is a survival measure, but once created and crystallized, it will not allow the real master to come in its place.

Then there are so-called teachers who will say, "Be humble. Be egoless" – and then we begin to cultivate humility. With the ego on the throne, we begin to cultivate humility; then the ego takes on the garb of humility. And really, it is difficult to find a more egoist person than the so-called humble one. So what to do now?

I feel it as a necessity: ego has to be developed. As far as the child is concerned, ego has to be developed – it is a necessary evil. It has to be developed, but a moment comes where it becomes useless. The moment you are mature, the moment you are conscious, the moment you are alert, grown-up, you need not have the ego – you can step beyond it. One has to be on the step of the ego, and then one has to step out of it. It is a necessary evil; up to a limit it is needed. Beyond that limit it is not needed at all; rather, it becomes a hindrance. So as far as outward life is concerned, ego is a need; but as far as inward life is concerned, ego is a hindrance.

The moment you become aware that now you need a new growth, an inward growth, ego becomes a hindrance – the basic obstacle. And because you have strengthened it, you have fed it, and you have lived with it, it simply rejects that you can be without it. It becomes just an old habit, and you cannot conceive how you can be without it. You have always known yourself, felt yourself as an ego. For example: A child needs a nine-month pregnancy; it is a basic need. It is difficult, and in a way a long death: nine months, absolute bondage, no possibility even of movement, no thinking – not even breathing. The child cannot even breathe. He is so dependent on the mother that he only breathes through the mother – he cannot breathe. He has no heartbeat; mother's heartbeats are his. But these nine months are needed.

Then there is a crisis: the birth. The child resists being born, because it is a very traumatic experience; it is just being thrown from your so-conditioned existence. In a way the child was absolutely safe – the bondage was a safety. The child was absolutely free of responsibility – even the responsibility to breathe was not there. In a way, the child was an absolute slave, and in a way, the most free, because there was not even the botheration of breathing. These nine months create a conditioning and the child resists.

Even the mother also resists. That's why there is pain; otherwise, there is no need of pain. Nature is throwing the child out and the child resists. Of course, it has been his home – and such a safe home. The mother also resists, because something so drastic is going to happen. There is a natural resistance – that's why there is pain in birth.

But this pain has to be passed through if the child just declines to be born – that is the case with us. Ego is a shell; ego is an egg. There comes a moment when the egg is to be broken and you have to be born. Of course, there is going to be a painful birth. And you have lived with this ego so easily, in a safety – in a deep safety. This ego has been your home, and then comes a moment when this ego itself becomes the bondage – it is the bondage and one wants to be free of it.

This is the spiritual urge: to be free from the ego. If you have not felt that you, your ego, is the bondage and you want to be free from it, the spiritual urge has not yet come into being. The spiritual urge means to be free from this egg, from this shell, from this ego – from this long pregnancy. And this long pregnancy is really millenia long – lives and lives and lives. And we are in the shell, enclosed, imprisoned. It is a necessity; one has to be in it. But again, one has to break it and come out of it.

There is fear. There is fear, when for the first time some bird comes out of its egg. The bird has fully-grown wings, but he cannot just go into the sky, fearful of the unknown. The bird waits, waits, looks around; there is fear – with full-grown wings! But how can the bird know that these are wings and he can fly; that he can go into a totally free space and move, and can experience ecstasy? How can he know? The same happens with us – we are in an eggshell. It is difficult to come out of it, but even if we can, if we come out of it, then again there is fear to go into the unknown, into something uncharted, into something we have not known before. Fear....

What to do? One thing is to be aware of the whole fact of the ego – what it is. The moment you become aware, then you know it is just a safety measure; it is not so substantial as we have been thinking. It is just a safety measure; it is just a functional thing. It was needed; now it is not needed, so it is just an old habit. The minute you see the ego as an old habit – as a functional unity, not anything substantial; as a necessity but not as a reality – ninety-nine percent of the ego will have disappeared just through this knowledge. The one percent will need a jump.

That jump...I was talking about a bird just waiting, and looking around with fully grown wings - with fear; but the bird takes the jump, takes the challenge. And once taken he becomes aware that now there is no fear; the whole sky is his - he has wings. In that moment what happens in the psychic realm of the bird? What happens?

That happening has been known as faith - that happening. What happens in the mind of the bird? There is fear, the unknown is there; he doesn't know that he has fully-grown wings and in a moment he can be the master of the whole sky and totally free. What to do? But other birds are in the sky moving freely, flying freely. Seeing them thus, a faith is born: to take the jump.

A Buddha, a Mahavira, a Christ, a Mohammed - just birds flying in the sky. And you, waiting with fully grown wings - with fear, not knowing what to do. By faith, by *shraddha,* only this, this trust is meant. Seeing a buddha flying, you take the jump and you become a buddha yourself.

Faith is not blind belief in someone else. On the contrary, faith is faith in oneself, seeing someone else fully grown.

Faith is not in someone else.

Faith is always in oneself.

Seeing the possibility - that "this can happen to someone else; why cannot it happen to me?" - one gathers courage; one becomes potent. One has always been so, but now one remembers - one becomes potent.

Sariputta came to Buddha to thank him, and said to Buddha, "I have come in a deep gratitude to thank you."

Buddha said, "I have not done anything for you, Sariputta. You have not even come to me before. I have not even uttered a single word to you. How is this thankfulness?"

Sariputta said, "I have been looking and looking. Wherever you have moved, I was moving just behind, like a shadow. I have been watching and watching, and suddenly a faith is born in me that I can also be this. So I have come to give you my gratitude and show you my gratitude. You have not uttered a single word; you have not taught me anything. You have never been my teacher; I have never been your follower, but I have followed you like a shadow. I have moved with you from village to village – just seeing that if this can happen to this man, why not to me? A faith is born in me, a faith is born unto me and I am transformed."

This is how a teacher works: as a catalytic agent. The moment you take the jump from the "I," you are in the "thou." So the rishi says, the second definition – deeper, higher – is to know existence in the form of "thou." We have known only the "I" existence – a very minute fragment of existence, we have known what is known as "I-existence." Take the jump from the "I," and you become aware of existence, of the total existence as "thou." We discussed before what this "thou" means.

But now the rishi says that even this "thou" is not the ultimate. It is just a step ahead of the "I," but not the ultimate. You have even to jump from this "thou," because to thank the universe in the form of "thou" is still to continue the memory of the "I." The "thou" can only be meaningful in relation, and in reference to, and in context with an ego. How can I say "thou" without there being a "me"? Only the "I" can say meaningfully, "thou." If there is no "I," what does it mean? What does this "thou" mean? Is it only an old memory habit that we again call this world, this existence, "thou," because we know only the language of "I"? The "I" has dropped, but not the language.

The rishi says, "Now drop even that language, and take a jump from the "thou" also – then the universe becomes a "that." From "I" to "thou," and from "thou" to "that" – simply "that.""

You must have heard one of the deepest insights of the *Upanishads: tat twamasi – That art Thou,* in which both are used, "that" and "thou." That art Thou, or Thou art That, but "that" is still higher, because now no reference to the ego is implied. "That" becomes pure existence – "that." You are irrelevant now. "That" can exist even without you; but "thou" cannot exist – thou needs you. "That"…"That" doesn't need. "That," is a simple statement of the fact. But these deeper journeys need a still deeper jump.

The rishi says that even "that" is not the ultimate, because still it is your assertion. And when you say "that" you indicate something. You are not addressing now; "thou" is an address. "I" is there to address. "That" is simple assertion, not anything addressed; but you are indicating – a finger is there indicating "that." A very nonpersonal indication, but still indication; someone is showing "that." The rishi says, one step more. This "thou" and this "that" both are again limitations. Even drop "that," then nothing can be said. Then it is sheer existence, mere existence, pure existence.

Buddha says it is nothingness, shunya; because he says all that we knew has been denied and eliminated; all that we could indicate is irrelevant. Language cannot go further; mind now cannot reach further; expression is not possible – not only not possible, it is absurd, it is nonsense. Whatsoever you say becomes nonsense. You say "I" – it is nonsense. You say "thou" – it is nonsense. You say "that" – it is nonsense. It may be higher nonsense, but it is nonsense, because it makes no sense at all.

So Buddha says, "Do not say anything," or if you insist, he says, "Say, now it is nothingness." But by nothingness he doesn't mean that there is nothing. By nothingness he means there is no-thingness. "Now there is nothing" means no-thing, no *thinghood* which can be indicated, showed and expressed; otherwise, there is all. Otherwise, there is all: pure existence, the is-ness.

Buddha chooses a negative way: he says shunya, nothingness. This rishi chooses a positive way: he says when "thou" and "that" have fallen, all the limitations are gone; limits cease, boundaries are no more. That which remains is simple existence – *satta math*, simple existence.

Simple existence.... What does he mean by simple existence? A table exists, a man exists, a tree exists – these are not simple existences. A table exists.... There are two things: the table and existence – the table exists. The table is something which exists; existence is something more, a plus. When the table is not there, only the table is lost; but the existence which was a plus, remains behind. You cannot see it, of course, because we can only see the table. The table is not there, but where has existence gone? Existence is still there.

If every thing-hood is not there, then the ocean of pure existence remains. The rishi says that this is pure existence – nothing exists, only existence is. This, he says, is parabrahma. By parabrahma is meant: that which is even beyond brahma, because brahma can be defined. We have been defining brahma, we can indicate something about it; even if we say it is indefinable, we define it. Even if we say we cannot say anything about it, we have said something. So we go on contradicting ourselves. If we say nothing can be said, then this much has been said, and we have contradicted ourselves. If we say something, it becomes nonsense. If we don't say something and say that nothing can be said, we have said something.

But with brahma there is some possibility to define it – in relation to us we can define it. We can say it is bliss, because we feel bliss. When we come near it we feel bliss. It is just as you feel near a garden…the air becomes cooler, you begin to feel the flowers, their scent, the perfume. But really, this is *your* feeling – this is in relation to you.

We can define brahma. In relation to us, we can say it is blissful, because we, deep in misery will come near it – really it is a bliss. We can say it is knowledge, because deep from ignorance, darkness, when we come to it, it is light. But it is in relation to *us.* These assertions are relative.

Now comes the absolute: parabrahma means the absolute, about which only this much can be said: "Whatsoever we say about it, it is beyond and beyond. Whatsoever is said, falls down, doesn't reach it – and it always goes beyond." Parabrahma means the transcendence which always transcends everything.

This is the ultimate goal, because this is the ultimate existence. And unless one achieves it, one remains in death, in misery, in *samsara.* By samsar is not meant the world; by samsar is only meant the wheel of life and death.

The word "samsara" means the wheel, the constantly moving wheel – birth, life, death; birth, life, death – and the wheel goes on moving, and on and on. This constant wheel in which we are caught is samsar. If we can jump out of this wheel, these are the three steps: from the "I" to "thou," from "thou" to "that," and from "that" to the all – or to the nothingness, or to the transcendence, or to the beyond and beyond.

---

*That which is beginningless and yet which ends,
which is neither being nor non-being and which in
itself is seen as the purest of energies is called
maya or the magical world.
It cannot be described in any other way except this.
This maya is ignorance-like, petty and unreal,
but is seen by the deluded persons as real
at all times – past, present, and future. Therefore to say
that it is such cannot explain its real character.*

Now, the enquiry goes into *maya*. After brahma, it must be discussed. By maya is meant something which is *and yet is not*, which appears to be – the appearance.

Things as they appear to us are not as they are. Immanuel Kant says somewhere that we cannot know the thing in itself; a thing cannot be known in itself. Whatsoever we know about a thing is a projection; it is a contribution, we have contributed something to it. When you fall in love with someone, it is your projection. You contribute to your beloved, to your lover, something – you give something, and then you are impressed by your own contribution. This is maya.

We go on creating illusions around us. We go on creating dreams around us. The real, that-which-is, is engulfed with our dreams, projections. This force to create illusions around oneself is maya – this magic, this power of the mind to create things which are not, or to give things qualities which are not. And we live in this world, this created one. Of course, obviously, disillusionment is bound to come. It may take time, but it comes – any moment the reality asserts, the dream is scattered.

And we also help each other to create dreams. Someone falls in love, and then they both help each other to create the dream; they both bring qualities, show appearances which are not real – masks, faces. They help each other deceive themselves. All that is beautiful comes up, and all that is ugly goes down. All that is lovable is brought out, and all that is not lovable is just forgotten; it goes into the unconscious and we create a false face. Because really, no one can love unless he can hate – so whenever someone loves, it means that there is every possibility of hatred as intense as love. They both exist simultaneously, they are part of one phenomenon.

You cannot love if you cannot hate; both are one energy. But the hatred part is suppressed into the unconscious, and the loving part is brought out. Both are bringing the loving part above and suppressing the other, inevitable part, which cannot be denied. They create dreams around themselves, and because of these dreams which *they* have created, they fall in love.

But how long can you continue? The denied part will assert; it will have its revenge. It will explode. The more suppressed, the more dangerous is going to be the explosion. You can go on having faces when you are not so near and intimate. The moment you are near and intimate, and love demands now be near, now live in one house, now be married, now we cannot live apart.... It is impossible. This demand, that "now we cannot live apart," creates the situation in which the other suppressed part will have its revenge; it will come up. It will begin to assert, then the dream is shattered.

But again, again we begin to believe that, now this person is just hatred. First, we believe this person is just love, now we again fall into the second trap, the other trap; now this person becomes just hatred, poison. This again is just a projection: the other part is being projected. And we go on living in these projections.

This is the power of maya. This is the inner magic of your mind. It can project, and then it can create disillusionment for itself. It can create dreams and then it can believe in them – *both*; it can create and can believe in them! And when those dreams are shattered, it is not that one becomes aware of this whole fallacious game. When the dream is shattered, again you begin to create another dream. This shattering of particular dreams is not the shattering of the maya.

The rishi says that maya is a natural capacity to hypnotize oneself, it is auto-hypnosis. This auto-hypnosis can create things which are not, and can hide things which are. And for a seeker of the truth, of the real, this has to be understood; this has to be felt very deeply. This power, this maya must be understood deeply, because this is our bondage, this is our ignorance, this is our insanity, this is our suffering – creating dreams and then creating frustrations; creating illusions then disillusionments. And one goes on repeating – lives and lives one goes on repeating, and the power goes on working again and again.

But whenever we are disillusioned, we are not responsible for it; the other one, the situation, the object, is responsible. When we create this illusion, then again we are not responsible; the other one, the object, the lover, the beloved, the world – they are responsible. This happens because the projector is within. We never become aware of the projector, we always become aware of the projected scene, of the projected phenomenon. Just as in a cinema hall the projector is behind – no one looks back to see the projector; the projector is behind. Everyone is facing the screen, and on the screen are just projected images. The real, the power is behind. The film, the power to project, is behind, but no one looks at the projector; everyone is looking at the screen.

The whole world is just a screen; the whole objectivity is just a screen, and the projector is within. And we go on projecting images on the screen of the world, and then we begin to believe. Whatsoever we see on the screen, we begin to believe. This is maya: the capacity to project images on the screen of the world. If you stop your projections, the whole world just withers away, just disappears. And when the world disappears with your maya, with your projective mechanism…when the screen remains just a screen without the images, you are face to face with the brahman.

Brahman is the screen. But we have never seen the screen, because there is a continuous flow of images. One image is followed by another, one image is replaced by another. There is a gap, but we are so concerned with images that the gap is never felt. Slow down your projecting. Slow down your projecting machinery. Sometimes it happens in a cinema hall, some defect in the mechanism, and the film is slowed, and then you see the gaps. One image has gone, another has not come, and there is a sudden gap and the screen is seen.

By meditation we try to slow down the mechanism of projections. If the mechanism is slowed down and even for a single moment you begin to be aware of the gap – imageless gap of the screen – you have the glimpse.

Suddenly you know that you have lived in the dreams of your own creation; and whatsoever you have known as the world was not the world really, it was *your* world.

Pearl Buck has written her autobiography; she has named it *My Several Worlds*. It is good; the title is good – everyone is living in several worlds, in several dreams, in several projections. And you can continue forever. That's why the moments of suffering sometimes become blissful; the moments of suffering sometimes suddenly create a situation in which the mechanism stops, falters, and you see the gap. Someone has died, you loved him. Suddenly there is a gap; suddenly you cannot project – now the person is dead, you cannot go on projecting on him. You will need some time to find another object to project the same dreaming; there is a gap. So sometimes death, sometimes deep suffering, sometimes illness, sometimes sudden dangers and the mechanism falters and you have the gap.

But we are cunning. We are so cunning we just close our eyes. The moment there is a gap, we just close our eyes. Someone has died, you begin to weep, and your tears will become a screening phenomenon, and you cannot see the gap. The gap is there. Someone has died! Now be aware and see that the object has disappeared, and your dreams are just in a vacuum, and they cannot find an object! Be aware in this moment and you may be able to see the gap, the screen, not your world.

But no, the mind is cunning. The moment there is a sudden gap, our eyes are filled with something else. Again, we are not able to look in the interval. One is weeping and crying; and he will weep and cry unless he can find another object again to laugh, again to live, again to create the old illusion.

Buddha says when there is death, meditate – meditate on it.
 This is the moment.
When there is suffering, meditate on it.
When there is disillusionment, meditate on it.
This is the moment!
Don't lose this moment in anything which deviates you from the gap.
This mechanism, this capacity, this power to create illusions is maya. It

is there, and very real because it works. Very real, and very actual because it works and we are in it. This auto-hypnosis must be broken; otherwise, you are never face to face with the reality. And unless one is face to face, unless one is in an encounter with the real, one is not.

You can dream only if you are asleep, and you can project only if you are in ignorance. So ignorance means spiritual sleep, a spiritual somnambulism. This ignorance you cannot destroy by learning more and more. By any information, by any accumulation of knowledge, this ignorance cannot be destroyed, because this ignorance is not the *lack* of knowledge. So one can be a very learned man and still in illusion, and still in the same hypnotic trance, in the same sleep.

That is the difference between knowledge and wisdom. Wisdom comes when there is no ignorance–ignorance conceived as a positive force of maya, not just absence of learning, information – not just absence. And wisdom comes only when there is no ignorance. This positive energy which is creating illusions just stops to create. Knowledge means ignorance is still there, but hidden, hidden in information. And you can hide it, you can cover it, you can create a false sense of knowing without knowing at all.

Scriptures can help; teachers can help; religions can help; philosophy systems can help. Only meditation will not help you to create a false sense of knowing; everything thing else can help, help this dreaming. Only meditation cannot help you; only meditation can destroy the whole structure of ignorance and so-called knowledge. And then there is a sudden burst of wisdom. Then you are face to face, encountering the real.

Meditation is a technique to destroy another, another natural technique of auto-hypnosis, maya. Maya can be destroyed only by meditation, because meditation brings your mechanism of projections to a halt. And if you can go deep, it comes to a full stop. The moment it comes to a full stop, the whole changes; you are transformed and you are in a new world, in a new consciousness. That consciousness is brahma. As we are, we are in maya; as we can be, as is our potentiality, is brahma. This seed of brahma, this seed of supreme consciousness is covered in ignorance, in maya.

Use meditation as a technique of de-hypnosis.

Maya is hypnosis; meditation is de-hypnosis.

Of course, it looks like hypnosis, because it is going back on the same path you have come. It is retracing your steps back, so it looks like hypnosis. In a way it is hypnosis, only the direction is different. In hypnosis you are projecting things; in de-hypnosis you are taking your projections back, collecting back your projections, bringing back the web of your projections into the projector. It looks the same, only the direction is just the opposite.

In hypnosis you go far away from yourself on the same path. In de-hypnosis you come back – on the same path but towards yourself. So meditation is de-hypnosis, the technique to de-hypnotize yourself from a natural hypnosis, from a natural power called maya.

Now we should start de-hypnosis....

I am never born as a body.
I am not the ten senses.
And I am neither intellect,
nor mind nor everlasting ego.
I am eternally pure self-nature
without vital breath and mind.
I am the witness without intellect,
and I am the everknowing self-nature.
There is no doubt, whatsoever, about it.

A very long journey from "I" to "thou," from "thou" to "that," and from "that" to the beyond. And now again the rishi begins to talk about "Who am I?" Obviously, the first "I" is not referred to, that has been just disposed of. This is a second "I."

The first "I" constitutes the ego; constitutes whatsoever we have done, whatsoever we have achieved, whatsoever has been our accumulation. This second "I" is not our doing; this second "I" is our being. So we must distinguish between these two: the doing and the being.

The being is something which is there, has been there; it is *a priori*. It is not your creation, it is not your construction, you have not contributed anything to it, because you *are* it. So how can you do anything? And whatsoever you have done is just an accumulations around – never on the center; the center has always been there.

The child is born. The child is born with a being, with a center, but with no periphery, with no circumference. The child is born with a being, but with no doing at all. Now the doing will grow; now the child will cultivate the ego. Whatsoever the child is going to do will become part of his ego. If he succeeds, then a superiority is accumulated; if he fails, then an inferiority is accumulated. And whether you begin to feel to be inferior or superior, a certain ego is formed. Even when you feel inferior, you have an ego which feels to be inferior. If you succeed, you have an ego which feels to be superior.

The ego means whatsoever you have done – whether you succeed or fail, it is irrelevant, you create an ego. You begin to assert, "I am this, I am that." And the more this feeling grows, the more the center is lost, and by and by forgotten. In the end we are nothing but our doings. The being is just lost; we have lost the track.

So first we discussed the "I," the ego, the superficial, the one created by us – our own creation. Now the rishi is talking about the being – what we are, not what we have done; what we are, pure, simple beingness. Of course when we say "I" and use "I" for it, the meaning is totally different. We again refer to it as an "I," because this is the innermost center of our existence. But now there is no feeling of "I- ness," only a reference, only a word to be used and forgotten. This pure "I," this pure being, can only be described in a negative way, through elimination. We have to say, "This is not, that is not," and go on denying. And when nothing remains to deny anymore, it is revealed.

There are two ways to indicate a thing. One is direct, positive; another is indirect, negative. The more sublime a phenomenon, the more deep a thing is, you cannot indicate it positively, you cannot figure it out. You cannot say, "This is." No, that's not possible. How can you say what love is? How can you say what goodness is? How can you say what God is? If you say something positive, you will feel that much has remained unexpressed, and your word has given a limitation.

Saint Augustine has been asked by someone, "What is God?" Saint Augustine says, "When you do not ask me, I know very well, but when you ask me, everything is lost. So don't disturb me; go and find out. Please go and find our for yourself. I am not going to answer, because the moment I begin to answer, I feel guilty. Any expression becomes just criminal, because whatsoever I say is nothing compared to that about which I am saying." This has always been felt, very deeply felt, and so many have just remained silent, mm? – not to be guilty; it is better not to say.

Wittgenstein has written in his *Tractatus*, "It is better not to say than to say something about a thing which is inexpressible. So be silent, it is better, because at least you are right." At least you are right! The moment you say something you are bound to be wrong, *any* assertion is bound to be wrong. So infinite a phenomenon as the deeper "I"...it is better to be silent.

But it needs expression. It may be better for the person who is going to say, but it is not better for the person who is going to understand it, to enquire about it. Silence will not do.

So the rishi uses the second method, the negative one. The *Upanishads* have been using the same method always. That has been their technique, to negate. They will say, "I am that which is never born. I am the unborn one. All that which is born, I am not. So whatsoever is born, I am not." This is the eliminating process. Whatsoever is born, I am not. Breathing has been born in me. It is born because a child is born without breathing, then he breathes. So the being precedes breathing; being comes first, and then there is breathing. Then there is thinking, then there is ego – all this is born.

If we go still deeper, when the mother becomes pregnant, the first egg has no senses, but the being is there. Then by and by the egg grows and then senses come into being; they are born. After the being is, it is born.

So the rishi says: "I am not the senses, because I am always prior." I always precede. And whatsoever has succeeded me, I am not."

"I am not the senses" – that is, I am not the body – "neither I am the mind," because mind is a later growth, and sometimes mind can be destroyed without destroying you. Sometimes it happens that accidentally the mind is destroyed, and you are.

In the second world war, one English soldier fell down into a ditch. He became unconscious, and he remained unconscious for one week. And when he came back from unconsciousness, he was not the same mind again. He couldn't recognize anyone – not even himself; he couldn't recognize his face in the mirror, because all his memory was lost; the whole mechanism was destroyed. But the being was still there. So the mind is a mechanism – something added to you, but not you. It is something instrumental to you, but not you.

The rishi says, "I am not the mind. Neither am I the feeling of being a self." Neither am I the feeling of being a self, because how can you feel yourself as a self without the mind? The feeling of self is part of the mind, that, "I am." Go deep into it. We use "I am." This feeling of "I" is part of our mind. The rishi says, "No not this either. This feeling of being a self is again not my reality, my being." So when the rishi says, "Not even the feeling of self," then what remains? "I" drops completely, and only "am-ness" remains. The feeling of "I" belongs to the mind, but "am-ness" belongs to my being itself. A feeling of "am-ness" is what is meant by *atma* – just "am-ness."

If you can drop your thinking, you will be, but in an oceanic feeling of "am-ness." Even this formation of "I," this formation of self-hood, is not there. That is a later growth.

The rishi is really trying to bring into consciousness, the purest possibility of existence, with nothing added to it – the purest, just a clean slate, nothing written on it. So he is washing everything that we have written on it, and just cleaning the whole thing. When nothing more remains to be washed, he says, "This is the being." Because whatsoever is written is just doing – howsoever subtle, howsoever hidden, howsoever unconscious – whatsoever is written is a later growth.

So go back, retrace, regress to the original "am-ness." That, he says, even when there is no breathing, where there is no "minding," this being is there – without mind, without breathing, without senses. What remains? But what remains? Just a vacuum? Just a nothingness? No, all remains, but in its purity, in its potentiality, in its absolute see.

Only one positive assertion is made, and that is, "This innermost center is aware, is conscious." The very nature of it is consciousness. When everything has been eliminated – thoughts, senses, body, mind – when everything has been eliminated, only pure consciousness remains. This is the nature of it.

What is meant by pure consciousness?

By pure consciousness is meant that there is consciousness; not conscious about anything – just a mirror, mirroring nothing. Towards this purity is the whole search. And the rishi says, "There is no doubt about it," because this is not a doctrine, this is not a philosophical system; this is experience, this is realization. The rishi says, "This I have known; this I have lived; this I have reached.

This is not just a mental projection; this is not just a thought-out system; this is what I have lived and known and experienced."

This must be understood because this is one of the most emphatic characteristics of Eastern *darshan* – I will not call it philosophy. It has been called and translated as philosophy very wrongly – not only wrongly, but the very meaning is perverted. By darshan is meant that which you have *seen*, not thought. By philosophy is meant that which you have thought.

Philosophy means love of thinking. *Philo* means love, *sophy* means thinking – love of thinking. Darshan is not love of thinking; it is love of seeing. So only one man, Hermann Hesse, has rightly translated it; he has coined a new word to translate darshan into English, and that word is *philosia* – *philo* for love, and *sia* for seeing – not *sophy*, but *sia*.

The Eastern mind has been constantly concerned, not with thinking, but with seeing. They say thinking is a pale substitute. You have seen the sunrise, that is one thing. Someone who is blind can only think about the sunrise. Can there be any parallel? Can there be any comparison? Whatsoever you have seen and whatsoever he may have thought – can there be any link between the two? A blind man thinking about the sunrise is really a very complex phenomenon, primarily because a blind man has never known what sunrise is, what light is. What does rising mean to a blind man? What does light mean to a blind man? Simple words – only words, mere words with nothing in them – meaningless. He has heard "light," "sun," "sunrise"; he can think. What can he think? He can think in a chain of words. He can create a chain of words – simple – a chain of words, not of meanings, because meaning is something which is always felt. A word is meaningless unless you have felt the substance of it. A blind man cannot think about the sunrise because he cannot even think about light; really, he cannot even think about darkness.

We always think, we assume that the blind man is living in darkness. That is simply absurd, because darkness is a phenomenon of the eyes, not of blindness. You have to be not blind to know darkness: darkness is seen, and a blind man cannot see. So a blind man is not in darkness – remember this. A blind man has never known what darkness is, because for darkness to be felt, you need eyes. Even darkness has not been known. So if you eliminate, negate, and you say to the blind man, "Light is what darkness is not," it still means nothing. You cannot even use the eliminative process; you cannot say, "Light is not darkness." He will ask what darkness is.

A blind man can think. Thinking is a dimension which need not be experienced. He can think, he can create concepts in his own way – in his own blind ways he can create concepts. He can create some parallelism; he can create some synonyms. He can begin to think in terms of his own experience about light, darkness and sunrise, and he can create a philosophy. Really, only blind men create philosophies, because those who can see will not bother to create philosophies. If you can see, there is no need.

This is the basic difference between Eastern thinking and Western. Western thinking has always remained with thinking; Eastern thinking has always stepped out of thinking, because they say even thinking is a barrier to seeing. If your eyes are filled with thoughts, you cannot see. The eyes must cease all thinking, all ideation, all minding – then the eyes are clear, then you can go deep into reality.

So the rishi says, "There is no doubt about it. Whatsoever I am saying, I have seen, and there is no doubt." So it is not, "I don't know, but I propose…perhaps…it may be so…." It is *not* so. The rishi is not saying, "Perhaps it may be like this," or "Perhaps it may be like that." He is simply saying – he is *describing*. So it is not that he is proposing any ideology; it is simply this, that he is describing something he has gone into. So he says, "There is no doubt. I myself have know this: this *pure consciousness*."

How to go? – because for us still there is doubt. It may not be for him – for the rishi it may not be – but for us there is still doubt. And it is good – if you also say, "Now there is no doubt," then you are lost, because if there is no doubt for you, you will not go for the journey where the certainty is. You will create a pseudo certainty; all believers create pseudo certainties. They also say, "We believe it is so," and they have not known.

Unless you know, do not believe.

Unless you know, do not say, "There is no doubt."

Remain with the doubt.

Doubt is healthy; it pushes you.

152

But don't get stuck in the doubt – go ahead, find the state where you can also say, "Now there is no doubt. I know it." But not before that – not before that.

Live with doubt, go with doubt; search, enquire.

Don't make your doubt suicidal – that's enough – don't make your doubt suicidal. Let it be a healthy push. Let it be an enquiry, an open enquiry.

So be with doubt. Don't create any false belief. It is better to be sincerely in doubt, than to be insincerely into belief, because at least you are authentic. And authenticity is very meaningful. An authentic, sincere person can reach – will reach. But a non-authentic, insincere person may go on believing for lives and lives together. He is not even moving a single inch; he cannot move.

So when this rishi says, "There is no doubt," it is not meant that thereby you begin to believe. The rishi is simply giving a statement about his own stage. He is saying, "For me, there is no doubt. Whatsoever I am saying, I mean it, and I have known it."

Really, the *Upanishads* have never given any arguments. Whatsoever they say, they say without any arguments, without any proofs. This is rare! They don't say why this is so; they say, "This is so." Why? It is significant. It is very significant, because whenever you try to prove something – you argue something, you gather witnesses for it – it means that you are creating a philosophy, a rationalization, a reasoning, a logical system; but you have not known.

If you have known, then a simple statement is enough. So the rishis give simple statements, and then methods – not proofs. Whatsoever they say, they say, "It is so; now this is the method, you can also know it." They never give any proofs; quite the opposite.

There are Greek thinkers: Aristotle, or Plato, or even Socrates. They go on giving proofs. They go on giving proofs, arguments. They say, "This is so *because*....And in "because" they will never say, "because I have known it." They will say, "because this proves it, that proves it; that's why it is so." It is a syllogism, a logical syllogism.

These rishis are just illogical. They say, "This is so." And if you ask, "Give us proofs," they say, "This is the method. Experiment with it and you will get the proof." In a way this is more scientific – less logical, but more scientific – not concerned with arguments at all, but with experiment. Really, this is what scientists are doing. If you ask them, "Why is this so, why does fire burn?" they will say, "Put your hand in it. We don't know why, we know *how* it burns."

So the basic approach of any philosophical ideation is "why?" And the basic scientific approach is always concerned with "how," never with "why." The rishi will never ask why we are not minds; he will ask "how" – the method. This is religious science, not philosophical systematizing. Of course, the experiment has to be different, because the lab has to be different. For scientific experimenting a lab is needed outside you; for religious experimentation you are the lab.

How? How can this pure consciousness be achieved? The very description is the process also – this eliminatory method of saying a thing is also the process. When the rishi says, "I am not the body; I am not the senses; I am not the mind" – this is also the method. Go on, go on being more and more conscious of the fact that "I am not the body." Remain with this fact: "I am not the body."

Remember this fact – let it go deep in you:

I am not the body.

Begin to feel the gap between you and the body, and soon the gap is known, because the gap exists there – you have only forgotten it. It is not to be created; it is there already – you have just forgotten it. You have just escaped from the gap. The gap is always there, but we never go in to see the gap.

Really, this is miraculous in a way, and very strange, that we know our bodies from the outside – even our own bodies we know from the outside. This is as if you live in a house but you have never known the inner walls of the house; you have known only the outer ones – your own house! You cannot describe your body – how it looks from within? You can describe how your body looks in the mirror. But the mirror cannot see the inside; it can only see the outer, the outer shell.

But there is an inside also, because no outside can exist without an inside – or *can* an outside exist without an inside? But we have never become aware from the inside of our own body.

So be aware:

Close your senses, remain in, and be aware.

And begin to feel your body from the inside. There will be a gap, because there is always a gap. You will come to know that gap, and then you will know what this rishi means when he says, "I am not the body, I am not the senses, I am not the mind." Go on, deep. Begin to look into your *minding* itself, into your mind process itself, and then you will begin to be aware that there is still a gap, between you and your mind.

Go on eliminating, and a moment comes when you explode into simple am-ness – without any I, without any self, without any selfhood – into pure authentic, existential being.

I am not the doer. I am not the consumer.
I am simply the witness of nature.
And just because of my nearness, the body, et cetera,
have the feeling of being conscious, and they act accordingly.
Beyond a shade of doubt, I am still, eternal,
everlasting bliss – everknowing pure self or soul.
And I pervade all beings as the witnessing soul.

How does this bondage happen? How is it that we never feel that we are *in* the body, but feel that we *are* the body? The witnessing self is never felt. We always feel some identity; we always feel some identification. And the witnessing consciousness is the reality. So why does this happen? And how does this happen?

You are in pain – what is really happening inside? Analyze the whole phenomenon: the pain is there, and there is this consciousness that pain is there. These are the two points: the pain is there, and there is this *consciousness* that the pain is there. But there is no gap, and somehow "I am in pain" – this feeling happens – "I am in pain." And not only this – sooner or later, "I am the pain" begins, happens, starts to be the feeling.

I *am* pain; I am *in* pain; I am *aware of* the pain" – these are three different, very different states. The rishi says, "I am *aware* of the pain." This much can be allowed, because then you transcend pain. The awareness transcends – you are different from it, and there is a deep separation. Really, there has never been any relation; the relation begins to appear only because of the nearness, because of the intimate nearness of your consciousness and all that happens around.

Consciousness is so near when you are in pain – it is just there by the side, very near. It has to be; otherwise, the pain cannot be cured. It has to be just near to feel it, to know it, to be aware about it. But because of this nearness, you become identified, and one. This is a safety measure again; this is a security measure, a natural security. When there is pain you must be near; when there is pain your consciousness *must* go in a rush towards the pain – to feel it, to do something about it.

You are on the street and suddenly you feel a snake there – then your whole consciousness just becomes a jump. No moment can be lost, not even in thinking what to do. There is no gap between being aware and the action. You must be very near; only then this can happen. When your body is suffering pain, disease, illness, you must be near; otherwise, life cannot survive. If you are far off and the pain is not felt, then you will die. The pain must be felt immediately – there should be no gap. The message must be received immediately, and your consciousness must go to the spot to do something. That's why nearness is a necessity.

But because of this necessity, the other phenomenon happens: so near, you become one; so near, you begin to feel that "this is me – this pain, this pleasure." Because of nearness there is identification: you become anger, you become love, you become pain, you become happiness.

The rishi says that there are two ways to disassociate yourself from these false identities. You are not what you have been thinking, feeling, imagining, projecting – what you are is simply the fact of being aware. Whatsoever happens, you remain just the awareness. You are awareness – that identity cannot be broken. That identity cannot be negated. All else can be negated and thrown. Awareness remains the ultimate substratum, the ultimate base. You cannot deny it, you cannot negate it, you cannot disassociate yourself from it.

So this is the process: That which cannot be thrown, that which cannot be made separate from you, is you; that which can be separated, you are not.

The pain is there; a moment later it may not be there – but you will be. Happiness has come, and it will go; it has been, and it will not be – but you will be. The body is young, then the body becomes old.

All else comes and goes – guests come and go – but the host remains the same. So the Zen mystics say:

Do not be lost in the crowd of the guests.

Remember your host-ness.

That host-ness is awareness.

That host-ness is the witnessing consciousness.

What is the basic element that remains always the same in you? Only be that, and disidentify yourself from all that comes and goes. But we become identified with the guest. Really the host is so occupied with the guest, he forgets.

Mulla Nasruddin has given a party for some friends and some strangers. The party is very boring, and half the night is just lost and it goes on. So one stranger, not knowing that Mulla is the host, says to him, "I have never seen such a party, such nonsense. It seems never-ending, and I am so bored that I would like to leave."

Mulla says, "You have said what I was going to say to you. I myself have never seen such a boring and nonsense party before, but I was not so courageous as you are. I was also thinking to leave it and just run away." So they both run.

Then, in the street Mulla remembers and says, "Something has gone wrong, because now I remember: I am the host! So please excuse me, I have to go back."

This is happening to us all.

The host is lost –

The host is forgotten every moment.

The host is your witnessing self.

Pain comes and pleasure follows; there is happiness, and there is misery. And each moment, whatsoever comes you are identified with it, you become the guest.

Remember the host.

When the guest is there, remember the host.

And there are so many types of guests: pleasurable, painful; guests you would like, guests you would not like to be your guests; guests you would like to live with, guests you would like to avoid – but all guests.

Remember the host.

Constantly remember the host.

Be centered in the host.

Remain in your host-ness; then there is a separation. Then there is a gap, an interval – the bridge is broken. The moment this bridge is broken, the phenomenon of renunciation happens. Then you are *in* it, and not *of* it. Then you are there in the guest, and still a host. You need not escape from the guest, there is not need.

Then you can be in the crowd and alone. And if you cannot be alone in the crowd, you can never be alone anywhere, because the capacity to be alone in the crowd is needed to be alone when you are really alone; otherwise, if you cannot be alone in the crowd, the crowd will be there when you are alone. The mind will be crowded even *more*, because the mind has a tendency to feel absence more than presence.

If your beloved, if your lover is present, you can just forget very easily. But if he is not present, you cannot forget. The mind has the tendency to feel absence more, because through absence is desiring. And mind is just desiring, so mind feels absences more; otherwise, there can be no desiring. If you can forget absences, then desire becomes impossible. So we forget presences, and we go on feeling absences. Whatsoever is not, is desired; and whatsoever is, is just forgotten.

So when you are alone, the crowd will be there; it will follow you. If you escape from the crowd, the crowd will follow you. So do not escape, do not try – it is impossible. Remain where you are, but don't be centered in the guest.

Be centered in yourself, remember the host.

This host is your being in its purity.

Do not fall in love with the guest.

Do not fall in hate with the guest.

Really, this word is very good: "falling" in love. Why falling in love? Why not rising in love? No one rises in love, everyone falls in love. Why? Why this falling? Really, the moment you are in love, or in hate, you fall from your host-ness. You just fall from your host-ness; you become the guest. That is the misery, that's the confusion, that's the darkness.

Wherever you are – doing, not-doing, lonely, in the crowd, active, inactive – wherever you are, go on remembering the host. Remember that whatsoever is happening is just a guest, and you are the host, and don't be identified with anything. Anger comes – remember you are the host; anger is just a guest. It has come and it will go.

I am reminded of a Sufi story.

A great emperor asks his wise men to give him a mantra of such a type that it can be used in any dangerous, fatal situation – *any*. Advice is always particular, and he wants a mantra, an advice, the essence of all wisdom, so that it can be used in any situation whatsoever, whenever there is danger.

The wise men are very confused, very disturbed, and in a deep anguish. They cannot find such an essence of all wisdom. Then they go to a Sufi mystic and he gives a piece of paper and says, "This should not be opened unless there is *really* danger! And then the advice will be there." So the king put the piece of paper under the diamond of his ring.

There are many moments when the danger approaches, but the Sufi has emphatically said, "Unless you feel this is really the last hope – that nothing can be more dangerous – only then open it!" Many dangers come and go, and the king always feels this is not the last; something more can still happen. Even death approaches, and the king is just on his deathbed, but still he cannot open it, because he remembers still more is possible.

But his wise men say, "Now please open it. We want to see what is there." But the king says, "The promise must be fulfilled. Really, now it is irrelevant what is there; the mantra has worked upon me. Since having this mantra with me, I have not felt any danger at all. Whatsoever the danger was, I have felt still more was possible, and I have remained the host. I was never identified."

Danger can never become the ultimate unless you are identified with it, and then anything can become the ultimate – just anything! Just anything ordinary can become the ultimate, and you are disturbed. And the king said, "Now I am not worried at all, whatsoever. The man is wise; the Sufi knows – I am not concerned about what he has written."

Then, the king died without opening the ring. The moment he died, the first thing his wise men did was to open the ring. There was nothing; it was just a piece of paper . . . just a piece of paper – not a word, not a single word of advice.

But the advice worked; the mantra worked.

So be centered in you host, and remember nothing is happening to you. All that is happening is just the guests, visitors; they will come and go. And it is good that they come and go; it enriches you, you become more mature. But don't follow them, don't be involved with them. Don't become one with them. Don't fall in love and hate; don't fall into identification.

Remain the host, and then the ultimate happening happens.

Then the ultimate explosion becomes possible.

Once the witnessing soul is known, you will never be the same again. The whole world disappears and you are transmuted into a new dimension of bliss. Identification is misery; non-identification is bliss.

To fall in love and hate with the guest is misery. To transcend them, and to be centered in oneself, is bliss.

I am the brahman known by the whole vedanta
*(that which is beyond all knowledge). And I am
neither ether nor air, nor anything that I appear to be.
I am neither form, nor name, nor action, but
only brahman which is* satchidananda
*(existence, awareness, and bliss).
I am not the body, so how can I be
subject to birth and death?
I am not the vital breath, so how can I be
subject to hunger and thirst?
I am not the mind, so how can I be
subject to sorrow and attachment?
I am not the doer, so how can I be
subject to bondage and freedom?
Such is the mystery.
Here ends the Sarvasar Upanishad.*

Now the last assertion, the last thing to be said: The rishi says that knowledge must cease, because only then is knowing possible.

Knowledge means the accumulation of dead experiences – of your own, or of others, but knowledge means the dead past. Knowledge is always of the past. Knowing is always here and now, and knowledge is always of the past. The past must cease for the present to be, and knowledge must cease for the knowing to be.

Knowing is alive; knowledge is dead.

So really knowledge is not a help towards knowing; on the contrary, knowledge is the hindrance, the obstacle. The more you know, the more you accumulate information, the less is your capacity of knowing. That's why the capacity of children to learn is more, because they are fresh; knowledge is not there as a barrier for their knowing; their knowing is fresh. The old man cannot learn so much – not because the consciousness is not capable to learn, but because the consciousness is so much burdened with knowledge that the burden itself becomes a hindrance. Knowledge creates a barrier, and destroys the capacity to know.

All knowledge, whatsoever its nature, is a burden. So the rishi says:

Knowledge must cease for the knowing to be.

And the knowing, this knowing can happen only in total innocence. Knowledge is cunning; knowledge can never be innocent. So the more knowledge grows in the world, the more cunningness comes into existence. Why? – because the more you know, the less you begin to be spontaneous. You become calculating, and the more you calculate, the less you are conscious, and the more you are mechanical.

Really, calculators can do more calculation, and in a better way, and more efficiently than you. Soon computers will replace man, because they can accumulate more knowledge and in a better way.

Our own brains are also doing the same. The rishi says that the *veda* cannot reach to that supreme consciousness, brahman. And veda means all accumulated knowledge. So in India we have created a very strange word: *vedant*. It means the end of the vedas, just going beyond the vedas, just throwing the vedas far away, just being unburdened by the vedas. Veda means "knowledge," and vedant means "beyond knowledge." So in the end the rishi says: Now understand one thing – and this is one of the ultimates – that by knowledge you will never be able to know, to know the being; because being is always prior to knowledge.

We discussed the fact that being is prior to doing. Now the rishi says that being is prior to knowledge also.

You *are* before you know.

Being precedes knowing, knowledge, doing, everything.

That which precedes knowing cannot be known by knowledge. That which precedes doing cannot be reached by any doing whatsoever.

So the mystics say, "Reach there by non-doing; know that by not-knowing." These become very contradictory statements; that's why they are called mystics. Mystic statements are absolutely illogical, but not meaningless; rather, because they are illogical they carry more meaning, more dynamic meaning. Mystic statements are not just mad statements; they appear to be, but they are the most sane possible.

When the rishi says that you cannot know by knowledge, he means that knowledge is always concerned with something else, never with truth. My eye cannot see itself – why? When the eyes can see everything else, why not themselves? Of course I can see my eyes in a mirror, but that is not really seeing the eyes themselves – just a reflection, and the reflection becomes something else. The same is the phenomenon inside: the being can know by knowledge everything other than itself. Knowledge is just an opening, an eye towards the whole world.

Really, this will be very significant to understand. The word "science" means exactly what veda means: knowledge. We can put it in very modern terminology: by science you can never know the being, because science means knowledge, systematized knowledge.

So how can you know it? If knowledge itself cannot know it, then how? If eyes cannot see a thing, if it is impossible to see it with your eyes, then what to do? The only possibility – and you may not be able just to remember it – is that if the eyes cannot see a particular thing, then *close your eyes and see.* That's the only alternative possible. If it is not possible at all to see with the eyes, then close them and see. If knowledge cannot know the innermost being, then throw away the knowledge, and know. This is what vedanta means – throwing away knowledge – because it is felt that by knowledge, we cannot know the knower. Then throw it, don't carry it, because it may prove a hindrance. Just throw it; just put it aside as if you are taking your clothes off. Take you knowledge off, and be without knowledge.

Be without knowledge.

In that innocent moment of not knowing, one happens to be there, where one has always been. One is just thrown to the center. Suddenly the periphery disappears, suddenly you are not whatsoever you have been, and you are something which you have never known yourself to be…this is the secret.

So the rishi says: This is the secret; by not knowing, is that known. He is not saying by ignorance. Ignorance is not not-knowing; ignorance is just absence, absence of knowledge. Not-knowing is cessation of knowledge, not just absence.

So there are three steps: ignorance, knowledge, and supreme ignorance. You can call it supreme knowledge or can call it supreme ignorance; it means the same. It is supreme because it is beyond both knowing and not-knowing.

This is the secret of all secrets. *Upanishads….* The very word *upanishad* means the "secret doctrine." Why call it secret if you are going to call it a doctrine? If it is a doctrine it cannot be secret; if it is secret it cannot be a doctrine. So why call it a secret doctrine? Why use two contradictory words? The mystics have always felt that the moment you use one word without at the same time using the contradictory one, you divide life. And life exists in contradictions. The negative and the positive of electricity exist in a deep communion; the male psyche and the female psyche exist in a deep communion. The darkness and the light – we may think of them as contradictions, opposites, polar opposites, but they exist in a deep communion.

Have you ever seen any fight between darkness and light? Has there ever been any war between darkness and light? – they co-exist; they co-exist so silently. Really, there is no contradiction in existence; all contradictions are created by our minds, because we can look at a thing from a standpoint alone. We can never look at a thing as it is in its wholeness. Even a very small thing – just a pebble – you cannot look at the pebble from all sides simultaneously; the other side always remains in darkness. But the pebble is one. For you it is always an aspect that is known, and the remaining begins to be another aspect, but you can never know both simultaneously. But the pebble exists simultaneously.

Darkness and light are just two aspects of one thing. Birth and death – two aspects of one thing.

That's why the *Upanishads* are called the secret doctrine. Secret and open at the same time – simultaneously, because "doctrine" means open, a known thing, and "secret" means something unknown. So it is better to call it an open secret. It is open for everyone; but it is a secret, because even if you know it you can never claim the knowledge. By the very knowing the claimer is dissolved.

Socrates says, "When I was ignorant I thought myself to be wise; and now, when I have known, I know nothing else but ignorance."

This is the essence of all mysticism.

Polar opposites exist in a dynamic unity.

And by this statement that even knowledge is not you, everything else but pure being is negated.

And then the rishi asks the same question he was asked in the beginning. He has not answered it. He was asked, "What is bondage, and what is freedom?" He has not answered. He has answered many things which were not asked; he has gone deep in many dimensions; he has discussed and analyzed everything that is needed for a seeker, but he has not discussed bondage and freedom.

And now in the end he *asks* the disciple, "Now tell me who is there to be in bondage? Where can bondage exist? – because we have dissolved the ego. If the ego is there, bondage is possible. If the ego is not there, who can be in bondage, and how can bondage happen? To whom can it happen? And if there is no bondage, then what do you mean by freedom? On this question the *Upanishad* ends.

This is a strange book. A question has been raised in the beginning, an enquiry has been made: What is bondage? What is freedom? And on the same question the enquiry ends: What is bondage? Who is in bondage? Who can be in bondage? How can bondage happen, and what do you mean by freedom? Who is going to be free?

Who is the agent to whom bondage and freedom can happen? What type of a book...answering nothing, and the question comes back! But now the quality of the question has totally changed. The question was asked in the beginning by the disciple; now it is asked by the master. And the disciple was asking in ignorance; the master is asking in supreme knowledge. The disciple asked because he didn't know; the master is asking because he knows.

Really he is saying, "You have asked absurdities. Your question was irrelevant; it was not a question at all."Just because the form of it was that of a question, doesn't make it a question. You can ask anything and it may look grammatically right, linguistically exact, and it may not be a question at all.

There are many questions the human mind goes on asking without knowing the fact that those questions are just absurd, they cannot be answered; because really there exists nothing in reality corresponding to them.

The disciple asks, "What is bondage?" One thing is implied – there is someone who can be in bondage. That has not been questioned at all. He asks, "What is bondage?" – with an implication, taken for granted, that bondage is possible. Someone can be in bondage, and someone exists who can be in bondage – that has been taken for granted, that has not been questioned at all. It has been accepted and assumed that there is bondage.

Then he asks, "What is freedom, and how to be free?" You can go on asking, but the basic assumption is false, pseudo. There is no one inside who can be in bondage. Really, if you don't ask the basic question – is there someone inside who can be in bondage?...if you miss the first basic question, you may ask and ask, and many answers can be given to you, but no answer will be an answer. And no answer will satisfy you, because the basic question has not been asked. These questions are secondary.

The rishi goes on talking about things which raise the basic question again and again. And then he goes on dissolving the basic factor upon which creates bondage, and freedom also. Then ultimately when the agent is no more, when the doer is no more, when the knower is no more, when the ego is no more, when the center is just dissolved – in that very moment, in that total silence and egolessness – when the guru sees, when the master looks into the eyes of the disciple, and feels that now there is no one inside but total silence, nothingness or pure being, then he asks. He must penetrate deep into the eyes of the disciple, and ask, "Now tell me: who can be in bondage? And for whom are you asking freedom?"

The book becomes still more strange, because the disciple remains silent. This is the last; here the secret doctrine ends – with a question mark. The master has asked, and the disciple has not even nodded his head. He has not said anything, not even a thanks. He remains just silent, as if he is not. The disciple has disappeared, and this disappearance is the real essence of disciplehood.

The disciple has disappeared.

When the disciple has disappeared, only then the master can ask. This disappearance of the disciple, this total evaporation, is the answer. No verbal answer has been given, but an existential answer has been conveyed. Now the disciple knows, but the disciple is not.

That's why the teacher asks. The question is raised not because any answer is expected; the question is raised only to know whether there is still someone who reacts. But there is no reaction; the question just echoes in the disciple and disappears. This is the answer from the disciple. They have come to the end of their journey, for which they prayed. They prayed to the divine, to God: "Help us, help us both in our common endeavor, in our common effort. This is going to be a deep communion, so help us" – teacher and taught both, the master and the disciple both – "help us both so that we may endeavor and find out the truth."

The truth has appeared, but only when the disciple has disappeared. And the master has never been there, so there is no problem, no need for him to disappear – he has not been.

The master means one who has disappeared already. The disciple means one who has to disappear.

When the disciple also disappears, there is neither master nor disciple, and then exists *that* – that which we once called "I," then "thou," then "that"...and then, even beyond that.

There is a tradition in Tibetan Buddhism: when the disciple disappears, the master puts his head at his feet, at the disciple's feet. The circle becomes complete – because now there is no disciple; in a way there is only the master. And by master I mean one who has disappeared.

You can be two if you *are*, but if you have disappeared you cannot be two. We are so many here because we *are*. If we all disappear, and there are so many nothingnesses, will there be so many nothingnesses? – nothingness is bound to be one. How can you count absences? You can count only presences; absence is always one. You can count egos; you cannot count consciousness. There is no way to count egolessness, nothingnesses, absences.

In this moment who is the master, and who is the disciple? They have both disappeared. This disappearance of master and disciple is the culmination, is the climax; is the peak of communion, of love, of intimacy. Neither husband and wife, nor mother and son, nor brothers, nor friends, can come to this disappearance. Only a master and disciple relationship can come to this highest peak of non-existence, of dissolving one into another.

That's why in the East, nothing was more sacred than this relationship of the master and the disciple – nothing was more sacred, nothing whatsoever! No love was higher than that; it cannot be. Because in any other love and intimacy, you never disappear; you remain, and you continue to remain. And that continuity of the presences becomes a constant conflict, a continuous misery and anguish.

Love fulfills itself, becomes a perfect flower only in a relationship between two, of whom one has already disappeared, and the other is ready to disappear. In all other relationships both are present, too much present, and each one is trying to be more and more present. Of course they also try for the other's disappearance – but that disappearance is different. Both try so that "the other should disappear, and I should be completely, totally, the master of the whole." And both are trying, so there is conflict.

A master is one who has disappeared already, so there is no question of his domination. He is not. And the other has come to him, not to possess him, but to be dispossessed of himself. That's the reason that when the master says something it has to be obeyed. Not that it is the master's domination; on the contrary, because the master cannot dominate, he is not. So his order becomes just an order from the source of all being. There is no ego, so there is no question of domination.

Again the paradox: a guru cannot dominate, so he dominates totally.

We tried to understand, to discuss, to analyze something which cannot be discussed, cannot be analyzed. We have discussed and analyzed not in order that whatsoever I say may be meaningful, but the way I say it, and the way I convey it to you may be meaningful. Not my words, but these silences between words may become glimpses to you. This is just beating around the bush, because the bush cannot be beaten directly. The truth cannot be indicated directly. So round and round about, I have been beating the bush in the hope that it may be...perhaps just by going around and around the bush, you may have a glimpse of the bush itself.

And that's why I am more more emphatically interested in meditation than in discussions. These discussions are just to give you a push, to satisfy you in an intellectual way; just to give you a feeling that whatsoever you are doing is very intellectual, rational. It is not.

So whatsoever I have been saying is in a way quite the opposite of what I have been trying to pull you into. My approach, as far as these discussions were concerned, was rational, just to satisfy you – just to give you some toys to play with, so that you can be persuaded into something else. That something else is not rational; that is irrational.

Someone came to me and said...he is new here, he has come just two days ago, and he is not acquainted with the Eastern mind at all; he is from the West. So he came to me and said, "I am bewildered, because whatsoever you are saying, and whatsoever is being done in meditation...there seems to be no connection at all."

I said to him, "Of course there is no connection; but still there is. But it is very indirect." I try to pacify your mind just to help you take a jump out of it. I go on rationalizing things, talking logically, arguing about, only in order that your argumentative mind is just exhausted, and you can take a jump out of all the nonsense that is called rationality.

So our meditation has been just a jump into irrational existence. And existence *is* irrational – it is mystic, it is a mystery. So please don't cling to what I have said to you; rather, cling to whatsoever I have persuaded you to do. Do it, and someday you will realize that whatsoever I have said is meaningful. But if you go on clinging to what I have said, it may give you knowledge, it may make you more knowledgeable, but you will not attain to knowing. And even whatsoever I have said may become a hindrance.

I don't know. I may have helped you to create a hindrance – I don't know. It depends on you.

Now our last meditation. Because it is going to be the last, do not withhold yourself at all. Just be in it as totally as possible.

PART TWO

Mt. Abu

Kaivalya Upanishad

March 25th - April 2nd, 1972

AUM.
May the different limbs of my body – my voice,
my nose, my eyes, my ears, and my strength,
and also all the other sense organs be nourished,
and become intelligent.
All the Upanishads *are manifestations*
of brahman itself.
May I never deny brahman
may brahman never deny me.
May the dharma *described in the* Upanishad
belong to me, I who am devoted to brahman.
AUM, peace, peace, peace.

The *Kaivalya Upanishad* enquiry into the ultimate freedom is an effort to know the secret of total loneliness without feeling lonely. Man can be lonely because others are not present. In that case, even in loneliness, the absent crowd is present. But one can be alone, so totally fulfilled, so totally oneself, that the other is not felt – not even as an absence. The other is not. When the other has dissolved totally, absolutely, you become free.

By freedom, the *Upanishads* means not a political thing, not a social thing, not even a psychological thing; by total freedom, they mean a spiritual, basic, ultimate freedom. One becomes so fulfilled that the whole universe is felt not as an other, but as oneself. Really, one has to go deep into it. We feel the other because we are unfulfilled: We feel the other as *the other* because we are unfulfilled. Once we are fulfilled, the other is dissolved. In a fulfilled mind there is no feeling of the other. Totally fulfilled, the universe and you become one.

This is the search: how to be one with the total universe. And if it is possible to be one with the total universe, then one is lonely without the feeling of loneliness. This phenomenon is known as *kaivalya*: loneliness without feeling lonely.

This *Upanishad* is concerned with this ultimate aloneness, what Plotinus has called, "a flight of the alone to the alone." This is the flight; this is what Plotinus means.

This is the flight, but this flight begins with a prayer. Nothing religious can begin without a prayer. Really, whatsoever begins with a prayer is religious, because a prayerful mind means many things – much is implied in a prayerful mood. Man is not enough; alone he is not enough. Alone he is helpless, alone he cannot go on this flight, a divine support is needed.

The support of the total is needed, the support of the whole. Unless the whole supports man, man cannot proceed, because we are not something separate from the whole. We belong to it as an organic part, not as a mechanical part. A mechanical part can be pulled out from the whole, but not an organic part. My eyes are part of me, organically one with me. If my eyes are pulled out, they will not be eyes then, because they can only be eyes when I am seeing through them. My eyes, out of me, will be just dead. Even to call them eyes will be wrong, because they cannot be called eyes if they are not seeing. My eyes see only when they are one with me.

This is organic unity: parts are not parts, they cannot be parted, so they are not parts. In an organic unity the part behaves as a whole. In a mechanical unity, the part behaves as a part.

If you pull my eyes out, the eyes will not be eyes – not only that, I will not be a see-er, because how can I be a see-er without the eyes? Eyes pulled out will be dead eyes; without eyes I will be a dead see-er. Eyes and me exist in an organic unity. The eyes are not my part, they *are* me. I am not something apart from my eyes, I *am* my eyes.

This is what I mean by organic unity. Man exists in his wholeness as an organic unity; that's why prayer is meaningful. Prayer only means alone, helpless, I am nothing. I cannot even move, I cannot even be, so help me. The total is invoked through prayer. The whole is invoked, the whole unity is called forth: Help me; only then I can proceed, only then this enquiry will be possible.

Prayer means this: a call for help from the whole. Prayer also implies that unless the whole desires it, it is futile, unless the whole helps it, it is not even desirable. So first, the whole must be with me. Unless the whole is with me, my efforts are futile, and not only futile, they may be even dangerous. They may be even against myself.

Man is ignorant. He can go on a search which is meaningless; he can ask for things which which are not really for his benefit; he can ask for things which will prove poisonous to himself; he can desire his own death;

he can desire his own destruction. The whole must be asked first. The whole must be taken into confidence, so to speak.

The whole must be with me; only with the whole with me, can I go any-where. And the going will never be harmful to me or to anyone else. This is one thing to be understood.

There is a proof for it also. Science begins without prayer – man endea-voring by himself, without any participation, without any call, without any prayerful mood for the whole – man, endeavoring by himself, without any participation, without any call, without any prayerful mood for the whole – man, struggling alone. That's why science becomes a conquering, a struggle, a fight, a war. And that's why, as I see it, science has led humanity into a cul-de-sac.

Science has promised many things, but not a single promise has been fulfilled. On the contrary, everything that was felt, propagated as a bless-ing to humanity, has proved quite the contrary. Why? Why so much effort, so much concentration, so much energy wasted by scientists? And human-ity is going on every day, deeper into its hell – why? Any endeavor begun in a non-prayerful mood is going to be dangerous, because the whole has not been asked. The whole has not been taken into confidence. The whole has not even been considered.

Prayer means, the whole is significant.

I am nothing, I must ask permission, and I must ask for help. If my prayer is answered, only then is any step to be taken. And with a prayerful start man never goes astray; the very prayer changes the whole conscious-ness. The very mood creates a surrender, creates a surrendering mind, a surrendering consciousness. The very prayer creates in you, not a fight with the universe, but a love.

In another way, two things are very significant in human consciousness. The Freudian psychology says man has two types of wills, or man's will is divided into two conflicting centers. One, Freud has called *eros* – love. An-other, Freud has called *thanatos* – death. If your mind is functioning from the center of death, thanatos, then a fight is created. If your mind is func-tioning from the center of eros, then a love towards the universe.

I would like to say, that to begin with prayer is to begin with the center of eros. To begin with prayer is to begin the effort as a love effort. It is advancing towards existence in a love-ful mood. It is through love that one prays. If you are going to fight, then prayer is not needed. Science is fighting with the universe; religion is a love effort, it is falling in love with the universe.

So this *Upanishad* begins with a prayer, and the prayer is very strange, because the *Upanishad* says, ask that the senses – eyes, ears, nose...the senses should be strengthened first. "Let my senses be strengthened."

This is the first prayer – very strange, very un-Indian looking! Very un-religious because a religious man is against the senses. He can pray that "I should be away, beyond, transcendent to my senses; how can I dissolve my senses completely?" That seems logical, rational, consistent, but *this* prayer is very strange. "Give strength, more energy, more growth, more maturity to my senses" – Why?

Really, any authentic religious mind lives in a non-duality, not in a duality. For really authentic religion there is no duality between consciousness and body, no duality between the divine and the world, no duality between mind and matter; the duality is just a mental construct.

Duality exists nowhere, the whole is one. If we take it as two, or if it appears to us as two, it is because of our way of looking, not because it is so. Through senses it appears to us as matter, and through a non-sensuous approach it appears as mind, as consciousness. But it is one!

Matter is just a very deeply asleep consciousness; consciousness is just awakened matter. Matter becomes conscious. So a stone by your side is just in a deep sleep, a very deep sleep of a mind. It may take millennia for it to be awake, but it is. Even in a stone, deep down a soul is asleep, a possible consciousness is there, a potential consciousness is there. And even in you, it has come only to an awakening – it is there.

Matter and mind are two states of one thing, of one phenomenon: asleep it is matter, awakened it is mind.

So for the *Upanishads* there is no duality between body and consciousness. So he asks, prays that, "my senses should be strengthened to become more mature, more strong, more sensitive, more penetrating. Why? – because if my eyes can become more penetrating, I can see the divine even in matter, in a tree, even in a stone I can see it. If I am not seeing it, there are two reasons. One, the stone is asleep; second, my eyes are not so penetrating that they can reach even into its sleep and know it. These are the two reasons.

Matter is consciousness asleep, and I cannot feel it because my eyes are not so penetrating. My senses are not even so alive that I can feel the consciousness asleep in the stone. So there are two possibilities: either the stone must become, must flower into consciousness, then I can know – or my eyes must come to their perfection, then I can penetrate. And then even if the consciousness is asleep, I can know and feel.

The *Upanishad* prays, "Let my senses be strengthened, so I can penetrate your mystery." Your mystery is here but I cannot see it, my eyes are weak or just blind. My eyes are blind, they don't see you, they don't feel you. Wherever I see, wherever I feel, only matter comes to my knowledge. My feeble senses are not capable of feeling you. Make my senses more alive, more strong, more acute, so I can go deep in your mystery, which is all around.

This is a strange prayer and a very beautiful one. Strange, because we have been fed a very wrong conception that the senses are your enemy. So kill the senses, destroy them. With a deadened sensuality, with a dead body, you will be more spiritual. This has been given to us, fed into our minds, this totally wrong conception. It is a very pathological conception towards life – ill, diseased, neurotic.

The *Upanishads* are very healthy, life-affirmative. They say one is not to be dead in the body; rather, more alive. If you are more alive, more and more alive, then you will not feel the body at all. A moment comes when the body is totally filled with aliveness – every particle of the body alive, awakened – then there is no body at all. You become just energy, just consciousness.

So this is a transformation, not a suppression. The prayer is not for suppression. The rishi is not praying, "Let my eyes be weak or blind so I cannot see that which must not be seen." On the contrary, he is praying, "Let my eyes be so strong that I can see that which cannot be seen. The unseeable, the unknowable are not seen; so give me strength, give me more energy, more consciousness to my senses." He is praying, "Let me come down, down to my body, to every fiber of my body. Let me be deep down into every particle of my body, so alive, so full of energy, so full of consciousness and sensitivity, that I can know you and I can feel your mystery."

Really, those who have ever felt the divine mystery were basically the most sensitive minds in the world.

Our so-called ascetics – who are just trying to deaden their bodies, trying to destroy the instrument of knowing – may come to a point where they become just an enclosed stone. The body has become completely dead, and now they are just enclosing themselves. They can become very perfect egos, but never souls, never enlightened ones.

They can be perfect egoists, because the more you are closing yourself the more your are self-centered, and the self is strengthened. You become a monad, completely enclosed and dead in yourself. Then you can live in your illusions, then you can live in your dreams, then you are in a coma. You are broken from the whole by your own effort. This is a spiritual suicide. Really, this is suicide; all else is just changing from one body to another. This is a spiritual suicide.

The rishi is saying quite the contrary, "Let my body be more alive, let me come down to my body. Let my fingers be my soul, so when I touch something, it is not only that I am touching by my fingers, but *I* am touching and fingers are dissolved. I become prominent, significant, I go *through* my fingers, and then only, I can touch something which cannot be touched." If I take your hand in my hand, and if I can move with my whole consciousness through my fingers, only then I am touching *you*, not your hand. Then your being is touched, and then your mystery becomes something alive to me. Then the doors of your mystery are open to me; then I begin to participate in your existence. Then a window opens and we are not two.

This can happen with the whole of existence, and when this happens only then one can achieve total freedom.

INSTRUCTIONS FOR NIGHT MEDITATION

Now close your eyes and put both your hands in a *namaskar* posture to pray. Close your eyes, bow down your head in a surrender. Now begin to pray in your heart, "Man alone is helpless. I am helpless. What can I do without the divine help? Without you, what can I do? Help me...help me-...help me." Open your heart towards the divine, to be filled by his grace. With this thought we begin this prayerful camp, that on the last day we will be able not only to pray but also to thank him.

The sage Asvalayan approached the Lord ParameShwar,
the creator Brahma, and said, Bhagavan,
teach me brahmavidya, *the highest science of reality,*
the path treaded always by the good people,
which is ever a hidden secret to a man.
Due to which, discarding all their past sins,
the wise men reach the highest purusha, *the buddha-self.*
To him, the grandsire, Pitamaha, Brahma said,
"Know this by means of faith, devotion, meditation and yoga."

The *Kaivalya Upanishad* begins with an enquiry into the ultimate. What is the ultimate *brahma*? How can it be known and achieved? Not only known, but *achieved.* Knowing is secondary, being is primary; and the basic enquiry is concerned with being, not with knowing.

But the disciple who is asking, who is enquiring, is not an ordinary man. He is a great rishi, a great scholar, a great so-called knower. He knows, still he enquires because whatsoever he knows has not become a transformation to him. The knowing has remained just knowing, it has not changed his being. His being has remained the same, has remained unconnected, unrelated to his knowing, to his knowledge. Knowledge has become something else – a growth in itself – and the being has remained untouched.

The disciple is not an ordinary one; the disciple is extraordinary. He knows everything that can be known about brahma; but he doesn't know the brahma itself. He knows *about,* he knows everything about, but to know *about* brahma is not to know brahma. You can know everything about, and still the brahma remains absolutely untouched, absolutely unknown. Knowledge can be gained without knowing, knowledge can be accumulated without knowing.

By this I mean, if your being is not transformed simultaneously with knowing, it is worthless. You can become a person who knows, but you will be a person who is untransformed. A deeper mutation is asked for.

This wise man, this well-informed man, this well-learned man, comes to the teacher enquiring how to to be transformed into brahma. How to achieve the being of the cosmos? How to be one with the center of existence?

It is not an intellectual enquiry at all; it is existential. And unless an enquiry is existential, it is not religious. One can go on enquiring philosophically, and one can go on ad infinitum, but one reaches nowhere. Knowledge can go on growing infinitely, it reaches nowhere. It *cannot* reach. It is intrinsically impossible because knowledge grows in memory, not in being.

There have been persons who were absolutely ignorant in the ways of knowledge, but they had being, they *were* being; they had something more substantial, more inner, more authentic. They cannot tell you anything about the brahma, but just being near them you feel something. You are in contact with a live wire. You are in contact with something alive.

In a way intellect is just a dead thing. Memory is just past. The moment you know something, it has become a past, dead thing – it has become material. The moment you know it you can accumulate it – it has become a gross thing. The moment you have experienced something, it has become part of your memory.

But the being is always alive; it is life itself. Being must have a growth, an explosion; only then, you know authentically, only then you are wise. Unless that happens your wisdom is just a hidden ignorance.

So this wise man comes to the teacher to ask how to achieve that being, that oneness with the ultimate, with the substratum, with the center of existence.

The teacher says that you come to know by four things. *Know this by means of faith, devotion, meditation, and yoga.*

The word *faith* is difficult to understand; it doesn't mean belief. A belief is an intellectual thing based on reason; you can reason about it. A belief is a rationalization; has proofs around it, behind it, below it, above it. A belief is supported by reasons, proofs, arguments, and is always argumentative.

So a believer is not a man of faith.

A Christian is a believer, a Hindu is a believer, a Mohammedan is a believer. By belief, I mean, they believe in some concepts, in some system.

And every system has become intrinsically a very rational thing. They go on producing proof – they even produce proof for the existence of God, which is absurd because no proof can be given for the ultimate.

The ultimate remains unproved, because if even the ultimate needs proof, then the proofs become more ultimate. And if the proofs can be destroyed then the ultimate is destroyed. If your God needs proof, then he can be disproved, because there has been no proof which cannot be disproved. There has been no logical argumentation which cannot be disproved, that cannot be argumented against. No belief is such that it cannot be converted into a disbelief. So a believer is potentially a disbeliever. He has, deep down in himself, doubt, disbeliefs. He puts his own doubt underground in the unconscious by using arguments, reasons, proofs; he is simply suppressing his own doubts. But a suppressed doubt is not faith.

A mind with no doubt is faith. A mind in a state of no-doubting is faith, but you cannot achieve no-doubting by using proofs. Proofs can help to suppress, proofs can help you to believe, but not to have faith.

To have faith is one of the most impossible things – *the* most impossible. Really, to be in faith is to take a jump into madness. And all religious people, all religious minds, are in a way, mad. When I say mad I mean they *leave* reasoning; they don't use reasoning because faith is absence of reasoning, absence of argumentation. Faith is a sort of love. It is a happening, *not* a mental construct.

How can it be achieved? It becomes very difficult because if you can achieve it, you can achieve it only by your mind. If you can achieve it, you can achieve it only by reason. So how can faith be achieved? It cannot be achieved really, only doubts can be destroyed. And the moment there is not doubting, faith flowers.

So faith comes negatively. If you become totally disgusted with your reasoning, if you come through your reasoning to nothing, if all reasoning leads you to absurdity...when your whole reasoning becomes just absurd and meaningless, only then it drops. And the dropping of reasoning is the flowering of faith.

So faith cannot be achieved; it happens when there is no reasoning.

How to achieve faith means how to go beyond reasoning. And the only way is to reason to the very extreme. Reason so much that you come to the point where you can see that this whole effort has been basically wrong; reason so much that you become aware of the futility of the whole effort.

Faith is not achieved by those who have never reasoned, remember this. Those who have never reasoned cannot achieve faith. Only those who can reason to the very climax, to the very peak – only they fall into the abyss, the abyss of faith.

That's why faith has been mentioned as the first thing, because the person, the disciple, is a man of reasoning. He is not an ignorant man, he is wise, learned – well-learned. He was known as a Maharishi Asvalayan, one of the most learned persons. He knew everything that could be known by intellect. He has reasoned in every way, in every way possible. He has gone through reasoning through all its dimensions, and now he has come to a point where he has become aware that his whole reasoning has led him nowhere – he remains the same. That's why faith has been mentioned as the first thing. It is possible for Asvalayan to take a jump now. It may not be possible for you; it may not be possible for a person who has never reasoned.

Reasoning *is* a necessity, so when I say a no-reasoning has to be attained, I do not mean that I am anti-rationalist; I am not. Neither is this *Upanishad*, nor is anyone who has ever said something meaningful been anti-rationalist. Reasoning is a part. Of course, you cannot reach through reasoning, but you have to pass through it. No one has reached *with* reasoning, but no one has reached *without* reasoning also. Reasoning has to be there, and then it is to be discarded. It will be good if we try to understand through something else.

A beggar on the street begging, a poor man deep in poverty...then comes a Mahavira, a Buddha from a royal family, from a luxurious life, from riches, and becomes a beggar on the same street. They are beggars who are poles apart.

One, the first beggar, is *just* a beggar; his poverty is very poor, it is not rich. But a Buddha, a Mahavira begging alongside, is a rich beggar: his poverty has a different dimension. He has *known* riches and has discarded them.

In a way, a buddha is not poor; he cannot be, because poverty consists of longing, of desire, desire for riches. Poverty cannot be measured without the desire for riches – a man is poor in the same proportion in which he is desiring riches, wealth. He is poor only because he desires riches; he is poor against the riches.

A buddha is not desiring riches; on the contrary, he is desiring poverty. In the same way your riches can be measured only by your desire for poverty. If you can discard riches for poverty, you are rich in your poorness.

The buddha is a royal beggar; his begging has a different dimension, a completely different quality. The second beggar has to pass through riches; only then will he really become a royal beggar.

The same happens in reasoning also: A person who has never reasoned and has come to believe, is a poor believer; he cannot attain faith. Deep down he remains a disbeliever, because reasoning has not been transcended. A person who has reasoned totally, completely, with his whole heart and mind, with his whole being, has left no stone unturned. He has done whatsoever can be done; he has passed through all the bypaths of intellect and now he has come to a point where he discards reasoning. He says, "I have reached nowhere. This whole effort was meaningless!"

But this meaningless effort has been meaningful in a way. Now he can discard it without leaving any scar behind. And he will not be poor now, he will not be ignorant. He will not be a man without reasoning; he will be a man who has gone beyond reasoning. His faith will not be belief. His faith will be rich – a richness that comes to a Buddha, to a Mahavira when they begin to beg on the street. The same richness in a different realm of being, the realm of mind, will belong to this man who has reasoned absolutely. And unless you reason absolutely, you will not come to the point where reasoning can be transcended.

That is why faith has been mentioned as the first thing, the first step. Go through reasoning, pass through it; but go beyond also. When one goes beyond reasoning, faith is attained.

Then devotion: When faith is attained, it begins to be express in devotion. By devotion is meant a loving attitude towards existence, what Schweitzer calls, "reverence for life." By devotion is meant a reverence for existence as such, unconditional. That word "unconditional" has to be remembered. If it is conditional, it becomes love; if it is unconditional it becomes devotion.

If it is conditional it becomes love, the so-called love. A lover and a beloved, whatsoever they may say, remain conditional. Whatsoever they may *dream*, they remain conditional. They go on expecting, and they go on continuing in a subtle bargain: "I can love you only if you are this way, if you are like this. I can love you only if you are doing this – if you are *not* doing this, love is broken. If you are not according to me, love is broken. If my conditions are not fulfilled then love evaporates.

Love is a conditional relationship.

Devotion is unconditional.

Devotion means you are not to be in any way conditioned by me, and I do not expect anything from you.

Devotion is not objective, it is subjective; love is objective.

I love someone because the object of love is such; it is lovable. Or, I am in devotion because in me there is devotion; the object is irrelevant. My subjectivity is the source of it, and then anything – a stone lying on the street – begins to be an object of devotion. A tree, a river, a hill – anything, anything that exists – simply by being there it begins to be an object of my devotion. The whole of existence becomes the object.

And the difference is that in love hate is implied. If you love someone, you hate someone else. If you love one, then you have to hate many, because love is a choice. If someone says, "I love everyone equally," then you will not feel his love at all. If your lover says, "I love everyone equally," then the beloved is going to depart, because if you are loving everybody equally, it means no love. Love exists against hate; you must hate others. Against all, you must choose one. That's why lovers are so possessive.

Possession comes because love should not be dissipated, it should not be given to others. It must be taken whole, totally. You must give your hate to everyone else, and love to one. Every love is a monopoly, and a lover is chosen *against* the whole existence. The whole of existence must be unloved, only then is the lover satisfied; anything else will become a distraction.

That's why persons who exist as sensitives for many things, are not good lovers. A Socrates is not a good lover to his wife, he cannot be, because sometimes the wife feels he loves philosophy more; philosophy becomes the competitor. A musician, of course, loves his wife, his beloved, but loves music even more; then the wife feels that music has become the competitor. So any genius begins to feel that love is a hindrance. The feeling is only because every love wants to be a monopolizer.

Devotion differs. Devotion exists for the total existence, without the counterpart. There is nothing against devotion. There is hate against love; there is nothing against devotion. No-devotion is not against devotion, it is just absence.

So when someone says, "I am devoted to Rama," really he is using a wrong word. If he loves Rama, then he cannot love Krishna. If someone says, "I am devoted to Krishna," then he cannot love Christ. He is using a wrong word. He is continuing the love phenomenon; it is not devotion.

Devotion means for the total; it is never for Rama, never for Krishna. Of course, Rama and Krishna are implied in the total, but it is never for a chosen one. Love is always for the chosen one, devotion is for the whole. So you cannot be a devotee of Rama. If you are for Rama, you are only a lover; and when you are a lover, then competition is bound to be there. Then Krishna will be a competitor, and Christ will be a competitor, and the same jealousies, the same conflicts, and all the same nonsense will follow. It has followed.

The whole religious world is really in conflict because of this love phenomenon being misunderstood as devotion. It is not. A devotee is simply a devotee of no one; a devotee is simply a devotee of all. A devotee is just devotion; it is not addressed to anyone. Love is addressed; devotion is unaddressd – or it is addressed to all which means the same.

Then meditation. Really, this is strange, strange because meditation should come first. Ordinarily, we think meditation is the beginning; it is not. That's why it looks strange, and that's why meditation becomes such an arduous thing.

So many people come to me and say, "We cannot meditate; it is so difficult." It *is* difficult; I know it, but the difficulty is *not* in meditation, it is because there is no faith. It is because there is no devotion. If faith is there, if devotion is there, then meditation is just a shadow which comes by them, by itself, it comes spontaneously.

They say, "We have also felt it, but we never think about it, we never reflect." If you love someone, your mind becomes silent. If the beloved is near you, you cannot think; thoughts cease. The moment a lover begins to think, it means love has waned. When you are with your beloved or with your loved one, and you are thinking many things, it only means one thing, that love has ceased. Because when there is love, thinking ceases. You are in such a deep communion that thoughts will be a hindrance, thoughts will be a disturbance.

That's why real deep lovers will not ever talk, they cannot. They will sit silently, but they cannot talk because talking will be a disturbance. Only husbands and wives talk, because if they don't talk then silence becomes heavy. So they go on talking – anything, any nonsense. They go on talking, because if silence is there, then is is very heavy. And then it is bound to explode in some conflict, so it is good to go on talking.

Talking is avoiding. It is just trying to escape from a situation which can become ugly. Once two lovers begin to talk it shows that the love has waned, it has gone, it is not there now. And then they are bound to talk nonsense. The talk is just to evade the situation, just to escape from a situation which can become explosive any moment.

But two *lovers* are always in silence, they cannot talk. If this happens even in love, you can imagine what can happen in faith. When someone is in faith and devotion, the whole of existence begins to take the shape of a loved object. Then you can be with the trees silently, then you can be with the river silently, then you can be with the wind silently. Then you can be with anything silently, because devotion creates silence. And meditation is

190

nothing else but silence.

Then yoga, and the last, the fourth. Ordinarily, we start with yoga; in this sequence it is put last. If the mind is silent then the body is integrated. If the mind is in meditation then the body becomes tranquil and quiet itself. Then every gesture of the body, every posture of the body, just reflects what is happening deep down in the mind. What is happening to the center is reflected by the periphery and the body is just the periphery.

This is the right sequence: to begin with the cosmic, then to come to the self, then to the mind, then to the body.

The cosmic, the brahma, is the absolute center of existence. Second comes the individual soul, the self; then the third circle. The third concentric circle is the mind, the thinking soul, and the fourth concentric circle is the body, the embodied soul – from the cosmic to the material.

Begin from the within and then come to the without; start from the center towards the periphery and then everything becomes easy. Everything becomes so easy and so spontaneous that one begins to feel that it is effortless.

Effort is felt because we begin from the without towards the within, we begin from the body. But there is a problem because we exist in the body, and we don't know anything else; we know only the body, and not even that. We know it only in a very illusory way. We are not even aware of our body, because we are so asleep. That's why we have to begin with the body.

This sequence cannot be told to anyone; it was told to a very extraordinary disciple. Ordinarily one has to begin with the body, then go to meditation, to devotion, and *then* to faith, because ordinarily we are so asleep that only at the body are we a bit aware. Everything else is in darkness, deep darkness. And then it is difficult, very difficult.

It becomes difficult because to begin with the body is the most gross instrument. If you can begin with faith, then you have begun with the most subtle, most powerful, most potential instrument. If you can begin with faith, it is okay. If you cannot begin with faith, then it is better to begin with the body than not to begin at all.

THE MORNING MEDITATION

The morning meditation is divided into four parts. The first part is ten minutes of vigorous breathing, chaotic, violent – just be nothing. Just be a breathing instrument for ten minutes – mad breathing. Then for ten minutes, body movements used as catharsis. So whatsoever happens to your body, cooperate with it. The body begins to dance, to jump, to cry – anything. Whatsoever happens with the body, allow it; cooperate with the body. And third, go on dancing and jumping, but use "hoo" as a mantra. Go on crying, "hoo! hoo! hoo!" Go on for ten minutes and then in the fourth we will relax and go in a deep silence.

Make a space around you so that you can jump very freely and easily....

Neither by work nor by progeny nor by wealth,
but by renunciation alone immortality is attained.
Higher than heaven, the ultimate truth abides
in the cave of the heart, shining,
and the sincere seeker attains.

For religion, death is the basic problem – not life, because life *is*. Life is not a problem; you have it, you are it. But death is a problem. Death is not here and yet is here. Death has not occurred to you, yet it has occurred all around; it will occur to you. Life is the present; death is the future. The present is never the problem – the future is the problem, because future has to be tackled, because future has to be encountered, because future has to be transcended. So man is always face to face with death, not with life.

That's why animals have no religion, because they cannot imagine death; they cannot conceive of death. They live, they die, but death is never a problem for them. It is never comprehended, it is never conceived, it is never encountered as a problem in their consciousness. They don't know death – they are alive or they are dead, but they don't know death. When is death known? How is death known? Death is known – you are alive, you are not dead, but there is death somewhere in the future.

A dead man has no problem with death, he is already dead. Then death is not a problem. Alive, death faces us somewhere, just around the corner, waits for us. This waiting death – this constant awaiting, somewhere near, just any moment it can happen – is the problem. So man goes on fighting it, and the whole of life becomes just a fight with death. The whole of life is just wasted – just wasted in arranging, in making securities – in defense against death.

We cannot be alive, because there is death. We cannot live, we cannot live authentically because death will not allow us to live. How can you live when there is death? When you are going to die, how can you live peacefully? How can you live blissfully? Then every step in life is just a step towards death. Then any movement is a movement towards death, or any movement is a movement of your death coming towards you.

Religion has death as the problem – what to do about it? We are doing many things – through wealth, through science, through health, through protection, through medicine, through philosophy, through theology – we are creating many different measures for how to be deathless. We are creating many things, but everything proves futile, meaningless, absurd. Death comes, and every arrangement is just proved futile. It has always been so and it will always be so, because death is not really just in the future, it is also in the past.

The moment one is born, death is born within him. Death is not only in the future – if it were only in the future then it could be avoided, but it is part of the past. It is just a process of the same thing which we call birth. Birth is the beginning of death – or, death can be said to be just an ending of the process of birth. So your birth day is also your death day. The beginning is the end, because every beginning implies its end. Every beginning has its end as a seed. If death is just in the future, then it can be avoided. It is not; it is part of you, it is here and now – just in you, progressing, growing.

Death is not a fixed point somewhere, it is a growth within you; it is growing constantly. When you are fighting it, it is growing. When you are feeding it, it is growing. When you are escaping from it, it is growing. So whatsoever you do, one thing is constantly going on – that is, you are dying. Whatsoever you do – you are asleep, you are relaxing, you are working, you are thinking, you are meditating – whatsoever you do, one thing is certain: death is growing constantly, continuously. It doesn't need your help, it doesn't need your cooperation. It doesn't care about your defenses; it goes on growing. Why? – because it has come into being with your birth; it is part of birth. So death cannot be escaped in the ways man and the human mind have always tried.

This *Upanishad* says that death can be escaped, but you can become deathless. You can know something which is immortal, which will never die. So how to know it? Where to search for it, and how to discover it? Because every effort that we know is just meaningless, irrelevant.

The *Upanishad* says: Don't fight with death; rather, know that which is life. Don't try to escape from death; rather, try to enter that which is life. The very flame of life must be entered. Don't create the sort of life which is negative; don't go on trying to avoid death – this is negativity. Be positive and try to know what is life. Really, death is not against life. In the dictionary it is; in existence it is not. Death is not against life; death is against birth.

Life is something else. Life is before birth, life is *born*.

Birth is a phenomenon which happens in life.

Birth is not the beginning of life – if birth is the beginning of life, that means you were born dead. Birth is not the beginning of life – life *precedes* birth. Life is presupposed, it is before birth – because life is there, birth happens.

Life comes first, then there is birth.

You *are*, even when you are not born.

You are born because you were there before.

And the same is the case with death. If you *are* before birth, then you *will be* after death, because that which is before birth is bound to be after death. Life is something which happens in between birth and death, and beyond birth and death.

We must think of life as a river: in this river one point is known as birth, another point is known as death, but the river continues. The river continues beyond death. The river was continuing before birth. This riverlike life must be penetrated – only then we can know that which is deathless. Of course that which is deathless is bound to be birthless... but our whole focus is just misguided. Our whole focus is on how to escape death, not how to know life. It is against death, not for life.

This is the only flaw, and because of this we can never know the deathless. We will go on, continue, constantly searching, discovering new methods, new techniques, new ways of how to escape death. And then death will be coming – and death will come.

Know life.

Jesus has said, "Search for life, for more life." Don't be satisfied with that which is with you as life. Search more, find out more, find *in* more – go for more life. We are for less death, we are not for more life; the whole focus is turned towards death.

It is like this: If there is darkness, you can do two things – either you can begin to fight with darkness to destroy it, or you can begin to search for light, which is quite a different search. You can fight darkness directly, but then you will be defeated. And darkness will be victorious – not because it is stronger than you, not because you are powerless against it. No, darkness is not powerful, you are not powerless – but darkness is just an absence, and you cannot fight any absence.

Darkness is simply *not*. You cannot fight it, and if you fight it you will be defeated – not because it is powerful, but because it is *not*. How can you fight something which is not? A darkness means nothing; it means simply absence of light. So if you fight darkness, then you continue for millennia; you will never win. And the more you are defeated, the more you will search for new methods to fight it. The more you are defeated, the more you will feel impotent, and darkness will feel like something very potent. You will think that you have to find something which can be more powerful than darkness. The whole of logic is fallacious; you can continue it and you will move in a vicious circle. The more you will be defeated, the more you will be frustrated, the more you will fight with new means – and again you will be defeated.

The defeat is not concerned with your power or powerlessness at all.

The defeat is because you are fighting something which is not.

The same is the case with death. Death is not something positive, it is just absence of life. When life goes somewhere else, death occurs. Death is just the going of something; it is not something which comes to you. Death is not something which comes to you; rather, it is only that life goes somewhere else. The river of life begins to flow somewhere else, and death occurs – death is just an absence.

The light is not, darkness happens; the light comes, darkness is not there. So find the light, find life; don't fight with death, don't fight with darkness. Don't be negative; be positive. And by positive, I mean always search for something which is present; never go on any search for something which is absent – you will never find it.

Death happens daily, but no one has encountered it, no one has known it. No one can know it, because how can you know it? You are life – how can you know it? Darkness is there, but the sun has never known it – how can he know it? The moment the sun is there, darkness is not; so they have never encountered each other – they cannot, that is impossible.

If you bring light into a dark room, do you think your light will encounter darkness? The moment light is there, darkness is not. So only one can be; both cannot be together – either darkness can be there or light can be there. Light has not known darkness, darkness has not known light, because darkness is simply the absence. So how can light know its own absence? If it is to know, then it must be present. And if it is not present, only then is the absence there – but then light cannot know it.

You cannot encounter your own absence – how can you encounter it? Death is your absence. When you are absent, death occurs. So allow me to tell you this way, that death is a social phenomenon, not individual. No individual dies – individual rivers continue somewhere else. But when from this crowd the individual river moves somewhere else, then for this crowd someone has died; for this crowd, someone has become absent.

If my friend dies, it means he dies for me; not for himself. Death is a phenomenon which happens to *me*, not to him. How can it happen to him?

Life cannot face death; life is a movement which has moved somewhere else, so *we* face it. Death is a social phenomenon, it is not an individual phenomenon. No one has died ever – but everyone dies, we know everyone dies, because someone becomes suddenly absent.

We are here. If I become suddenly absent, I will die – not for me, but for you. For *you* I will be absent. How I can be absent from myself? – it is impossible.

The *Upanishads* say, don't fight death, it is fighting absence; rather, search for the presence which is in you. Who is present in you? – find out.

What is present in you which you call life? What is there which you call life? From where does it come in you? What is the center, the source of it? Go deep into yourself and find the source. The *Upanishad* says, this source is hidden in the heart.

This source of life is hidden in the heart.

Go in your heart and find the original source.

Once you have known that source then there will be no death for you. Then there will be no fear, then there will be no problem. Once you have known life itself, you have become immortal. You *are* – unconsciously, un-knowingly, unaware. Everyone is immortal. Nothing dies, nothing can die – but everyone feels the fear. This fear also comes because of the society, because we see – now today "A" has died and tomorrow "B" will die, and yesterday "C" has died. Then we become aware: *"I* am going to die." I am going to die – this fear grips the mind because death occurs in a society.

Think of it in this way: If you are alone and you have never known any death, will death be a problem for you? If you are alone on an island, have never known any death, never heard about it – will you be aware of death at all? Will you be able to conceive that you are going to die? How can you conceive? – it is a social thing; the society teaches you death. The society shows you that death happens. Alone, you will never be able to know it; alone, you cannot even imagine it. Alone, the very word "death" will be meaningless. And in a certain, subtle way, everyone is deeply aware of this. That's why, howsoever you become aware of death in others, somewhere deep down you continue to think that you are not going to die. Deep down everyone thinks, "Death may occur to anyone else but it is not going to occur to me." That's why so many deaths are occurring yet we continue; we continue to live; otherwise, we would be paralyzed, totally paralyzed. A single death occurring and we would be paralyzed. But somewhere deep down one knows: "It may have occurred to him, but it is not going to occur to me." Everyone goes on deep down believing in something in himself as immortal...it is very unconscious; otherwise, there would be no fear.

The *Upanishads* say, make it conscious. Go deep down and know it very consciously: something that is life in you, that flame, will continue; that flame is not going to die.

How to go into the heart? How to penetrate it? – the *Upanishads* say, by renunciation. Renounce every outward-going effort, all that leads you outward. All that becomes a vehicle for your consciousness to move outward – renounce it. In the deep inactivity of renunciation, you will come to the center.

For example, how does the mind move outward? It moves for wealth, it moves for prestige, it moves for power. Any movement means a deep desire for something outside, a deep desire for something which doesn't belong to you inside, but belongs to the objective world. Any desire for any object in the world is a movement outward. Renounce this movement. Even for a single moment, if you can renounce all outward-going movements, you will be in. This means that this in-coming doesn't need anything to be done directly. It needs something to be done indirectly.

Don't move outward and you will find yourself in the heart, in the cave of the heart.

Mind moves with desires, outwards. Then it can continue, continue, and go on and on – to the very end of the world it can go. Don't move with any desires. Desirelessness is the method to come in, and desirelessness is meditation. Do not desire anything. Even for a single moment, if you are in a desireless moment, you will find yourself in. And then you can encounter the flame of life which is immortality, which is non-dying, which has never been born and will not die. Once known, there will be no fear of death. And when there is no fear of death, only then you can live authentically. Then your life will have a different quality altogether. It will be aware, it will be alive, it will be fresh. It will be blissful, it will be a deep ecstasy, a continuous ecstasy.

With no fear, with no longing, with no desire, there will be no pain. There will be no suffering there will be no anguish. With no desire you fall into a deep abyss of ecstasy. This is what is known in the *Upanishads* as the *brahmalok*, the world of the divine.

We live in a world of material things, mm? This is outward-going movement. When consciousness comes in, we penetrate a different world, the world of the divine. With outward movement there is suffering; with inward movement there is peace and bliss. It doesn't mean that one who moves inward will not be able to move outward; he will be *more able*, more capable. But now he will move with his whole "in-ness," now he will move in the outward world but untouched by it. Now he will move, but constantly rooted in himself. He will not be uprooted from himself. Now he can go anywhere, but he will be rooted in himself.

This rootedness in oneself is the source of all bliss that is possible.

*Those who have purified the mind by the
practice of sannyas and yoga, and those who
have come to understand the exact meaning of
the spiritual science indicated in the* Upanishad's Vedant,
they in the end become capable of attaining brahmalok – *the world of
brahma. And liberating themselves from everything,
they strive to achieve immortality.*

The basic problem before a spiritual seeker is not how to know, but how to be. Knowing is not the problem, it is easy. The real problem is how to be, how the being should be strengthened. Knowing can grow easily; knowing has its own ways of growing. But knowing is a parasitic growth.

Knowing grows in the memory, and memory is just mechanical. That's why we now have mechanical devices which can be fed with memory – we have computers, and a computer is more efficient than any human brain. A computer can do anything that a human brain can do – and a computer can do many more things which a human brain cannot do. Sooner or later, human memory is going to be replaced by mechanical devices. A mechanical device can do whatsoever your mind is doing, and more efficiently, and in less time. A computer can do a mathematical problem in seconds for which you would need an Einstein, or a person of the caliber of Einstein, to work on for at least three months.

Mind is just a mechanical device. It can grow – you go on feeding it with knowledge, with information, and it can grow. You may not be aware of it, but nothing comes out of your mind which has not been put in it before – nothing. Nothing comes out of your mind which is original. In that way, nothing is original as far as mind is concerned; everything is just repetition. Mind is the most repetitive mechanism. You have to feed it, give it something: it will reproduce it. Not a single thought comes to you which is your own – it has been given to you by society, by education, by study, but always it has been given to you. At the most you can make new combinations, that's all. Nothing more can be done with the mind. This is one growth, a parasitic growth at the cost of your being.

By being, I mean the consciousness with which you are born. And by mind, I mean all the accumulation that has come to your consciousness through society, through education, through culture. You are not born with a mind; you are born with a consciousness. Mind is a later growth. That's why if a person is not taught, if a person is not educated, then he has a lesser mind, a poor mind. If no language is taught to you, you will know no language. If nothing is taught to you, you will know nothing. Mind is a social growth.

Consciousness is part of you, but mind is not part of you; mind is given to you. The whole process of social cultivation, of social imposition, is to produce a mind in you. That's why a Christian mind is different from a Hindu mind – because a Hindu society is feeding something and a Christian society is feeding something else. A Mohammedan mind is totally different from a Hindu, or a Christian, or a Jaina mind. But a Hindu consciousness or a Mohammedan consciousness or a Christian consciousness, are not different.

Really, a consciousness cannot be called Christian or Hindu or Mohammedan – but minds *are*. So unless you go beyond your society – you are imprisoned in your upbringing. This mind, which the society gives to everyone…it is a necessity; a society has to give it to you. It is good as far as it goes, but it must not become an imprisonment. A moment must be attained where you are freed from your own mind. Then mind begins to work as a mechanical thing in you; you can use it but you are not identified with it.

Of course one has to use language, one has to use mathematics, one has to know history and geography and everything. But it must not be identified with your consciousness. You must remain a witness to it. You must remain separate, unidentified, different from your own mind. This is what meditation means: how to be not identified with the mind – how to create a space between yourself and your own mind. It is difficult because we never make any separation. We go on thinking in terms that the mind means *me*: mind and me are totally identified. If they are totally identified, then you will never be at peace; then you will never be able to enter the divine, because the divine can be entered only when the social has been left behind.

When whatsoever the society has given you has been renounced, only then you enter the divine, because only then, you enter pure consciousness. Mind is an overgrowth; it must be put aside. By renunciation, I mean renunciation of the social. And your mind is nothing but a social by-product, it depends on your society.

This mind can go on growing. Then you grow in knowledge; go on studying, go on learning new things, more things, and your mind goes on growing. And a mind is infinitely capable to grow; yet scientists cannot say to what extent this mind can grow. It can go on growing, the process seems infinite. It has so much potentiality – seventy million cells working in the mind, and a single cell can have millions of bits of information in it. A single cell of the mind can have so much information stored in it, and the mind has seventy million cells in it. We are not using even a single cell's capacity – ordinarily, we are not using a single cell's capacity – and we have seventy million cells. And each cell seems to be capable of infinite accumulation of information. The mind seems to be infinite in its own way – and it is not you! It is just something which has been given to you.

It is useful, it is utilitarian; that's why we become identified with it. One has to use one's mind constantly, and one has to use it so constantly that there is no gap. You don't remember any moment when you were not your mind, that's the problem: to remember it, and to create a space, a gap, when you are not your mind. You are yourself and mind is just a device which can be used or not used, and you are the master to choose whether to use it or not.

Ordinarily, the mind is the master and you have to follow it. The mind gives you something to think about and you have to think about it. The mind gives you some dream and you have to dream it. And the mind goes on.... And sometimes even if you say to your mind, "Stop!" it is not going to stop, it is not going to listen to you at all. Because you have cooperated with it so much, and you have given it your energy and identification so much, that the mind doesn't remember your mastery at all. You are just a slave.

Meditation means to create a gap so that you can become master, master of your own mind. And mastery means that you are not identified.

I can order my hand to do anything – to move or not to move. Why? – because I am not identified with the hand; otherwise, who is going to order and who is going to be ordered? I can order my hand to move; it moves. But if my hand begins to move and I say, "Stop!" and it is not stopping, what does it mean? It means only one thing: my order is impotent because of too much identification with the hand. The hand has become a master in its own right – it goes on moving. It says, "I am not going to follow your order at all."

This has happened with the mind. The mind goes on working in its own way; no order can be given to it. There is no intrinsic impossibility – it is only because you have never ordered it, so it doesn't know that you are the master. The master has remained so silent, has remained so hidden, that the slave has begun to feel himself the master.

If one goes on growing in this mind, one goes on more and more hidden deep down. And the mind becomes such a great thing, it is difficult to assert your consciousness. That's why a very ordinary villager with a lesser mind, is with more consciousness. An ordinary person – not very educated, not knowing much – has always, of course, less mind but more consciousness. So sometimes a person who has more mind may behave very foolishly, because he has less consciousness. A person who has a developed mind can work very wisely, behave very wisely if the situation is such that the mind knows what to do and what not to do. Then he can behave, work, do anything very efficiently. But any new situation in which the mind is not aware, and he will be stupid, he will behave stupidly.

A villager – an uneducated person, a primitive, with less mind – will behave more consciously in a new situation, because for him new situations are occurring daily, every moment. With no developed mind, he has to work with his consciousness. That's why the more the world has grown knowledgeable, the less wise it has become. It is difficult now to produce a

Buddha, not because we are more ignorant, but because we know more. It is difficult to produce a Jesus, not because anything is lacking – on the contrary, something has grown too much. Knowledge has grown too much, and if knowledge grows too much, the being begins to feel poor.

We value a person because of what he has: knowledge, wealth, power. We never value a person for what he is. If I am a powerful man, then I am valued; if I am a wealthy man, then I am valued; if I am a man of knowledge, then I am valued – but never simply for what I am. If wealth is lost, then my influence will be lost; if knowledge is lost, then my influence will be lost; if power is lost, my influence will be lost, because I was never valued for what I am. Something which I have – having has become so important, and knowledge is also a subtle having.

Being means: the purity of my inner existence, nothing added by the outside – neither wealth, nor knowledge, nor anything else – just my inner consciousness in its purity.

This is what I mean, what this *Upanishad* means by the growth of being. This being can be achieved only by two methods: renunciation – sannyas – and yoga, the science of positive growth. One must renounce identification: one must come to know that I am not the body, I am not the mind. One must renounce all that which is mind, but I am not. One must come to the center point which cannot be renounced.

A Western thinker, Rene Descartes, begins his theosophical speculation with doubt, and he goes on doubting. He goes on doubting everything that can be doubted. He was a very keen and penetrating intellectual; really, he was the father of modern Western philosophy. He goes on doubting everything, he makes it a point that "I will not stop doubting unless a moment comes and I encounter something which cannot be doubted. If I can doubt, I will continue to doubt, unless I stumble upon some fact which is indubitable." So God can be doubted very easily. It is difficult to have faith; it is very easy to doubt, because for doubt you have only to say no. Nothing else is needed.

"No" is a very non-involving word. If you say yes, you are committed. If I say "Yes, God is," then I cannot remain the same. If I say, "No, God is not," I will continue to be the same. "No" is the easiest word in a way: you say it, you are not involved, you remain outside. If you say yes, you are involved. You have come in; now you are committed. To say no to anything is very easy, because then you need not prove anything. If you say yes then you have to prove it – and proofs are, of course, very difficult. Even if things *are*, proofs are very difficult. Time is. We know time is, everyone feels time is – but can you *prove* that time is?

Saint Augustine says, "Don't ask about time, because when you don't ask, I know it is. When you ask, I begin to hesitate – whether it is or not? And if you persist, I become doubtful." Can we prove time? It is; everyone knows it is. We cannot prove it.

Can we prove love? Everyone knows it is. Even if one has not felt love, one has felt very deeply its absence. Love is felt – either as presence or absence, but no one can prove it. So anyone can say, "Love is not," and you cannot disprove their statement.

Descartes goes on denying, doubting: God is denied, then the world itself is denied – even the world which is here and now. You are here, but I can doubt; it may be just a dream to me. And how can I tell the difference whether it is a dream or not? – because sometimes I have dreamt about talking to people. And when I was dreaming and talking, those who were present were as real as you are – and really, in a way more real, because in a dream you cannot doubt. But if you are really present, I can doubt: it may be just a dream, you may not be there at all, but just a dream, a dream happening to me. And I am dreaming that you are, and I am talking to you, to my dream construct. How can I prove that you are really there? There is no way. There is no way to prove that you are. I can touch you ... but I can touch someone in a dream, and even in dream I can feel someone's body

It is difficult – really, in a way, impossible to make any distinction between reality and dreaming. That's why Berkeley says that this whole world is just a dream, or a Shankara says that this whole world is just a dream. They can say it and they cannot be disproved.

So Descartes says, "This world is not. It is only a thought, a dream. God is not." Then he goes on denying everything. Ultimately he comes to himself, and then he begins to think "whether I am, or not." Now there is a fact which cannot be denied, because even if all is dreaming, someone is needed to dream. Even if everything is dubitable, someone is needed to doubt. Even if Descartes says "I am not," this statement has to be made by someone – even to doubt, he is needed. Then he says, "Now I have come upon a point which is indubitable. I can doubt everything, but I cannot doubt myself. If *I* doubt, the doubt proves *me*. So he gives a very meaningful formula: He says, *"Cogito ergo sum.* I think – I doubt – therefore I am."

This "I-am-ness" must be broken apart from mentation, from mind, from thinking. This "I-am- ness" is the being, and to know it in its purity, one has to renounce all that can be renounced – just like Descartes who says, "I must doubt all that can be doubted, unless I come to a point which cannot be doubted." Just in the same way, one has to continue renouncing – renouncing all that which can be renounced, unless you come to a point which cannot be renounced.

You cannot renounce your being; all else can be renounced. All else you can say, "This is *I-am."* All that you can say, *"This is I,"* you can renounce. You can say, "No, this is not *I-am.* This body, I am not; this world, I am not; this thought, I am not; this thinking, I am not." Go on, go on denying. Then there comes a moment when you cannot deny more. Simply "I-am-ness" remains. Not even "I-am-ness," but only "am-ness." That "am-ness" is the existential jump.

This is the first part of the sutra: renunciation, sannyas.

So sannyas is a negative process. One has to go on eliminating: "This is *I-am-not."* Go on – "This, that, I am not." This is renouncing, a negative process, elimination. But this is only a part: you have renounced whatsoever you are not; then you have to grow that which you are – that is yoga; that needs the positive, of growth. That is yoga. Now you have to grow that which is in you. How to grow it? – we have been discussing that – by faith, by devotion, by meditation, by practices, bodily and other. That is yoga.

Sannyas plus yoga means religion. Renounce that which you are not, and grow in that, create in that, which you are. Only by such negative and positive processes in a deep harmony, the brahma, the ultimate, is achieved.

This much for today's morning talk. Now we will go for meditation. You have to do it so totally that nothing is left behind, no energy untouched. Every energy must be brought to it totally.

*They have undisturbed space, resting in a
comfortable posture, clean and pure, with the neck,
head, and body in one line; held erect, in a mental
attitude of sannyas, having controlled all the
senses, saluting one's own teacher, guru, devotedly,
meditate within the lotus of the heart;
the untainted, the pure, the clear and the
transparent, the griefless principle of devotion.*

Meditation is a very complex phenomenon. It looks simple; it is not. It is a science, a complete science in itself. It is bound to be, because meditation means a deep mutation of your total being. The whole being has to be transformed, so it is obviously going to be a complex affair.

Man is a complexity; the mutation is bound to be also a complex thing. Some basic elements must be understood. One: your body – your body must be in a deep cooperation; otherwise, meditation will be unnecessarily difficult. Your body must be in such a state that it helps, not hinders. As it is ordinarily, it is a deep hindrance. Your body goes on hindering you; it becomes an obstacle, and if you want to transform, you must purify the body first. And by purifying the body many things are meant. First, you must not be identified with it; that is the first and the most basic impurity.

One must not be identified with one's body. One must remain in a beyondness, in a transcendence. Neither one should think, "I am the body," nor one should think, "I am in the body." Rather, one should remain in a constant remembering: "I am something beyond the body – neither one with it, nor *in* it, nor within it, but beyond." Constant remembrance that "I am beyond my body" gives a different dimension to your whole being. Try it, constantly! You are moving, walking, sleeping – whatsoever the state – remember constantly that you are as if something is hovering over the body, beyond the body. Not in it, not within it, not one with it, just something beyond, moving with the body, living with the body, enveloping the body.

Think of it this way. Ordinarily we think, "I am enveloped by the body." That's why the word "body" – body means that in which we are embodied. We are within and the body is without: "Body is a casket, a house, and I am in it. Change the thing totally, upside down. Let the body be in and *you* be out – beyond the body, hovering, enveloping.

If you can change this attitude from yourself being within, to yourself being beyond, you will feel a sudden change: your body will become light; all the heaviness will be gone and your body will become something with wings. You will feel that now you can fly; you can go now, any moment, beyond the forces of gravitation. Try it! From this very moment, begin to think that the body is within, and you are without, encompassing it. And then the body is purified.

Why? – because identity becomes impossible. You can identify only with something which is greater than you. No one identifies himself with something which is lesser; identification is always with the greater. You are within a very small point and the body is big and great and everything; that's why you begin to be identified. Let yourself be the greater one, and let the body be just a minor thing. You will never be identified with it.

Secondly, if you are within, you will have limits; if you are without, you become unlimited. If I am within my body, then I am encircled by my body, I have a finitude, a limitation. If I am beyond my body, then there is no limitation; then I am not only beyond my body, I am beyond all. Then there is no ending to it – then suns will rise in me, stars will move in me, creations will come in me and go out and will cease – then I become the whole universe. Body becomes the center – just a minor center, an atomic existence – and I become the whole universe, encompassing it.

Heidegger has used this word "encompassing." It is beautiful – encompassing. Feel it, try it, imagine it, and you will come to a new understanding of your own being. When I say imagine it, I say it consideredly. Really, this feeling that "I am the body" is just an imagination. This feeling that "I am *in* the body" is also just an imagination. Because the society has taught you, this imagination has become unconscious.

For example, I would like to tell you: Many cultures, in different ages, different religions, different thinkings, have considered the body center to be in different places. For example, as far as this contemporary world is concerned, more or less everyone thinks that he is somewhere in the head – not in the legs, not in the hands, not in the belly. If someone insists and asks you, "Where are you? Point it out!" Then you will begin to feel something in the head; you are in the head. But ask a Japanese and he will say that he is in the belly, not in the head – because the whole of Japanese culture has always thought that the spirit lives in the belly. So if you think with your head, the Japanese think with their belly – they say, "We think with our belly." They say, "The belly must be strong. The belly is the center." But there have been other cultures – some cultures think that the heart is the center. Then if that culture has been imposed on you, you begin to think that the heart is the center. Really, these are just imaginative identifications.

In a sense, the spirit is nowhere in the body; it encompasses it. Or, it is everywhere in the body and everywhere outside of the body. If any center is maintained in your imagination, the body becomes impurified, burdened with the center – tense, diseased. Let there be no center in the body; let yourself be outside, just encompassing the body. And then the body becomes fresh, young, flowing, liquid, an energy – without any burdened feeling upon it. Then the body cooperates. This light feeling of the body becomes a basic source of help for meditation.

Not only the body, but your heart also must be prepared for meditation to flower in it. Unprepared, much energy is wasted unnecessarily. Prepare the heart.

This sutra says you can prepare the heart by throwing all the impurities out of it. But instead we go on accumulating. You can forget if someone has helped you, but you cannot forget if someone has harmed you. You can forget something which has been a bliss, but you cannot forget something which has been a suffering. We go on accumulating negatives; these negatives become the impurities for the heart. Everyone goes on accumulating negatives. If someone is friendly to you for years, and for a single moment is not friendly, then all that friendship will go down and that moment of unfriendliness will become the most significant thing – and you will remember it. This attitude must be changed. One must go on accumulating positives and throwing out negatives; then the heart becomes purified. Go on accumulating positives. Never accumulate anything negative; it is not going to help you, it is going to destroy you.

Someone has been angry to you: don't remember it. What to do? – one has to remember something – find something positive. Someone is angry – why be so much concerned with the anger? Why not be concerned with the *phenomenon* of anger? There are some people who are beautiful only when they are angry – why not look at the beauty of it? Even if they are not beautiful, everyone when he is angry, is vital. Why not look at the vitality, the energy, the aliveness, the radiance of it?

Why be so much concerned with anger? Why not be concerned with the phenomenon? Something is happening – a beautiful phenomenon in itself, a very radiant phenomenon – energy expressing, alive. Why not look at it in that way? Why not look – when someone is angry – why not look at yourself? What happens to *you* when someone is angry? If you are also angry then he has won, you are defeated. Why not be victorious? Why not be indifferent? Look at the anger, look at it as if you are looking at a psychodrama – someone is playing a role and you are just a witness. Why not be a witness? And then you will feel grateful to the person who has been angry with you. If you can be a witness when someone is angry, you will feel grateful, because he has given you a situation in which you could know your own mastery.

Whenever someone was with Gurdjieff, he would create many situations. He would create unnecessary situations in which someone would become angry, so angry that everyone would feel that he was going to explode. And then suddenly Gurdjieff would tell him, "Now be aware! Now be a witness to it!" – and everyone would begin to be a witness. Anger becomes a situation, an object to be studied, and that person himself who is angry feels a sudden change, because it has become a study project. Now it is not anger, it has become a drama. So why not look at a thing from the positive, with something to learn from it? Why go on accumulating the negative? This is just a habit – it is not inevitable; it is not.

Buddha could send his disciples to the burning places, to cemeteries to look at dead bodies, to contemplate death, to meditate on death: The body is burning – the dead body is there – it is burning. And Buddha would send his disciples there, to sit there and meditate on death. And meditating on death, the disciple would soon come to realize a different quality of life which never dies. Then he would come dancing, singing, to Buddha – from the dead body burning in the cemetery, he would come running, dancing – why? He should come sad, sorrowful, depressed, dead himself in a way. But he has not accumulated the negative even from a dead body. He has accumulated something positive. He has been meditating on death, and if you meditate on death you become more and more aware of life. He comes running, dancing, grateful – grateful to Buddha, grateful to the dead man also.

Why go on accumulating the negative? – we go on; that's just a wrong habit. Change it! Always look at the positive, and soon you heart will be purified. Negativities are the diseases of the heart. It begins to feel sore, and then the whole of life will become just a suffering, because you live through your own heart. You go on accumulating negatives; then you have to live through this negativity; then everything becomes just a suffering, a long suffering – meaningless, purposeless, leading to nowhere.

This is suicidal. A negative attitude is suicidal. Purify the heart by looking at the positive. Find everywhere something which can become a cherished accumulation in the heart. When I say, now remember, remember the face which was angry at you in the past – remember the face. Feel the beauty of it, and the whole thing suddenly changes. Someone was abusing you…remember the past, and feel when someone abuses; feel the energy, feel the aliveness, and everything changes – it is up to you.

The body must be purified by encompassing it. The heart must be purified by a positive foundation given to it, negatives denied. Be negative only to negatives, and then, then you can meditate.

On what is one to meditate? – the untainted, the pure, the clear, and the griefless.

Meditate on the untainted.

What is untainted? – only the sky, space is untainted. Meditate on space, pure space, and you will become like it. Whatsoever one meditates on one becomes.

Meditate on purity.

Everyone has felt somewhere a glimpse of purity...a flower, a virgin – anywhere. Many moments are there when one begins to feel purity. Meditate on purity...a flower, a virgin – anything. Meditate on purity and you will become pure. Whatsoever one meditates on one becomes.

The clear, the transparent – meditate on any transparency. A silent lake – you can look to the very bottom, everything clear; a glass window – so pure, so clear that even you don't see the glass, that the glass is there. Meditate on any transparency, and you will become transparent, you will become clear.

The griefless – meditate on the griefless... anything which is blissful, which is a beautitude. We go on meditating on grief; we go on meditating on grief continually. We go on meditating on suffering, then we become part of it. Meditation is the way to make oneself just like the object of the meditation.

Remember a Buddha, a griefless one. Remember a Krishna, a joyous one. Remember anything – a Chaitanya dancing, a Meera singing. Remember anything – a cloud passing in the sky, dancing, rays of the sun coming to you. Remember anything which is blissful to you. Meditate on it and you will become blissful. Don't continue to meditate on things which you would not like to be like. We go on meditating on wrong things.

Everyone is a meditator, remember. It is *not* that there are a few people who meditate. Everyone meditates, no one can be without meditation. So what is the difference between a meditator and a non-meditator? The difference is not of meditation, the difference is only of objects. The difference is only of objects. Someone is meditating on sex – he becomes sexual. Someone is meditating on anger – he becomes angry. Someone meditating on some sad event, he becomes sad. Everyone is meditating.

Only Mahavira has divided meditation into four types. Really, this is strange because Mahavira alone has divided meditation into four parts.

Many divisions are there, but nothing like Mahavira's, because Mahavira divides two such things, two such types which no one would like to call meditation. The first he calls *raudradhyan* – anger meditation. The second he calls *artadhyan* – suffering meditation. No one has named these. The third he calls *dharmadhyan*, and the fourth he calls *shukladhyan*. Dharmadhyan – religious meditation; and shukladhyan – the purest meditation. But he calls all four meditation. The first two, anger meditation and suffering meditation – no one will call these meditation.

If someone is angry, have you felt that he is in deep meditation? Everything has gone out of his mind, only one point, of anger, remains. He is focused, the whole world has dropped. Really, when someone is in anger, he is not in this world at all. He is not looking at you, he is not looking at anything; he is not even aware that the whole world exists – only anger exists.

When someone is suffering, deeply suffering – some loved one has died – then he is not aware of anything, only of his own suffering. His suffering encompasses him. Only now the suffering is there, everything has become just illusory. He is in a deep meditation, of course of the wrong type.

Everyone meditates. The difference is: someone meditates on wrong objects, and someone meditates on right objects. Meditate on some blissful moment. Meditate on something you would like to become like, then meditation becomes a mutation. First, wrong objects are to be dropped, then ultimately right objects are also to be dropped.

When there is no object, and only a meditative consciousness remains, you have achieved the ultimate.

Thus, by meditation, they achieve the ultimate reality,
which is unthinkable, unmanifest; the one of endless forms,
the ever-auspicious, the peaceful, the immortal,
the origin of the creator, the one without a beginning,
a middle and an end; the only one, the non-dual,
the all-pervading, the consciousness, the bliss,
the formless, the wonderful.

This sutra is basically concerned with meditation: What is to be attained by meditation? What is meditation, and for what does it stand?

The Hindi word for meditation is *dhyana*; the connotation is very different. By meditation, one thing is meant in English; by *dhyana* something else is meant. So first we must understand the basic difference between these two words. Meditation is not a right translation, because by meditation thinking is implied. When we say someone is meditating, it means someone is thinking about something. In meditation an object is implied. In dhyan, no-object is a basic condition. By dhyan is meant a meditative mood without any object.

Objects must cease, mind must become just a pure mirror – a mirroring, not mirroring anything – just a mirror without any object in it, a pure mirror. By dhyan, this purity of the mind is indicated.

So first, no object should be in the mind. Mind must remain alone without thinking about anything – with no thought, just a consciousness, just an awareness, just an alertness.

This alertness without any object is meditation.

So go on dropping objects. Even if one has to use some object as a help to withdraw other objects from the mind, that one object has to be dropped ultimately. Unless that is dropped, it is not meditation.

For example, there are many thoughts in the mind. You can use a mantra; so now there are not many thoughts, just one thought. You can use a name – Rama, Krishna, Jesus, Maria, anything. You go on repeating, "Rama, Rama, Rama, Rama." Between two "Ramas" no gap should be left, because only from that gap a thought enters. If your "Ramas" go on over-lapping each other there will be no gap for any thought to enter. Now you have a mind with one thought. It is still not meditation, it is still thinking – thinking one thought. Ultimately this "Rama" has to be dropped. When you have become attuned with one thought and other thoughts are not entering the mind, then drop it and remain without thought. Many thoughts have been dropped except one; then drop the one, so you come to a state of no-thought.

This state of no-thought is meditation.

This is dhyana, this is pure consciousness.

In this pure consciousness is achieved that which is known as *brahma*. This sutra is concerned with the definition of that indefinable.

It cannot be defined, because definition needs something which becomes impossible with the ultimate reality – definition needs comparison. You cannot define anything without comparing it. That divine is non-dual; it is one, so no comparison is possible. How to define it?

Can you say that the divine is man, or woman? You cannot say, though many religions have defined it in that way. Some religions are man-oriented, so they define God as father. Some religions are woman-oriented, so they define God as mother. But He cannot be defined, because "man" and "woman"...these words are relevant in human language; they become irrelevant for the whole universe. The whole universe is neither male nor female. How to define it? What to say about it?

The moment we use any word to define it, it looks absurd, because every human word implies the contrary also. If you say, "He is light," then where to put darkness? Then what is darkness? Either you will have to deny darkness absolutely from divine nature, or you will have to imply it somewhere; He must comprehend darkness also. So what to say about Him? – light or darkness? If you say both, they become meaningless. He is both, and He is not both. That is the problem; that's why He cannot be defined. Every word implies duality: the polar opposite must be there to make the word meaningful. Every word, with the total existence, becomes meaningless.

But this sutra tries to define the indefinable – this is only an effort, it never succeeds. But it has to be made. Even in its unsuccessfulness it helps, it indicates. It may not be able to define the divine; it is capable of indicating it.

Wittgenstein has said somewhere, "There are experiences which cannot be said, but which can be shown." And he is right. There are experiences – you cannot say what they are, but still you can indicate them. This sutra is an indication.

Some terms have been used; one is: *Thus by meditation they achieve the ultimate reality, which is unthinkable – which cannot be thought.* Why? – because thinking is not, is not something. It is a process of the known; it never leads to the unknown. The unknown is always beyond thinking: You can think something you know; how can you think something which you don't know?

And then the whole of thinking becomes absurd. If you can think only that which you know, what is the use of it? You know already, so what is the use of thinking it? If only the known can be thought, then the whole process becomes circular: it leads nowhere, you go on in a circle. You know and you think; and you think and you cannot think the unknown. So you go on in a circle – mind works in a circle.

The mind never achieves anything from the unknown. So mind must cease, thinking must cease; this circle must be broken. You must come to a standstill: not thinking, not thinking at all. And the moment you are in a no-thinking state, suddenly you enter the unknown.

It is not only unknown but unknowable also, because even if you have known it, you cannot make it known to others. By your being, they may feel it – by your movements, by your gestures, by your eyes, by your very presence, they may feel it – but still you cannot make it known to them. You may create a thirst in them for it, but you cannot give them a definition. You may lead them towards it, but you cannot make it known to them – unless they know themselves.

This knowing of the unknown is basically, foundationally, an individual affair. It can never be made collective. You cannot go to it *en masse.*

222

Alone one has to reach it; alone one has to drop oneself. Alone one has to enter it; alone one encounters it. It becomes known to you, but you cannot make it known to others.

That is the basic difference between science and religion.

A scientist discovers something, and then the discovery becomes that of the whole of humanity. But a religious mystic discovers, and the discovery remains his own. It never becomes a collective phenomenon. A Jesus knows, a Boehme knows, an Eckhart knows, but they are helpless; they cannot make it a common property. It cannot become an object of common knowing; humanity remains in the some grip of ignorance. Each one has to approach it by oneself.

The opening is individual; that's why it is not only unknown but unknowable. And for one reason more, and that reason is still deeper: even if one comes to know it, one never knows it totally. Even when one comes to know it, no one knows it totally! So the unknowable is infinitely unknowable. Even if you are satisfied, even if your thirst is no more, the infinite unknowability remains – that's why it is mysterious. And it is good, and it is beautiful that it is so. Because if you can know the divine totally – if the very moment the divine has been known, you have known it totally – it becomes meaningless.

Anything known totally becomes a thing. Anything known totally creates boredom. Anything known totally will again create a new thirst to know something else.

But once the divine is known, no desire to know anything remains – because you can go on in your knowing…deeper, deeper, deeper, infinitely deeper; the abyss is endless. You have a beginning in it, but no end. You drop into it, and then you go on dropping, and there comes no substratum, no bottom where you can stand again and say, "Now the dropping has ended."

This is the mystery. That's why this sutra says: *the formless, the wonderful*…the mysterious – God is a mysterium. And when I say a mysterium, I mean that you can know it, but still you cannot say, "I have known it." You can only say, "I have dropped into it"; you can only say, "I have ceased to be"; you can only say, "Now I am no more and He is." But you cannot say, "I have known it."

For one reason more it remains unknowable: because the knower is lost. The moment you enter the divine you don't enter as a knower, you enter as a drop of water entering the ocean. You become one with it. The knower is not separate, so how can you say, "I have known it"? How can you say that "I am," still? You are not; only He is.

This is one of the riddles of religious experience: when the knower is lost, the known is known. When the knower is lost, only then knowledge happens.

Kabir has said, "I was searching and searching and searching. Now He is found but the searcher is not. Now He is there but where is Kabir?" The seeker is no more. There has never been a meeting between the seeker and the sought. Never a meeting! – because the two cannot be together. The seeking ends only when the seeker is lost, and only then the sought is found.

You are, then He is not. When you are not, then He is; there is no meeting – or you can call this the meeting.

This is the riddle of religious experience.

...which is unthinkable, unmanifest; the one of
endless forms, the ever-auspicious, the
peaceful, the immortal, the origin of the
creator, the one without a beginning, a middle
and an end; the only one, the non-dual, the all-
pervading, the consciousness, the bliss, the
formless, the wonderful... is known through meditation.

These are just indications, and every indication is a negative. Remember that – every indication is a negative. He is *unthinkable* – you cannot think about it. He is *formless* – he is without form. He has no beginning, no middle, no end. He is *non-dual* – not two. All these are negatives. Why use so much negativity for such a positive phenomenon as God? He is the positivity; He is the only positive force. Then why use so many negatives? – *without* form, *without* the other, everything – everything that has been used to

224

indicate Him, has remained always negative. Why?

There are reasons. The moment you use a positive word, you create a limitation. If I say that He is beautiful, then the ugly is denied. If I say that He is light, then the darkness is denied. If I say that He is good, then the evil is denied. Whatsoever I say positively will deny something.

To use a negative term is to say that He is so infinite that we cannot use any positive term, because positivity becomes a limitation. We cannot say, "He is one"; rather, it is good to say, "He is not two." It is better to say that He is not two; then He is left totally without any positive demarcation. If we say, "He is one," then we have encircled Him.

In meditation, the deeper you go, the more deeply you will come to the positive. But when you want to express it, more and more you will have to use negative terms. The ultimate in using negative terms is Buddha. He has used for this ultimate experience the word *nirvana*. Nirvana simply means cessation. He has not used *moksha*, liberation, because it is positive; it says something. He has not used *brahmalok*; it is positive, it says something. He has not used bliss, consciousness – these are positive. He has simply said, nirvana – cessation of everything, nothingness. And he is right, absolutely right. In meditation you will achieve a positive experience. But when you are expressing it, you will have to use absolute negatives.

If we can create a world consciousness about this use of negatives, there will be no fight between religions. Every fight is because a religion has used something positive. This is strange, but one has to understand it. If you use the negative, then two negatives are never in conflict; but if you use two positives, then two positives are always in conflict.

For example, if Islam says that He is one, and Hinduism says that He is all, one begins to feel some conflict somewhere. Use negatives, and then there is no conflict. If you say that He is not two, then He can be both – He can be one and He can be all. When I say He is not two, I don't deny that He is not all – He can be all. "He is not two" – He can be all. "He is not two" – He can be one. In saying He is not two, both ends – one and all – are implied. If religions are created around negatives, there will be less fight and more understanding.

In the West, all the three religions which have come out of Jewish mystics have all used positives. Christianity, Islam, and the Jewish religion have all used positives. That is one of the reasons they are mostly fighting religions – too much fighting, too much arrogance. They have never used negatives; they have used positive terms. A linguistic factor has created so much violence....

All the Indian religions have used negatives, more and more negatives. And Buddhism is exceptional; Buddhism has used absolute negatives. That's why Buddhism has been one of the most non-fighting religions.

If you use a negative term to indicate the divine, there is no fight. If you use a positive term, a fight is bound to happen. Someone using another ...then two positives are always in conflict. Two negatives are never in conflict. That's why one other strange phenomenon can be understood: Two theists will always be in a fight, but two atheists will never be in a fight, so there are three hundred types of theists in the world, but only one type of atheist.

What is the reason? An atheist anywhere is the same. What is the reason? – the negative, because he stands only with one statement: that there is no God. So how can there be many types of no-Gods? Only one type, one negative, implies everything. The negative is a universal thing: an atheist anywhere – in Tibet, in Germany, in Japan, in China, anywhere – an atheist is simply an atheist. He stands on a negative.

But theists differ. Village to village, neighborhood to neighborhood, theists differ. There are so many brands, and so many types, and so many creeds. Why? The moment you use a positive you have defined an area, and all else is excluded. Unless theists also begin to use use negatives more, there will not be a universal religion. If theism also bases itself on a negative definition of the divine, then there can be a universal brotherhood.

Meditation leads you to all. But never define it as positive; always define it as nothingness.

So meditation has two parts: the creative part as positive, the expressive part as negative.

Two things more: If we understand by "meditation" a state of no-think-

226

ing, then this state of no-thinking can be created in many ways. One, I talked about: you can use one word, one mantra to deny many many thoughts in the mind – this is one way. But there is a basic difficulty in it, because you will have to use one word so much that you may be capable of throwing all else outside. But then this word will become so rooted in you that it will be difficult to throw *it* out. You have used it so much as a device that it will be very difficult to throw it out. Then it will take the whole place; then meditation is not achieved.

To use a name as a repetition has its own difficulties. It is easy to throw out all else, but then it is difficult to throw out itself. If you have used "Rama" to throw out all other thoughts, it will become rooted in you, and then you cannot throw it out. It will be very difficult and very painful. Then something else will be needed to throw it out. As far as I am concerned, I never suggest this method. It is better to begin with no word. Then how to begin?

Take the total energy of your body and mind as the beginning. Let you total body-mind energy be involved in it. Make it so active – let your body energy, your mind energy becomes so active, so active at the peak – that thoughts dissolve, because thoughts cannot exist at the peak. When your energy is moving vigorously, thoughts are thrown out. Even in ordinary things: if you are running fast, you cannot think. Try it! Go on round and round, running fast. You cannot think, because the whole energy is absorbed by running, and thoughts cannot get energy.

We are aware – we may not have understood – when you have eaten much, you cannot think; that's why one feels sleepy. If you have eaten much, you begin to feel sleepy. Why? How is the food concerned with your thinking and sleep? You cannot think; the energy is taken by your stomach. Now the stomach needs energy and the energy is withdrawn from the mind, so mind cannot think. Too much eating will create a very mediocre mind – it cannot think. So thinkers have always been, in many ways, good fasters. They can fast, because the moment you fast the stomach needs no energy, and then the energy can be given to the mind and the mind can think.

A Mahavira, a Buddha, a Mohammed, a Jesus – they are all fasters; they have fasted long. And then their total energy is released and their mind can use it.

So, as far I am concerned, my method is to let your energy work so totally that mind is devoid of energy.

This morning meditation uses this technique. Ten minutes of fast breathing – your mind just cannot get any energy. And fast breathing gives your blood more oxygen; the blood begins to run more quickly, your body electricity is helped by oxygen – it begins to be active. Then ten minutes' jumping, crying, laughing – just going mad – gives your total energy an outlet. Mind cannot get anything out of it; thoughts are dropped. Then using "hoo" – not as a word, but as a sound, remember. "Hoo" is not to be used as a word. It is meaningless, it is just a sound – a mad sound with no meaning. Then using this "hoo," the more vigorously you use it, it hammers the *kundalini*. It hammers the kundalini; it goes down to the very sex center and hammers. This "hoo" is to be used as a hammering, not as a mantra; it is a hammering, just a device.

Now when your energy is in a climax – at the peak – this "hoo" hammers the kundalini and the kundalini begins to go up. When it begins to go up, the kundalini needs your total energy, and mind cannot function at all. Total energy is now on a new route – the route is kundalini. First you have to make it alert and creative – alive. Then you have to force it into the kundalini route. This "hoo" helps to hammer it and to force it through the backbone, upwards – then the kundalini moves. Once the kundalini begins to move, your mind cannot get any energy to think.

Then comes the fourth step: just lying down as if dead, the energy moving upwards. That's why lying down is good. If you are standing, then for the movement of the energy it is a bit difficult. If you are sitting, then too it is a bit difficult. So lie down just as if dead, flat on the ground, so the energy can move easily.

Once energy begins to move in the kundalini, mind cannot think. No-thought is achieved. And in no-thought, meditation happens.

One thing more: no-thought can be achieved in another way also – that is unconsciousness. You can become unconscious; then there is no thought. But then there is no consciousness also. So one can hypnotize oneself into unconsciousness. That gives you a feeling as if you have achieved meditation; you have not achieved. So don't fall into a sleep.

But this meditation will not allow you to fall in a sleep. Such vigorous movement of body energy for thirty minutes will not allow you to drop into sleep; otherwise, many meditators feel that whenever they begin to make any *japa* – *Ram nam*, et cetera, they begin to feel sleepy, they begin to doze, feel drowsy. That too is a hindrance. If you begin to feel drowsy, if you begin to feel sleepy, and if you become unconscious, then nothing is achieved – except a deep sleep. It is good for health, but nothing for meditation is achieved. It is relaxing, it is refreshing, but only for the body – nothing for consciousness is achieved.

That's why I insist so much on this violent meditation, not on silent meditation. Through silent meditation also, the ultimate can be achieved, but sleep comes as a barrier. With this violent, active meditation, sleep is not a barrier at all. It cannot come. It cannot come; at least for ten or fifteen minutes after the exercise, sleep is impossible. You remain conscious and alert, with a no-thought mind. In this, meditation can happen – this is just a situation. You cannot force meditation, you can only create the situation.

And if the situation is created rightly, then meditation happens automatically.

By meditating upon the Lord Parameshwar,
consorted by Mother Uma, the highest lord,
the all- powerful, the three-eyed, and the ever-silent,
the meditator reaches Him who is the source of all manifestation,
the witness of all, and who is beyond all ignorance.

Meditation is object-less. If you use any object, then it is not meditation; it becomes thinking. It becomes contemplation; it becomes reflection, but not meditation.

This is the most essential point to be understood. This is the essence of a meditative state: that it is object-less. Only consciousness is there, but not conscious *about* anything.

Consciousness without being conscious of anything – this is the nature of meditation. But this may create a very depressed mood; this may create pessimism in the mind. It is so difficult to throw even a single thought out of the mind – how can one conceive of being totally thoughtless? It is so difficult to get rid of one object of the mind, that it is inconceivable how to be totally object-less; how to be just a mirror, how to be just conscious without being conscious of anything.

We are never conscious without being conscious of anything – something is always there. And there are some psychologists, some schools of psychology, who say that it is impossible to be conscious without any object. Consciousness to them means consciousness *of something*. Something must be there; otherwise, we will go to sleep; otherwise, we will become unconscious. But yoga says that ordinarily this is right: as far as the ordinary mind is concerned, if there is no object the mind will go down into sleep, slip down into unconsciousness.

We also are aware of it. If you are thinking something in the night, then sleep becomes impossible, because if some object is present in the mind then you cannot drop into sleep, into unconsciousness. So if you are thinking, then you cannot go to sleep; you go to sleep only when thinking has ceased. When thinking has ceased but there is no sleep, only then will you understand what is meant by meditation – but we never know any moment like that. When thoughts cease, thinking ceases, sleep takes over. You are not even aware when sleep has come; you become unconscious.

This is what hypnosis uses as a technique. Hypnosis – any method of hypnotism, any method – uses only this technique: to fix the mind somewhere on one object so intensely that the mind becomes bored of one object. This is the tendency of the mind – mind needs novelty; something new every moment, then it feels alert. If you are in a situation where you have to be aware of only one thing repeatedly then the mind feels bored, and boredom becomes the gate to sleep. So hypnotism uses it. It will give you any object to concentrate on, to concentrate your total consciousness on; then you will feel bored, by and by sleepy, and then sleep will take over. The very word hypnosis means induced sleep. So sleep can be induced if mind is devoid of thoughts.

But yoga says that this is right as far as the ordinary mind is concerned, but this is not right for a meditative mind. Through meditation, mind takes on a new quality, and it becomes possible to be conscious without thoughts. But it is difficult, and to take the jump is arduous.

In Zen there are two schools: one is known as the sudden enlightenment school, and another as the gradual enlightenment school. The sudden school says that any enlightenment is sudden. You have to take a jump from thought to no-thought, from ignorance to knowledge, from sleep to enlightenment. You have to take a sudden jump. But there are very few followers of the sudden school; there cannot be, because it is inconceivable.

There is another school which is known as the gradual enlightenment school. There are many many followers of it, because the moment one says "gradual," we are at ease – now we can do something. And in steps, gradually, in degrees we can proceed. In a sudden phenomenon there is no time, so you cannot postpone – you cannot say tomorrow. If the phenomenon can happen suddenly, this very moment, then your mind cannot excuse itself; there is no basis to postpone it. With a gradual school you can say,

"Okay, we will try in this life, and if not in this life, then in another life. Gradually we will reach the peak. One step, second step – by steps we will reach to the ultimate." Then you have to divide.

But this *Upanishad* belongs to neither. This is neither sudden nor gradual. This *Upanishad* takes a middle way. It says: It is difficult to take a sudden jump, and it is tedious and long to think in terms of degrees. Then you can go on thinking in infinite degrees. So this *Upanishad* says: Only one step is enough – neither sudden nor gradual. Only one step – only one step in between. To be object-less, to be thought-less and conscious is the goal. Only take one step: from many thoughts to one thought, and from one thought to no-thought. This one thought is suggested in this sutra.

This sutra says: *By meditating upon the Lord Parameshwar, consorted by Mother Uma, the highest lord, the all-powerful, the three-eyed, and the ever-silent, the meditator reaches Him who is the source of all manifestation, the witness of all, and who is beyond all ignorance.*

From the world to the ultimate, take any image of God as a single step. This will look strange because we think of God as the ultimate. But the *Upanishads* never think of God as the ultimate. They say, "God is a step towards the ultimate." And they always use for the ultimate the term *brahma*, the absolute. God, Ishwara, Parameshwara, is just a step towards the ultimate. God is not the ultimate end. God is just to be used as a technical help for the jump into the ultimate abyss.

Use God as a jumping board from the worldly mind to the ultimate abyss.

This image of God used as a technical help is very typical and strange, because ordinarily the religious mind feels that God is to be *achieved*. But yoga says, "God is also just a technical help." That's why there are systems of yoga which are godless – for example even Buddha's system. Buddha never talks about God – he discarded God. He created other steps; he discarded God. Mahavira never, never uses the word "God." He discarded it

233

– he used other techniques as jumping boards. But the ultimate remains the same: Hindus call it brahma, Buddhists call it nirvana, Jainas call it kaivalya. The ultimate remains the same: God is used as a technical help. Any imagery, any symbolism can be used. But it must be such a symbol that when you have used it, you are capable of discarding it.

Buddha has told a parable. He says:

Some villagers crossed a stream by boat. But then they thought, "This boat has helped us so much; otherwise, to cross the stream was impossible. So we must not discard this boat." Then they carried the boat on their heads into the town.

Then the whole village gathered and everyone began to ask, "What is the matter? Have you come to sell this boat in the town? or why are you carrying it? The boat seems so old – just a ruin. Who will purchase it? And we have never seen anyone carrying a boat on the head. Why are you carrying it?"

So they said, "This boat is not ordinary; this has helped us to cross the stream. Without this, it would have been impossible to come to this village, so we cannot be ungrateful to it. Now we will have to carry it."

Buddha always used this parable, and he said, "Every technique, every symbol, every ritual is just a vehicle. The moment you have crossed the stream, discard it. Don't go on carrying it; otherwise, you will be just stupid."

We can understand that those villagers were stupid, foolish. But as far as religious vehicles, techniques, boats are concerned, everyone carries them continuously. If I give you a name "Rama" as a japa, as a repetitive method for your meditation, then one day it is bound to happen that you will come to me and say, "Now I feel very blissful with this mantra. Now I am more at peace, more relaxed. Now I am more fresh, now I am less disturbed, now I am less tense. So now what more to do?"

And if I tell you to drop this name now that you have crossed the stream…now that you have come to the other shore, now drop this name also, then you will feel disturbed. I have advised many, and when I say to them, "Drop this," they say, "What are you telling us? How can we drop

234

this? It is inconceivable. We cannot do this. And this seems profane – how can we? This is a very holy name, and this has helped us so much that we cannot discard it."

No ordinary person – even a Ramakrishna…Ramakrishna used the name of Mother Kali as a mantra continually, for years. He achieved much through it, but not the ultimate. He became silent, he became purified, he became holy; he became everything that we can conceive of a religious man. He became totally a religious man – but still a discontent within, still a desire, the desire for the ultimate. He had not reached the end.

Then he met a Vedanta teacher, Totapuri. And he said to Totapuri, "I have reached a very deep silence but still something is missing; I feel it, something is missing. So what to do now?" So Totapuri said, "Now drop the name of Mother Kali. Drop it – you are carrying the vessel, you are carrying the boat. You have crossed the river; now don't carry this boat." Ramakrishna was absolutely disturbed. He said, "What are you telling me? – A person like you, a renowned teacher – what are you telling me? To drop the name of Mother Kali? This is simply irreligious, unholy! What are you telling me? Don't tell me such things!" He began to perspire, he began to tremble – a person like Ramakrishna.

Totapuri laughed and he said, "I knew this. You will feel much disturbed, your whole base has to be destroyed. You have made it a foundation; hitherto this has been your base. Now this has to be destroyed; otherwise, you cannot go further."

For three days Ramakrishna wept, because he had heard such irreligious words. He couldn't speak to anyone; he just closed his door, wept; cried, "Mother! Mother!" and wept. And Totapuri would come and knock at the door, and would say, "Ramakrishna, come to your senses. Drop this name."

After three days, fasting, weeping, Ramakrishna came out, and he said, "If you say, I will do it. But first let me go to the Mother and ask her permission. I cannot do it would her permission." This is how a boat can become so meaningful…and don't laugh at it; even if you are in the state of

Ramakrishna, this will happen.

Ramakrishna went to ask the Mother – of course permission was given, because deep down Ramakrishna himself felt that now this name is the only obstacle. If it drops, consciousness will be totally pure; there will be no disturbance. But he couldn't utter it, he couldn't say it. He went to Mother – there was no one; this was his own deep-down unconscious which gave the permission. He asked the Mother....If one goes in a very devoted way, continuously, to feel in an image the divine presence, one's own deep unconscious becomes projected. And even from the image, things can come which are just being put there by oneself. It was his own unconscious, it was his own deep existence which responded. So permission was given. He came back, of course weeping, because the conscious was still clinging, clinging to the name. His own unconscious was ready. He was totally purified, and this last step was to be taken – *had* to be taken, it was a must!

So the unconscious allowed him, but the conscious began to feel guilty again. He came back. Totapuri said, "Don't feel any guilt. When the Mother herself has allowed, now you drop it." So Ramakrishna sat before Totapuri, closed his eyes, went into deep meditation. Tears were flowing. Hours pass and Totapuri goes on saying, "Now drop it! Don't continue!" And Ramakrishna is continuing. Tears are flowing; he is weeping and trembling. He cannot stop.

He opens his eyes and says, "It seems impossible. I cannot stop. It seems it is absolutely impossible to stop! How can I myself drop the name? It is my heart of hearts. How can I drop it? This is just...it seems suicidal, as if I am killing myself. I cannot." And poor Totapuri insists, "Try again, try again."

Then Totapuri says, "This is the last, and I will not remain here for a single moment longer. I am not going to remain here; I will leave this place. So try again, only one." And he brought a piece of glass, and he said, "When you are meditating and when I feel that the image of Kali has come into your consciousness as an object, I will cut your forehead on the third eye spot with this piece of glass. And when I cut your forehead, you cut the

236

image inside."

Ramakrishna said, "But how can I cut it? And with what? How can I cut it and with what? There is no weapon!"

Totapuri said, "If you can create an image, so alive, by imagination, why can you not create a sword? You have created the image of Kali so loving, so radiant, so alive, so why not create a sword? You are so capable a man – imagine a sword and then cut it! Otherwise, I am going to leave and you will not find me again."

And Totapuri was a a rare man; to miss that man was to miss for lives. And Ramakrishna knew this, that this was the only man who could help; otherwise, one would have to wait, for lives even. And one is not certain that even after waiting for many lives, a man like Totapuri will be there. So Totapuri stood, and he said, "Now I'll leave. You try."

Ramakrishna closed he eyes – he was weeping, he was crying, screaming; and then Totapuri cut his head. And in a single stroke, Ramakrishna *dared* – this is the most daring thing – he dared: he cut the image within. The image broke into two. Tears stopped, crying stopped. And Ramakrishna began to laugh and Ramakrishna began to dance. And Totapuri said, "Now I am leaving. Just tell me in one sentence what has happened."

So Ramakrishna opened his eyes and said, "The last barrier has dropped." And Totapuri disappeared.

Ramakrishna tried and tried for many years to find the man again, to give him thanks, but Totapuri was not found again.

So don't laugh. This middle step can become a barrier, or it can become a jumping board – it depends on you. Use any image, but remember continuously that this is just a technical help. Remember continuously that this has to be dropped. If you can remember it, then you can use any method, any technique, any image, any help. It is artificial, but for our minds – which cannot take a sudden jump – it helps.

He is Brahma, he is Shiva, he is Indra.
He is indestructible, the supreme, the self-luminous.
He alone is Vishnu, he is Prana. He is sun, fire; he is the moon.
He alone is all that was and all that will be, the eternal.
Knowing him one goes beyond the sting of death;
there is no other way to reach complete freedom.
Experiencing one's own self in all beings and
all beings in the self, one attains the highest brahma,
and not by any other means.

The reality is unknown; the reality is unnamed. The reality is, but indefinable. It *is*; it is felt. We are part of it; we encounter it everywhere. Wheresoever you move, you move in reality; you live every moment in it; you participate in it every moment. It is not something different from you, you are not something different from it, but still you cannot name it, you cannot pinpoint it, you cannot give it a label. What is it?

This is a problem for a religious mind. It is not a problem for a philosophical mind; the philosopher can say it is existence, naked, pure – it is absolute. For a Heidegger it is not a problem; he can call it simple "is-ness," being. For a Shankara it is not a problem; he can call it the supreme, the absolute, the brahma. But these are not basically religious types.

For a religious person it becomes a problem, because unless he can name it he cannot be related to it; unless he can personify it he cannot feel the relatedness. The intimacy is impossible with a pure "is-ness." An intimate relationship is not possible with something absolute, with something just like a concept. Being, brahma – how can you feel related with being, with brahma, with "is- ness," with existence? Relationship is only possible when you personify it. That is the basic difference between philosophical speculation and religious search.

Religion is in search of an intimate relationship with existence; it is not only speculation. For a religious man it is going to be life itself. Philosophy seeks in terms of knowledge, religion in terms of love. When you are seeking in terms of knowledge, you can be an observer, an onlooker. But you are not a participant, you are not deep in it – you are just an outsider. A philosopher is basically an outsider; he goes on thinking, but from without. He will not enter into a deep relationship. He will not get involved, he will not be committed. But religion is nothing if it is not a commitment; religion is nothing if it is not an intimate love relationship. So how to change existence into a love object? This sutra is concerned with this.

This sutra says that he is nameless, but we cannot deal with a nameless. He is nameless, obviously, but we must give a name to it; otherwise, we cannot feel related. And to feel related is a great transformation. Not only is the divine nameless, everything is nameless. A child is born a nameless phenomenon, with no name – but if you don't give a name to him, he will be unable even to live. If no name is given to him it will be impossible for him to move. Not only that, but others will not be able to understand him; he himself will not be able to understand himself. Even to understand oneself, one has to be addressed, given a name; otherwise, one cannot even think about oneself – who he is. Of course this name is just a false label, but it helps.

This is one of the mysteries of life: even falsities help, even untruths help, even dreams help, even illusions help. So a person who is bent upon destroying every illusion, every falsity, every untruth, may prove harmful. One has to remember: something may be false, but don't destroy it. Let it be there, it has a utility. But the utility should not become the truth. Utility must remain a utility, it must not become the truth.

Man cannot feel in deep relationship with the divine, with existence, unless he names it. Many names are possible – it will depend on the man who is naming. Thousands and thousands of names have been given to him. In India we have a book, *Vishnu Sahastranam* – a thousand names of Vishnu. The whole book consists only of names – nothing else, just names. It is a very beautiful book, consisting only of names, but in its own way showing that the phenomenon is nameless. Only because of that, thousands of names are possible.

So you can name the divine any way. Call him whatsoever you like, but call him. The emphasis should be on the *call*, not on the name. Call him Rama, call him Hari, call him Krishna, call him Christ; call him any name –

but call! Let there be a deep invocation. Use any name. That name is just artificial, but it will help.

Make any image, but make it. The making is significant. Any image will do, but remember that this is just an artificial help; a technical use must be made of it. In this way also, India has tried many, many experiments – particularly Hindus. They make their idols of mud. Stone came only later on, with Buddhists and Jains; otherwise, Hindus were satisfied with mud images. Stone is a more substantial thing, more permanent; it give a permanency to a thing. A mud idol is just as impermanent as anything in the world. Hindus tried to make their idols only of mud, so that they remembered: this is just an artificial phenomenon made by us. And they insisted that it must be dissolved soon after.

A Ganesha is made, worshiped, everything done – called, prayed, invoked – and then they go and throw it into the sea. This is very symbolic. This means: this image was just an artificial thing. We created it, we used it; now the use is over and we throw it. Hindus are the least idol-worshipers in the world, but everywhere they are known as the idol-worshipers. They are the least, because they are so courageous to throw away their idols so easily, and with such a celebration. They go to throw their idols into the sea with such a celebration. The throwing is as necessary as the creating.

With the stone idols things changed. No stone idol should be there. Clay idols are beautiful, because even if you are not going to destroy them, they will destroy themselves. Sooner or later you will become aware that this was just something made for a particular purpose. The purpose is solved, now the artificial help can be dissolved with a thankfulness, with a celebration. No country, no religion, no race, has been so courageous with its idols. Really, sometimes strange things happen.

Hindus are the least idol worshipers, and Mohammedans the most – and they have not worshiped at all. They have not made any idol. Not even a picture of Mohammed is available – not even a picture. How did he look? They have persistently denied any picture, any idol, any image. Not only have they denied them for themselves, they have destroyed others' also. Others' images, others' idols they have destroyed – with a very good wish. Nothing is wrong in it, because they feel idol worship is harmful – harmful to a religious man. It must not be in between; god must be faced directly, immediately. There should be nothing in between – a very good wish, but it proved dangerous!

It proved dangerous; they went on destroying; they destroyed much that was beautiful – much. They destroyed Buddhist monasteries, Hindu temples, Hindu idols, Buddha's images – they destroyed. All over Asia they destroyed, with a very good wish that nothing should remain between man and God. But they became too concerned with idols. Idol-destroying became their sole religious practice.

This is worship in a negative way – too much concentration on idols; idols became too significant for them. This is how life is strange. I call Hindus the least idol-worshipers, because they can throw away their idols any time the purpose is solved. They use them, but the idols can never use the Hindus; Hindus can use the idols. Mohammedans are so against, yet so concerned; so against but still so attached. They turn really into nega-tive idol-worshipers. Create an image, create any name, create anything that you feel can help you move towards the divine. All names belong to him.

Old Mohammedan names – old, and still Mohammedans are orthodox and old....All old Mohammedan names are names of Allah. All old Hindu names – but now all names are not old – are names of Rama. Not only have we tried to give God a thousand names, we have tried to give everyone a name which really belongs to God. This is symbolic. Every name is God's name, and every name – to whomsoever it belongs – indi-cates a god.

This sutra says:
He is Brahma, he is Shiva, he is Indra.
He is indestructible, the supreme, the self-luminous.
He alone is Vishnu, he is Prana.
He is sun, fire; he is the moon.

He is everything. Call him moon, call him sun, call him Vishnu – call him anything. Whatsoever you call him, remember that the call – the heartfelt call, the prayerful mood – is important. The name is just a device to help you to call him.

He alone is all that was and all that will be, the eternal.

Knowing him one goes beyond the sting of death;

Knowing him one goes beyond the sting of life and death – why? This has to be understood. Why, if you can understand him, why will you go beyond life and death? – because life and death belong to the ego. If you say he is everything that was, if you say he is everything that is, if you say he is everything that ever will be, that means you are not. That means he is and you are not; that means the ego is not – and only the ego is born and only the ego is to die. If he is everything, then he is birth, he is death, he is life. Then how can you conceive of yourself as being born, and as dying?

Birth and death are just two poles of your ego – the feeling that "I am." If you drop this feeling, then birth is not the beginning and death is not the end. Then something always was, before you were born. Really, you are a continuity, a continuity of the whole past; and when you die, nothing is dying – only the continuity changes, takes a turn. Around the corner the continuity will continue. But if you begin to feel between birth and death that you are, then you will die, then you will have to feel the suffering of dying.

Remember that you are a continuity.

The whole universe is involved in you; you are not alone.

No man is an island, no man is alone and separate. The world exists as a net, as an interconnection, as inter-relatedness. The whole world exists as one. You are organic to it; you belong to it. If this feeling comes to you'". *Knowing him one goes beyond the sting of* life and *death; there is no other way to reach complete freedom.* And unless you are a non-ego, there is no way to attain complete freedom. Ego is the slavery, ego is the suffering, ego is the anguish. Ego is the anxiety, the tension, the disease. So unless there is ego-lessness...and egolessness and God-consciousness mean the same thing. If you become God-conscious, you will become I-unconscious. If you are

I-conscious, then you cannot be God- conscious. This is focusing. If you are focused on the ego, the whole universe goes into darkness. If you are focused on the whole universe, the "I" simply disappears. "I" is a focusing of all the energy on a limited link of an unlimited continuity – one link. One link of the whole chain is the ego. Remember the whole continuity.

It will be good if we can think in this way. Could I exist if something had been different in the universe? – I could not exist. Even a millennium before, if something had been different from what it was, I would not be here, because the whole universe is a continuity. Whatsoever I am saying ...if a Buddha had not been there in the past, or a Jesus had not been there in the past, I couldn't say this. The whole universe is a continuity. A single event missed in the past would make the whole universe different. And when I say a Buddha, you can understand. But I say, even if a single tree had not been there in the universe, I would not be here.

The whole universe exists as a continuity; it is an intermittent phenomenon. We are here because the universe was such that we could be here. The whole past was such that this meeting becomes possible. Something missing, and the whole thing will change. This feeling of eternal continuity in the past, of eternal continuity in the future, will dissolve the ego completely. You are not; you are just a part – a part which cannot exist alone.

Then the destiny of the whole universe becomes your destiny, then you have no separate individual destiny. That is what is meant by saying one goes beyond life and death. If you have no individual destiny, the whole destiny of the universe is your destiny. Then who is going to die? And who is going to be born? And who is concerned? Then a total acceptance explodes, a total acceptance comes. A *tathata*, a total acceptance happens. This is freedom; this is ultimate freedom.

Now you cannot feel any limitation.

The universe has never felt limitation. You feel it because you separate yourself. I will die as an individual, but I cannot die as a universe. The atoms in my hand will be there; my eyes will be there as someone else's eyes; my heart will be there as someone else's heart. I will exist in the trees, in the stones, in the earth, in the sky – I will be there as a universe. I will not be there as myself. My consciousness will be there as someone else's consciousness. Or even it may not be someone else's consciousness...just a cloud floating in the sky, or just a silence, or just a drop in the ocean. As myself I am going to die, but not as a universe.

This remembrance, this realization is the only freedom – the only and the ultimate. Unless this happens, you are a slave. You will go on feeling limitations, you will go on feeling boundaries, you will go on feeling that this is going to be death, this is going to be birth, this is going to be pain, this is going to be suffering. To create, or to go on believing in individual destiny, is irreligion. The beginning of the feeling that "I am not an individual destiny – destiny belongs to the universe, I belong to the universe" – is the beginning of freedom, is the beginning of religion.

Religion is the search for total freedom. And unless the freedom is total, it is not freedom at all.

Experiencing one's own self in all beings and all beings in the self, one attains the highest brahma, and not by any other means.

This is what I mean by being aware of a universal destiny: by dissolving one's individual, petty destiny one begins to feel then that he is everything – all. All penetrates into oneself, and one's own existence penetrates all. Really, it is saying simply that boundaries dissolve.

The observer becomes the observed.

The knower becomes the known.

The lover becomes the beloved.

Wise men make their conscience the lower arony, the churning
stick, and AUM, the upper churning stick.
And with the help of these two,
they practice the churning of knowledge.
In the fire of knowledge, born out of this friction,
they burn all their blemishes and become free.

With the natural, the spontaneous, the spiritual voice, everything is total. Acts become total, and the moment any act is total there is no continuity. You do it, and it drops – just like dead leaves dropping from a tree. The tree is not going to remember them. They were complete in a sense, they were perfect in a sense; and the moment has come for them to drop.

Just like this, actions go on dropping and the mind remains unburdened and fresh. This is the criterion: observe inside yourself and until you come to a point where division of the mind is transcended, don't stop; go on inwards. Ultimately the basic rock is attained. That basic rock is one part of the techniques shown here.

The second part is the word "AUM." The sutra says that by making the mind the lower *arony*, or churning stick, and AUM the upper churning stick, and by repeated churning, a wise man burns up all the causes of his bondage. In ancient India, for creating fire, churning sticks were used; they were called *aronies*. Two sticks rubbed together can create fire, so particular wood was used to make these sticks. Just by rubbing them, fire was created. So this sutra says: conscience is one churning stick, AUM is another, and by these two – constant churning by these two – an inner fire is created. That fire burns all the causes of bondage, and man becomes freedom – not free, but freedom.

This AUM has to be understood. This AUM is not a word, it is just a sound – just a sound, like the sound we are using in the morning meditation, "hoo." AUM is just a sound like hoo. I am using hoo rather than AUM for a specific reason: AUM can be used only when society is in a very innocent state. If the society is very innocent, unsophisticated – not very tense, relaxed – then AUM can be used as a churning stick, because if you say AUM, it never goes below the heart. Create the sound AUM, and it never goes below the heart. For those who are very innocent, this much is enough. But in our age, which has become specifically sexual, tense, anxious, pathological, psychotic, AUM will not help. That's why I am using hoo; hoo goes deep down to the very sex center.

Hoo is part of a Sufi mantra: Allah hoo – the last part. Sufis use it as AUM. They begin by repeating, "Allah, Allah, Allah." Constantly repeating, "Allah, Allah" becomes "Allah hoo." If you repeat it constantly then Allah will begin to look like Allah hoo. Then Allah is dropped by and by, and simply hoo is retained; and that hoo works very deeply. Why do Sufis use hoo? Because the Arabic race is one of the most sexual – one of the most sexual races on earth, Sufis had to devise a different sound to work with their race; they used hoo.

As I see it now, the whole world has become Arabic. Now AUM will not do; hoo will do – but both mean nothing. Neither does AUM mean anything nor does hoo mean anything, they are just sounds used as an inner hammering. If a person is heart-oriented, then AUM will do the work of an arony, a churning stick. Find your conscience – the authentic, real, basic, your own – then use AUM. But if the personality is not heart-oriented but sex-oriented, then AUM will not help; then hoo will help.

So it depends: Where is your energy? If it is in your heart – that means if you are more love-oriented rather than sex-oriented – if you are love-oriented then the energy of your body, of your mind, of your spirit, is in the heart center, and then AUM will do; AUM is mild. But if it is not in the heart, then hoo will be better. One thing more: if the energy is in the heart, hoo will also do. But if it is in the sex center, AUM will not do. Hoo passes the heart center, goes deeper. AUM goes up to the heart center; it cannot go deeper.

But in those days when this sutra was written, they never felt the need of hoo; people were innocent, more authentic to their being, less conditioned, nearer to nature, less nurtured, less cultured, less civilized – more authentic to their own being. Then both were simple; to find the authentic conscience was not a difficult affair, it was easy; then to use AUM was not difficult. With a natural conscience, this sound AUM hitting it continually, hammering it, creates an inner fire. And that inner fire burns everything that has become the cause of our bondage. It burns the whole past; not only the past, it burns the whole future. Then you are in an eternity, without any past and without any future. Then you are just in the present.

Then you begin to live moment to moment, free – totally free, with no bondage, with no commitment with the past, with no longing, with no investment with the future. Moving moment to moment, totally free, spontaneous; this freedom is the longing of all religions. This freedom is the flowering of the religious phenomenon.

Why can this constant hammering of AUM or hoo, or any sound, create an inner fire? For two reasons: one, words are electric forces, sounds are electrical – every sound is electrical.

In Tibet there is one famous yoga exercise known as heat-yoga. A Tibetan Buddhist monk has to pass an examination before he becomes a perfect ordained monk; he has to pass through the examination of heat-yoga. Heat-yoga means that the monk, the *bhikku*, stands in a cold night, surrounded everywhere by snow, naked. And he has to create an inner heat, so that his body begins to perspire. If he cannot pass this examination then he cannot be ordained as a Buddhist lama. So every lama, to be a lama, has to pass through this examination. And it happens; it happens!

An absolutely cold night, when even blood begins to freeze, and this bhikku who is being examined...and they are examined, many in one night; sometimes even one thousand are examined in one night. They begin to perspire – not only perspire, they begin to burn. If you touch them, they are burning. What are they doing inside? With no outside heat, fire, nothing...what are they doing? And standing naked! They are using a particular sound which, hitting inside, creates body electricity.

You may have heard – it is neither a fiction, nor is it just a superstitition – that sometimes yogis have burned themselves through their inner heat. Just ten years ago, a Sikh yogi burned himself in Uttar Pradesh, in front of hundreds of observers. Just sitting in a temple, meditating inside, then flames were seen, and the whole body was burning. It was examined medically and it was proved that no fuel was used – nothing from outside was found to be used. The fire came from somewhere inside, and the whole body became just ashes.

A particular sound can create fire inside; a particular sound can create coolness, because sound means electricity. If you hit a particular sound continuously, it creates heat – AUM creates heat; hoo creates even more heat. That fire created by AUM in the conscience, in the *antahkaran*, burns everything that was you, and a new man is born – a new birth, a freedom is born.

THE NIGHT MEDITATION.

Just because of the full moon we will be doing *kirtan*. So come near; the nearer you are the better....

The self, deluded by maya,
identifies with the body and does all actions.
In the waking states it is he, the same self,
who finds gratification through the various objects
of enjoyment, such as women, food, wine, et cetera.
In the dream state that very same
individualized ego experiences pleasure and pain
in a field of experiences created by its own maya,
the least apprehensive of reality.
During the state of profound sleep, when everything is merged,
it is overpowered by tamas, *inertia,*
and experiences it as happiness.

As we live, as we are, it is a deep hypnosis. Whatsoever we feel, whatsoever we think, is based on hypnotic projections. In some face I see beauty; that beauty doesn't belong to the face, because someone else may not feel it as beautiful at all. It belongs to my projection. When I say some face is beautiful, I am projecting something from me; and the face is just a screen, because someone else may see the face as ugly.

You can project whatsoever you have in your mind, onto anything. That's why philosophers have been trying to define what beauty is, but they have never been able. It cannot be defined; not because it is something indefinable, but because it is an individual projection. It is not something objective which can be defined. It is not objective at all; it is just a subjective feeling. So not only may someone think something is ugly while you are thinking it is beautiful, it may happen that in the morning you thought it was beautiful, and in the evening you yourself begin to feel it is ugly. And the thing remains the same – the object remains the same, the screen remains the same. You go on projecting, then the screen changes, and the object begins to look like something else.

This phenomenon of projection is basic to our minds. We live not in the objective world, but in a projected world. Once you being to understand this, the whole phenomenon changes. So there is not only one world, but there are as many worlds as there are minds. Everyone is living in his own individual world – multi-worlds, multi-universes. You have your own world that belongs to you; it is not something which can be participated in by anyone else. Participation is impossible when there is projection. When there is hypnosis, participation is impossible; we cannot share it. I feel someone is good, you feel he is not, and there is no sharing. I feel someone is a saint; he may be, he may not be, but it is my projection.

For example, Krishna is the perfect *avatar* for Hindus, but for Jains he is not – he is not even an avatar. For Hindus he is the peak: all that is beautiful, all that is good, all that is true is personified in him. But for Jains, he is not: they have put him into the seventh hell, because he was the man responsible for the great Indian war, *Mahabharata*. Jains judge everything by the criterion of violence or nonviolence. Krishna was responsible for this whole violence. Arjuna was going to be a saint; he was just escaping from the war, and this man Krishna persuaded him to fight. So the responsibility for the violence goes directly to Krishna – he becomes responsible. Jains have put Krishna into the seventh, the lowest hell.

It doesn't matter what Krishna is. He is "X," the unknown; but what he appears is a projection. Anyone can project anything; it depends on you, your attitude, your mind, your way of thinking – then you can project. And we are projecting every moment – that's why reality is not known. You can really know reality only when your projecting mechanism stops completely. Then the objective world appears, then things begin to look as they are: as they are, not as you feel them. Your feeling says something about you, not about the thing itself. This auto-hypnotic process, this projection mechanism in the mind is the problem. And unless this whole mechanism stops, you cannot enter meditation, because meditation means only one thing: a non-projective mind, a non-projecting mind, a non- hypnotic mind – a mind which is not hypnotized by itself – a mind which is absolutely devoid of the hypnotic process.

We can hypnotize ourselves. And the whole culture, civilization, society, education – everything; politics, the so-called religions – they all use this weakness. They all use it. For example, business uses it. What is advertising? It is simply going on repeating a particular thing so that it becomes hypnotic. Someone goes on saying that this cigarette is the ultimate in cigarettes – goes on repeating. You go on listening, you go on reading. By every possible media, by every possible method, this thought is being put into your mind: "This cigarette is the ultimate in cigarettes."

Then every other means is used – a naked woman is placed in the poster just by the cigarettes, a cigarette in her hand. Now your sex attraction, sex appeal is being exploited. Now the cigarette is being associated with sex, it will become more hypnotic. Continual repetition will put the idea as a seed in you. When you go to the market, to the shop, and you say, "I need a particular cigarette," you think you are choosing it; you are not – you have just been forced to choose it. Your hypnotic mechanism has been used and exploited, but you will think that you are choosing it, that you are the chooser – you are not. Whatsoever you are choosing, ninety-nine out of one hundred times you are not the chooser – you cannot be. Unless the whole mechanism stops, you cannot choose. You are being forced, manipulated to choose something.

Preachers go on convincing people about Christianity, about Hinduism, about Mohammedanism – they are doing the same. They are the businessmen of the market of religion. They go on convincing people, "This will do, this will do, this will do – all else is worthless." They go on repeating the idea. That's why every religious sect is very much interested in keeping children, because they are the most innocent, and their projective mechanism is very powerful, alive. So whatsoever you put in them, they will have to run their whole life accordingly. So every religion – the so-called religions – is very much interested that children must be taught religiously. Before they are seven they must be converted; otherwise, conversion will become impossible. Once they become aware, then conversion will be impossible. Before seven, seeds must by put in them. Then those seeds will work; they will become their base.

So a Christian child, even if he goes against Christianity later on, will be in a subtle way still Christian. Even his going against, will be in a Christian way. Even his rebellion, his reaction, will have a continuity with all that against which he has rebelled. Now he is in the grip, and it is difficult to come out of it. If you rebel, if you react, again the mechanism will work. That's why it is so difficult just to drop Christianity or Hinduism or Mohammedanism. You can go against it, but you cannot drop it, because in going against you are still in it – related, concerned. But if you can drop it without going against, without any reaction, then you are out of it. But that is possible only if you become aware of your own auto-hypnotic processes; otherwise, you can hypnotize yourself to the opposite extreme – that is easy. And people go on moving from one extreme to another.

This happens not only with individuals, this happens with societies also, – this happens with nations also. For example, this is happening now. The East has hypnotized itself that materialism is useless, *only* spiritualism is meaningful. This has been the Eastern hypnosis. Now they are bored so they are absolutely, absolutely going to the other extreme. Now the East is becoming every moment more and more materialistic, but their mind continues to talk in terms of spiritualism. And if you go deep down, Eastern people are the most materialistic in the world. They are moving to the other extreme.

The West tries to hypnotize itself to the other extreme: materialism became so significant that spiritualism is just a Sunday affair, mm? Not significant, not meaningful – just a social thing; not deep, not individual, not concerned with the inner being, but just a social phenomenon, just symbolic. Too much materialism in the West now creates a reaction, and the West is moving towards spiritualism – to the other extreme. Sooner or later, East will become West, and West will become East. It is going on; the process is there.

So whenever someone from the West comes in search of spirituality to the East, even the Eastern religions feel a bit of inconvenience, discomfort, unease. The Eastern intelligentsia cannot conceive why you are coming here. Here there is nothing; you have everything. Why are you coming here? The Eastern intelligentsia is going to the West for technology, for science, for everything that the material world can give; they are going Westward. And you cannot conceive, in the West, why these Eastern people are coming to the West. To learn? What can they learn here? In the West intelligent people, intelligent boys and girls are dropping out of universities, just because nothing can be gained there. They are dropping out of universities, they are dropping out of their society – they are creating an alternate society. And people from the East going there? It becomes inconceivable to them. But nothing is inconceivable. This is how opposites work; this is now hypnosis changes itself from one opposite to another. But the *other* is as dangerous. – The real thing is: how to go beyond hypnosis. From one hypnosis to another it is easy, it is nature, the way of things – how they work. But how to go beyond, how to go beyond this hypnotic process? How to dissolve this whole mechanism?

This sutra says that all our happiness and all our miseries are part of our hypnosis. They are. A person who has no hypnosis in him is beyond both. He is neither happy nor unhappy; he simply is. And that "is-ness" is bliss; it is not happiness, it is bliss. Never, never think of bliss in terms of happiness; it is not. Happiness is related to unhappiness, not to bliss.

If you desire happiness you will create unhappiness.

If you desire bliss, then let happiness and unhappiness both dissolve.

But how can they dissolve unless your mind is dehypnotized? Meditation means dehypnotization. The process looks just the same.

Many people come to me and they say, "Whatsoever is being done here, is it not hypnosis?" It is *dehypnosis*. The process is the same, but the dimension is reversed. You can hypnotize yourself – that is going further from yourself towards the object. You can de-hypnotize yourself – that is going back from the object towards oneself.

When you are centered in some object, you are hypnotized.

When you are centered in yourself, you are de-hypnotized.

When you are yourself, you are beyond hypnosis.

When you are not yourself, centered, but obsessed with something, then you are hypnotized. Look at a man who is hypnotized by a woman, or a woman who is hypnotized by a man. Look at the eyes, at the face, at the body: they are not in their senses – they cannot be. That's why traditional wisdom says that love is blind, because it is hypnotic. It is a sort of madness. – It is a sort of madness which comes from yourself, and then you project. And then something becomes so important and meaningful that you can even give your life for it – anything! It is not that love happens only between persons; love happens between persons and things also. A person who is in love with wealth is as much hypnotized – he is as mad. A person who is in love with power – he is as mad. He is as mad, he can give his life for it. At any cost he must have the loved object, whatsoever it is. He is centered in the object – this is what I mean by hypnosis – he is centered in the object, not in himself. He can lose himself, but not the object.

Mulla Nasruddin was robbed once. He was alone on a lonely road. He was caught and the robber said, "There are two alternatives: either you give whatsoever you have or your life. You can choose. So Mulla said, "You can take my life, but as far as my wealth is concerned that is what I am saving for my old age."

And he is right. This is how a hypnotic mind works; he is right. "What will I do with my life if there is no wealth? So you can take my life; it has cost me nothing. As far as my wealth is concerned, I have devoted my whole life to it. It has cost me much; and moreover, I am saving it for my old age."

Any love object, *any* love object becomes obsessive. You are not in your senses – that is, you are not conscious. You become unconscious, you begin to move in a deep sleep. That's how we are.

De-hypnosis, or meditation means to bring your consciousness – which has become projected onto the object, back home. The process looks like hypnosis – it is; in de-hypnosis the process is the same. If you have gone far away from your home, you have traveled a path, you have used your legs. Now if you want to come back, you will have to use the same legs and you will have to travel the same road, only in the reverse order. That will be the only difference. We have gone deep into the world. If we want to come back, the process is going to be the same, only in reverse order.

So hypnosis has to be used in the reverse order, and every meditation is hypnosis in the reverse order – *every* meditation. The only question is whether you are coming back or going away. If you are coming back, then it is meditation; if you are going away, then it is hypnosis. If something brings you to yourself it is meditation; if something takes you away from yourself, then it is hypnosis – the process is the same.

This sutra says that man lives in a deep hypnosis. Then he suffers unnecessarily, because unless you are centered in yourself you can never be in bliss. That centering is bliss. Unless you are centered in yourself, you will never be independent; you will be a slave. Centered in something else, you will be a slave, you will be in bondage. Centered in something else, you will be dependent; of course, you are bound to be dependent on something else. Your happiness, your unhappiness will be dependent on someone else – if you love me, if I love you. Then my happiness will depend on you – how you behave, how you are; only then will I be happy. If you behave differently, if you are different, then I will be unhappy. Then I am not the master of my own happiness or unhappiness; you are the master.

Then you can manipulate – and everyone is manipulating everyone else; this whole world is just a manipulation. The husband is manipulating the wife, the wife is manipulating the husband; the father is manipulating the child, and the child is manipulating the father; the disciples are manipulating the teacher, and the teacher is manipulating the disciples – everyone. And then everyone is unhappy, because dependence is unhappiness. How can you feel happy when you are dependent for it on someone else? He is the master, and he will be the deciding factor – not you. And a master needs sometimes to check, again and again, whether he still remains the master or not.

So if you are happy because of me, sometimes I will have to make you unhappy, just to check whether I am still the master or not. So lovers go on checking each other, examining each other – whether the mastery remains or it has gone. That checking creates unhappiness, and the more unhappiness is created the more longing there is for happiness. The more longing for happiness, the more dependence, and then more unhappiness results. It becomes a vicious circle, and it goes on and on with no end in view. There is no end really.

In hypnosis you can go on eternally; it is an infinite process – because once you have left your center, you can go anywhere. And there is no end. The end comes only if you come back to your center – then you reach somewhere. A point can be reached *only* when you come to yourself.

This centering is meditation.

Urged by these acts done in previous births,
the jiva *again comes back from the deep sleep*
to the dream or the wakeful state.
The jiva, embodied soul, thus born in the three cities –
gross, subtle, and causal body; from where
all diversities have sprung up.
When these three bodies have dissolved completely,
only then this soul becomes free from maya,
and attains eternal bliss.
From this is born prana, *all organs, space,*
air, fire, water and the earth that supports all.

Eastern psychology divides man's mind into three states: deep sleep – dreamless sleep – dreaming, and awake. Ordinarily, we are not aware even of the state which is called "awake." We are not aware. We feel we are awake, but we live as if we are asleep. We move, we do things in a somnambulism; there is no awareness. There is awakening in the the morning – when you come out of your sleep you are awake, in the first state – but you are not aware. You go, you move, you do things in a mechanical way – not consciously, not meditatively.

Any movement is possible unconsciously and consciously. You are eating: you can eat in a mechanical way, not aware of the process, not conscious, not mindful – just going on eating mechanically, unconsciously, robotlike. You can walk on the streets unconsciously, not even aware that you are walking, that your legs are moving – you go on moving, robotlike. Someone hits you, someone abuses you, someone condemns you; anger bubbles up – you are not aware.

It works as if someone has pushed a button, and the light is on: someone abuses you, someone has pushed the button, and the anger is on. You are behaving in a mechanical way, not aware of what is happening; not aware that anger is coming to you, that anger is surrounding you, that anger is taking charge of your mind, of your body; that now you will be pulled and manipulated by your anger – no, not even aware. You are not aware; it just happens and you go on following a mechanical trend.

This so-called awake state is the first – on the periphery. Deep down, just behind it, is the second state – dreaming. Western psychology has

260

taken note of dreaming only with William James, never before…just in this century, just in the beginning of this century. With William James, dreaming became important, and with Freud, it gained its own status. For the first time it was recognized as significant and meaningful in the West. But in the East, for thousands of years, dreaming has been thought very significant – more significant that the first, the awake. Because in dreaming you are more authentic, more real. Because in dreaming there is no fear of society, no inhibition, no suppression. So your mind as it is, begins to work. Freudian psychology studies not your waking hours – they are not meaningful – but your dreaming. That is meaningful; that shows your real face.

Indian psychology says that dreaming is the second state of the human mind. And it is not only a state, but it corresponds to a body also. The first state, the awake, corresponds with the gross body; it is part of the gross body, the material body that we know as the body. The second state, dreaming, corresponds to the second body, which is known as the subtle body. That second body is just a body behind this body, and Indian psychology says – and Indian yoga has experimented for centuries and has come upon many, many facts – that in a deep dream your subtle body can move out of your body. It can go, it can move, it can travel.

Now in the West also, astral traveling has become a prominent thing to be studied. Astral projection – how to project your astral body, how to move out from your body – is now an accepted fact of parapsychology. But only now is it accepted – and that too, not universally; only parapsychologists accept it – that a subtle phenomenon, a subtle body can go out from this body, and move, and travel.

This sutra says that dreaming is concerned with the second body, not with this body which is known to us. The second body is the dreaming body; second state is dreaming, and the second body is subtle. Then there is a third state of the mind: deep sleep, or dreamless sleep – total sleep, not even a dream. This corresponds to a third body which is known as the causal body.

You live in the outward world with your gross body; you live in a dream

261

world, in a subtle world, with your subtle body. And you move from one body to another, from one birth to another, from one life to another through your causal body – the third body. The causal body means the basic body. And beyond the causal is your real self. These are three bodies only, three surrounding bodies, three concentric bodies. And behind these three, and beyond them, is the center, the self, the consciousness.

This sutra says that unless one is capable of dis-identifying from these three bodies; capable of knowing oneself apart, separate, beyond all these three bodies – unless one is capable of that, one will go on coming back to this earth, in a circle. One will go on being born again and again, and then dying, and then being born again and again. If these three bodies can be known as the other, if you can recognize yourself as different from these three bodies – the awake, the dreaming, the deep sleep; the gross, the subtle, and the causal – if you can feel, realize, know that you are beyond these three, only then this vicious circle of life and death ceases, and you gain freedom, and you gain bliss.

What to do?

How to be aware beyond these three bodies?

The technique that can make you aware, that can make you transcend, that can create a situation in which you can witness all these three bodies – standing outside them – is meditation.

But here, by meditation is meant training the consciousness of each body in mindfulness. Buddha has used this word "mindfulness" for meditation. He says, "Walk, but mindfully; don't just walk. Eat, but mindfully. Think, but mindfully."

What is meant when I say, "Think, but mindfully"? It means, let there be thought, but let there also be an awareness that there are thoughts. Just like you are sitting under the sky, and clouds are moving. Look at the clouds, see the clouds, and constantly *and* simultaneously be aware that you are seeing the clouds. Let your consciousness be two- arrowed: one arrow pointing to the clouds; another arrow pointing to yourself *seeing* the clouds.

Let your consciousness be double-arrowed.

Ordinarily, our consciousness is one-arrowed. For example, if you are listening to me you will forget yourself completely. If I say it, then suddenly you will remember: you have forgotten yourself completely. You are listening to me, so your consciousness has become one-arrowed – your consciousness is arrowed towards me, the speaker. But where is the listener? You are not aware of yourself as the listener.

Experiment, make your consciousness double- arrowed. Listen to me, but constantly remember that you are listening. You need not repeat it, because if you repeat then you will forget me, the speaker. If you repeat it in the mind, that you are listening, in that moment you will not listen. Do not repeat it, do not verbalize it; words are not needed. Just be conscious, double-arrowed. Of course, when I am speaking you are listening. Speaking and listening are two points: *here* I am speaking, *there* you are listening. There is a relationship; these are two arrows. Be aware of both, then you will transcend both. Neither will you be the listener nor the speaker, but a witness of both.

This is what is meant by mindfulness. Do whatsoever, but remember the doer. Go on witnessing – *any* process. Thoughts are moving in the mind – look at them, observe them and remember; remember that you are observing your thoughts. Then thoughts are somewhere like clouds in the sky, moving, and you are an observer. This observation, this witnessing, this awareness is the technique to transcend any body.

But first, always begin with the gross, the waking state. If you succeed in that, then you can succeed in the second; then you can become aware of your dreams. You can dream and be simultaneously aware that a dream is floating, that a dream is unfolding, that a dream is going on. And if you become aware of your dream process, then you have transcended the second body, the subtle body.

And then the last and most arduous is to penetrate into deep sleep with consciousness, to become aware of your sleep also. There is sleep, no dream – sleep is surrounding you; still you are conscious that sleep is there.

But this can happen only in a sequence. Begin with the first; otherwise,

263

the third will be impossible, inconceivable. Go to the second; only then the third becomes possible. And if you can know that you are asleep – *in* sleep, not afterwards; not in the morning, that "I have had a very beautiful good night's sleep." Not afterwards – presently, when you are asleep, be aware. If you can be aware of your sleep you have transcended all three bodies and all three consciousnesses, and then you will know the fourth.

Indian psychology says that the fourth is your being. The three have been named, but the fourth has been just called "the fourth" – *turiya* – it has not been named. The fourth is your center. But that center is surrounded by three peripheries, concentric circles. Unless you transcend them, you will not know it. And unless you know it, no bliss is known, and no freedom is possible.

But always begin with the first. When the first is complete, only then begin with the second, because only then a beginning is possible. If you become aware of the first, then you are at the door of the second. If you become aware of the second, then you are at the door of the third. If you become aware of the third, then you are at the door of the fourth. Without experiencing the first, all else is just inconceivable.

Lastly, if you transcend all these three bodies, then there is no birth again, and of course, no death. The whole dimension changes. You begin to move in a different dimension: the dimension of the eternal, the dimension of the non-temporal, the dimension of timelessness. Then you are not moving in time from one birth to another death, then again death, and again birth. No; now you move from the circle of time to the ocean of timelessness. In this timelessness is the authentic, existence, the ground of existence, the ground of all being. And in that is freedom, because then there is no ego, then there is no boundary, then there is no "I." And with the cessation of "I" everything that is a disease, that is a misery, that is an anguish, ceases.

That which is the supreme brahma,
the self in all, the ancient support of the universe,
subtler than the subtle, and eternal, that alone thou art.
Thou alone art that.
That which illumines the world of related experiences
lives in the waking, dream, and the profound sleep state.
One who realizes that brahma and I are one,
is liberated from all bondages.

This is a very revolutionary sutra:

That which is the supreme brahma, the self in all, the ancient support of the universe, subtler than the subtle, and eternal, that alone thou art. Thou alone art that.

Any search, any inner search begins with elimination, begins with the negative. One has to know what one is *not* in order to know what one is. The "is not" comes first, and the "is" follows. The negative is the beginning, and the positive the realization.

If you begin with the positive you will never reach the real positive. If you begin with the negative, only then you can reach the positive. Why? Because negative and positive are two polar opposites. They look opposite to us; deep down they are not. Deep down, negative and positive are poles of one existence.

Existence is manifested into polar opposites. They are complementary, not opposites; they are contraries but not opposites – complementary to each other. They supplement each other, they help each other. Really, the one cannot exist without the other. The good cannot exist without the evil, and the light cannot exist without darkness, and love cannot exist without hate, and the friend cannot exist without the enemy.

A Jesus cannot exist without a Judas. A Judas is not opposite to Jesus. He is the complementary, the dramatic complementary of Jesus, the other aspect of Jesus. It is difficult to conceive, because as our thinking goes, it always divides. We see Jesus as the god, and then we see Jesus' opposite, Judas, as the evil.

Jesus cannot exist without a Judas, and a Judas cannot exist without a

Jesus. They both come simultaneously into existence. This story is very beautiful and meaningful.... When Jesus was crucified, Judas committed suicide. He was instrumental in Jesus' crucifixion, but when Jesus was crucified, Judas committed suicide. Really, Judas cannot exist without Jesus; when Jesus is no more, Judas becomes meaningless, irrelevant. Then he has nothing to do. He was here only for Jesus to be crucified, or for Jesus to be. He was the counterpart, the shadow. When Jesus disappears, the shadow is bound to disappear. A Judas cannot exist without a Jesus, and a Jesus cannot come into this world without a Judas.

The polar opposites are complementary, deep down; negative and positive are one. And the negative makes the boundary, negative surrounds the positive. The positive is the center, negative is the periphery. So if you want to enter the center you have to pass through the periphery. That's why a religious search begins with the negative – what you are not. You are not the body, you are not the mind. You are not the ego, you are not the self. These are all negatives. These negatives, these "nots" are the periphery, and only when you are past all the "nots," all the negatives, then you enter the positive – then you become aware of what you are.

If you begin with a positive, you begin wrongly, because then the positive will be just in your imagination, not an authentic experience. If you begin with, "I am brahma" without knowing that you are not the body, without knowing that you are not the mind, without knowing that you are not the ego.... If you begin with "I am brahma," this "I am brahma" is not the center; rather, you are outside the periphery and imagining it.

This statement, "I am brahma," can be of two types: one of imagination, the other of experience. The other is the authentic; the one, the first, is just imaginative thinking. If you have not denied thinking first, you can think that you are brahma, but that is you thinking; just a thought in the mind, not an experience. You have not known that you are brahma, you have only become acquainted through scriptures, through others. This is just a thought in your mind, not a deep realization.

So never begin with any positive. There are many who go on continually repeating, "I am brahma, I am brahma, I am brahma." And by their repetition they only show that they don't know. Because if you know, there is not need to repeat. Whatsoever you know, you never repeat – there is not need. You know; you know already – then why go on repeating? This repetitive mind shows that you are just suggesting to yourself that you are brahma, just trying to create an illusion by autohypnosis that you are brahma. But this autohypnosis will not lead you deep; it will not even be skin deep. So someone hits you, and the brahma evaporates – you begin to react out of whatsoever you really are. Then you begin to react as a body, then you begin to react as a mind, then you begin to react as an ego and *nowhere* as a brahma! Because that was only a thought – just a dream, just a cloud, not an experience in you.

Never begin with any positive, because beginning with the positive is bound to be illusory. Begin with the negative.

But we are fearful of the negative, we are afraid of the negative, because the negative means renunciation; the negative means renouncing something. Negative means destroying something, negative means eliminating something, negative means *dis*-identifying with something. It is painful, one begins to suffer. "I am not this" – then something has dropped from me. "I am not this" – then again something has dropped from me. It goes on dropping and I go on becoming poorer, and poorer, and poorer – that is the fear.

We desire to accumulate. We desire to go on identifying: "This is me, that is me." This is how the mind works. We go on identifying with more and more things, with more and more persons. And the greater becomes the periphery, the more secure we feel.

This is what lust means. Lust means a desire for accumulation – "This house belongs to me." Then suddenly I become the house. "This car belongs to me" – then I become the car. So when someone falls in love with a car – and many fall – then the car is not just something outside of you; it becomes part of you, it is your body. Then you don't feel that the car is a possession; you begin to feel identified with it. Whatsoever is attached to you becomes part of your body – this is how our mind goes on working, accumulating. So elimination becomes difficult.

Mind is the accumulator in you.

Meditation is the eliminator.

That's why mind and meditation are in conflict.

If you meditate, then you go on destroying your mind.

The Zen monk Rinzai has defined meditation as a state of no-mind, a deep freedom from the mind. It only means a deep freedom from accumulation. The reverse process is needed: elimination. Go on eliminating and saying, "This is not me, this is not me, this is not me" - go on. In the *Upanishads* the formula for this elimination is *neti-neti*. This formula means ...these two words are the base of the negative process.

Neti-neti means, not this - not that. The word means, not this - not that. Go on saying, "I am not this, I am not that" - go on.

When the negative is completed, you fall into the positive. When the negative is crossed, you enter the positive; and now the positive is not imagined - you experience it, you encounter it, you become it.

"I am brahma" is an experience, not a statement to be made before experience - it *never* should be made, never should be believed, never should be assumed. If you assume "I am brahma" without knowing it, you will never be able to encounter the reality which reveals to you, which explodes in you, and becomes brahma.

Pass through the negative and attain the positive. The positive should not be tried directly; it is always reached indirectly. Whatsoever you need is just elimination, and when all else which is not you is eliminated, *suddenly* that which is you is revealed. That's a revelation. You have nothing to do for it directly; indirectly, you have to do much.

Go on cutting and renouncing, go on breaking identities. Unless you come to a point where nothing remains which you can call "this" or "that" - only you, only the center; everything of the periphery eliminated, only the center without the periphery....Then suddenly the whole focus of consciousness changes. You enter into a different world, the world of the positive. You become aware what you are.

Meditation is negation.

Realization is positive.

Meditation is negating, negating to the extreme where nothing remains to be negated; denying to the very end, where nothing more remains to be denied. When everything has been denied and negated, and you cannot deny and negate anything, because nothing remains to be denied – then is revealed that-which- is, which you are, which everything is. Then you fall into the existential. Then you transcend the world and enter brahman; then you enter the beyond.

One thing more: When you enter the positive, you feel it as positive only because of the negative you have experienced. When you enter the positive – this center – you feel it as the center because you know the periphery. But once entered, both are lost – the periphery and the center both, the negative and the positive both. That's why the Indian term for it is *parabrahma*. It means that which is always beyond – beyond the duality. It will be good if we translate it as the "beyondness," as the transcendence; that which is beyond the duality.

First you eliminate; first you use the negatives. Then you enter the positive. And then both are lost.

Only when both are lost do you enter totality.

So remember, we have three terms: One is *samsara* – the world, the *maya*, the illusion, the world of the objects. Then we have brahma, the seer, the knower, the world of the the subject, the subjectivity. Then we have the beyondness, the world of the the beyond, which goes beyond both. First we have the objective world, then we have a subjective world, then we have neither this nor that – the remaining. The remaining consciousness which transcends both is *parabrahma*, the beyondness, the absolute existence, the ultimate.

Begin with negation; attain to the positive; then attain to the beyond where both are dissolved...or both become one, or both are known as one...but the twoness is not there.

That which illumines the worlds of related experiences lives in the waking, dream, and the profound sleep state.
One who believes that brahma and I are one, is liberated from all bondage.

Knowing this, realizing this, encountering this, that "I am that brahma which transcends all, I am that brahma which is expressed in all, I am that brahma which is the negative and the positive *and* the beyond," one is liberated, one becomes free; rather, one becomes freedom.

This is the religious longing, this is the religious thirst: How to be liberated? How to be totally free? How to be beyond suffering? How to be in the eternal bliss?

Only when you transcend duality do you attain it.

Begin with elimination; then you will come to the positive realization. And then that also dissolves. You have to do only the elimination; then you enter spontaneously, without any effort, into the positive. Then you have to do nothing – the positive disappears itself, because it can exist only with the negative. When the negative is not there, you have only a glimpse of the positive; and then the positive disappears. It cannot exist without the negative.

So whatsoever you have to do is only the process of elimination, meditation – nothing else; all else *happens*.

Renouncing that which you are not is the alpha and omega – all – the beginning and the end.

Now be ready for morning meditation....

Different from all that constitutes the experiencer –
bhokta, *the experienced –* bhogya,
and the experiencing – bhoga, *in the state of waking,*
dream, and deep sleep.
I am the witness, the ever-auspicious,
the pure consciousness.
I am the non-dual brahma.
In me alone is everything born;
in me alone that everything exists.
And in me alone, that everything dissolves.

This sutra is concerned with a very basic, foundational attitude. Man as he is, is always identified with something or other. Identification is our habit. By identification is meant that whatsoever we see, we become one with it; whatsoever we feel, we become one with it; whatsoever we know, we become one with it. Whatsoever happens as an object becomes part of our subjectivity. There is no space between the two, no gap. This no-gapness, this no-spaceness between the object and the subject is our misery.

For example, I have pain in my leg. The pain is there in the leg; the consciousness is in the head. The actual fact is that I become aware of the pain, I am a witness to it. But that happens rarely – what happens is quite different: I begin to feel pain not as a witness, but as an experiencer. I feel this pain happening to *me* – pain *happening to* me – not pain as *witnessed by* me. If I am a witness to it, there is a gap – pain is somewhere, and I am somewhere else, and there is space. If I feel that the pain is happening to me, the space is lost, the gap is bridged. Now there is no space between me and the pain – I become pain.

This is a fiction of the mind, but we live in fictions. This is a fiction, absolutely a fiction, because pain is not happening to the consciousness; it is happening before it. It cannot happen to the consciousness itself, it always happens before it. The consciousness is just a mirror. It mirrors...but when a mirror is mirroring something, that something goes deep into the mirror. It never really goes, it only reflects. But it appears that it has gone deep into the mirror. If the mirror could become conscious, then it would feel that "this thing has come into me, has become part of me. Now this thing is me." Because the mirror is not conscious, it never falls into this identification.

We are a conscious mirror, so whenever something is before us it goes deep down inside. And a conscious mirror catches it, identifies himself with it. Pain in the leg is something before the mirror of the consciousness. But then, reflected, the pain goes in. And then consciousness becomes identified and I begin to feel pain as happening to me – not happening *before* me.

This is the distinction between a non-witnessing consciousness and a witnessing consciousness, between an identified consciousness and a non-identified consciousness. And this is the distinction between the world and liberation, between the world and the divine. This distinction looks small, but it is not. This distinction is the greatest distinction possible, the greatest distance possible.

When you are identified with any object, you are in the world. When you are not identified, you are beyond the world. So how to achieve this witnessing consciousness? Consciousness, we have – but identified. This is what bondage means: consciousness identified with things which are not part of it, and can *never* be part of it.

Consciousness is intrinsically, inherently, an outsider; it remains always outside of whatsoever is reflected in it. It always transcends whatsoever is experienced, known, felt, looked at. It is a transcending mirror. But it becomes identified, it becomes one; whatsoever reflects in it becomes part of it. This is illusory – it cannot become part of it. But it appears to have become, and then we live as if it has become part of us. This living is bound to be just a dream, based on a very illusory thing, based on a very fallacious conception, based on an absolute error. The whole life becomes erroneous, illusory.

This sutra says that unless one becomes a witnessing consciousness, one is really not awake, one is just asleep – dead asleep. One is not really conscious unless one is witnessing.

How to create this witnessing? How to achieve it? What to do?

Always divide your experience, analyze it – analysis is the method. Ana-

274

lyze the experience into its constituents, and then look within to see whether there is something which is *not* analyzed, which is not in these analyzed parts. For example, I see a flower. There is the flower, the object; then in me there is the seer, who has seen. These are two things: the flower there, and the experiencer, the seer, is here. Here inside, something – the subject. There outside, something – the object. These two are related; that relationship is the third part. The known, the knower, and knowledge – the experiencing, the experiencer, and the experience.

So whatsoever you know, experience, feel, is divided into three parts. Is this all, or is there something more which is not in this this division? Is this all, or is there something more which is missing? Ordinarily, it seems to be the whole thing: the known, the knower, and the knowledge. But this sutra says there is something more hidden behind: the witnesser, who witnesses all these three – you.

Who is analyzing? Who is trying to understand the whole phenomenon of experience? – the flower, the object; the knower, the subject; and knowledge.

And who is this, who has become aware of this whole phenomenon? This fourth is the witness.

This witness is never involved in any experience.

It is always outside.

The ego is involved, the ego becomes the knower. Or, you can call it mind – the mind is involved, the mind becomes the knower. Objects are involved – they become the known. And then there is a relationship of knowledge. But within you and beyond, is a consciousness which witnesses all these three. This process of knowing, and experiencing, and feeling is witnessed by someone. That someone, that "X," that unknown factor, is basic.

For example, you have gone to a film, or to a drama, or to a theater. You have seen something, your were there. But have you ever tried it – to be a witness of the whole phenomenon? Try it here. I am speaking, so I am the object for you. Can you transcend both? Can you look at the whole thing? Look at me – be aware of the speaker, be aware of the listener; be aware of both the speaker and the listener. Don't think about it. Just here and now, this very moment, be aware of the speaker, be aware of the listener, make these two...just put them before your witnessing.

Then who are you? Who is aware of the speaker? And who is also aware of the listener? Who is he? He transcends both – he is neither the speaker nor the listener, he transcends both. And that witnesser, if rightly understood, doesn't belong to the speaker, and doesn't belong to the listener.

Then to whom does it belong? It cannot belong to you; you are the listener. It cannot belong to me; I am the speaker. Then to whom does it belong?

It belongs to no one, but everything belongs to it.

It transcends all, but everything is based on it.

It is the hidden source of all life.

It is the hidden source of all existence. To reach this witnessing is to reach the divine, is to reach existence, the being – or the ground of being, whatever one likes to call it.

One thing more: this witness is not yours; this witness is not mine. This witness is the source of all, the base of all. So the moment you are a witness, you are not an ego. You can remain an ego only if you are identified; then you are an ego. If you are not identified with your experiences, then you are not an ego. The witness has no "I" as a center; it is center-less. So we can say that witnessing has no center, or it has its center everywhere. This witnessing is just an unknown cloud. We are surrounded by it, or we exist in it.

This witnessing is the unknown sky which surrounds us all.

This witness is a space, inner space, in which we exist, in which we are born and in which we dissolve.

Find this witness; try to find this witness in everything you are doing, knowing, feeling. You are walking on the street; be a witness to it . See it, feel it, that the body is walking and the mind knows that the body is walking. Then be a witness of both; then be a witness that the mind knows that the body is walking, and the body is walking. The mind is the subject; the walking the object. Who are you?

You can witness both body and mind – *witness.*

Then suddenly you become aware that "the body is walking in me, the mind is knowing in me." And this me is not an "I" – this is just a pure consciousness, a mirror in which everything is mirrored: the walking, the body, the knowing mind, the flower on the tree, the moon in the sky, people all around, the speaker, the listener, everything is in it.

Just like there is space outside, there is space inside – that space is the witnessing consciousness.

So this sutra says:

Different from all that constitutes the experiencer, the experienced and the experiencing, in the three realms of waking, dream and sleep, I am the witness, the ever-auspicious, the pure consciousness.

Why is this witnessing consciousness *ever- auspicious?* – because it is always innocent, pure, virgin. You cannot make it impure; a mirror is always virgin. Whatsoever is reflected is only reflected; it never gets in it, it never becomes a part of it. So a mirror remains always fresh, new, because there is no memory of the past, nothing remains of the past. The moment the object is not there, the mirror is again the same. Really, it *has* been the same; it has only reflected, and reflection cannot make anything impure. Impurity means something has gone deep, it has become part of you; then you become impure.

This sutra says that the ever-auspicious, the ever pure, the ever holy, the pure consciousness... this witnessing will lead you to the land of virginity, will lead you to the land of ever-freshness, will lead you to the land of ever-purity. Impurity is impossible.

But we all have become impure, so how does this happen? Deep down, the consciousness is always pure. Then why have we become impure? We become impure only through identification, and that impurity is also just a fiction, not a reality. You cannot become impure, you can only think that you have become. You can only believe that you have become, you can only deceive yourself that you have become.

For example, there is something in front of the mirror – something impure, dirty, ugly – an ugly thing before a mirror. If the mirror could become conscious, then it might think, "I have become ugly," because ugliness is reflected in it. The same happens to us. Ugliness is reflected, impurity is reflected, sin is reflected, and we become sinners; we begin to feel like sinners, impure, ugly – but this is only a reflection. But unless you know that this is only a reflection, how can you believe it? One has to *know* it, that this is only a reflection.

Be a witness to your experiences and you will know that the whole world is just a reflection of you; it has not penetrated you. It *cannot*; it is impossible. It can only be reflected; a consciousness reflects. Once you become aware that you are only reflecting, all the impurities dissolve. It is not good to say "dissolve" because they were never there; they *disappear*. Even to say "disappear" is not good, because they were never there.

When Buddha attained this mirror-consciousness, when he became a buddha, an enlightened one, someone asked him, "What have you gained?" Buddha said, "I have gained nothing, because whatsoever I have gained has been always with me. So how can I say that I have gained it?"

Then the man asked, enquired, "Then have you lost anything?"

Buddha said, "How can I say? It is difficult, because whatsoever I have lost was never with me. So how can I say I have lost it? I have not gained anything, because whatsoever I have come to know has been always with me. I have not lost anything, because whatsoever I have lost, was never with me. I have lost ignorance which was not with me, and I have gained knowledge which is a part of me – my nature, my very being."

I am the non-dual brahma.

In this witnessing, in this awareness, one becomes aware; one becomes suddenly aware that "I am the non-dual brahma." Why? – because this witnessing consciousness has no "I," no center, no ego. It is just an infinite space with no boundaries – unbounded, with no limitations – infinite space within. Once you become aware of it, you know this is the non-dual brahma. This is the base, the source, the ground.

In me alone is everything born, in me alone does everything exist, and in me alone does everything dissolve.

278

But this must be experienced; otherwise, it becomes just a theory, a hypothesis. Then it is a philosophy and not religion – and I am not concerned with philosophy at all. I am absolutely non-philosophical; philosophizing is just stupid. It leads you nowhere, it never transforms you; on the contrary, the more you are involved in thinking about things unthinkable, the more and more you are far from the center where, if ever something is known, *it* knows. The more a mind is philosophical, the more it goes away from existential experiencing.

I am concerned, and this *Upanishad* is also concerned with religion, not with philosophy. And this is the difference: philosophy is thinking about the unknown – which is impossible – you cannot think about the unknown; you can either know it or not know it. Religion is concerned not with thinking but with realizing, with transforming, reaching, dissolving, entering, encountering.

Religion is an experiment in one's own depth.

It is not thinking, is is not speculation.

So this "I am the non-dual brahma" is not a theory. This "In me alone is everything born, in me alone does everything exist, and in me alone does everything dissolve" is not a theory. It is an experience, it is a realization.

Don't believe it unless you know it.

Don't make it a dogma unless you reach it.

We are so cunning with ourselves, and so deceptive – self-deceptive – that we can begin to think "I am the non-dual brahma." We can go on repeating this; we can make our minds up: "I am the nondual brahma," and then we can create the illusion that "I am the non-dual brahma" without reaching anywhere.

This is a statement, not a theory. So try for that state of mind where you also can make this statement. Never before utter these words, because words are dangerous. You can autohypnotize yourself with words, and you can begin to believe them if you go on repeating them. By constant repetition you begin to feel that you know. But that is not knowledge, and that is even more dangerous than simple ignorance. From ignorance there is a path, but from so-called, false knowledge there is no path. False knowledge is a closed prison. Ignorance is an open sky, you can move from it. You cannot move from false knowledge.

So whatsoever is being said here is not to make you more knowledgeable. I am not giving you principles; I am only hinting at some truths.

But they are not truths unless they are you own truths. One's own truth is the only truth. All else which is borrowed is even dangerous – more dangerous than simple lies. Borrowed truth is more dangerous than any untruth, because you can begin to feel that this is your own, and it is not.

So remember this: All these statements are made from a state of mind, from a realization. That's why this *Upanishad* never argues about it, because how can we argue about a statement? The *Upanishad* goes on just stating – there is not argument, there is no effort to prove anything. There is no rationalization, there is no argumentation, nothing – a simple naked statement that if you do this, this will happen; if you go through this, this will come to be encountered; if you pass through this state, this will be the realization.

These are simple statements, not theories. Don't make any theories out of them; rather, make some experiments so that one day you can be a witness, and then you also can state:

I am the non-dual brahma.

I am the pure consciousness.

I am that which never dies.

I am the deathless: I am existence.

I am being.

I am smaller than the smallest;
I am also the most vast.
I am the marvelous cosmos.
I am the ancient one,
purusha – *the base of all.*
I am hiranyamaya,
the effulgent one,
the ever – perpetual.

Mind can reason, mind can think, but thinking is a limitation – and reason also. So the moment mind encounters the unlimited, the infinite, difficulties arise, because mind itself is a limitation. Mind has a window to look at the sky, but then the window is imposed on the sky, and the the sky is cut by the window. Then whatsoever you look at from the window is not the infinite sky, it is a windowed sky, a patterned sky. You have given a pattern to it; it is not real. It has been cultivated by you, and the boundaries of your window will become the boundaries of the sky.

The same thing happens with the mind:

Mind is a window to look at the world, mind is a pattern to look through. When you look from the mind, through the mind, the whole universe is distorted. You give your pattern to the universe. You look at the universe with an attitude, with a thought-system, with a reason, with a logic, with a method.

If you really are interested to know the world as it is, to know existence as it is, then throw away this mind totally, then discard this window; then don't give any pattern to your experience. Let the experience happen as it is, and don't give any limitations to it – don't cling to your stupid logic. Every logic is stupid. Why? It is stupid because that which you are going to encounter, to know, is illogical.

Logic is man-made; the universe is not.

Logic is yours; the universe is not.

Logic has all the limitations which a human mind can give to it. Logic is a by-product of humanity.

There was a time there was no humanity, no human mind, but the universe was. It existed without your mind, it existed without your logic – it existed without you! And it existed quite at peace. It will exist when you are not. If there is no mind, the universe will still exist, but the mind cannot exist without the universe. The universe is greater, existence is original; mind is just a by-product, mind is just a flowering.

The tree can exist without this flower, but this flower cannot exist without the tree. Remember this: don't go on imposing things from the flower on the tree. If the flower wants to know the tree, the flower must go deep down into the tree, into the sap of the tree, be mingled with it, be in a deep communion with it. It should not be an observer from the outside. The flower can observe the tree from the outside. The flower can look down at the tree and begin to think that the tree is ugly, because the flower has its own conception of beauty. But the flower has come out of this tree, so how can something like a flower come out of an ugly tree? And the flower is there because of the tree, and the tree is helping, every moment – the tree is giving life every moment to the flower. And now the flower has it own conception, its own mind. Now the flower says that the tree is ugly, now the flower says that the tree seems meaningless, now the flower says that the tree exists illogically.

Mind is a flowering in the universe. It is good, it is beautiful if you accept the universe as it is. It is beautiful; it a great value. Mind is a great value added to the universe if you look into the universe, not through the mind as an outsider, but in a deep communion. This deep communion happens only when you drop your patterned thinking, when you drop your windowed outlook, when you drop your thoughts, concepts, theories, reasonings, rationalizations. When you drop everything of the mind, you just become conscious – thoughtlessly conscious, free from prejudices, conceptualizations, philosophy, religion, theology. When you just become conscious and become an insider, not an outsider, when you drop into the universe with your mind purified of its patterned thinking, then you come to know a different phenomenon. If you look from the mind as an outsider, you will know only the part, never the whole; and you will not be able to connect even, to relate even to the part. Then the experience will be atomic – that is what is happening to science.

Science is bound to come – reducing everything to its atomic existence – to the minutest part. Then the whole world becomes a chaos; there is no inter-relatedness. Really, with science there is no universe.

Universe means one. Science has created multiverses. The very word "universe" means one – "uni" means one. Science has created multiverses. Every science has its own universe, and no two sciences are in any way related. Every science goes into its own specialization, more to the part, and then the whole is lost.

You can know a part, but a part is always dead.

Life exists in the relatedness of the total.

Life is always of the whole.

That's why life is holy.

Both the words mean the same thing. Holy means of the whole, belonging to the whole. The moment you begin to feel a belonging to the whole, you become holy.

But science goes on dissecting, analyzing, cutting every phenomenon into its parts. The moment you have cut any phenomenon any wholeness, into parts, you have dead parts. Life belongs to the whole; it runs through the parts, it belongs to the whole. The whole is not just a combination, accumulation, or a totaling of the parts. The whole exists in its own right. The whole is something more than its parts; only then is there life. If the whole is just the parts, then the whole is dead. The whole is alive only when it is more – more than its parts, more than its constituent parts. It must go beyond the parts, only then life is there.

That's why science cannot encounter life. The very method debars it; the very approach closes the door. Science cannot come to consciousness, because consciousness exists as a whole. For example, my hand and my mind – they are not related physically, they are related in consciousness. My eyes see and my legs move accordingly. Somewhere deep down, seeing is related to my moving. The moving center is related to my cognitive center somewhere. Where is it related?

My body has parts the same as any mechanical thing. The parts are related mechanically, but they are deeply related as a conscious unit also. That consciousness is not centered anywhere in the body; that consciousness is just wholeness. It is everywhere in the body and nowhere. You cannot pinpoint where it is, it cannot be figured out – it is everywhere. Every part of your body is conscious; every part is related in a wholeness.

That wholeness cannot be found by scientific methodology, because the very methodology is based on analysis, on cutting, on dissecting. So science will never encounter life, and science will never encounter consciousness. And science is unable intrinsically to encounter the divine in the world, because all these things – life, consciousness, divinity – belong to the whole, not to the part.

Religion is the search for the whole.

Science is the search for the part.

So science ultimately comes to the atom, and religion ultimately reaches to God, to the whole.

But mind is the difficulty, the problem. Our minds are trained scientifically. Our minds are trained analytically, and the method of analysis has some basic qualities: one quality is always to be the outsider.

For example, someone came to me last night, and he said...he was here for the first time; he observed your meditation. He came to me and he said, "This looks absolutely foolish." He is right in a way; it *looks* foolish whether it is or not. But when he says it looks foolish, he is saying something about himself, not about the meditation. It looks foolish to him. But how could he judge? He was not a participant; he was not in it, he was not doing it – he was observing.

Science observes from the outside; religion goes deep.

Religion means involvement, looking at things from inside.

A religious person will never say, "It looks foolish." He will say, "It looks strange." He will say, "It looks mysterious." This judgment shows much about the person. He can judge a thing without knowing it; he can judge a thing without experiencing it.

So I told the man, "Rethink the whole thing – whether your judgment is foolish or the persons who were doing it were foolish. Rethink it, because to judge a thing from outside is not good; it is not good, it is fallacious. To judge so immediately is not even scientific. And to judge according to one's own fixed mind and attitude, according to one's prejudices is not just." But science goes on, logic goes on, mind goes on in this way: judging everything from the outside.

From the outside you can be aware only of parts. You can see my hands, you can see my eyes, you can see my face, you can see my legs, but you cannot see me. I am something else existing inside. Parts exist as my outside. I am the inside of my parts, and that inside is the whole. Someone jumping, crying, weeping or laughing in meditation, may look foolish – but from the outside. You don't know what is happening inside him.

What is happening inside him? How can you know from the outside? If he is weeping, what is going on inside him? What is happening to the whole inside? This weeping, if you take it as a part then it is foolish, it is meaningless. If you take it as a whole, deep down something must be happening there which is being released by the tears. Deep down something must be exploding which is being thrown out by his cries and screams. Deep down something must have been moving which is shown by his mad movements. Deep down something so new is happening, something exploding, some inner energy moving through new centers. But that is something inside, and you cannot observe it. You have to go through it.

You can be a participant but not an observer in religion.

You can be be an observer in science, never a participant.

Really, for science this is a basic condition: you should not be a participant, because if you participate you are involved in it, then you become a party to it. So you must be neutral, like a judge – outside. For science it is a basic condition.

For religion, quite the opposite is the basic condition. You must not be the observer, because how can you observe anything which is inside? You can observe only the outside. You must be a participant. This is a basic condition for religion: you must be a participant.

For science, non-participation is the condition, because it is a method to observe from the outside.

For religion, deep involvement, deep commitment, participation, is a necessary condition, because it is a knowing of the inside; it is a knowing of the whole. You can know it only when you are in it.

So sometimes it happens that for a scientifically trained mind, that which looks foolish, for a religious mind may be the very wisdom. And the vice versa is also true: for a religious mind, that which looks foolish may be very meaningful, rational, and logical for a scientifically trained mind. But it you are aware of the basic difference of approach, of the foundational difference of dimension, then you can say something can be scientifically foolish and religiously wise; and something can be religiously foolish and scientifically wise. And these two are not contradictory.

That is what is meant by the strangeness and mystery of life. If we look at life as a mysterious phenomenon, then contradictions are not there. They only appear, they are related, they are complementary.

A logical approach is good in itself within limitations...an illogical approach is also good in itself within limitations.

If you are approaching the whole then approach illogically.

If you are approaching the part then approach logically.

Logic is the door to the part.

Illogic, or meditation, is the door to the whole.

Meditation is illogical; it is a jump from the mind to the no-mind. It is a jump from reason to life itself. It is a jump from thinking to existence, so how can it be logical? It is a jump from thinking to existence. It is not thinking, it is experiencing. So I will say, "Be foolish." Scientifically, be foolish when you approach religion. That foolishness pays; that foolishness ultimately proves to be wisdom. Be mad when you are approaching the whole.

Be mad, I say, when you are approaching the whole.

Don't cling to so-called sanity, which is based on the experiences of the past.

Be mad!

But this madness is divine, and this madness has a method of its own. Religious madness is methodological. Religious madness is a method to approach the whole, the mystery of life, existence itself; to take a plunge, to take a jump, to suddenly take a jump from the mind – because the mind is your past and mind is your thinking, your thoughts, your culture, your civilization, your theology.

Mind is just thoughts, an accumulation of thoughts; existence is not. And thoughts are dead, all thoughts are dead; existence is alive.

All thoughts are borrowed, and existence is always original. And all thoughts are just dust on the mind, accumulated in your movement, accumulated through your life, death, birth. Existence is ever-fresh just like a flower, fresh, flowering this very moment, a river flowing this very moment, a sun rising this very moment – existence is ever-fresh.

Don't cling to the dead mind.

Take a jump into the freshness of existence.

Existence is always here and now, and mind is never here and now. Mind is always there and then. Either the mind is in the past or it is in the future – it is never in the present. Have you ever observed it? Have you ever become aware of the fact that mind is never *here*, it is never *now*; it is always either in the past or in the future. And neither is there past nor is there future. Past is that which has gone dead, and future is that which has yet to be born. Only this moment, here and now, is in existence.

When I say take a jump from the mind, I am saying take a jump from past orientation, from future orientation. Take a jump here, this moment into the present. Existence is here; mind is never here, so they never meet. Mind never meets existence.

Mind is just like a radar – it can look far away; it cannot look just near here. Radar cannot look near; it can only look far. Mind is a radar. It is a useful thing but it always looks far away. Either the expanse must be in the past or in the future; it cannot look here and now. Here and now is just missed by the radar. It is good for looking to the future, it is good for looking to the past. It is good to go down for memory, it is good to go down for desire; but it is never good – absolutely useless – for going down here and now into existence.

Meditation means a jump – it is foolish, it is mad.

But be mad in it and be foolish in it, and then you will gain a strange wisdom which comes only to the mad mind, the religiously mad mind.

Life is a mystery; it is not a mathematical problem. It is more like poetry than like mathematics, it is more like love than calculation. It is love, not logic.

Now be ready for the madness....

I am the incomprehensible shakti *(energy),*
I am without hands and feet.
I can see without eyes,
hear without ears,
know without intellect.
Devoid of all forms, I know all;
but there is none who knows me,
the ever pure consciousness.

This has been one of the most foundational questions for a religious seeker: whether the divine can be known, whether the divine can become an object, whether the divine can be encountered, whether one can meet him. A religious mind has always been asking, enquiring, searching, seeking knowledge of the divine.

This sutra says that the divine knows all, but no one can know the divine. The divine is the knower and everything is the known. The divine is the subjectivity and everything is just an object. And the divine can never be reduced to an object - it is impossible. The very nature of the divine is subjectivity.

Soren Kierkegaard has said that subjectivity is spirituality. By subjectivity is meant the knower. When I know something I am the subject and the thing known is the object. Can I, myself, ever become an object of myself? Can I encounter myself? Can I have an interview with myself? Is it possible to make myself into an object? It is impossible. My intrinsic nature is subjectivity.

I can make anything an object, but I remain continuously, constantly, eternally, the subject, the knower. I cannot know myself in the same way that I know other things, but still I can know that I am. This knowledge must be qualitatively different from all other knowledge.

How do you know yourself? Everyone knows he is. Who has informed you about yourself? Who has introduced you to yourself? Who can be a witness that you are? Have you known yourself through the eyes? Have you known yourself through the hands? Have you known yourself through any sense? No, no sense gives information about me. My eyes say many things about other things – the whole world. My ears inform me of a different dimension of the universe – the sound dimension. My eyes inform me about the light dimension. My senses go on giving me information about the world, but no one, no sense gives me any information about myself.

All that I know about the world is through the senses, and all that I feel about myself is not at all concerned with the senses. Then who informs me? Who gives me the feeling that I am? How do I stumble upon it? How do I come to know it? And it is deep-rooted. I can doubt my eyes, because sometimes they inform me in a very misguided way. Sometimes I see something and it is not there. Sometimes I see something as real, and it proves to be a dream. Sometimes I see something, go near to it, and it is not there; it was just a deception, a hallucination.

So I cannot believe my eyes absolutely; I cannot believe my ears absolutely – every sense can be deceptive. But this information which I have about myself, this feeling, this rootedness in existence...no sense informs me and yet it is indubitable, I cannot doubt it.

Can you doubt yourself? You can doubt everything: you can doubt the divine, you can doubt the world, but you cannot doubt yourself, because even to doubt you will be needed. Even to doubt you will have to assume that you are: the doubter is. This "I," this feeling of I-amness....From where have you got it? It seems from nowhere. It bubbles up in yourself; it is not something coming to you from outside, but something from yourself.

This word "information" is beautiful. Really, when we use information, we should use *out*-formation. Only one information is there: that is the feeling of myself. This is *in*formation – it comes from *in*, from nowhere. There is no source other than me. This is the only information – the *only*, I say. But it is, and it is absolutely there; you cannot doubt it. Doubt is impossible. This feeling that "I am," is not knowledge in the ordinary use of the word, because knowledge means a division between the known and the knower. Here, in me, the known and the knower are one, they are not divided.

If we say that someone is seeing God, again it is wrong.

So how to call it knowledge? Or if we insist on calling it knowledge, we have to qualify it, we have to give a different meaning to the very word. Knowledge means: the division between the known and the knower. If I call this self-knowledge, that means: without any division between the knower and the known. How can knowledge exist without the division? So, this is not knowledge; rather, this is an existential feeling. This is less like knowing and more like being.

This being is not known by anything else – it is known by itself – so this being can never be made an object. It can never be put before; it is always behind. It always transcends; it always goes beyond. You can never put it before yourself, because you are it and you will always be standing out and out and out. In English the word "ecstasy" is good, and "existence" is also good, and very relevant.

The word "existence" means to stand out. Heidegger, Sartre, Marcel, Camus – they all have played with this word "existence." They say existence means to stand out. This being always stands out. Wherever you put it, it is always out. It is never involved in the known – it always goes beyond. The word "ecstasy" also means the same. Ecstasy also means standing out.

This subjectivity, this knower, is always deep in existence, in deep ecstasy, and it can never be reduced to an object. Why? This sutra insists that this can never be reduced to an object, because God can never be known. You have a God within you; it goes on transcending. If all objects are dissolved from the mind, then you become suddenly aware of your own being. This being has no limitation, and this being is not yours; this being belongs to the whole universe.

Without object, without thought, when you become aware of your being, you also become aware of the whole being, of the whole ground of the being. The being-ness in all existence...you become aware of it not again as a knower, because no being can be known in that way. Again you are dissolved into it, you become one with it. Again you know it as an existential feeling. So the way we express that someone has known God is wrong.

293

But language has to be used, and any word is going to be wrong. So any word can be used, because all words are equally fallacious – because all words are invented for objects, things; and God is not an object, consciousness is not an object. And there is no word for something which is known without any objectivity, as a subject. This becomes a problem.

But this is only a problem if one tries to understand it intellectually.

It is not a problem if one takes a jump into it and knows it existentially. That's the difference between a philosophical approach and a religious approach. The philosophical approach is to understand; the religious approach is to be.

So a religious mind is never searching after knowing; a religious mind is always seeking being. A religious mind means a search to be deep in God, not to know him; to be one with him, not to be a knower; to live in him, to live him, not to know him. If you are trying to know him then only your intellect will be involved. If you are trying to live him, love him, be him, then your totality will be involved. And unless your totality is involved, nothing is possible. Unless you are totally involved, dissolved into it, the ultimate cannot be known, cannot be felt. It remains always beyond. With your intellect it always escapes.

Go into it as a whole. Try to live the divine, not to know it. Try to be divine; do not try to make it an object. Only then it is known. And to be the divine, what is to be done?

We cannot do anything with the divine. We can do only something with ourselves. We can dissolve ourselves, we can surrender ourselves. We can commit a deep suicide – not of the body, but of the mind. And that deep suicide of the mind is *samadhi*.

That deep suicide of the mind is meditation.

294

I, alone, am the theme taught
in the various Vedas. *I am the revealer of the*
Upanishads, *the* Vedanta, *and of the* Vedas.
I alone am the real knower.
For me there is neither virtue, punyam, *nor sin,* papa.
I suffer not destruction, neither have I birth,
nor body, nor senses and mind.
I, alone, am the theme taught
in the various Vedas. *I am the revealer of the*
Upanishads, *the* Vedanta *and of the* Vedas.
I alone am the real knower.

Some words must be understood first. *Veda* is a very meaningful word. Ordinarily it indicates the four compilations: *Rig, Yajur, Sama, Attharva.* But that is not the real meaning of it.

The word "veda" means knowledge, authentic knowledge. The English word "science" is the exact meaning of it. Science means knowledge, authentic knowledge. When I say authentic knowledge, I mean experimented, experienced, not speculative. You can speculate, you can think without going into any experience. One can think about love and can create theories, and can create a system, but this will not be authentic knowledge. You can speculate about love, but you cannot know it that way. One has to love, not to speculate, to know what love is. One has to live it, experience it, suffer it. One has to go through all the pain, all the suffering, all the blessing, everything. One has to know the unhappiness of it, and the happiness. One has to pass through it – then only one grows in love, and then only one knows. To live is the way, not to speculate.

You can go on speculating infinitely without ever touching the reality. By authentic knowledge, by veda is meant: something which has been experienced, not speculated. That is the difference between science and philosophy. Philosophy is speculation; science is experiment. And that is the difference between philosophy and religion also. Religion is also an experiment. So we can say, philosophy is speculation about everything, science is experience, experiment about the objective world, and religion is experience and experiment about the subjective world.

Veda is authentic knowledge about the inner one. Veda is the supreme science: science of the inner one, science of the subjectivity, science of the knower, not of the known, science of the consciousness itself.

This sutra says: *I, alone, am the theme taught in the various* Vedas. All the authentic sources of knowledge talk about me. I am the theme. The divine is the theme, the absolute is the theme, the ultimate is the theme. This can be understood.

I, alone, am the theme taught in the various
Vedas. I am the revealer of the Upanishads, the
Vedanta and of the Vedas. I alone am the real
knower.

But the translation seems somewhere fallacious: I am the theme of the *Vedas*, and also I am the creator of them. This will look strange. I am the creator of the *Vedas* and also the theme; I am both. Why? – because there is no one else. The divine can talk about the divine, the divine can live the divine, the divine can express the divine.

For example, a painter paints something. The moment the painting is complete, the painter and the painting are separated. The painting becomes something in its own right. The painter can die, but the painting will live. The moment a painting is complete the painter cannot say, "I am my painting," because the painting can be destroyed and the painter can live – they become two.

So God is not just like a painter; rather, he is like a dancer – a dancer dancing. The dancer is the dance, you cannot separate them. If the dancer dies, the dance dies. And if the dance stops, there is no dancer, because a dancer is a dancer only when he is dancing.

If there is no dance then the dancer has stopped; he is not a dancer at all. And if the dancer dies there is no dance. So what is a dancer doing? He is dancing himself. He is the dance, he is the theme, he is the creator – everything. That's why India has chosen a dancer as the symbol of the divine – *Nataraj.* It is meaningful, it is significant. It shows something, it indicates.

The world is a dance of the divine. The dancer is involved in the dance, and the dance is nothing but dancer expressed.

So this sutra says: I have created the *Vedas*, but I am the theme of them. I have talked about myself, because there is no one else to talk about; there is no other reality.

For me there is neither virtue nor sin.
I suffer not destruction, neither have I
birth, nor body, nor senses and mind.

This part of the sutra is even more strange. It says there is neither virtue nor sin for me.

To a Christian mind it will seem inconceivable, because God means virtue. To the Jewish tradition, to Islam, to Christianity, God means virtue. Sin cannot be conceived in any way related to God. That's why Christianity, Jewish tradition, Islam, all have to create a second God: the devil, Lucifer, Satan, Beelzebub. They have created many names for the other god, the god of evil. But if you create two gods in the world – one of good and one of evil – you create a deep conflict which can never be reconciled.

How can two gods, totally contradictory and opposite, polar opposites, be reconciled? When? And how? – It seems impossible. Once you have made the rift, it become unbridgeable.

Who will win in the end? The devil, or God? The religious mind hopes that in the end God will win. But why in the end? Why not now? Is God impotent just now? Why cannot he win this very moment? Why in the end? And the devil goes on winning. The devil goes on winning not in the end, but just now, just here! It seems that this is just a hope; this end is just a hope, just a long postponement.

What to do with the devil? He goes on winning. So how to help good, how to help virtue? So we create a long postponement...in the end God will win. Why in the end? And how can he win in the end when he is defeated every moment? – because ultimately these moments will count. And if the devil goes on winning continuously, how in the end can God win? These defeats of the divine and these victories of the devil will count. In the end the devil seems more likely to win than God.

And how can God win if the devil is a force, an entity independent of God in itself? How can you destroy an independent force? And if you say that the devil is just a rebellious child of god, then again you make God very impotent. This child goes on winning, and God cannot do anything. And if this child is just a rebellious child, then rebellion is possible against God; some force can rebel against him.

Anyway, you create a rift, unbridgeable. And this rift creates a deep tension in the mind, because then you are also divided. Some part of your being becomes the devil and some parts divine. That's why Christianity proved so sadistic, and so masochistic – both.

Christianity created a very anti-body attitude, so torturing oneself became virtue. Really, in the West the rebellion that exists today is just a part, a reaction of the whole Christian anti-body attitude. If you go to the extreme, then somewhere the pendulum comes back, begins to come back. The body became something devilish, part of the devil in you, so you have to fight it. So Christian mystics are doing much violence to themselves – unnecessary violence, unneeded. But because of the rift between the devil and God, you have to choose in you what part belongs to God and what part to the devil.

The world, if divided into two, will create a division in you also, and then there is tension, anguish, anxiety. Silence becomes impossible; there is only a fight, a war, a continuous fight.

Look at the face of Jesus; look at the face of Buddha. There seems to be a vital difference: Jesus looks sad; you cannot conceive of a sad Buddha. Of course, Buddha is not laughing, but Buddha is also not sad. Christianity has a tradition which says that Jesus never laughed. If you look at the picture, the tradition seems right. Jesus looks sad, sorry, in anguish, in pain, in suffering. Jesus cannot dance; it is inconceivable. Jesus cannot laugh – why? The rift, the division: a constant fight within creates this sadness. Buddha is a reconciled one. The conflict has disappeared; he is now at ease with himself – nothing to fight with, nothing to fight for. He has accepted: whatsoever is, is.

This acceptance comes only if you can think and conceive, "For me there is neither virtue nor sin."

The whole of Christianity revolves around the idea of sin, original sin.

The whole of the mind is burdened by the sin Adam committed – the original sin overshadowing everything; and you are born a sinner, because Adam committed a sin. We are born in sin. Sadness is bound to come. Sadness, suffering, and ultimately a fight – how to overcome this sin?

So the basic thing becomes guilt. If I am born in sin, if I am a sinner, if sin is all around me, then guilt is a by-product. So I become guilty. That guiltiness will create sadness, futility, a life without a song, a life without a dance, a life without a laugh.

This sutra has to be understood deeply: *For me there is neither virtue nor sin.* God is not the virtuous one; God is both and neither. He expresses himself in both, and he can express himself in both because he is neither. These are his expressions, not his being.

But why put evil and good both in the divinity? The Indian concept is that good and bad balance existence; they are not contradictory, they are complementary. This conception of complementariness is very basic to Hindu thought. Nothing is contradictory, there is no deep opposition in anything; everything is interconnected and complements each other. The Hindu mind says that good cannot exist without evil, so evil is just a soil for the good to flower – a lotus flowering in dirty mud. That is the concept of the Hindu mind: the lotus out of dirty mud. The dirty mud is not against the lotus.

If you look at the lotus and the dirty mud, there seems to be no connection at all. The petals of the lotus – fresh, young, beautiful....How can you conceive of any relationship with the mud, the dirty mud? But it is born out of that; it comes out of that. This beautiful lotus is just a growth of the dirty mud. So the dirty mud is not against the lotus, but just part and parcel of the whole process. At the one end is the lotus, at the other end is the dirty mud. At one end there is Rama, at another end there is Ravana, but they are interconnected – they are two parts of one process.

We cannot conceive of a lotus without dirty mud. Can you conceive vice versa? Can you conceive of dirty mud without a lotus? It may look like vice versa is possible. We can conceive of dirty mud without a lotus, but if there is no lotus, how can you call it dirty mud? The lotus gives you the concept of beauty, cleanliness. The lotus gives you the concept of cleanliness, freshness, beauty. If there is no lotus there will be no dirty mud; there will be mud, but not dirty. The dirtiness comes into the world with a lotus flowering. That lotus comes out of that dirtiness.

The Hindu concept is of a deep complementariness; nothing is opposite. Even virtue is not opposed to sin, it is only supplemented, complemented. It is only how it is supported, and they both support a deep symphony, they both are part of it. If you can conceive of virtue and sin as one process, only then you can conceive the Indian concept of God.

A Christian god is qualitatively different from a Hindu god. For a Christian mind, a Hindu god is not a god at all. Sometimes he looks profane – a *Krishna* dancing with women looks profane for a Christian mind. A Krishna fighting, or trying to convert Arjuna to fight, looks absolutely non-religious for a Christian mind. A Jesus saying, "If someone hits you on one cheek, give him the other," and a Krishna converting, convincing, arguing with Arjuna for a war – go into war; they become inconceivable.

But the basic problem arises because of this concept of non-contradictoriness in existence. Existence is dual but not contradictory! And the duality is only in the expression, not in the ultimate source. The ultimate source remains the same. These contradictions are there, because without contradictions, without a dual nature, things cannot exist, the world cannot be. The world is there through duality.

Can you conceive of silence without noise?

Can you conceive of birth without death?

Can you conceive of beauty without ugliness?

They balance, they exist together.

They have a deep togetherness.

And you cannot deny one, and you cannot destroy one, and you cannot save one against the other. So really, many problems arise because of this choosing – one has to be chosen against the other. Look at it in this way: the whole of humankind has been trying to create a world which is without poverty. And the West has succeeded in it; it has created a world now which is without poverty. But look at the problem; it has many dimensions. One is, that whenever there is someone rich, someone becomes poor. The richer someone gets, the more someone else goes deeply down in poverty. It has existed in many dimensions. One person going up, one person going down, mm? That has been the old pattern.

That pattern has changed. Now the West is going up, the East is going down; the dimension has changed. Now the West goes on becoming richer, and the East goes on becoming poorer – one going up, the other going down. We can even conceive of a world where even this dimension dissolves. The whole earth becomes rich, but then a new dimension opens. The moment the whole earth becomes rich, everyone deep down becomes poor.

That is happening in the West. With affluence, everyone feels poorer, deep down empty, poor, just a beggar – nothing within. Everything all around...a new dimension of duality. When you have everything all around, deep down you become poor. No one else is now becoming poor because of you. You yourself, you have everything – every possession is there – and now you feel that you are poor, buddha feeling inner poverty, having everything, but not being.

When you have everything then the dimension of poverty has changed. You have everything and the being becomes poor. Now you are divided – not the world, but you are divided into two. Go on accumulating riches outside, and you will go on creating a deep valley of poverty inside. So only a rich man becomes really conscious of inner poverty.

We have created much to help the human body – many medicines, much science, many instruments, many things. This century has created much as far as medicine is concerned, human health is concerned. But are you aware that new diseases have come in? – they go on balancing. You create a medicine and a new disease bubbles up, but the balance remains the same. The balance remains the same, the proportion remains the same. You create a new medicine and a new disease comes up and brings the balance again to the same level. You create laws, you go on creating laws, and new criminal acts are invented – they go on balancing.

If we look at the world it is a deep balance, always balancing itself with

302

the opposite. So what to do? Stop fighting and poverty? No, go on fighting. But remember, it cannot be destroyed; it can only be changed from one dimension to another. And a deeper dimension may be more painful.

We solve one problem and another comes up, but the total number remains the same. The total number always remains the same. If you are aware of this totality, this duality, this complementariness, then what to do?

This awareness will tell you that this is just the dynamics of the world, you cannot change it. This is the very dynamics of the world: to be in duality, to be in antithesis, to be in a dialectical process. The world works through dialectics, through duality, and the antithesis is not *anti*. It is anti only in language – the antithesis is just a balance.

I have been studying much about intelligence, and I have become aware that if one percent of the human minds are geniuses, then one percent balances them by being idiots. If ten percent are talented, highly talented, nearly geniuses, then ten percent are highly untalented, nearly idiots, fools. Fifty percent are divided on the right and fifty on the left. And now this is a problem for psychologists: if you create more talent, you create somewhere the opposite also.

For example, in American you have come to the point where universal education is possible, but now boys and girls are dropping out of universities. This is the only country which has come to a point where universal education has become possible – a dream fulfilled, but what is happening? American boys and girls are dropping out. Everywhere in the world in poor countries, everyone is running, rushing for education; and in America they are running away from education, rushing away from education. What is happening? – a deep balance.

You have created intelligence to a high peak, now you will create foolishness to a deep valley. Only then there is balance. If you have created a highly structured society, you will create hippies – that is the balance. If you have come to a highly structured, planned society for the first time in the history of the world – everything planned, structured, patterned – you are bound to create an alternative society: unstructured, unplanned, chaotic. That gives the balance.

But we are not aware of this deep complementariness: sin and virtue are complementary.

This sutra says: *For me there is neither virtue nor sin.* It means that for me sin is not sin, and virtue if not virtue. It means that for me sin and virtue are not two opposites. It means that for me the totality is both and neither – they both complement each other and negate each other. So God is neither good nor evil; God is neutral. But the expression of the neutral is both good and evil. Expression is inevitably dual; existence is non-dual.

I suffer not destruction... because the total can never suffer destruction; only parts suffer destruction. How can the total suffer destruction?

Scientists say that nothing is added in existence, and nothing deleted. Not a single atom has been added, cannot be added. From where can you bring it... when we talk about the total, from where can you bring a single atom? Or if you want to destroy a single atom, how can you destroy it? Where can you push it? Science says that nothing can be destroyed and nothing can be created. The totality remains the same, but the parts change. A tree is destroyed, a body is dead; a flower is coming up, a tree is alive.

Things come up, things go down; things are born, things die.

But the totality remains as it is.

A tree dies because a tree is a part. When it dies it goes back down to the total, but the total remains the same. This sutra says: *I suffer not destruction, neither have I birth....* How can the total be born? This point also must be looked at deeply.

All the religions have tried to think how the world came into being. Where is the beginning? Christianity says that before Jesus Christ, four thousand years back, the world came into being, suddenly, in a week. In six days God created the world, and on the seventh day he relaxed. That's why the seventh day is a holiday. In six days he created the world – on a particular date. This is absurd, because this total cannot come out of nothing. And even if the world came into being, God was before it. So there was a world of a certain kind. God was there, so existence was there.

Hindus say this is beginningless and endless; existence is beginningless and endless. So worlds may be created and worlds may be destroyed, but existence continues. The Hindu mind says that one world is created and another is being destroyed simultaneously. A star is born and another star is dying. Our earth is just now old, and soon it will die. Whatsoever we do, the earth is going to die; now it is old. Many things will happen which will help it to die: the population explosion will help, atomic research will help, pollution will help, chaotic trend, revolutions, rebellions will help; everything will help this earth to die.

Man going to the moon is a very symbolic act. Whenever some planet dies, life tries to go somewhere else. It happens only then, never before. Whenever some planet is going to die, life begins to try to go somewhere else, to be replanted somewhere else.

Still scientists are not able to find out from where life came to this earth; there seems to be no reason how it can come up suddenly. It must have come from somewhere else. It is possible that some old earth dying, some ancient planet dying, and its sun....Even one man and one woman transplanted to this earth would create the whole thing. It may have been Adam and Eve coming from some other planet which was dying; and two are enough to create millions.

It is felt deeply that this earth is going to die soon; that is why there is so much search to go beyond this earth – to the moon, to Mars, or to somewhere, somewhere to find a home again. Life is just going to die here. Neither politicians can help us, nor pacifists. This earth is going to die. Everything born is bound to die some time. And for the earth, one thousand, two thousand years are nothing. So it may continue, but it is just on the verge. Every symptom shows that it is just on the verge. So one earth may be born, another may die.

One world may be born. When I say world, I don't mean total, because there are many, many worlds. Our world consists of the solar system: this sun and the family of this sun. We don't know. Out there are other worlds; there are many universes. We are totally unaware of them. Every day a new star is born and every day a star is dying, disappearing. But the whole remains, and the whole remains the same. It is neither born, nor is there any possibility of its being dead. It is beginningless and endless.

Lastly, this sutra says that *I have neither body nor senses nor mind*. It is easy to understand that the total can have no body, the total can have no limitation. A body is a limitation; the total is bound to be infinite. Where can it end? If it ends somewhere that means something else begins. Every end is a beginning. Your house ends then the neighbor's house begins. Your village ends and another village begins – or a forest begins. Every ending is a beginning of something else. Where can this total end? Where is the boundary? It can never be anywhere.

This is inconceivable for the mind, because the mind goes crazy if you think about it. If you think of the world ending nowhere, going on and on and on – infinitely on...the mind thinks, "Maybe if I can go on, the end may come." How can the world go on and on without any boundary where it ends? Mind cannot conceive the infinite. That is the difficulty with the mind – not with the world, not with the universe. The universe is infinite and the mind is a window. It cannot think about the infinite; it can think only about the finite.

So there is no body, because body means a definition, body means a definite limit.

Nor senses....The divine has no senses, the total has no senses. Senses are required to know the other. I can see you only because I have eyes. If you are there, then eyes are needed, but for God there is no you. He cannot say to anyone, "You." For the total there are no senses.

And lastly, mind – the divine has no mind. It appears absurd. We would like rather to think that the divine has the perfect mind, the absolute mind. But this sutra says: I have no mind. This is absurd, because we go on thinking about God on our own lines. We make God a perfect man; we conceive of God as a perfect man. So whatsoever man is, we go on perfecting in God. That's why the concept of God goes on changing with every age.

If you go back to the old Jewish God, he is angry, violent, because the whole of the human race was angry and violent; it was just coming out of the animal world. So no one objected to Moses, and no one said, "What type of God is this?" – because man was like that. So it was not a problem that God was angry. He must be totally angry – that was the only thing; he must have total power in his anger. So God could destroy cities, God could destroy the whole world if he became angry. Moses' God is a very violent God, very jealous, angry – everything! But no one thought about it, that these things are ungodly, undivine – no one thought about it.

With a Christ everything changes, because with a Christ, humanity has progressed much. Love becomes more human a quality than anger and violence. And when man begins to think in terms of love, he has to change his god again. Then Jesus says that God is love. Mm? That was the problem between Jesus and Jewish priests, because their god was angry, their god was jealous, their god was violent; and this man was saying that God is love – a different god comes into the world. We go on changing our god, because we go on changing. But our god always remains a perfection of ourselves, nothing else.

This sutra says that God has no mind, because God is not a man. With man, mind is a necessity, because man is ignorant, so he needs a mind to think about things which he doesn't know. Mind is part of ignorance. Mind is an instrument of ignorance – to know. God is not ignorant, so mind is not needed. He knows. Nothing is unknowable to him, nothing is unknown to him. The total knows, so mind is not required at all.

And it is logical that if there is no body, there can be no senses; and if there are no senses there can be no mind, because mind, senses, body, are one mechanism. Mind is the most subtle thing in the body, body the most gross, and senses in between created a duality in this also, that mind and body are two things – that is absolute nonsense. Mind is part of the body, the most subtle part, and body is just an outgoing of the mind in the gross – they are one. So man has not a body and mind; man has a body-mind, a psychosomatic oneness.

But the duality, the thinking of duality creates everywhere opposites, dualities. God has neither body, nor senses, nor mind – then what has he? To say that he has anything, will be again wrong. He has nothing; he is.

He is not a having; he is a being. He possesses nothing because he is all. He has no possessions because he is all. What he can possess? He is no-thing. When I say he is nothing, I mean he is no-thing; he is all.

Finally, even to say that he is, is wrong. We can say a man *is*, because a man can be *not*. We can say a thing *is* because a thing may be *not*. Is-ness implies the possibility of going into nothingness. We cannot say God is, because he cannot be; he cannot go into nothingness. We cannot say God is, because to say that God *is not*, is not possible. So what to say?

When we say, "God is," linguistically we are saying, "Is is." Or we are saying, "God God." "God is," is not accurate; rather, it is better to say, "Is-ness is God; existence is God." Existence and God mean the same thing. Isness and God mean the same thing. So to say, "God is," is just to repeat – it is meaningless. That's why a Buddha remains silent. He cannot say he is not, he cannot say he is, so he remains silent.

Now we must take a jump from the mind to the mindless....

For me there is neither earth, nor water,
nor fire, nor air, nor ether, akasha.
Thus realizing the nature of paramatma,
the supreme self, the one who is in the cavity of the heart,
who is without form, without comparison, advidya *the witness of all,*
beyond both existence and non-existence,
one attains the supreme self.
Thus ends the Kaivalya Upanishad.
AUM, peace, peace, peace.

For these eight days we have been doing something very strange. I say strange, because the human mind goes on asking for things of the world but never, never for something concerned with the inner being. We go on desiring objects, but never desiring our own self. That's why I say we have been doing something very strange here: not asking for things, not asking for riches, not asking for any object of the world, but asking for the inner being. Not asking anything concerning any utility, concerning any utilitarian object, but asking and desiring something of pure being, which is not a utility at all. Not going out, but coming in. That's why I call it strange.

And it has been still more strange because for these eight days we were not only asking, we were doing something – and doing madly.

This phenomenon has become rare. It was not rare in the past. A buddha was moving, and thousands and thousands of seekers were around him doing very strange things, going on a very strange journey. A Jesus was there, a Mahavira was there, a Zarathustra was there, a Lao Tzu was there...and many many people were deeply involved in knowing "Who am I?" Now, this question has become absurd – if you ask, "Who am I?" your neighbors will feel that you have gone mad. Everyone knows who he is, there is no need to ask. But really, no one knows who he is, and there is a very deep need to ask it.

But just asking will not do. You have to penetrate in; you have to break many barriers, and you have to put aside many hindrances. You have to transform your energy to make it capable of moving into a new dimension – the dimension of the inner.

So we have been doing something strange here, and very madly. And it was good to see so many people so deeply involved with themselves. Ordinarily we are involved with others – sometimes even madly; but no one is involved with himself. That is the last thing to be searched for, that is the last thing to be asked, that is the last thing to be enquired. But here, for these eight days, we were searching after our own selves.

Whatsoever you have learned here, it is only a beginning. You have to continue it consistently, persistently. No interval, no gap should be allowed. Mind is very cunning: if you give it a gap, all that you have learned will be washed away. Unless a certain point is reached where energy transforms, everything can go back.

It is just like heating water. Up to a certain point it becomes hot water, but it can fall back unless it evaporates. Unless it evaporates, it can fall back and become cold again. We also have such points inside. Unless the energy passes through those points, those chakras, it will fall down again. So you have to be aware: if you have begun something, then go on doing it. Go on digging in, go on continuously. Unless you feel that now something has changed and you have come to a point of no return, the energy cannot fall back, how can you know that your meditation has come to a point of evaporation?

There are certain signs which make you aware. One is, the more your meditation goes deep, the less and less you will feel the burden of the mind. The more and more meditation goes deep, the less and less you will be a mind. Thoughts will become rare, and ultimately they cease. That doesn't mean you become unthinking; it only means that your consciousness becomes clear, transparent, without thoughts moving continuously as clouds. Whenever you need to think you can think; but now thought becomes an instrument to you, not an obsession as it is presently.

Thoughts are an obsession without meditation.

They go on in their own right; you cannot stop them. You cannot say to them, "Now you are not needed." They move, and you have to be in them; you are not the master. The more meditation goes deep, the more you will become master of your own thoughts. You will say, "Stop!" and the mind stops. You will say, "Move!" and the mind begins to move. Once this capacity comes to you, you will not fall down again. Unless this is achieved, if you discontinue meditation, soon every result will be washed away.

Secondly, as meditation goes deep you will feel less and less desires, more and more contentment with whatsoever you have. There will be less and less desire for that which you don't have, and more and more contentment with whatsoever you have.

As meditation goes deeper, a very contented consciousness evolves.

Ultimately there is no desire, only contentment.

They are contraries, contradictories:

More desires, then less contentment.

Less desires, then more contentment.

No desires, then absolute contentment.

When you feel this deep down – there is no desire – every movement of the mind has ceased.

Desire is the movement of the mind.

When thoughts cease, desires cease; when desires cease, thought ceases – because both are movements. And a non-moving mind – quite at ease in itself, relaxed, centered in itself – is the point from where your energy transforms into a different dimension. Unless *this* mind is achieved, you remain in the world in bondage.

When you pass this point, transcend this point, you enter into another – the *Kaivalya Upanishad* was concerned with that other world, the world of the beyond.

This sutra says that you can know the divine hidden deep in the cave of the heart. You *can* know – two are the ways to know. One is, if you go on becoming more and more aware, more and more a witness and less and less a doer, then you can know that reality hidden in the heart. This path is known as *samkhya* – the path of knowledge, the path of knowing, or the path of awareness.

Make awareness a continuous process.

Whatsoever you are doing, do it with an alert mind.

Do not do it sleepily.

We are doing everything as if asleep. You are listening to me; you can listen in two ways. You can listen as if you are asleep; then you will hear the words but not the meaning. Then your ears will go on working, buzzing, but your consciousness will be absent. Or you can listen alertly – with full awareness, with an intensity of awareness, with consciousness, with a focused mind. If you listen with a focused mind, alert, conscious, aware of what is going on, then not only the words, but the meaning can also be heard.

Words don't carry meaning; they become meaningful only when you are alert. Your alertness gives them meaning. Words carry only sounds. If you are not alert, then your ears will hear, but your consciousness will remain untouched.

By being alert, I mean that whatsoever is going on is going on with full consciousness – you *know* that this is going on. Buddha walks – he walks differently; the quality is different. Outwardly, you may see that he is walking the same as anyone else; but he walks differently, because each step is an alert step. He knows it. When he is raising his leg, he knows it. When he raises his hand, he knows it. When he moves his head, he knows it. There is no movement of the body, and no movement of the mind without being conscious of it.

So Buddha has said...and he was one of those most deeply gone into the path of knowing, one who has touched the ultimate on the path of knowing, the path of awareness. He has said that no other means, methods, techniques are needed if you can practice only awareness. But then, it is hard – because we are so asleep that to talk about awareness is to talk about just the polar opposite to us. We are just asleep. Not only asleep but unconscious; not only unconscious but as if in a coma.

You have been angry without knowing when the anger has come. You have been violent without knowing when the violence has come. I have heard many people say, "I can't say why I became so angry. I became angry in spite of myself." How is it possible that in spite of yourself, you became angry? It means you were not conscious.

Buddha has said, "If there is anger, close your eyes. Feel the anger arising. Feel the anger clouding you; feel the anger coming up; go on seeing it. Do not do anything with it – go on seeing it. Then, by and by it will evaporate; then see it evaporating. First see it coming, arising, spreading – then see it going away, dying, evaporating."

Once you have seen the anger in all its stages, you will never be angry again, because your anger needs your identification. You must be identified with it, you must be not conscious of it.

So Buddha has said that if you are doing something unconsciously, it is sin. If you are doing it consciously it is virtue. There is only one difference between virtue and sin: consciousness or unconsciousness makes the difference. This is one path to enter into the innermost reality of the heart, or into the beyond, or into the *parabrahma*.

There is another. That other one is not directly concerned with awareness; that other path is known as yoga, the path of means, methods, techniques. The other is not directly concerned with awareness; it is directly concerned with some methods which create awareness. You are not required to be aware directly, immediately; you are required to do something which creates the situation in which you become aware.

For example, we have been doing in the morning, and in the night, two yogic methods. If you do fast breathing, *bhastrika*, so chaotically, then the energy inside is hit, and the energy comes up. In that awakening of energy you cannot fall asleep, you cannot be unconscious; so much energy makes you aware. Then in the second step, allowing yourself to go completely mad – and understand it: when you yourself allow yourself to go completely mad, you can never be mad; because madness can never be allowed, it happens. So if you can allow yourself to go completely mad, it shows that you are a very sane person. A madman cannot allow it. A madman is just mad; madness happens to him, it is not his will; it is against his will.

But if you can will madness, and allow madness, you will be saner for two reasons. One, that you are capable of allowing madness means you are above it, you are master of it. And secondly, if you allow it, then many many suppressed complexes will be released through it; it will be a catharsis. When so many suppressed complexes are released, when so much suppressed energy is released, it is an explosion. In that explosion you can never be unconscious. It is such a big explosion, as if your house is on fire – how can you be unconscious? You will become suddenly conscious. Your whole mind has gone mad; your house is on fire. You become suddenly aware, it is an emergency. You cannot fall asleep. Awareness will happen in this situation.

And in the third stage, when we are hitting the kundalini with "hoo".... Kundalini is the reservoir or all our energies. If this reservoir is hit, the energy begins to spread in ripples all over the body. It goes on spreading. Every fiber, every cell of the body becomes more alive, vitalized; more energy is given to it. Every cell becomes more aware and the whole body feels a sudden rush of awareness. In that rush of awareness you cannot be unconscious.

These three steps are yogic steps to create a situation in which consciousness becomes an automatic result. And then in the fourth you just wait – fully aware, conscious, waiting. What is going to happen? In this awareness happens that which is known as brahma. In this awareness happens that which is hidden in the cave of the heart. Samkhya and yoga are two ways. I have made both into one. Three steps of the morning meditation are of yoga, and the fourth is samkhya.

In the night meditation the beginning – gazing constantly, hammering your energy with "hoo!" and jumping belongs to yoga. And the last part belongs to samkhya.

In the afternoon meditation, the kirtan belongs to yoga – *bhakti yoga*. It belongs to yoga, it is a means. It again creates energy in you, it again creates a situation – it creates a situation in which awareness can happen. Then in the second stage we are waiting, and in the third, whatsoever has been felt, we are expressing.

To me, religious life is not only experience, but also creativity. You must know the divine and you must express it also, because then, when it is expressed, it can create the same thirst in others. When expressed it can hit other's sleep also; it can make them aware of a different dimension also.

When someone is dancing madly in a blissful state, in ecstasy after

315

meditation, he is creating vibrations around him. They may penetrate into anyone. They can become infectious; they do become infectious. This ecstasy can go to others also; this ecstasy can be felt. Others' hearts will be touched by it. And if you can create ripples around you, vibrations, you have served the world, and there is no other way to serve it – you have served the divine, and there is no other way to serve it.

This last sutra says: Here ends the *Kaivalya Upanishad.*

The *Upanishad* ends, of course, but your journey only begins. When you go back, remember whatsoever you have done here and felt, and make a continuity of it. If you have taken sannyas, if you have renounced deeply the nonsensical world, the absurd world, and have taken a step towards the real, towards the truth, then continuously you will have to remember this renunciation. This remembering will help to change everything around you and inside. Just remembering that now you are a sannyasin will make a lot of difference. You cannot react in the same old ways, because you are not the old man.

That's why I have given you new names, just to make you feel and remember that the old identity is dead – a new one has come into existence. And now you have to create your mind, your body, your soul around this new center.

Sannyas must now become your self.

Do, live, be, but now from this new center.

And soon, if you continue in your effort, in your awareness, you will come to a point where the transformation, the mutation happens – where you are lost forever and only the divine remains.

PART THREE

Mt. Abu

Adhyatma Upanishad

October 13th - October 21st, 1972

This is the invocation of shantipath:
AUM, let the sun be beneficent to us.
Let Varuna be beneficent to us.
Let Arya be beneficent to us.
Let Indra and Brahaspati be beneficent to us.
Let Vishnu be beneficent to us.
Salutation to that supreme, the brahma.
O air, salutations unto you, for you are the
immediate brahma, the supreme.
I shall call thee alone, the immediate brahma.
I shall also call thee Ritam and Satyam,
the law and the reality. Let them protect me,
let them protect that acharya, the teacher.
AUM shanti, shanti, shanti.

Jean-Paul Sartre has named his auto-biography, *Words.* This christening of his autobiography as *Words* is significant, deeply significant.

Everybody's biography is just words and nothing else because what is your mind? – words and words and words.... If you analyze the mind, then what are you? Just words? A long sequence, a long procession of words; this is everybody's autobiography. But if you are nothing but words, then you are not. Then you are yet unborn, then you are yet to exist authentically. Because words are just words, sounds; they mean something, but basically they are meaningless. The meaning is given to them.

And mind is just a mechanism, a natural computer. It feeds on words and then creates more words out of them. Then you go on associating those words, you go on creating principles, philosophy systems. And ultimately, where are you?

Truth is not a by-product of a long process of words. Truth is not a word at all. Truth is outside of words: truth is beyond words or below words. Truth is experience, not words. Truth cannot be said, because when you say something, language has to be used, words have to be used. And truth is not a word, so when you say it, you miss it. The moment you say it you have missed it – it cannot be said. It can only be experienced; it can only be lived. Unless you live it, you cannot know it.

But we know – that's the problem; rather, we know too much; we know more than enough. What is our knowledge? – words accumulated. You can accumulate them logically, rationally. You can create an edifice, a beautiful system, just as you can make a house with playing cards, but you cannot live in it. It is a house just in name; you cannot live in it. Out of words you can create a palace, a system, a philosophy – but you cannot live in it.

Philosophers create beautiful systems, but they always live outside of them. They cannot live in them, that is impossible. Nothing is wrong with them; the very system is such that it cannot be lived in.

An Immanuel Kant or a Hegel…they create principles and hypotheses out of words; they go on explaining the whole universe, but they themselves remain unexplained. They can explain the whole cosmos; they can say how the world was created; they can say what destiny is. And look inside them, dig deep and you find very miserable men, just as unhappy as anyone, as much in hell as anyone.

Don't believe in words.

They are the greatest deception created by humanity.

And the word has become our world: we live in it, we eat it, we write on it; the word beats in our hearts, and the word circulates in our blood. We are just a collection, a big collection of words. Mind is very miserly about words, it goes on accumulating.

But remember, the word is never the reality.

I can use the word "love," but love, the word, is not love the experience. I can go on repeating, "Love, love, love," and I can create a sort of auto-hypnosis, and I can believe that I know love because I know the word. To know the word is easy. To know love is difficult – not only difficult, but impossible, impossible not because the experience is impossible, impossible because you are incurable. Because love can come only to you when you are not. And that is the path of everything that is great, deep – love, truth, God – they come only when you are not; your non-being becomes the passage.

Someone was asking Mozart…Mozart was one of the greatest musicians of the world – rare, unique. Someone asked him, "Which music do you like most?" And Mozart is reported to have replied, "No-music, sir. No-music I like most."

Difficult to understand, difficult to penetrate, but very significant. The reply is just unique, unexpected – and from a musician. He says, "No-music is the best." Have you ever heard the music which Mozart calls "no-music"? You have heard sounds. And if sounds can be put in a system, in a rhythm, it becomes music. Music means rhythmic sounds, but sounds. If they are unrhythmic it becomes noise; if they are rhythmic it becomes music. But what is "no-music"? No-music means no sounds, silence.

Silence has a music of its own, but you cannot hear it as you are.

You are filled with words, so you can understand sounds. You are filled with noise; that's why music has so much appeal. You are so filled with noise, crowdy noise, mad noise, that when someone creates music outside you forget your noise inside. You are magnetized by the music outside. You forget yourself, you become concentrated on the music outside; that's why music is loved so much. Music is a hypnosis created by sounds, rhythms, technique. Unless your inner noise ceases; unless your constant inner talk, chattering, ceases; you cannot hear no- music.

The *Upanishad* is concerned with no-music. No-music means meditation, the state of mind when there is no noise within. Then suddenly you become aware of a silence without. When you are silent the whole universe becomes suddenly silent.

When the whole universe is suddenly silent, for the first time you are authentically existent.

For the first time you have being.

For the first time you know who you are.

No-music is meditation. No noise inside creates the possibility, the situation in which you can hear the soundless silence – which is everywhere. Just here and now it is there, but you are chattering inside; you cannot hear it. You are too engaged, too occupied; it cannot penetrate you.

Become silent, and silence begins to penetrate you. And when your silence and the silence of the universe meet, you have encountered God; you have come face to face. This is what is meant by "immediate brahma," immediate experience of the divine – when your silence meets the silence of the universe. When these two silences meet they become one, because two silences cannot be two. Remember this: Two noises are two; two silences

321

cannot be two, because there is nothing in between them which can become a wall, which can become a division. Two silences immediately become one. They cannot remain two, because where is the point which can divide them? So when your inner silence meets the silence of the universe, you are no more, neither is the universe. A new oneness…you explode into a new oneness. You *are* brahma – not really encountering, because there is no *other*.

Note this point, because the *Upanishads* are the first teachings in the world which say, "You cannot see God." All the religions go on talking about "seeing God." The *Upanishads* are the first teachings, the oldest which say, "You cannot see God, because in seeing, two are needed: you and God."

God cannot be made an object of knowledge.

God is your subjectivity, so you cannot put God before you, or there is no way of meeting God; you can only dissolve in Him; or He can dissolve in you.

Oneness is God.

When two silences meet, oneness is created.

Two silences meeting transform everything.

In this camp, we will try to create a silence within you. We have not to do anything for the silence of the universe; it is always here and there, it is always the case. Only you are missing your silence. Once you gain your silence, suddenly you are transformed into a different world, in a different being. You are no more the same – the old man is dead, and a new is born.

Creating this inner silence is all that is meant by meditation; remember this. We are not interested in teachings. Teachings are of no use in themselves, unless they are practiced. We are interested in this *Upanishad* only as a practical device.

The *Upanishad* is not, for me, some doctrine to be believed, or some system to be believed, or some philosophy to be believed. The *Upanishads* are practical guides. They believe not in changing your mind, but in changing *you*. They are not concerned with you directly, with your being.

Remember this: Knowing is your periphery, and being is your center.

Knowledge is added to you, being can never be added.

Being is that which you are already.

Knowledge is that which goes on being added to you. And it happens – unfortunately it happens for many – that their being becomes just more and more burdened with their knowledge. Knowledge is going to be piled up on you by the society, by culture, by everything.

Knowledge is utilitarian; it is needed. So everyone goes on accumulating knowledge. Knowledge is power, it gives you energy, particularly to move in the world, to act in the world; it helps, it is instrumental. But if you become too identified with this knowledge, you forget that you are more than what you know. Then you forget that you are prior to your knowledge; then you forget that your foundational being is not your knowing.

What you know is just your memory. How to penetrate this knowing and reach the innermost center which you are? – silence, no-music, no chattering, no inner talk. But how to do it? It is difficult. It is difficult because you can start a new talk inside. How to stop it? How to meditate?

You can start a new talk. That will not do. The way to do it is to throw this inner nonsense out completely, to go through a catharsis. Whatsoever goes on inside, make it outside – throw it out! Express it. If you can throw all your mind out, you create space within. In that space silence happens.

So we are not going to sit silently here with closed eyes, and make an effort to stop the inner talk, the inner noise. You cannot do it that way, you can only add something more to it. Your efforts for stopping anything inside will create more noise. So here we will be concerned with a technique of expression, not suppression. We will be throwing the mind out – throw it out completely! Throw it out so much that inside, no mind happens. If even for a single moment you can find that inside there is no mind, no talk, no words, you have tasted something of the beyond. Immediately ... *immediately* you are in tune with the infinite.

This, we are going to do; this is not a camp for teaching anything. I am not going to teach you something; I am going to help you to grow into something, to be something different. Cooperate with me, because unless you cooperate, nothing can be done.

Not only is this cooperation needed from you; you must ask, you must request, you must invite and pray, so that all the forces of the world, all the forces of the universe cooperate with you. That's why this *Upanishad – Adhyatma Upanishad* – starts with a prayer. This prayer is beautiful.

> *AUM, let the sun be beneficent to us.*
> *Let Varuna be beneficent to us. Let Arya be*
> *beneficent to us. Let Indra and Brahaspati be*
> *beneficent to us. Let Vishnu be beneficent to us.*
> *Salutation to that supreme, the brahma.*
> *O air, salutations unto you, for you are the*
> *immediate brahma, the supreme.*
> *I shall call thee alone, the immediate*
> *brahma. I shall also call thee Ritam and*
> *Satyam, the law and the reality.*
> *Let them protect me, let them protect that*
> *acharya, the teacher.*
> *AUM shanti, shanti, shanti.*

With prayer we start. Why? – because man alone is helpless. Man alone cannot do anything, because man alone is nothing.

Man is just a meeting point of millions and millions of forces. In you, every universal force is crossing. You are just a crossroads. The sun, the air, the earth, the fire, the ether, everything is passing through you. You are just a crossroads. Remember this, because then you become part of this cosmos. And this is very significant to remember, because the modern mind thinks itself to be isolated – not in tune with the universe, but in conflict, in struggle.

The Western attitude has always been of a struggle, conflict; and now the Western mind has become the universal mind. Now there exists no such thing as the Eastern mind. This *Upanishad* belongs to the Eastern mind; it existed once. It is totally different.

The Western attitude is of fighting with the universe, of conquering.

324

How to conquer nature? How to conquer natural forces? This makes man alienated – man becomes a stranger in this universe. A conqueror is bound to be in conflict. And ultimately a conqueror is bound to be violent. And ultimately, a conqueror is bound to find himself isolated, alone.

The Eastern mind is totally different. The very approach is not of fight, but of deep resonance: The universe and I are not two; I am part of it, just a wave in the great ocean. I belong to it, and it belongs to me – there is a belonging. I am not a stranger in this world, I am not forced on this world. I am not an enemy and the world is not inimical towards me. I am part of it – and not a mechanical part, but an organic part, just like my eyes are my organic part, my hands are my organic part. I touch through my hand, I see through my eyes; my seeing has become my eyes and my touching has become my hand.

The universe has become man in you.

The universe has become a particular individual in you.

You are not different from it –

You are just a wave.

And the universe is flowering through you.

This is the Eastern way of looking at the world – man in tune. That's why prayer. Prayer is a bridge, it makes you feel again at home. Even the sun is not so far away.

The *Upanishad* says: *Let the sun be beneficent to us.* Let everything be beneficent to us; let everything be a blessing to us, and a help. Why? – because truth is not yours or mine. Truth means the center of this universe. And if you are in conflict with the universal forces, you can never reach it. Only in a deep friendship, deep intimacy, the universe opens its doors for you. So prayer is just creating a forgotten intimacy.

Look at it in this way. A child is born. The moment a child is born he is separated from his mother. Before birth, in the womb, he was one with the mother. There was no separation, the child and the mother were one. The child existed within the mother as part, an organic part. The child was even not breathing; the mother was breathing and the child was alive through the mother's breath. The child's heart was not beating. The mother's heart was beating and the child was alive through the mother's heart. The child was not eating, the child was not doing anything. The child was just part and parcel of the mother. Then the child is born and separated. Then the child grows as an individual, and the child goes away from the mother.

The same happens with human consciousness. Before consciousness is born, you are one with the universe. In deep sleep you again fall into that oneness. When there is no dreaming and no thought, there is no mind; and when there is no mind there is no ego. In deep sleep you are no more, because your mind is no more. Who are you in your deep sleep? Can you say what your name is? When you are deeply, dreamlessly asleep, who are you? What is your name? There is no name, because if there is a name you are not deeply asleep. The name is just a surface thing.

Who are you? A Hindu or a Mohammedan? A Christian, Catholic or Protestant? Who are you? Educated, uneducated, poor or rich – a beggar or a king? Who are you? Man? Woman? Young or old? In deep sleep you are none of these, still you are. You cannot say that you are absolutely not. You *are*, but you are not that which you are when awake. While dreaming, while awake, you are a mind; while deeply asleep, you are a no-mind. The mind is lost, dissolved, but the being is.

Deep prayer gives you this feeling of no-mind, of deep oneness, as if the whole universe has become a womb; you have become just a child in the womb of your mother. The whole universe has become motherly, no conflict, just prayer, just a feeling, and a trust.

Prayer is a trust.

The child in the womb of his mother cannot distrust – or can he? How can he distrust? He trusts his mother totally. He is no-mind, so how can he doubt, how can he distrust? Whatsoever the mother is, is good, is beneficial.

When you pray, you are throwing yourself back into a motherly universe; you are back into the womb of the world, of existence itself. And you trust; this trust is shown in the prayer. The sun will be beneficial, the air, the earth, everything. All the forces of the universe will be helpful. This is a deep trust.

How does it work? What is the mechanism of it? Is it that all these forces are going to help you? No. No one is going to help you, but the moment you create this trusting, this prayerful attitude...once you create this bridge, all the barriers are withdrawn. Those barriers were created by you; now they are withdrawn. You are not in fight; you are ready to surrender. You are not going to conquer; you are ready to surrender. You are ready to withdraw your ego.

They are not going to help you positively, but now negatively all the problems, all the barriers, all the hindrances that were bound to be created by your ego will not be created anymore. Now you will not be your enemy. Understand this deeply: these forces, once taken as deeply related with you – intimate, friendly, homely – and the whole universe taken as a home, a motherly womb, then your fighting attitude dissolves. Then your conflicting mind dissolves. Then your violence, then your ego – the effort to *be* constantly this or that; the very becoming – dissolves. And if you have no ego and a prayerful mind, suddenly – with full awakening – you fall into deep sleep. This is the mystery: Suddenly, with full awareness you fall into deep sleep.

That's why the *Upanishad* says, constantly declares, that *samadhi*, the ultimate ecstasy which is achieved by meditation, is just like deep sleep, with one difference: and that difference is awareness. In deep sleep you are unaware, unconscious. In samadhi, in ecstasy, you are conscious, aware. But the phenomenon is the same: in deep sleep you become part of the cosmos; in samadhi, ecstasy, you become part of the cosmos. In sleep you are unconscious of what is happening; in samadhi you are fully conscious. And once you can become consciously a part of this universe, you have achieved the goal.

So from tomorrow morning we will try to reenter the womb of the universe by dissolving ourselves, by throwing away the main disease of the human mind, the ego – by surrendering, by being receptive.

We are not going to conquer the truth; rather, we are going to allow the truth to conquer us.

Now, for some instructions for the morning meditation:

First, don't be serious at all. For this whole camp, don't be serious at all. I consider seriousness to be a fatal disease, so please don't try to be long faces. Why do I particularly say this? – because religious people are usually trying to be that. Don't be serious. Be more and more laughing, enjoying like small children; because before the divine force we are small children. So don't be serious. You cannot approach the divine force with a serious, sad face – that's a barrier. Laugh and dance and enjoy like small children, and you can enter the temple very easily. The doors are always open for children – be childlike.

Jesus is reported to have said that only those who are like children will enter the kingdom of God. And look what Christians have done: they have created a very serious, sad religion – Jesus on the cross, a weeping religion, crying. Christians say that Jesus never laughed. This is unbelievable, because the man who said, "Only those who are like children will enter the kingdom of God," cannot be a man who never laughed. Vice versa can be believed: that he continuously laughed, never stopped laughing, even in his sleep. But this cannot be believed, that he never laughed.

Be like children. Forget your ages, your experience, your knowledge; throw them all away, wholesale. Don't try by and by to throw them away, because unnecessary time is wasted. Just *throw* them; forget them. You may be someone – everyone is someone; if not in other's eyes, in his own eyes, everyone is someone; you *must* be someone – here, be nobody; forget. Leave your identities outside the campus ground. You may be a doctor, you may be a professor – leave all these diseases outside. You may be a rich man, you may be a politician – there are thousands and thousands of types of diseases. Please leave them outside. Here, come like small children. Then something is possible; otherwise, nothing.

So the first thing, be completely non-serious.

The second thing: for all these eight days, laugh as much as you can. Why? – because you don't know the mechanism of the mind; suppressed energies can be thrown out in many ways. Laughter is the easiest. Any energy...try it. Someone has abused you, you feel anger coming in. Immediately laugh! And this same energy, the same energy which was going to be anger, will become laughter. You are sad, something has happened; the moment you remember you are sad, immediately laugh.

Don't wait for someone to help you – laugh. And suddenly you will feel the change: The same energy which was going to take a shape, a sad shape, is transformed into laughter; it has been released. The laughter I give you is a technique of release, and don't try to be miserly about it. And don't try to find any reasons for it; no reasons are needed. Take it as a help for meditation and the whole thing takes a different dimension.

Thirdly, for all these days to come, remember one thing constantly, that you are to create a situation in you in which the divine can be invited. So don't do anything, don't behave in such a way that the situation is disturbed. What do I mean? Be more graceful, be more loving, be more compassionate, so that you can create a situation in which the divine can become a guest. Be a host. Just think of it – the divine coming to you as a guest. What will you do? How will you behave? How will you clean your house, how will you celebrate? How will you create space in your house?

Constantly, for all these eight days, remember this, that you are going to be a host, a host to the divine, so behave always thinking of that.

Remember, your laughter can become many things. It can be violent, it can be angry, it can be insulting to someone – then you are not behaving like a host. Your laughter must become a grace; it must not be insulting to anybody. It must not be insulting, disturbing. It must not create something which can become a barrier. So do whatsoever you like, but constantly remember that in these eight days, any moment the divine can enter into you. Any moment the divine can enter, so remember that you are ready to receive.

Don't talk much. Fourthly, don't talk much. If you can be silent completely, that's better. If you cannot be, then talk less and less. Be telegraphic. Use only as many words as are absolutely necessary. That will conserve energy. Our talking is very much a wastage. Conserve energy; don't talk, don't read. In the morning we will be doing meditation, and in the afternoon, and in the night. The remaining time, be more and more silent, happy, blissful. Sit somewhere, don't waste time in talking, and just wait.

Remember this word, "wait." Everyone knows the meaning, but no one knows the experience. Or sometimes when you really wait – you are waiting for your beloved or your lover to come – you are a different man, a different quality enters into you. You are waiting for your beloved; someone passes by the door, you just become eyes. The whole energy is transformed into eyes. Someone knocks on the door, you become attentive; the beloved may have come. Even the rustling of the leaves outside – dry leaves falling on the ground – and you feel the beloved has come. You are constantly alert – alert but not tense, alert, but waiting.

For all these eight days, wait. Do meditations, be happy, and wait. Don't be impatient. That's what I mean; be alert and not tense. Don't be impatient!

You cannot force the guest to come.

You can only invite and wait.

So give the invitation and wait: any moment the guest can come, and if you are not alert you may miss the moment. Any moment the guest can come – and you are angry, and talking to someone else; you may miss him. Any moment the phenomenon is possible; but if you are not there, you may miss for lives. No one can say when the next moment of such opportunity will come. Wait.

And lastly, meditation needs you in your totality. Nothing less will do. If you withhold something, and just do it halfheartedly, it is better not to do it, because the whole effort is useless. You will be simply tired and nothing will happen. So why unnecessarily tire yourself? If you are half in it you will be tired. And if someone feels tired – remember this, and find out – he will be half in it. If you are totally in it, you will be refreshed, not tired. This is the difference. If you are *totally* in it – nothing has been retained, nothing has been withheld; you were in it totally, the doer was not standing outside; the doer has become the doing – then you will come out of it fresh, fresh like the dew in the morning, fresh like a rose just opening; fresh, full of energy, light, dancing...blessed. And not only blessed, in such a state of mind that you can bless others.

But that happens only when you are total in it; it never happens when the major part is just standing, and only the minor part has moved. Then there is a tension between you standing, and you moving. Then you have become two, then you are split. That split, that inner tension between two, creates tiredness. You feel exhausted, not vitalized. You feel just as if your energy has been sucked out. You will feel it. So whenever you feel it, go deep and ask: Are you split into two? Divided? Is the effort partial? Then either stop completely; don't do it – that's better, because you are not deceiving yourself; it is honest – or, be totally in it; move into it. When you move totally into it, it has a different quality. Suddenly there is no tension, no conflict, no struggle within. Your whole being has gone into it.

And you have never gone into anything totally. You have not loved totally, you have not observed totally, you have not done anything totally – always partially. That's why your life is just moment-to-moment exhausted, you feel as if you are dying every moment – no beauty, no flowering out of it, just death. Out of lie, only death? That shows what you are doing with yourself.

Otherwise, life is every day, every moment, a new flowering; every day a new achievement, every day a new height and a new depth, every day more life. And if you can go on moment to moment moving totally in your life, death itself becomes the deepest experience of life. There is no death then. But it is difficult to move totally in anything.

At least try this meditation. If you can move in meditation totally, then you can also move in other dimensions totally.

And a total life is a religious life.

Religious life doesn't mean any ritual, doesn't mean any formalized religious worship, doesn't mean any religious affiliation; it means energy moving in its totality. And when you move totally, you become holy. Why? – because all that is known as sin is possible only when you move in parts.

You can love someone totally, but you cannot hate someone totally – that's impossible. You can be compassion totally, but you cannot be anger totally. Really, a very strange phenomenon happens. If you can, just try to be totally angry: suddenly, when the anger comes nearer and nearer to its totality, it will change into compassion. If you can try just to be angry totally, with your full being, you will reach to the ninety-ninth degree of anger. Then if you move more, just nearing a hundred percent, suddenly you will know that the anger has disappeared. And the object of your anger has now become the object of your compassion.

Anger can never be total. I define sin as that which can be done only partially, with only one part; and I define virtue, *punya*, as that which can be done only totally. If you do it partially, it cannot be done. The sin cannot be done with your total being, and virtue cannot be done with your partial involvement. You have to move with your whole being, and when the whole being moves into something, you become holy. This is what I mean by being a religious man.

Wait, try for these eight days. The thing, the happening is positive for everyone. It is also possible for you; no one is excluded, everyone is called and invited. Be courageous and take a jump. We start with a prayer; we start with a surrender to all the universal forces. Let them be beneficent to us. Let their blessings be with us.

Enough for today.

*In the cavity of the heart, which is situated
in the body, dwells the unborn who is eternal.
The earth is Its body. It dwells in the earth,
but the earth does not know It.
Water is Its body. It dwells in water,
but water does not know It. Fire is Its body.
It dwells in fire but fire does not know It.
Air is Its body. It dwells in the air,
but the air does not know It. The sky is Its body.
It dwells in It, but the sky does not know It.
The mind is Its body. It dwells in
the mind, but the mind does not know It.
The intellect is Its body. It lives in the
intellect, but the intellect does not know It.
The ego is Its body. It dwells in the ego,
but the ego does not know It.
The consciousness is Its body.
It dwells in the consciousness,
but the consciousness does not know It.
The unmanifest is Its body. It dwells in the unmanifest,
but the unmanifest does not know It.
The indestructible, the akshara, is Its body.
It dwells in the indestructible, but the
indestructible does not know It. Death is its body.
It dwells in death, but death does not know It.
He is the innermost self of all living beings.
All his sins have been destroyed
and his is the luminous god Narayana.
The body, the senses, et cetera,
are objects which have no soul.
The projection of the ego on these, is adhyasa, illusion.
Therefore the wise man should destroy this illusion
by having faith in brahma.*

Man is a periphery, but also a center. Man is a circumference, but not only that. Your body is your circumference, but not you.

This sutra is concerned with the identification of consciousness with the body, identification of the center with the periphery. The body is just your abode, just a house – not even a home, just a house. You *are* in it, but you are not it. But the mind believes itself to be the body. That is known as *adhyasa*, illusion, projection.

Why does this mind take the body as identical with it, as one with it? The nearness, the constant nearness, the intimacy between the two, and the body begins to be reflected in the mirror of the mind. Constant association – not only in this life, but of many lives – and by and by you become one with that which has been in association with you. It becomes a habit.

For millions of years consciousness has existed in bodies, and because of that, it is identified with the body. This identification is the only error, the only ignorance, the only sin. For the Eastern approach, this is the original sin, to be identified with the body. How to be non-identified again? How to be aware that you are not your body, you are not your mind? How to go in and find the forgotten center? It is always there, you are standing on it; you are it! But your eyes, your senses have taken you far away; you have gone on a journey.

This journey is very miraculous, it is like a dream journey. You sleep in Mt. Abu, and in the night you dream you are in London, or in New York, or in Calcutta. You have gone on a journey in the mind. The journey ap-

334

pears to be actual, real. You cannot remember in your dream that this is a dream. The moment you remember this is a dream, the dream will be broken. This is a basic condition of the dream, that you should not remember it as a dream. The dream must be taken as reality; only then the dream can continue, that's the basic condition. The dream must appear as real; otherwise, it is broken.

So in the night when you dream, the dream appears not only real, but really more than real. Real life seems pale before it; the dream is more colorful, more intense, more alive. You can go on a journey in the dream and still you continue to be here in Mt. Abu. In reality you remain in Mt. Abu, but in the dream you have moved. Nothing has moved, only the mind has moved.

The whole world, for the Eastern mind, is just a dream journey – you go on moving. You remain constantly at the center, but you go on moving to the periphery, to the circumference. You look at some beautiful face, some proportionate body...it appeals; the mind has moved. Now you are not at your center, you are not at your home; you have gone away. Now you will follow, your mind will move. Any desire is a movement, any motivation is a movement – a movement of the mind.

You see a beautiful car, or you see a rich palace, and the mind starts desiring, you start moving. You remain at the center, but the mind is not there. You have forgotten the center; now the mind is attached with the objects of desire. Those objects of desire become your clinging. That's why the mind goes on and on, out and out – and you are at the center. This creates a division; this divides you in two. And because you never return to the center, you never go back to it, ultimately you forget that you have a center.

The more civilized, the more cultured, the more educated the world becomes, the more it is centerless. Everyone is just a circumference – the master is missing. The house is there; the center is not there. And even if you try to reach the center you cannot reach it because you don't know how to reach it. And the ways and the means you try to reach it really are not means and ways. They are barriers, because you try to reach the center in the same way as you reach the circumference. You know only one way: how to move to the circumference, how to desire.

You desire riches, you desire power, you desire facts – you desire so many things. The mechanism of desire is that you desire something which you have not. You desire something which can become possible only in the future, never in the present! Desire is meaningful only in reference to the future. You cannot desire immediately, here and now; you will need time. Desire needs time to move. So you desire for tomorrow. You say, "Tomorrow," or "In the next life this will happen. This I would like to happen; I hope for it." Desire is basically future oriented, and desire means something which you don't have.

This mechanism, if you apply it to the inner journey, will become a barrier. This mechanism cannot help, because the basic situation differs; not only differs, it is absolutely diametrically opposite. Your being, your center is not something to be achieved in the future, it is here and now. It is already the case – you can have it immediately! No time is needed to move to it; really, no movement is needed.

Just an awareness and you are there.

You have not moved away, you are just unaware.

You have not gone anywhere so that you have to come back.

You have never gone in reality, only in dream.

You are sleeping in Mt. Abu and dreaming of London, and someone suddenly wakes you. Will you be awake in London or in Mt. Abu? Or will you say, "Wait, I am in London, and now I need to come back to Mt. Abu?" No, from a dream, if you are awakened, you are suddenly here. The dream world, the dream journey disappears completely. You have not come back, because you have never gone away.

Your being, your center is here and now.

It cannot be made the object of desire.

You cannot desire it, and if you desire it, you will miss.

Your very desire will become the barrier.

Lao Tzu says, "Do not seek; otherwise, you will miss. Do not seek, and find." This looks absurd! Do not seek *and* find, looks illogical; it is not. It looks illogical because we know only one logic: the logic desire. If some-one says, "Do not seek riches and you will find," it is illogical, you will never find. If someone says, "Don't long for worldly things and you will find them," nonsense; you will never find them. You will have to seek; then too, it is difficult to find them.

But it is not illogical for the inner journey. Note it, understand it deep-ly: the inner journey is just the reverse – from the center to the periphery, this is the way. Create an object of desire and then move towards it – just the reverse is the way which goes in. Don't create any object of desire, and don't move – and you will reach it, because you are already there.

Any movement anywhere, and you will miss your center. No movement and you are there, suddenly awakened.

Because we know only one logic, one method to reach a certain thing, we go on applying it towards the inner journey. That creates hindrances – they are self-created. Nothing is to be done to reach the center. I repeat, nothing is to be done to reach the center – it is there. If you can be in a non-doing moment you will find it. Or, we can say:

Non-doing is the doing for the center.

Non-desiring is the way for the inner center.

Just being, not becoming, is the gaining of it.

But the mind will ask, "What to do?" Even if I say, "Don't do anything," the mind will constantly go on asking, "But how? How not to do any-thing? What to do to achieve this non-doing, this non-action? How is it to be achieved?" And "how" means that something is to be done.

So one secret I will tell you.

All the techniques of meditation, and the one which we will be doing just after the talk – *all* the techniques are really just toys to play with, be-cause the mind goes on asking, "What to do?" So the technique supplies you: Do this. By that doing you are not going to reach the center, but by that doing, suddenly you will be exhausted. Suddenly, totally moving in that doing, the doing will stop. As I said last night, you cannot be angry totally. If you try to be totally in anger, anger will disappear and compas-sion will arise. You cannot be in hate totally. If you hate totally, at the climax, hate will disappear and love will arise. You can try to be in love to-tally; the same will happen.

If you do, in no doing can you be total – your being remains out of it. You go on doing a certain thing, your being remains out of it, it can never be total. You walk – can you walk totally? You cannot, because at a certain inner point is non-walking; it will never walk. Even if you go on to the moon, it will never go anywhere; it will remain there inside, just sitting there.

That's why if you love and your love is an act, an action, then your love, too, cannot be total. If you are "doing" love, if you are making love, love cannot be total. Because no action can be total – the being remains out. The love can be total only if you become love. It is not a doing; you *are* love. You are not making love, your very being is love. That's why hate cannot be total, because your being can never become hate. You can hate someone, but your being can never become hate; your being *can* become love.

— No doing, no action can be total. —

Only being can be total.

So I will suggest a method to do, and the trick – I may be allowed to call it a trick. And the trick is this, that if you go totally into it, suddenly a moment will come when all doing will cease, all effort will cease. And you will be thrown back to your center, and there will be no doing, no effort – simple existence, innocent existence, just being.

Tankar, one Zen master was standing on a hill, just standing. Three persons were walking, just taking a morning walk, so they started talking about Tankar. What is he doing there? The first one said, "Sometimes he goes there to find his cow. The cow it seems, didn't return in the night, so he has gone there, and he is just looking from a high point to see where the cow is."

But the second one said, "This does not seem right, because Tankar is just standing without moving. If he was searching for something, he would move. His face seems fixed, and even from this faraway point, we can infer that his eyes are closed." The second one said, "I propose another hypothesis: He is not looking for his cow; rather, he is waiting for some friends who might have accompanied him, but are left somewhere behind. He must be waiting."

The third one said, "He cannot be waiting, because if someone waits, sometimes he looks back. He never looks back; he is just standing like a statue. So I propose a third idea; he is meditating."

It was difficult to decide and they argued. So ultimately they decided, "We must go to him and ask what he is doing." So they went. They asked Tankar, "What are you doing?" The first one said, "Are you in search of your cow? The cow has not returned home?"

Tankar is reported to have said, "I have no home in this world and nothing to miss. Who has said to you that I have a cow? The cow is there, of course, but I don't have it; so there is no question of finding it, searching for it."

So the second one was delighted, and he said, "Then my hypothesis is going to be right. You are waiting for some friends who are left behind?" Tankar laughed and said, "I have no enemies so I cannot have friends. And I am alone so I cannot leave someone behind. I came alone in this world, I am alone in this world, and I will leave this world alone. So I am neither disturbed by enemies nor by friends."

Then the third one was, of course, delighted. And he said, "Now, nothing is left, and my hypothesis is right. You are meditating, are you not?" Tankar said, "I am not meditating, because really I am not doing anything. I am just standing. I am. I am existing, not doing anything."

But this *is* meditation. Meditation is not doing something. But you cannot take a jump immediately into non-doing. So I suggest that you make your doing total. Move into it so deeply, and so totally that suddenly the doing drops, and you alone are left, just existing.

Just like a tree - of course aware, but just like a tree.

Just like a flower - aware, but just like a flower, existing.

Just like a stream flowing - aware, but just like a stream.

No mind, just you alone, no thoughts.

When there are no thoughts you cannot move from the center. You move through thoughts. Thoughts are the way towards the periphery, and no-thought is dropping back to the center.

Now I will tell you something about the technique we are going to use.

Four steps. First step, ten minutes fast, chaotic breathing with no system. This is not a yoga exercise...chaotic, anarchic. Why? – because if you use any systematic breathing, any rhythm, the mind can control it. Mind can control any system. Mind is the great systematizer. So we are here to break the systems, the system of the mind. So breathe chaotically, like a madman – fast. Take the breath in as much as you can and throw it out – fast, with no rhythm; so that the mind is just shocked. And breathing is a great device to shock the mind.

You must remember that with every emotion, breathing changes. And every emotion has its own system of breathing. When you are in love, breathing is relaxed; when you are angry, breathing can never be relaxed. When you hate someone, breathing is different; when you are in compassion, breathing is different. When you are at ease, breathing is so silent that you cannot even feel it; when you are tense, breathing cannot be silent – you can feel it.

This chaotic breathing belongs to no emotion. So simply by doing it you transcend emotions, the mechanism of the mind. And the mind is just thrown off; it cannot continue. Ten minutes of mad, fast breathing.

The second step is a deep catharsis. You have to throw yourself out – the mind has to be thrown out. Laugh – but madly, totally; cry, weep or whatsoever comes to your mind – but madly. Jump, dance, do whatsoever comes to you; and if nothing is coming then too, try something, because mind is a long suppression. So sometimes you feel nothing is coming, start; choose anything – laugh, cry, scream, jump, dance – but do something; don't just stand there. Do something, and whatsoever you are doing, do it exaggeratedly.

The second step you must throw away your whole civilization, your whole culture. Just be like children with no fear – the fear of the others. Your eyes are to be closed; you have to use a blindfold.

In the third, when all the nonsense that is suppressed is thrown out, when all the madness is thrown out, you have to use a mantra. The mantra is the sound of "hoo, hoo" – meaningless. It is just a sound with no meaning attached to it – just "hoo." It is not "w-h-o"; it is "h-o-o, h-o-o." Loudly you have to make it; and dance with it, and move in it totally, so that you are exhausted completely.

And in the fourth step, you are not to do anything. You are just to fall down, and be as if dead....

By knowing oneself as the individual
witnessing self of the intellect, and all its moods,
and cultivating such feelings as "I am that,"
one should renounce any identification with all
things except the self.
After ceasing to follow others,
one should create a distance with one's own body.
Then one should stop following scriptures and give up one's
identification with the self also.
When a yogi is rooted in the self,
his mind is destroyed by following right method,
right listening, and his first hand experience,
and by seeing others as his own self.
He then, contemplates the self, inside the heart,
without giving an ear to what people say,
withdrawing his attention from the objects of the senses:
sound, touch, sight, taste and smell collectively;
and he does not give in to sleep or
forgetfulness of the self.

The word "witnessing" is one of the most significant words, particularly in Eastern spiritual alchemy. This word is a key word. So we must understand what witnessing means.

We act, we do something, and the moment we do it we become the doer – you walk, you become the walker. But there is one more possibility – to remain a witnesser, to remain a witness. Walk, eat, or do whatsoever; don't be identified with the act, don't become one with the act. Remain a witness. Walk, eat, or do whatsoever; don't be identified with the act, don't become one with the act. Remain a witness, an observer, looking from afar. You are walking; remain a witness to your own walking, don't be identified with it. And suddenly, if you can remain in witnessing, you will feel the body is walking, not you. You have never walked – how can you walk? Only the body can walk.

You are eating. If you can witness this act, if you can observe the very process of eating.... The body eats. You have never eaten; you have always been on a fast. The consciousness inside has never eaten anything. How can the consciousness eat? That is impossible. Hunger belongs to the body, the food goes to the body not to the consciousness. Food is a fuel. Your body is a mechanism, it needs fueling constantly – water and food – but you are not your mechanical body.

Look at it in this way: You are driving a car – the petrol goes into the car, not into the driver. The body is just like a car; the only difference is that your driver, you, cannot come out of it. That's why you become identified with it. If a boy is born in a car as a driver, and is not allowed to move out, he will become identified with the car. When the car is hungry, the boy will feel "I am hungry."

The body is just a vehicle. You are born in it, and you have never been out of it; that creates the problem. There are ways to be out of it. And once you are out of your body, then you will never be identified with it. One out-of-body experience will make you free of the identification that you are the body. Then you will know you are the driver.

And this witnessing is the process of going out of the body.

First, one has to destroy the identification; only then you can move out. You have to destroy the inner clinging with the body, and then you can move out. If you go on clinging with the body you cannot go out of it – and it is not difficult to go out of it. The out-of-body experience is easy, and it is beautiful to have it. It is worth experiencing, because once you can feel yourself a little bit out, the body becomes different. Then you can never feel yourself *as* the body. Then you will feel *in* the body, but never as the body.

Witnessing is the method.

Whatsoever you are doing, remember you are not the doer. Here, you are listening. Just now, I am talking. While I am talking, I know I am not talking; I am a witness to my talking. The talking is done by the body, by the mind; it is a mechanical thing. I go on witnessing myself – not as the talker, but as the witness of the talk. If you can also do this while listening – if you are not identified with the listener, with your mechanism; if you can witness, if you remember yourself as the observer of listening – if you can observe your own listening, if you can look at your own listening as a witness, suddenly a new point of consciousness arises in you. And this point has to be created continuously; only then will this point become crystallized.

So whatsoever you are doing – laughing, laugh, but be a witness also. When someone else is laughing, you are a witness; when you are laughing, be a witness to it also. Look at it as if someone else is laughing. Run, and be a witness. Do anything, go on witnessing it. Witnessing can continue with your usual day-to-day life; there is no need to ask for time. Whatsoever you are doing – taking a bath, eating, whatsoever, any trivial thing –

remember only one thing, that "I am not the doer, I am just a witness." This will create in you a new consciousness.

That's what is meant by being an actor in life. One man is acting as Rama, another is acting as Ravana. They fight on the stage, but they remember: Rama knows he is not Rama; he is only acting, doing a part, and he remains a witness. He is not identified with what he is doing. If you can take this whole world as a big stage, a big drama, and if you can perceive yourself as acting, then you can become a witness. And if you can witness, you have gone beyond, you have transcended.

Look at life as a drama – it is. And once you can look at it as a drama, you will feel a different energy arising in you, and a different mind being born. That different energy, that different consciousness, will help you to go out of the body very easily. And if you can go out of your body, you can go out of the world, because world is nothing but a big body.

Your body is just part of a big body – the world. If you can go out of this capsule body, you can go out of the cosmic body. Then there is no problem, the process is the same. Once you can jerk yourself out of the body, you have gone out of the world. Then you can come back, but then you will not have to remember that this world is a drama – you will know. That will be the difference: you will *know* it is a drama. Then you will not have to remember that you are acting and you have to witness – you *will* act and you *will* be the witness.

While meditating, continue witnessing. Your body is dancing; don't get identified – and there are two ways of getting identified. When you are dancing you feel that you are dancing – this is one way. When you are dancing, you feel "What will others say if I dance?" so you stop – that too is identification. In both the cases you miss the point. Dance, dance as madly as possible, but still remain witnessing; still remain constantly aware of an inner center which is not dancing, only the body is dancing.

There is a method, a Sufi method know as dervish dancing. Sufis dance. Their sect, a particular sect of Sufis is know as the whirling dervishes. You might have observed small children whirling, dancing round and round and then getting in a whirl. They get dizzy and their parents will stop them, check them, prevent them: "Stop! You will get dizzy! You may even get nausea!" But small children often like it very much, and the reason is that small children are still not too much in the body. They are entering by and by. Remember this: when a child enters into the womb, he has to adjust; the soul has to adjust with the body. It takes nine months, but still it is not completely adjusted. When the child is born, then by and by the soul adjusts. And small children like whirling. Why? – because when they whirl, they get a deep kick, and in that kick they again feel themselves beyond the body. And that's a beautiful experience – that's why they like it.

Studying this whirling of children, Sufis have developed a method, a meditation method – they turn, whirl. If you go to them, they will tell you to dance, and go on in a mad whirl, and remain a witness – as if a wheel is moving, and the axis is there and on the axis, the wheel is moving. The axis is just non-moving, and the wheel moves on – just like a wheel of a cart, the wheel goes on moving. It moves on the axis which is unmoving, non-moving. The axis remains constantly in one position, centered, and the wheel moves on it. Whirl like a wheel, and remember your witness inside as a center. Suddenly you will feel you are the center and the body is just a wheel.

If you can feel this, you are separated – you have become different from the body. You have know that the center and the periphery are different. Once you know this you will be a different man – and this is not knowledge, this is not information; this is a lived experience.

So while doing meditation here – just now, after this, we will be doing meditation – you will be jumping and crying and screaming and staring at me, remain constantly a witness. Feel yourself jumping, screaming, crying, "hoo! hoo!" staring at me.

But remain a witness to the whole thing.

Know that "the body is jumping, the mind is crying, I am silently standing inside." When the body is jumping and crying and in so much movement, and you are standing still, inside, you will be thrown out of the body. Sometimes the balance will be lost, and you will be out of the body. Even if a little bit you miss the body, and your body and you go on in different directions, you will become aware of the deepest experience *vedanta* can teach you – or any religion can teach you. The deepest experience is to know that "I am not the body, I am not the mind, I am the self." And ultimately even not the self – "I am the no-self, or I am the universal self."

Now we will be doing out last meditation of the day. First, let me explain it to you. The process is very simple: I will be standing or sitting here; you have to stare at me constantly. Don't waver your eyes; just stare at me. Go on jumping and crying, "hoo!" Both your hands will be raised towards the sky. Go on staring at me so that an inner communion is established. And remember yourself as a witness of the whole process. Don't inhibit, and don't withhold yourself. Move totally, so the wheel moves completely. And with the complete movement of the wheel, you can stand still inside.

This body is born out of excreta of the mother
and the father, and is full of filth and flesh;
therefore discarding it like chandala,
the lowly person, become one with brahma and be fulfilled.
O sage, just as an inner space of a pot is
merged with the outer space, once the pot is broken,
merge your own self with the universal self;
become indivisible and attain eternal silence.
Be a light unto yourself; become the self
which holds everything in itself, and give up your
own body as well as the universal body,
the brahmanda, *as if they are pots full of dirt.*
Establish your intellect, which identifies
itself with the body, in the blissful self which is
pure knowledge – thus discarding your subtle body, lingasharir.
Become the absolute, for all times to come.
O innocent! This illusory world is seen like
one sees the reflection of a city in a mirror.
Therefore, realizing that "I am the brahma," be fulfilled.

Man is embodied, but man is not a body at all. The body is just the periphery, the circumference; the body is just clothing. And not only this, this sutra says that the very attraction towards the body, the attachment to the body, is based on a very false notion about the body.

We never encounter our bodies. Whatsoever we know about our bodies is known from without – as if you have seen your body in a mirror. So you don't know what the body in reality is.

Look at your body from within; then you will not encounter beauty, then you encounter filth, ugliness. Then you will encounter something totally different. Then it is not a beautiful face – the mirror has given you the beautiful face. When you look at your body from within, when you enter your body from within, you will meet bones, skeleton – a totally different world, never encountered. Go to a hospital; look at the ill bodies, diseased bodies. Go to an operation table; look into the body being operated on. Go to a cemetery; look at the dead bodies. Go to a funeral; then you will encounter what a body really is.

But the body can carry on a deception because you look only at the skin, just the outermost clothing of the body. This creates an illusion, and this creates an attachment with the body. This attachment is one of the greatest barriers. Unless it is broken, unless you are removed, away from your body, you cannot enter into the dimension of the spiritual. Attached to the body, you are not facing the spiritual dimension; you are facing the body – and through the body, the world. You are facing the body and through the body, through the senses, the world.

That's why you encounter matter and matter and matter. People go on asking: Where is the soul? Where is the divine? Is there a God. Does God exist? Their questions are relevant, not because there is no God – their questions are relevant because their way of looking at things is through the body. Through the body you cannot know anything except matter. Through the body you can know only other bodies. Bodies cannot feel the bodiless; bodies can feel only bodies. That is their capacity and limitation.

When I want to touch you, I cannot touch anything immaterial in you. If I want to touch, I will touch the material. Touch cannot penetrate to the immaterial; touch is limited to the material. All the senses of the body can lead you only to the world of matter. And because the whole scientific edifice is nothing but extensions of the senses, that's why science goes on denying anything like godliness, anything divine in the world.

Science is the extended body of man. That's why science never encounters God, cannot encounter. Not because there is no God, but because your very approach is through matter. Through matter, only matter can be encountered. Unless you are removed from the body – not only removed, transformed totally, turned....An about-turn is needed, so that you are facing the body. Now through an about-turn you are not facing the body, but facing the bodiless; both are there in you. Both are there in you – both dimensions.

The body is there as a door towards the world.

Consciousness is there as a door towards the divine.

But you know only one door, you have never opened the other. The other remains there unopened; and not only unopened, you have forgotten it completely because you have never opened it, never tried it. It is there.

Scientists say, biologists say, that only half of your mind is functioning; half the mind is non-functioning. It is difficult for biology to account for it – why is half of the mind non-functioning? It seems useless. It can be operated on and thrown away, and you will not feel any absence; it was not used at all. Half your brain can be cut out and thrown away like an appendix, like anything unnecessary, and you will not feel even the absence, that you are lacking something. You have never used it.

Science is still unable to say anything about this. They go on saying this is just an accidental growth. But really this is very unscientific – to accept accidents is basically unscientific, because nothing can grow without any cause. Science means the link between cause and effect, the discovery between cause and effect. If there is some effect, it means there must be some cause.

Nothing is accidental, nothing can be.

It looks accidental if we don't know the cause.

Ignorance creates the illusion of accident.

Otherwise, there is no accident in the world.

Science goes on throwing things to the law of accident. Whenever science cannot explain anything, they will say, "This is accidental, unnecessary growth."

Either there is some cause behind it somewhere.... So there is one explanation that somewhere back in the history of man, man using that part, and we have forgotten how to use it. Or, somewhere in the future, man will need that part, and we have not yet discovered how to use it. Only these two explanations can be scientific, and in a way both are true. Both are true.

There have been civilizations in the world which have used that part, that non-functioning part of the mind. There have been individuals who have used that part, that non-functioning part – a Buddha, a Jesus, a Krishna. They are not just bigger brains than you, they are not just more intelligent than you; they are totally different. They use a different type of intelligence. The difference is not of degrees – the difference is qualitative, not quantitative. A Krishna, a Christ is not just quantitatively bigger than you, no. An Einstein is quantitatively bigger than you; the difference is of degrees – he is a great mind, a giant. You are just children before him. But a Buddha is not different quantitatively. He is not a great mind; he is a different mind altogether. His mind cannot be measured with your mind.

An Einstein can be measured through your mind. You may have a small mind; he may have a bigger mind – but you are both on the same path. You may be very much behind, but the path is the same. Einstein is with you on the same path – leading, on the peak. You may be the valley and he may be the peak, but you are both related; you are not different. A Krishna, a Christ is totally different; they are using something which we are not using at all. They are using a different door. They are not looking at the world from the body; they are looking at existence from consciousness. They are not coming to meet you through the body; they are coming to meet you through consciousness – that is the second door.

This sutra is concerned with the second door, how to open it. The first basic requirement is to create a distance between you and your body. A distance is needed; otherwise, you cannot take the about-turn. Space is needed. Create a distance. How can you create a distance? You cannot force a distance; the distance happens if you can become aware of the reality of the body, what the body is. If you become aware of the ugliness, the filth, the inner reality of the body, your attraction disappears. You are not to make it disappear; it disappears. The moment you know the filth of the body, suddenly your attachment is no longer there; you have taken the about-turn. In the disappearance of attachment, attraction, the turning, the about-turn happens. And for the first time you encounter another door in you.

Jesus says, "Knock, and the doors shall be opened unto you." About what doors is he talking? – "Knock, and the doors shall be opened unto you." What doors? He is talking about this door: Move away from the body, create a distance, let your back be towards the body, and suddenly you are facing a door you have never faced – and this door is not locked. That's why Jesus says, "Knock," and knocking is enough; this door is not locked. Just a knock and the door shall be opened unto you. They have been waiting for centuries and centuries – for millennia – to be knocked on. That's why Jesus says, "Ask, and only for asking, it shall be given to you. Knock, and just a knock is enough." No key is needed, there is no lock.

So the only key is how to face the door. Once you face the door, knock, and it opens.

This sutra says: Know the filth of the body, the death of the body, the deadliness of the body; the body is just a tomb. Look at it, but don't go on saying that the body is filthy; sayings will not help. Don't go on saying that the body is ugly; just repeating these things will not be of any use; on the contrary, your repetition shows that you don't know that really the body is a filthy thing; that's why you repeat. Through repetition you want to create some auto-hypnosis.

No, this sutra is not a suggestion for auto-hypnosis, so don't say the body is filthy. Don't believe in the teacher in this *Upanishad* – don't believe. Just try to find out whether he is right or not. Just feel the body from the inside. From your head, go on down, down, down – feel the whole body. Then suddenly you will become aware that the *Upanishad* is saying a truth, a very valuable truth. And truth itself is the turning. Then you need not turn yourself; truth itself is the turning.

You see a diamond; you are attracted, you are pulled. You begin to move towards the diamond. Suddenly you see it is not a diamond but just an ordinary stone. The pull has disappeared, the movement stops.

If you are attracted towards the body – and everyone is attracted, remember. How do you know that you are attracted towards the body? You may not have felt it consciously that you have ever been attracted to your own body. But if you are attracted to anyone's body, another's body, that shows you are unaware of the fact of what your body is. If you are attracted to a beautiful body of a man or a woman, it shows you don't know what the body is. If any body becomes attractive to you, it shows that you have not known your body; otherwise, *no* body can be attractive.

If you know your body and the reality, then all attraction towards bodies will disappear. Suddenly, then this whole world of bodies becomes a filth. Then you are not pulled, the pull disappears. Then you don't gravitate towards bodies, the gravitation disappears. And then a new law begins to function.

Remember, there are contrary laws in nature. While one law operates, another cannot operate. When the one law disappears, is not operating, the opposite law starts operating. If you are pulled by bodies, you are pulled by matter. If this goes on, you will be again and again pulled towards matter. This is what sex is, this is what biological reproduction is. One goes on reproducing oneself again and again – more bodies, more bodies, more bodies. You go on being pulled by matter continuously.

When you are attracted to a beautiful body, male or female, to what are you attracted? If you ask the biologists, they will say, "To certain hormones, to certain chemicals." A feminine body is constantly creating certain hormones; those hormones create the pull – you are attracted. A subtle pull is there, it is chemical. A feminine body has a different magnetism; a male body has a different magnetism. That magnetism goes on working.

If you have a magnet, then the iron is attracted, pulled.

Man-woman attraction is again a gravitation, a magnetism – biological, hormonal, chemical – but material.

If you are attracted to bodies, know well you have not known your own body at all. Then, try to know your own body. Don't believe what the *Upanishad* says, just go in and find out. Observe, analyze, and find out what your body consists of – what is the stuff the body is made of? If you can be daring enough, courageous enough to know the truth about your body, one law will disappear and you will enter a world of a different force.

Gravitation is one force.

Gravitation means being pulled downwards.

Grace is another force.

Grace means being pulled upwards.

You can say gravitation means being pulled outwards or downwards – both mean the same, they are synonymous. And you can say that grace means being pulled inwards or upwards – again both are the same; they are synonymous. Once you are not in the grip of gravitation, you will be in the grip of grace. Then God can pull you upwards and inwards; then you are open, vulnerable to grace – receptive.

So find out the facticity of the body. Then, attachment disappears; sex becomes meaningless, the pull of bodies is no longer felt. You enter another world, of another dimension, of another law: grace. Now you are pulled inwards and upwards; you are available for the divine.

As you are now, you are not available for the divine. The divine cannot do anything with you; you are just closed.

Meditations, methods, techniques, systems, schools – they exist only to make you available, to create the situation in which you can become available to the second law of existence – grace.

How is it possible? What to do?

Be more conscious of the body, be more conscious of what constitutes the body. Be more conscious of the desires of the body. Be more conscious of the totality of the body, and then nothing more is needed. You will be facing the door, the closed door. Knock, and the door shall be opened unto you. And once you enter the second door, you are no longer limited to the body. You become joined with the infinite space.

That's why man is anguish – man *is* anguish, constant anguish, conflicts, tensions, anxiety, insanity. Because a very infinite space is being confined, forced to live in a very small body. The infinite is being forced to live in the finite; that creates anguish, that creates uneasiness. Unless you can be infinite again, your anguish will remain.

Man remaining as man is incurable. Man remaining as man is the basic disease, and there is no medicine to cure it.

Man is a disease.

Unless man becomes divine, he cannot be cured.

Create the distance between you and the body, and the more the distance, the nearer you will be to the divine. And this nearness goes on transforming you. Then no effort is needed to transform you; the very law of grace starts transforming you.

So remember this: *you* are not to transform you; you are only to take a turn. Then you are available for the forces of transformation – *they* will transform you.

The meditation which will follow just now is just a turning. It is to create a turning in you, just a turning. It is not concerned with your character, it is not concerned with your morality. It is not concerned with what you have been doing – not at all. You may be a sinner – everyone is. You may be a criminal – everyone is. Some are caught, some are not caught – that's another matter.

This meditation is not concerned with what you are doing or with what you have been doing, no – not with your doing at all. You cannot do otherwise. As you are, all that you do naturally follows from it. So we are not going to change your doings. That's absurd, and cannot be done. And if you go on thinking that you can change your character, your action, your doings, then you are in an illusion, because if you remain as you are, available to the gravitational force, you cannot change anything. Your actions will be the same: you can change the names, but you cannot change anything substantially. Remember, in the whole life – this life at least, you don't remember the others – in this life, this whole life, you have been trying to change many things. Have you succeeded?

You have tried not to be angry. Have you succeeded? Fifty years, sixty years, seventy years…really, have you succeeded in creating a state of no-anger? You have been trying to be non-sexual, have you succeeded?

But man goes on in deceiving himself. He goes on thinking, "I will change." You cannot change as you are, because you are in a pull, in a gravitational force. You cannot do anything unless you change the law. Unless you become available to another law, you cannot change. You will remain angry, you will remain sexual, you will remain greedy. Moral teachings are just useless, just consolations. But they give you a certain ego…even the conception, "I can change myself, and if I am not changed, I have not made much effort – that's the reason. Any day I will make the necessary effort, and I will change."

No sir, you cannot change. Whatsoever you do, you cannot change. And if you become aware of this fact that just ordinary things…. One man smokes, and he goes on thinking he can change, he can stop smoking. He goes on thinking and he will go on smoking. And many times he will stop, and will start again. And if he stops smoking, then he will substitute something else for it; he will start chewing gum – it makes no difference. It makes no difference; only the thing has changed, not the mind.

The mind has to be occupied somehow, so he was smoking. Smoking is an effort to be occupied. You cannot remain unoccupied, you become un-easy. One goes on smoking; it gives you a feeling of occupation, you don't feel alone. The cigarette becomes your companion. This is the reason: you cannot be alone, the cigarette gives you company. You feel you are doing something – one of the reasons; there are many, because everything is multi-causal.

Everyone wants to go on feeding the body, because everyone is afraid of death, and food seems to be the antidote of death. So go on, but you cannot go on throwing food in the body. That's impossible. You can throw the food twice or thrice a day. But the mind says go on, go on feeing the body. One starts smoking, one feels one is feeding something without feeding.

So there are many reasons. You can stop smoking; then you will substitute it by something else which will do the same – the inner needs will have to be fulfilled. You cannot change *as you are*. But don't be disappointed. I am not saying you cannot be changed at all. But the change can come only if you start a journey towards another law of existence.

Change the law.

Don't change yourself.

Become unavailable to the law of gravitation.

And become available to the law of grace.

You will be changed – completely transformed.

THE MORNING MEDITATION

Now we shall try to become available to the law of grace. Be in a complete let-go.

Now start the first step: ten minutes of fast, vigorous, anarchic breathing. Just let yourself go totally. Move into breathing. Forget everything. Just be the breathing.

Go fast, only breathing. Forget everything. Just be breathing – fast, fast, fast.

Two minutes more. Just go mad in breathing. Only breathing remains; you are no more.

He alone realizes the self, who is free
from the clutches of egoism, and spotless like the moon;
he remains ever-blissful and self-illumined.
Cessation of action leads to the cessation of anxiety,
and cessation of anxiety leads to the ending of desire.
The ending of desire is freedom,
and this is what is called jivan mukti,
or freedom in life itself.
To see the divine everywhere, in every direction,
and in every thing is right attitude;
and being firm in this attitude brings an end to craving.
Do not be slothful and wavering in your
faith in the supreme, because this is death –
so say the knowers of the divine.
As water weeds cover up the water,
even as they are removed, so does illusion take hold
of a wise man if he swerves a bit from his
faith in the supreme reality.

The ending of desire is freedom. Freedom is not something that you can achieve from without. You are not imprisoned by someone else, by others, by the world; you are imprisoned by your own desiring mind. Desiring is the slavery. The more we desire, the more we become slaves – by why? Why is desire a slavery? Because the moment one desires, one has become dependent. If the desire is fulfilled, only then you can be happy; if the desire is frustrated, you will become a victim of suffering. And no desire is ever fulfilled. Desire as such, leads into frustration. That's why, the more one desires, the more suffering one creates around himself – not only suffering, but dependence also.

If I desire someone, something, now my attention, my being, everything depends on that. If I get – it is okay; if I cannot get…now I am always secondary; the primary thing has become the object of my desire. This primariness of the object of desire creates dependence, and we are all dependent. And there are so many masters, so many desires.

We live in a flux of desires. Every desire creates dependence – this is way is meant by spiritual slavery. And the Eastern mind, particularly, has been searching for freedom through religion – not heaven, not happiness, not bliss, but freedom.

The search of religion is for freedom, and freedom means freedom from desire. If I am in a state of mind where no desire arises, where I can say, "I am desireless," then slavery becomes impossible. Then for the first time I am in myself – rooted, centered in myself; I am not moving. Desire is movement. Then for the first time I am here and now, in the present; because desire is the future. Then for the first time I become existential, because desire is postponement. You desire – and you can desire only if you desire the future. Desire needs time, desire needs space to move; some day there will be the fulfillment, but it can never be here and now.

So you cannot desire in the present. Really, future is *created* by desire; it is not part of time. Future is not time; times is always the present.

We go on dividing time into three categories: past, future, present. That division is false, existentially false.

Future is desire and past is memory.

Time is always present.

There is no future time and there is no past time.

Time is always now.

Past means memories, and future means desires. You need future to move, and when you move into the future you miss the present. And missing the present is missing everything.

Missing the present you miss existence.

Missing the present you miss your being.

Take it from another direction: desire is becoming; it is to become something. A wants to become B; the poor man wants to become a rich man; the ugly face wants to become a beautiful face; the stupid mind want to be intelligent. Desire is from A to B, from here to there. It is goal-oriented. Somewhere in the future, there will be fulfillment – but now there can be only discontent; now there can be only frustration. Now there can be only suffering, but you can deceive yourself: You can forget this suffering by moving into desire, by moving away from it. By moving into the future, you can forget the present. So desire is really a drug. Desire is alcoholic, desire is like an intoxicant. It makes you postpone, it helps you; it creates the situation in which you can forget the situation – *that which is* – and can concentrate somewhere on some heaven, on some fulfillment in the future, in the future life.

Desire moves in the form of becoming, and your existence is in the form of being. You *are*. Desire means something that will be. That which is already here and now in me is my being; and that which I will be somewhere in the future is my becoming. There is a tension between being and becoming, and then anguish is created, anxiety.

Basically, psychologically, anxiety is just the tension between being and becoming – between that which is and that which is desired. That which is desired is not, and that which is – you can never desire it. You cannot desire it, it is here and now. You can move into it immediately.

Desire creates becoming; becoming becomes your slavery. You go on missing yourself, you go on missing your being. And that being is *satchidanda*; that being is existence, consciousness, bliss.

Be desireless, and you will attain everything that can be attained. But how to be desireless? How to go beyond desire? It creates a vicious circle: when we ask how to go beyond desire, we are creating a new desire – to go beyond. You cannot create a desire against desire; that's not possible, because the second desire will be as much a desire as the first. So what to do?

Understand desire, analyze desire, penetrate desire, and see how suffering is created, how slavery is created, how you create your own hells out of your own desires. Dig deep into desiring. Don't ask how to go beyond; rather, ask how to go more into the desire, to know and to understand. If you can understand that your suffering is created by your desire, that very understanding will become your transcendence. Because no one asks for suffering, but everyone desires, and suffering comes through desire. No one wants to be dependent, in slavery, but everyone desires, and slavery comes through desire.

If you go deep into desire, then you will become aware of the whole of the desiring mind, what it is. It is suffering, it is dependence, it is hell. But don't believe me, because by believing me – or by believing the *Upanishad* – you will be escaping your own effort to understand. Believers are always deceivers; they go on deceiving themselves. But they don't want to understand desire, so they say, "If you say that desire is suffering, we will believe it. But belief will not be of any help. You can believe it, but you will go on desiring. Belief will not destroy your desiring. You will have to understand; and no one else can understand for you.

It is like death: I cannot die for you; you will have to die to know it. Understanding is like love: I cannot love for you; you will have to love, you yourself will have to love – servants cannot do it for you. Howsoever rich you are, you cannot engage servants for your love.

Love, death, understanding, freedom –

These are the three deepest possibilities of the human being.

They cannot be transferred to anyone.

So don't *believe* that desire is suffering; try to know, try to understand your own desires. And if you understand your own desire, you will see that suffering follows as a shadow. And if you want that suffering to go, then desire must go.

But I say desire must go, I don't mean that you have to force it to go. I mean you have to understand it. The moment you understand your desire and the hell that is hidden in it, you have transcended it, you have gone beyond it.

The ending of desire is freedom.

And this is what is called jivan mukti,

or freedom in life itself.

And remember this: Don't wait for death to come and make you free. Death will not help you. Unless you become free in life, death is not going to help. But there are many who go on postponing....

Someone was asking me, "Why do you give sannyas to young people? Sannyas is for old men." Sannyas is *not* for old men, I don't mean that if you are old, don't take sannyas. It is late, but never too late. Why do we think that religion is not for young people? – because we think religion is something related with death, something to do with old age when one becomes impotent, when one becomes powerless. When one cannot move in desire, then it is good to be desireless, then it is good to renounce. When you cannot do anything, renounce the world.

But remember well: When the world has renounced you, you cannot renounce it, mm? That's a deception. While you are young, full of desire, that is the right moment to understand desire. Because when desire is young, when desire is powerful, you can understand it in a very clear perspective. When desire has become dull, muddled, muddied, dead, you cannot understand.

When desire is fresh, understand it – this is the moment. And a fresh desire understood, releases much energy; and that energy become freedom. When desire is already dead, you are not free from it. When desire is alive, that is the right moment, because desire is filled with energy, If you understand it and desire disappears, the energy will remain there. Desire will disappear, but the energy? – the energy will be left behind. That energy can become a medium to go beyond.

Without energy, no inner movement is possible. Desire is wasting your energy in downward movement. When desire disappears through understanding, energy remains, and energy goes on accumulating. You become a reservoir; and when you are a reservoir of energy, you can move now, inwards. It would be better to say you need not move really; the energy itself begins to move – because energy *is* movement. Energy needs movement; if it is not moving downward, it will move upward; energy *will* move! Energy cannot be static.

Energy means dynamism; energy is dynamic. Energy needs movement. If there is no desire, then energy cannot move downward – desire is the downward movement. Then energy cannot move outward – desire is the outward movement for something which is there in the future, for something which is outside, for something which you don't have, so energy moves outward.

When there is no desire and you have energy, the energy itself begins to move inward and upward, and you are carried by that energy to newer realms, to a transformed being. Do it in life. Do it while you are young.

Do not be slothful and wavering in your
faith in the supreme, because this is
death – so say the knowers of the divine.

A very beautiful definition of death....Death is not what you call it. A man is dying – we call it death; it is not. Really, while you are living, if you are living without the divine around you and within you, that life is death. We are all dead in a way, because a life which is not deeply rooted in the divine, will be rooted in the body. The body is death; the body is matter already dead, and we are rooted in the body.

Be rooted in the divine source which is deathless.
Be rooted in the divine which is life eternal.
Only then you never die.

Rooted in the body you will die again and again. Every moment you are dying; our so-called life is nothing but a long death. From the moment of birth we go on dying, and dying, and dying, and then we reach death. That death is just a culmination of a long process. The sutra says:

Do not be slothful and wavering
in your faith in the supreme, because this is
death – so say the knowers of the divine. But how to be rooted, and how to attain the faith?

Remember: Faith is not belief. This one moment more, this one point more to be understood: Faith is not belief. Belief is always borrowed, someone else gives it to you. Faith is inner search, you yourself attain it. Belief can be given by the tradition; faith cannot be given. Belief can be given by the scriptures; faith cannot be given. Belief can be given by the parents, culture, society, education; faith cannot be given. Faith you have to discover; it is a deep, hidden treasure – deeply hidden in yourself. You have to uncover it.

How to uncover it? How to attain to faith in the divine, and how to be rooted in the eternal source of life?

There is only one way, and that is take a jump from body consciousness to divine consciousness. In meditation we are doing that, trying to do that – to take a jump from body consciousness to divine consciousness.

Just now, we will be doing a deep meditation. Remain for a few moments more, sitting.

This is a jump – a jump from the body. This process....I must tell you what this process means.

You are staring at me. If your stare is total, you will become related to me immediately through your stare. The eyes are the least material part of the body; the energy that moves through the eyes is your consciousness, your attention. For thirty minutes, if you are staring at me, your energy is moving towards me through the eyes. If the energy moves in a total, in a whole process – not fragmentary, not partial – you will forget your body completely.

And then you will be jumping constantly. That jumping is to help your energy to jump inside; the jumping is not just a body exercise. The body is jumping, and you are staring at me. Your jumping body, your jumping exercise will help the energy to jump inside. Sparks will come through your eyes towards me. While you are jumping, you are constantly using the sound, "hoo! hoo!" That too is a hammering inside. When you say, "hoo," your energy moves upwards. When you say, "hoo," the sound goes deep to the sex center and hammers it; and the sex energy hammered, begins to move upward. And you are jumping, and you are staring at me – this whole pattern helps you towards a jump from the body to the divine consciousness.

Now get ready....

*One who has attained to the eternal absolute
shall remain so even after death. So, oh innocent,
attain* samadhi, *the highest state of unity with the
supreme, and be free of the choices.
The knot of ignorance in the heart is
destroyed, the moment one achieves self-realization,
through* nirvikalp samadhi, *choiceless awareness.
One should give up the self based on ego by
steadying oneself in unity with the higher self. And
one should be indifferent to egoism, et cetera, as
one remains indifferent to pots, clothes, and other
things.
From* brahma *the creator, down to the stone, all
appearances are false; therefore, see everywhere
your own excellent self, which is ever-unchanging.
The self is the* brahman, *the self is Vishnu,
the self is Indra, the self is Shiva, the self is
the world, and the self is everything; and there is
nothing other than the self.*

This sutra is concerned with choicelessness. Mind is always choosing – choosing this against that. Mind is the mechanism of choice. Have you observed this?

Observe:

Mind is always choosing this against that.

There is not a single moment when the mind is not in a state of choosing. We go on choosing – choosing pleasure against suffering, choosing happiness against unhappiness, choosing respect against insult – choosing, and choosing, and choosing. But if you go on choosing, you go on living in the mind.

Mind creates a dichotomy, it divides. Existence is one everywhere, in every dimension, but mind divides: Mind says, "This is black, this is white – choose white, don't choose black. This is good, this is evil – choose good, don't choose evil." But good and evil are not two; black and white are not two. In reality, only gray exists. One pole of the gray is black, another pole of the gray is white. White and black are just two poles of gray; the difference is only of degrees. White means less black, and black means less white. There is no absolute black and no absolute white.

Life is not a dichotomy, a division; life is one. Even in polar opposites life is one – but mind goes on dividing. Mind says, "This is good, this is bad; this is love, this is hate." But have you observed or not? – hate can turn into love any moment; love can turn into hate any moment. You love someone, and suddenly you start hating – if love and hate are opposites, then love can never become hate; then there is no possibility of its being turned into hate. But your love can turn into hate any moment – what does this mean? This means love and hate are not two – just two polarities of one thing.

Love and hate are polarities of attachment.

On one pole, attachment becomes love.

On another pole, attachment becomes hate.

That's why you cannot hate someone directly. You cannot hate someone suddenly; first you have to love him, to hate. You cannot create an enemy without first creating a friend. Can you create an enemy without creating a friend? First, friendship has to be established; only then it can grow into enmity. It means friendship and enmity are not two things, but just a growth of one. But mind goes on choosing, so mind creates a false world of divisions which exists nowhere.

In existence there are no divisions. Existence is liquid, flowing from one pole to another, moving again to another. Existence is like a pendulum moving from left to right continuously – from hate to love, from love to hate. But mind divides; and mind says, "This is to be chosen and this is not to be chosen." Then suffering comes in, because when you choose one part of a long movement, you have chosen the other part also. If you choose love, remember, you have chosen hate also. And when love turns into hate, you will suffer.

You have chosen happiness; you have immediately chosen unhappiness also. And now when happiness turns into unhappiness, you will suffer. But you will never become aware that this is your choice. You will not become aware because of the mind which divides. The mind says, "Happiness is something else. Unhappiness is opposite to it." Only in dictionaries is unhappiness opposite to happiness, not in life. Only in dictionaries – and dictionaries are not life; they are created by the mind. In words there are opposites – in existence, no; there are no opposites.

When you choose love, know well you are choosing hate. When you make a friend, remember you are making an enemy also. When you get respect, wait – insult will be following, it will come. It will take a little bit of time, but it will come. When you choose one part of one unity which cannot be divided; you will suffer.

Either choose both, or don't choose at all.

Remember, in both the ways you become choiceless.

Choose both, then mind cannot function – choose love and hate both. The moment you fall in love with someone, know well you are falling in hate also. Don't make any division; know that love is hidden hate. Choose both.

See the beauty of it…if you can choose both, you have not chosen at all, because choice always means choosing *against* something; you can choose love against hate. If you choose both, it is not a choice; you have chosen both love *and* hate. You can choose happiness against unhappiness. How can you choose both? If you choose both it is choiceless.

So either choose both, or don't choose at all, and mind dissolves.

Mind dissolves only when you don't choose. And when there is no mind, you are for the first time in your crystal clarity, for the first time in your original freshness. For the first time your real face is encountered. Mind is not there – the divider. Now existence appears as one. Mind has dropped; the barrier between you and existence is no more. Now you can look at existence with no mind. This is how a sage is born.

With the mind – the world.

With no mind – freedom, *moksha, kaivalya, nirvana.*

Cessation of the mind is cessation of the world.

So really, you are not to renounce the world, you are simply to renounce the mind. Don't try to renounce the world, don't try to escape to some monastery or to some mountain, to some Himalaya; that will not help, the mind will go with you. The mind is subtle. Just by leaving the world you cannot leave the mind. Really, now your mind will create a new division: the world and the monastery, the world and sannyas, renunciation. Now you have created a new dichotomy. You choose renunciation against the world; then it is no longer renunciation . When you don't choose, it is renunciation; or when you choose both simultaneously, it is renunciation. Because in both cases you become choiceless.

To be choiceless is to be in meditation.

To be choiceless is to enter the eternal.

To be of choice is to enter the world: the dream world, the divided world, the false, the pseudo, the illusory world.

So how to be without a mind? – That's the basic enquiry.

This sutra says, be choiceless and you will be without the mind, because mind is choice. Try it: whenever the mind says, "Choose this," choose also the opposite – *immediately*. The mind says, "This face is beautiful, this body is proportionate. Love this body, this is beautiful." Immediately remember, "This body is also ugly. Love this body because it is ugly also." Don't create the division between beauty and ugliness; they are two poles of one phenomenon.

The mind says, "Make this man your friend, he is so loving." But remember, whosoever can love, can hate. The mind says, "This man is good, he respects me so much." Immediately make your mind aware: the man who can give you respect is capable of giving you insult also. Only one who never respects you will never insult you; otherwise, the other is bound to come. So whenever you are choosing, and the mind says, "Choose this; this is good, gratifying," don't allow the mind to choose. Tell the mind, "I am going to choose both."

The mind says, "Life is good and death is bad." Tell the mind, "I am going to choose both" – and whether you choose or not, you cannot escape death. Once you have chosen birth, you have chosen death. But the mind will go on saying, and deceiving itself, and thinking, in the hope that somehow death can be escaped. You cannot escape; death has entered with birth. Birth is the first step of death; death will be following. It will take a little bit; it will take time. Wait – when birth has come, wait – the other pole will be coming. Don't choose.

Don't choose life against death.

Choose life *and* death.

Choose life *plus* death.

When I say, choose life plus death, what I really mean is, then you cannot choose; choice becomes absurd – choice becomes impossible! If you can see life and death as one process, you will not choose; you will become choiceless. Then things will go on happening, death will come ... but when death comes to a choiceless mind, it is a very different phenomenon. When death comes to a choiceless mind, you can enjoy death as you have enjoyed life.

Death is beautiful when it faces a choiceless mind. When death is mirrored in a choiceless consciousness, it has a beauty of its own, a silence – a deep silence of its own, a depth – a very dark depth of its own, a bottomless abyss, infinite.

When it faces a choiceless mind, death is divine.

But when it faces a choosing mind, death is ugly, death is the enemy. Not that death is the enemy, death appears as the enemy, because you have made friendship with life. You have chosen life; death appears as the enemy. You have said, "Life is beautiful," you have longed for life; that's why death becomes ugly. Otherwise, if you don't choose, if you don't divide, the totality of life is always bliss. It is always beautiful.

But remember, when I use the word beautiful I am not using it against ugly. When I say, "beautiful," I mean not against ugly, because division is ugly; and when beauty is against ugliness it is ugly. When I say life becomes bliss I'm not saying it against misery. When bliss is against misery, bliss itself is a misery. When I say "bliss," I mean the division has disappeared, the dichotomy has gone, the dilemma is no more; the mind is not there to divide.

Choicelessness is the deepest state of consciousness. Mind is the surface; choicelessness is the depth. Don't choose, or if you feel it is difficult not to choose, then choose both the polarities immediately, simultaneously.

Now be ready for the morning meditation. Make space for yourself so that you can move easily. Close your eyes. Use the blindfold. Close your eyes. Now start the first step....

The appearance of things has only been imposed upon oneself.
By eliminating it, the self becomes absolute brahma,
who is the whole, one without a second and without action.
The appearance of the self in the form of the
world of division is false, because one that is
without change, form, and organs cannot have any divisions.
The conscious self is free from
the feeling of the observer, the observation, and the observed.
It is innocent and full like the sea of the ultimate flood,
which destroys the whole existence.
As darkness dissolves in the light,
so the cause of illusion dissolves in the
supreme who is without a second.
And that supreme being without organs . . .
how could that supreme have divisions?
The supreme reality being one,
how could there be divisions in it?
In the state of dreamless deep sleep,
sushupti, there remains only blissfulness.
So how could there be divisions in it?

This *Upanishad* is basically against mind, and not only this *Upanishad*, upanishadic teaching as such is against mind.

Really, religion is against mind, because mind creates all illusions, all dreams. Mind creates everything that we call the world. Mind *is* the world; try to understand this. This is one of the basic truths.

Ordinarily we think we live in one world. That's absolutely false. You live in *your* world, I live in *my* world. So really there is not one world; there are as many worlds as there are minds. Each mind is a world of its own. My mind creates my world; your mind creates your world.

A poet lives in his own world. A scientist never passes through that world, can never pass. A scientist and a poet may be neighbors, but they are poles apart. A scientist passes through a garden; he looks at a flower, but the flower is never seen. He looks at the structure of the flower, not at the flower. The flower of the poet, he can never see. When the scientist looks at a flower, it is a chemical phenomenon. It is a mystery for him, but a mystery which can be decoded. It may be unknown but is is not unknowable. It can be known – if not today, then tomorrow, but the mystery can be de-mystified. Reason can penetrate into its structure and know what this flower is and how it flowers – the material structure, the atomic structure can be known, can be penetrated. So the flower is never a mystery for a scientist in the sense it is a mystery for a poet.

When a poet passes through this garden and looks at the same flower, this is not the same flower – know this. The same flower is looked at by two minds – one of scientific attitude, another of poetic attitude. The flower is the same, but not the same, because the scientist is thinking of a different flower – chemical, electrical, material, structural. He is thinking of atoms; he is thinking how this flower happens to be. What is its mechanism? How does it happen?

The poet is not concerned at all with atoms, with matter, with molecules, with mechanism, with structure. No, the poet is concerned with beauty; the scientist is never aware of the beauty. The poet is aware of a certain mystery which he calls beauty, and this mystery is not the same. This mystery to a poet means it can never be decoded. If it can be decoded, then it is not a mystery.

To him, mystery means something which will remain unknowable, not unknown. The unknown can become known; potentially there is no difficulty to make it known. Unknowable means: which cannot be made known – never! For a poet, a flower will remain a mystery forever. That mysteriousness is its beauty, and beauty has no structure; beauty has no molecules, no atoms, no mechanism. What is beauty? Beauty is not material; it is immaterial. Really, the poet is not looking at it; he is feeling it.

We can bring a mystic also to the garden. A mystic also passes – a saint, a Sufi, a Zen monk. For him the flower is neither a scientific structure to be understood, analyzed, known, nor is the flower just a beauty, a poetic sense, aesthetics; no. A mystic observing a flower becomes the flower himself; the barriers dissolve. It is not that the flower is there, and the mystic is here – here and there become one. So the mystic can say, "I have flowered in you." The division is not there. The mystic enters the very spirit of the flower; or, the flower enters the mystic and becomes one. A feeling of oneness, a feeling of divine oneness comes to the mystic.

The scientist approaches the flower through the intellect; a poet approaches the flower through the heart. A mystic approaches the flower through his wholeness, through his totality. The flower is the same, but not the same, because three minds create three worlds, and they never meet. The poet can never understand what the scientist is talking about – what flower is he talking about? The scientist can never understand the poet – he looks childish, talking nonsense. And the mystic...is a madman

– "What do you mean by becoming a flower yourself? Have you gone mad? How can you become a flower? And how can the flower become you?" Science depends on division, so the mystic's non-division, no-division world is absurd; he is mad.

There are psychological studies of Jesus. They say he was neurotic, a madman. Your Mahavira, Krishna, Buddha – they are as yet untouched, fortunately. Sooner or later some psychologist will say they were mad, not because they were mad, but because their approaches are different. They are talking of different worlds, different languages. They cannot meet, they cannot communicate. It is difficult to communicate poetry in scientific language; it is difficult to communicate science in a poetic language. If you create poetry out of science, the very scientific-ness is missed. If you try to translate poetry into scientific language, the beauty disappears. They cannot be translated.

That's why Indian scriptures have been translated many, many times, yet they remain untranslated; they cannot be translated. They all are written in poetry; that is the problem.

If you write a certain thing in poetry, it cannot be translated. Prose can be translated, because prose is basically rational. Poetry cannot be translated; it is the world of the irrational – feelings become more important, emotions become more important.

And mysticism, the lore of the mystics – that is impossible to translate. Because really it is not concerned with language; it is concerned with being, with the totality. A buddha looking at the world says something which cannot be translated – why? Because Buddha's outlook is so vast, so total, that no word can carry it.

I wonder whether you know it or not.....Buddha made it a point, continuously, for forty years while he was preaching, not to answer eleven questions. A certain eleven questions he would never answer – and they are the most basic questions. Really, it is a miracle how we could accept Buddha as an enlightened man, because those eleven questions are basic to religion. God, soul, *moksha* – all are included in those eleven questions. And Buddha said to his listeners, "Never ask about these questions. You can ask anything, but never about these eleven questions."

One of his disciples, Mahakashyap asked him, "But these are the most basic. If we don't ask them then nothing remains to be asked. You are playing a trick. In these eleven questions you have included *all* questions. If we cannot ask about God, if we cannot ask about the soul, if we cannot ask about liberation, then about what can we ask? And these are basic, so please don't make it a point not to answer them."

Buddha said, "Because they are basic, that's why I am not going to answer them. They are so total that language cannot convey them; and if I convey anything, that will be erroneous. So don't ask them. But I am not forbidding you to know them. I will give you methods; through those methods you will be able to know them, but I am not going to answer them."

Really, religion has no answers; religion has only methods. Those methods give you certain perspectives, certain situations from where you can look and penetrate into problems. But religion has no answers.

Every mind, each mind, is a world unto itself. That's why there is so much conflict. No one understands another.

You may live with your wife for forty years, fifty years – but have you observed the fact that you cannot understand each other's language? The husband says something, the wife immediately understands something *else*. Forty, fifty years they have been living together – what is the problem? Have they not yet been able to understand each other's terms and definitions? It is difficult.....They have two minds – each mind has its own world, and whatsoever penetrates into this world takes its shape and color. The husband has his own world: whatsoever he says, it means something in *his* pattern of thinking. When this penetrates his wife's world, it becomes something else – they never meet.

You can meet only when you are silent; when you are talking you cannot meet. That's why love is silent. When you love someone you don't talk, you are just present to each other; talking ceases.

So remember, when two lovers begin to talk, know well that love has ceased to be. When two lovers are silent there is love; in love they can understand each other. Why? – because in love, mind is not allowed to be. Language is not there, talk is not there, words are not there – mind is non-functioning. For a few moments, mind is not allowed to function; love becomes communion.

Talk, and it becomes a debate, a discussion, a controversy. You say something, and you will be misunderstood. To say something is to be misunderstood, because you are approaching another world, with different attitudes, different orientations, different languages. There is not one world; there are as many as there are minds.

Why insist on this? Just to tell you that *really* there is one world. And you cannot know that one world unless your mind is dissolved. If you go on clinging to your mind, then you go on creating your own world, you go on projecting your own world. When mind is no more, you face the oneness, the undivided, the undifferentiated existence.

That existence is bliss.

That existence is consciousness.

That existence is truth.

Anywhere you move towards religion, you move towards no-mind. Throw out the mind, and remain mindless, but aware. If you can remain mindless and aware, you will penetrate the deepest layer of existence.

Remember, just mindlessness will not do, because in deep sleep everyone becomes mindless. When there is no dreaming.....

Indian psychology divides human consciousness into three stages: deep, dreamless sleep – the deepest; then above it, dream sleep; and above it, on the surface, what we call the waking state. In the morning you get up from your bed; you enter the waking state. In the evening you go to your bed you enter dream sleep. And then deep in the night somewhere, dreams disappear and you fall down into the abyss of dreamless sleep – that is known as *sushupti*.

This dreamless sleep is without mind, because there is no thought, no dream, no ripple; everything has ceased, mind has dissolved. You *are* – without a mind. That's why the insistence – "without mind *and* alert." That's the only difference between samadhi and sushupti – samadhi, the ultimate peak of ecstasy, and sushupti, the deepest center of dreamless sleep – only one difference; otherwise, they are one. In sushupti there is no mind; in samadhi also there is no mind. In sushupti you are unconscious; in samadhi you are perfectly conscious. But the quality of consciousness is the same. In one there is darkness, in another there is light.

Through meditation one has to achieve a dreamless sleep with full alertness. Once this happens, the drop falls into the ocean and becomes the ocean.

Now be ready for meditation....

Desirelessness is the perfect knowledge.
And the peace that flows from this experience
of inner bliss is the proof of desirelessness.
That which doesn't happen in succession from
among the above-mentioned steps indicates that
the step preceding it has been fruitless.
To shun the objects of enjoyment is the
highest contentment, and the bliss of self
is itself incomparable.

Many things have to be understood – and not only to be understood, but to be lived. The first is that knowledge is not knowing.

Knowledge and knowing are different dimensions. Knowledge is information. You can collect it, you can accumulate it; you can become a man of great knowledge, but that will not lead you to knowing.

Knowing is experience.

Knowledge is information. For example, you can know everything about God that has been said anywhere, anytime, by anyone. You can collect information about God through Krishna, Christ, Mohammed, Mahavira, Confucius, Lao Tzu, and thousands of others. You can collect in your mind all the scriptures of the world. You can become *The Bible*, you can become a *Gita*, you can become the *Vedas*, but you will remain the same. This knowledge is not going to affect you at all; you will remain unaffected. Knowledge will become something in the head, and nothing in the heart. The head will go on becoming bigger and bigger, but the heart will remain the same. And it may happen – unfortunately it happens – that as the head grows bigger, the heart is forgotten completely.

The heart is the center of knowing; the head is the center for knowledge. You know throught the heart; you become a man of knowledge through the head. The head-oriented personality can know much without knowing anything. You know everything about God, but that doesn't mean you know God. Because to know God, one has to die first – but to know *about* God, no transformation is needed, no inner transformation is needed. To know about God, you can know as your are – but to enter knowing you will have to be transformed first. You will not do as you are, you cannot be accepted as you are.

Knowing needs a deep transformation first.

Your totality will have to be rearranged; only then you enter knowing. You can know about love – poets have written, and generally those poets who have not known love at all, because their writing is just a substitute. If you know love, it is one thing; if you have not known love, it is different – the quality is different. The difference is not quantitative, it is qualitative.

Poets have written about love – you can collect all that knowledge. You can go on singing about love, you can become a master of the knowledge about love, you can write a Ph.D. thesis about love – but that doesn't mean that you know love. To know love, libraries are not needed. To know love, a loving heart is needed; scriptures won't do, a loving heart is needed.

This sutra says: Knowledge is not knowing. Don't be deceived by knowledge; remember: Knowledge is not knowing. If you want to enter knowing, throw away all knowledge.

But how does one enter knowing? To enter knowledge is easy: there are schools, colleges, universities – the whole mechanism of knowledge is there. How to enter knowing?

Knowing is an individual effort; knowledge, a social effort. Society needs knowledge, because every generation which is dying has to impart knowledge to the coming generation. Teachers are the link; they go on giving knowledge to new generations, and knowledge goes on accumulating more and more. Society needs knowledge because society cannot function without knowledge.

The individual needs knowing, because the individual can never reach bliss unless he knows through his heart. Society is not interested in knowing. You will have to make an individual effort. What is that effort? These are the steps....

Knowing is the fruit of non-attachment. This looks absurd – "Knowing is the fruit of non-attachment" – *vairagya*.

This is a very beautiful Sanskrit word, *vairagya*. The word "non-attachment" carries the meaning, but just so-so. Vairgya means one who has turned away from the world, one who has known the futility of the world, one who has come to understand that you cannot achieve bliss through senses. Vairagya means: the outward search is futile; you have come to conclude this as your experience.

This conclusion cannot be transferred to you. If someone else is saying, "This world is futile," this conclusion cannot become your conclusion. You will have to pass through experience, fully aware. Whenever you feel desire, move into desire fully aware and when you reach the fulfillment of the desire, know well what has happened – whether any hope has been fulfilled or just frustrated. Go on moving in desire, alert, and then you will come to understand that all desire is futile, all attachment is meaningless; it creates misery, it never creates any bliss. Vairagya means this conclusion reached through awareness, reached through experiencing – and knowing is the fruit of vairagya, of non-attachment.

Why? Why is knowing the fruit of non- attachment? Because when you are not attached to the world, suddenly you are thrown inside. There is nowhere to move; all outer directions have been stopped by that non-attachment. Now there is no dimension to move out – you cannot move without, so your consciousness for the first time returns home. It moves inside.

The *Upanishads* say there are eleven directions. Eight directions we know: north, east, west, et cetera, eight directions. The *Upanishads* say there are eleven directions: the eight directions we know; and two directions of going up and down, so they become ten. The *Upanishads* say there are eleven directions: ten going out; one coming in. When these ten directions have become futile, this is vairagya – but the energy has to move. Energy means movement; energy cannot be static. Ten directions – in which energy was moving and moving for millenia – have become futile; this is vairagya. Now you don't want to move out. Suddenly the whole energy which was being dissipated without, begins to move within. And the more within it moves, the nearer the center, the energy becomes more and more one.

Make one circle, and then start from the circumference to move towards the center. You can draw many lines from the circumference to the center. Two lines drawn from this periphery, this circumference, to the center...as they come nearer the center they will come closer and closer. They will come nearer and nearer, and at the center they will meet. When this energy which has been dissipated in ten directions, begins to move towards the center, all this energy goes in; all the flowing currents of energy come nearer and nearer. And at the center they meet and crystallize. That crystallization becomes a flame - that crystallization, that intense crystallization becomes a flame.

That flame is known as knowing.

By that flame, for the first time your world is enlightened.

Now there is no more darkness.

Now you move in light; now you have light inside.

Concentrated energy becomes light. Concentrated energy, crystallized energy, becomes inner light. That is known as knowing.

And desirelessness is the fruit of knowledge. The Sanskrit word is beautiful again: the word is *uparati*. Uparati means total relaxation. Knowledge is the fruit of *vairagya*. Knowing is the fruit of non-attachment, of energy not moving without. Knowing is the fruit of energy not moving without.

If there is no knowing, and you don't attain the inner flame, then know well that your non-attachment has been false, pseudo. Knowledge, the flame, is inevitable if non-attachment has been real, authentic - not borrowed.

I say to you that knowing comes through non- attachment. So you can force yourself to be non-attached - that will be borrowed, and then knowing will not follow. Life is an authentic process; you cannot borrow anything from anyone. You have to live, you have to pass through, you have to move into experiences and attain. I say to you, "Knowing comes through vairagya." So you try to be non-attached - that effort will not help. You will become a *vairagi* - you will become a "non-attached man," but there will be no knowledge, no knowing. Your vairgya, your non-attachment is a borrowed thing; it is not a conclusion in *your* life. It is just foreign to you...someone has said, it has entered into your mind, but your mind has not come to conclude it by itself.

So this sutra says that if knowledge is not following, then know well that the first step has been futile and pseudo, unauthentic. If knowledge comes, if the flame of knowing is there, then you will feel a deep relaxation. This is *uparati* – deep relaxation, existential, not physical, not mental – existential, total relaxation. What is meant by total relaxation, uparati? It means, energy moving nowhere – not even *within.*

First the energy was moving outward in ten directions. Then energy began to move inwards in one direction – but it was moving. Movement cannot be relaxed; movement creates its own strain, effort, struggle – any movement is a struggle. When this inner moving energy becomes a flame, there is no movement; all motivation is lost. Energy is for the first time not moving but just is. You *are* – going nowhere.

First the ten directions became futile; now the eleventh also has become futile. You are neither moving out nor in; you are not moving at all. This is total relaxation, this is uparati. Your existence has become relaxed. For the first time you are simply existence, nothing more – simply existence. If uparati, this total relaxation, does not follow knowing, then know well that the knowing was pseudo, false. Then you must have deceived yourself, you must have quoted scriptures. You must have borrowed knowledge and you must have deceived your self that this was your knowledge.

We go on deceiving. Pundits are the great deceivers. But by repetition, continuously reading, they begin to feel that they know. They have not known, but they begin to feel that they know. This is auto-hypnosis. If you go on reading the *Gita, The Bible*, the *Koran* – go on, go on, go on for lives together – that constant repetition creates an auto- hypnosis. You begin to feel that you know. Really, you know too much! So it is bound to happen – this deception, this feeling that you know. You know everything! – really, if a Jesus is there to compete with you in an examination, he cannot compete. If Krishna himself is there to compete with a pundit, he is bound to be a failure; because a Krishna cannot repeat the same *Gita* again; it is impossible. Only a pundit can repeat it exactly as it is. For a Krishna, repetition is impossible. If he is going to say something, it will become another

Gita, but the same *Gita* can never be repeated. He cannot remember what he said in Kurushetra to Arjuna, but a pundit can repeat it.

Knowing is not repetitive; knowledge is repetitive. Knowledge is mechanical repetition.

Knowing is existential experiencing.

So if your knowledge is not knowing but just knowledge, information, then uparati, total relaxation, will not follow. So, if total relaxation is there – if you find a person of *knowing* – he will be totally relaxed, like a child, totally. Even a child is not totally relaxed. He is like a flower – but even a flower is not totally relaxed, because a flower is moving, the energy is moving; a child is moving. Total relaxation is incomparable, unique. You cannot find any comparison.

And inner silence, inner peace, is the fruit of total relaxation. Inner silence – *shanti* – inner peace, is the fruit of total relaxation.

One who is totally relaxed becomes silent. Nothing happens in him now. There is no happening, because every happening is noise, every happening has its own noise. Now there is no experience inside, because every experience disturbs silence.

The man of total relaxation is absolutely silent.

Now nothing happens in him.

He is; simply he is.

No experiences now – *no* experiences, remember this.

You will not have visions, because visions are a disturbance. You will not see light, you will not hear sound; you will not be taking an interview with God. No experience. Silence means no experience now. Everything has fallen. You have become just existence – no knower, no known, no experiencer, no experience.

This is what is meant by silence.

If silence doesn't follow total relaxation, uparati, then know well that the relaxation must have been a deception; it was not total. It may have been physical relaxation, it may have been psychological relaxation, but it was not total.

The relaxation was not spontaneous; you must have forced it.

We can force even relaxation. We can go on forcing things upon ourselves. We can force silence: you can sit like a buddha, like a buddha statue with closed eyes, just like stone – but you remain the same stupid man inside, it makes no difference. Forced, stupidity cannot go; you cannot force it out because who will force it out? The same stupid mind forcing itself; it becomes a vicious circle.

So you can find many stupid minds; particularly in India you can find them sitting like buddhas. They have just forced it, they have become like statues, but inside nothing has happened, because the silence is not there which is an inevitable consequence of total relaxation.

I am reminded....

Rinzai, one of the greatest Zen masters, used to ask whenever someone would come to him to be accepted as a disciple, "What do you want? For what have you come to me?" Generally those seekers would reply, "We want to be like Gautam Buddha, Shakyamuni. We want to be like that." So he would say, "Go away immediately, because we have one thousand stone Buddhas in our temple and we need no more. Go away immediately. Don't come again. The house, this temple is already too crowded with Buddhas – one thousand."

Rinzai lived in a temple where there were one thousand stone Buddhas. He would say, "Go away. There is no room, it is already crowded." And he was a lover of Buddha; he revered Buddha like anything, but he said, "Just by sitting like a Buddha you will not become a Buddha. You can force yourself, but the spontaneous flame will not come that way. So try to be yourself; don't try to be a Buddha."

You can try to be a Buddha, but how can you try to be yourself?

Leave all effort, leave all trying to be someone else.

Then you will be yourself – and that being yourself is relaxation.

If you want to be a Buddha or a Jesus or a Krishna, you can never attain relaxation. The very effort to be someone else is strain, tension, anguish, conflict.

So if silence doesn't follow, then know well your relaxation has been forced.

To shun the objects of enjoyment is the
highest contentment. And the bliss of self
is itself incomparable.

If you go through these four steps: *vairagya, gyan, uparati, shanti* – non-attachment, knowing, total relaxation, and the ultimate silence – then you achieve the incomparable self, the unique self that you are.

Now get ready for the meditation.

The supreme self is formed by the word "that"
which has maya, *illusion, as its disguise –*
which is the source of the world, which is invested with the
quality of omniscience, omnipresent, et cetera;
which is mixed with the indirectness, and which is
reality itself.
And that which is the shelter of the I-
experience, and of the word "I" and whose knowledge
about his own inner being is false, is called by the
word "thou" – twam.
The supreme has maya, or illusion, as its disguise, and the self has ignorance as
its disguise. Being shorn of them, only the supreme self remains, which is indi-
visible: satchidananda *– existence, consciousness and bliss.*

*T*he *Upanishads* do not believe in a personal God. Neither do they believe in any personal relationship with the divine. They say that personal relationship is impossible, inconceivable. Why? – because the *Upanishads* say that personality itself is illusory. Try to understand this.

I am a person. It means I am separate from existence – personality means separation. I cannot be a person if I am not defined, I cannot be a person if I am not different. I cannot be a person if I am not separate. Personality exists as an island, defined, demarked, different, separate. The *Upanishads* say, personalities are false; you only appear to be persons, you are not.

The inner being is impersonal; it has no limitations, no boundaries. It begins nowhere and ends nowhere. It goes on and on to the infinite; it is the infinite and eternal. In space and in time both, it is undefined, undifferentiated; it is not separate like an island.

This word "personality" is very beautiful; we don't have such a beautiful word in Sanskrit or Hindi. This word "personality" comes from a Greek root which means mask. The Greek root is *persona*. "Persona" means mask. Actors used it to deceive or to create the impression of some face in a drama. The original word means just a mask, a face, artificial. So if you are playing in a drama, acting as Rama, you can use a false face which gives the impression that you are Rama. Inside you are not Rama, only the face is Rama. The word personality comes from "persona."

We all have personalities, which are simply masks. Inside there is no person at all; inside you are just eternal energy, infinite energy. Outside you have a face. That face is not you, that face is just like any mask in any drama. The world is a great drama and you have faces to play – and that's why one face is not enough. The drama is so long and so big and multi-dimensional, so everyone has many faces. You are not one person, you are many persons together.

When you are talking to your friend, you have a different face; you are not the same person. When you are encountering your enemy, you have a different face; this is not the same face. You are with your beloved, this is a different face; you are with your wife – this is a different face. You can see: a couple is passing, and you can say whether they are husband and wife or not. If they are happy, they are not; if they feel blissful, ecstatic, they are not – the man must be moving with someone else's wife. With one's own wife it is a suffering, a pain, a burden – a duty. Any duty becomes a burden; it is not fun, it is not play.

Look at a person moving with his wife … he cannot look here and there; if a beautiful woman passes, he will remain a monk. Then you can know the man is moving with his wife, because the wife is observing him every moment – "Where are you looking? Why are you looking?" And he will have to explain everything back home. Of course, no explanation is ever accepted, but still explanations have to be given.

You are talking to your servant; look at your face in the mirror. You are talking to your boss; look – look at your tail, which is absent but still working, wagging. It is not there, but it *is* there.

Man has many faces, has to have, because every moment you need a new face. And the more civilized, the more faces; and the more civilized and cultured, the easier it is to change faces immediately. Really, you are not even aware that you go on changing faces; the whole thing has become automatic.

So personality is not personality, it is really personali*ties*. Every man is many men – a crowd inside, and many faces constantly changing moment to moment. But are you your faces?

In Zen, in Japan, whenever a seeker comes to a master, the master says to him, "Meditate – and this is the object of your meditation; I give you this object for your meditation: find your original face. Find out how you looked before you were born; or find out how you will look when you have died. Find your original face – which is *yours*, not for others."

All our faces are for others. Have you any face of your own? You cannot have, because faces are basically for others. You do not need them for yourself, there is no need. You are faceless. Really, the original face is face*less*. You have no face inside – all the faces are outside; they are for others, meant to be for others.

The *Upanishads* say that you are impersonal inside – just life, not a person; just energy, not a person; just vitality, not a person; just existence, not a person. So how can you create a relationship with the divine? How can you create any relationship with the original source of life? When you don't have any face, how can the divine have any face? The divine is faceless. The divine has no face, he need not have any. The divine is just pure existence with no body and no face. So you cannot be related personally.

Religions have talked in terms of personal relationship. Some religions call God father, mother, brother, beloved, or anything you wish – but they go on thinking in terms of relationship, of being related. They go on thinking in terms of anthropocentric attitudes. The father is a human relationship. Brother, mother, beloved, all – all relationships are human. You think in terms of relationship with the divine; you miss the point, because the divine is not a person, and there is no possibility of personal relationship. That's why the *Upanishads* never call God the father. They never call God the mother; they never call God the beloved or the lover. They simply call God "that" – *tat*.

This word "that" is very basic to upanishadic teaching and philosophy. When you say "that," it gives no sense of personality. When you call existence "that," you cannot be related to it – there is no possibility. How can you be related to "that"? You cannot be related to "that." What does it mean? Does it mean that you cannot be really related to the divine? No, but this shows that to be related to the divine is going to be altogether a different relationship; the quality cannot be human. Rather the relationship with the divine is going to be the very reverse of a human relationship.

When I am related to someone as husband and wife, or brother and sister, or father and son...two are needed in any relationship. Relationship can exist only between two points – two relators. This is how human relationship exists: between two. It is a flow, a bridge between two; it is dual. Human relationship is dual: two points are needed, then it can exist between these two. But with "that" – pure existence, divine, or God – you cannot be related in a dual way. You can be related only when you become one. You can be related only when you are no more. As long as you are, there can be no relationship. When you are not, then you are related. But then the very word becomes absurd, because relation always means between two. How can there be relationship when only one exists?

But this is the reverse of relationship. To call the divine "that," indicates many things; there are many implications. One, you cannot be related in the ordinary sense of relationship with the divine. You can be related in a very extraordinary sense, absurd sense, when you have become one. Secondly, you cannot worship "that"; that's impossible.

The *Upanishads* don't preach any worship, any prayer – no. It would be good to understand the difference between prayer and meditation. The *Upanishads* teach meditation, never prayer. Prayer is always personal, a dialogue between you and the divine. But how can you have a dialogue with "that"? Impossible – the person must be there; only then a dialogue is possible.

One of the greatest Jewish thinkers of this age, Martin Buber, has written a book, *I and Thou*. Jewish thinking is dual, just the contrary of the upanishadic thinking. Buber says, "*I and Thou* – this is the basic relationship between man and man, and between man and the divine also. Because this is the only relationship: *I and Thou*.

When you stand before God as "I," and God becomes "thou," you are related. Buber says that when God becomes "thou," you are in love. The *Upanishads* will not agree. They say if God is "thou," then you are still there to call him "thou." The "I" exists, and "I" is the barrier: the ego exists and the ego cannot be related. And if you think that the ego is related to the divine, then this thinking is false and pseudo. Really, you are in imagination. If God becomes "thou," it is imaginary. The *Upanishads* say: "that." But we can say "I and thou"; we cannot say "I and that," because there is no relationship between "I" and "that." The "I" must drop; only then the "that" evolves, arises. With the dropping of the "I," the "that" is born. It is there, but the "I" is a barrier. When the barrier drops for the first time you realize existence as it is – *That Which Is*.

So the *Upanishads* always call the ultimate truth "that" – *tat*.

The second thing to be understood in this sutra, is that the nature of "that" is *sat, chid, ananda* – *satchidananda*. *Sat* means existence; *chid* means consciousness; *ananda* means bliss.

These three are the attributes of "that":

It exists, it is conscious, and it is bliss.

The very nature of it is bliss.

If you can attain these three qualities, you have attained "that." You exist – go deep. Everyone says, "I exist." You were a child and you said, "I exist." Where is that existence now? You have become young; you again say, "I exist." You will become old.

The child said, "I exist"; the young man said, "I exist"; the old man says, "I exist." And the child is no more, and the young man is no more, and the old is dropping himself, disappearing. Who says "I exist"? Who is that which goes on existing? Childhood transforms into youth, youth into old age; life becomes death. Who is that which says, "I exist"? Have you known it?

When you say, "I exist," you always identify your "I" with the state you are in. If you are a child, you mean "I, the child, exists." If you are old, you mean, "I, the old man, exists." If you say, "I" . . . and if you are a man, you mean a man exists; if you are a woman, you mean "I exist, a woman exists." Always the state is identified with the "I," and states go on changing. So really, you have not known that which exists; you have known only that which goes on changing.

The *Upanishads* say that which goes on changing is not existential; it is dreamlike. That which is always eternal, is existential. So attain in yourself the point, the center, which can say, "I exist, never-changing, eternal, absolutely eternal." If you can attain this point of existence, you will attain the two automatically, immediately: you will become absolutely conscious and you will become absolutely filled with bliss. Or, try from other routes. There are three attributes, so there can be three basic routes. Either attain existence – then the other two will follow, or attain any other one of the two, and the remaining two will follow.

Attain consciousness, become fully conscious; you are not. We are asleep, unconscious, moving as if in somnambulism, asleep. You are doing things like an automaton. Look at a man eating: he is eating here, but his mind is not here. His mind may be in his office or somewhere else. If the mind is not here, then he is eating in his sleep. It has become a routine, so he is going on. You are walking, your legs are walking but you are not in the legs. You are no longer there; you have already reached the goal where the legs have to reach. Or, you may be lagging behind, but you are not there with the legs, fully conscious that "I am moving, walking, eating."

Attain to consciousness. Whatsoever you do, do with a fully conscious mind, mindful, aware, alert. If for a single moment you can be totally aware with no sleep inside anywhere, with no unconscious mind in your being...if you have become fully conscious, you have become enlightened. The other two will follow immediately – *immediately*! It is not right to say "follow" – they will happen immediately. There will be no following – immediately, *yugapat*. The very moment you are fully conscious, you will be existence, absolute, eternal, and you will be bliss – total.

Or, try to be blissful. Don't allow your consciousness to be vulnerable to misery. Don't allow your consciousness the weakness to be miserable. Be strong, resist the temptation of falling into misery. We all have temptations to fall into misery. There are reasons, psychological, because when you are miserable people pay more attention to you.

A child is sick and the whole family moves around him; when the child is not sick, no one cares. The child learns the trick: be miserable, be ill, and then the whole world will just go around you. It never does, but man goes on trying. Do you remember that when you are sick, you have a certain enjoyment in it? A certain satisfaction? Now you can throw everything on your sickness: your business is failing, so what can you do? You are sick. Your mind is not working well, what can you do? You are sick. Now you can throw everything on your sickness. And when you are sick you become a dictator. Now your wife has to follow, your brother has to follow, your children – you are sick. So the old man says to his children, "I am an old man. I am sick, I am going to die." This creates authority. He says, "You have to listen to me."

We have investments in misery; that's why we go on inviting misery. If misery is not coming, we become miserable. No misery? Then where to stand? What to do? When you are in misery, going from one doctor to another, you feel good.

I have heard about a great surgeon, Kenneth Walker. He has written somewhere that he was studying with his teacher...he was studying surgery with his teacher. The teacher was a very well-known professor. One day he was sitting, checking some notes, and a patient came to the great doctor, his professor. And the professor said, "Where have you been? For two years I have not seen you. Have you been sick? For two years I have not seen you!"

"Have you been sick?" – of course, when people fall sick they cannot come to the doctor! Those who come are enjoying the trick; they go on changing doctors – from this to that, and they go on saying, "I have been to this doctor and to that, and no one can help me. I am incurable. I have defeated all the doctors."

I know it in a different way. Many people come to me. They say, "I have been to this guru, I have been to that mahatma, I have been to this and that, and nothing happens." They have defeated all; now they have come to defeat me – "Nothing happens. Can you do something?" As if someone else is responsible for them, that nothing happens. Really, if something happens they will become miserable: now they cannot go anywhere else; now they cannot say, "I have been to this man and nothing happens." They will become miserable if something happens, so they continue....

Feel blissful. Don't allow yourself to be miserable. Don't help yourself to be miserable. Don't cooperate with misery; resist the temptation. It is very alluring – resist it! And try to be blissful in every state of mind. What-soever happens outside, don't allow it to disturb your bliss. Go on being blissful.

I will tell you one anecdote. Chuang Tzu, one of the great Taoists of China, was sitting in front of his hut playing on an instrument and singing. Just that very morning his wife had died, and he was singing. The emperor came, just to offer his consolations to Chuang Tzu. Chuang Tzu was a great man, and the emperor respected him very much. It was rare that the emperor should come to a fakir, a poor man. But the emperor felt very awkward when he saw that Chuang Tzu was singing and laughing and sit-ting under the tree alone. But he had come, and he must have prepared …as many of you know by experience. When someone is dead, someone has died, you go and prepare the whole dialogue – what is to be said, how to console, and how to escape immediately! It is a duty to be done, and a very ugly duty. Someone has died and you have to do something, to say something; go there, make a face, be sad, and then escape. The king was prepared, but this Chuang Tzu disturbed everything.

The king came, he saw Chuang Tzu laughing and singing and playing on some instrument; he felt very awkward. Now all that he had thought of could not be said. Chuang Tzu was not sad at all; it was as if there had been no death. Or, he seemed even to be celebrating. So the king said, "Chuang Tzu, I know you are a great sage, but it is enough, more than enough not to be sad. This is going too far…to celebrate? Don't be sad, that's enough; it suits a saint. But this is going too far. Your wife has died this very morning, and what are you doing? – singing, laughing, and you look so cheerful. Is it your marriage day? Are you going to be married again? What are you doing?"

Chuang Tzu said, "I have made a vow to my teacher that I will remain blissful – whatsoever happens, it is not going to disturb my bliss. So what-soever happens I always interpret it in such a way that it helps me to be blissful."

Remember, everything is an interpretation. If you want to be miserable, you will interpret it in that way – everything! If you want to be blissful, the same situation will be interpreted in a different way.

So the king says, "Please let me know, because I have really too many wives, and sometimes wives die. So tell me the trick, the secret: How can you be blissful in such a state?"

Chuang Tzu said, "Everything that happens there outside, happens *outside*; it is not happening inside. One has to remember constantly. And whatsoever is happening outside need not disturb you, because you are not the outside; you are the inside. So a division, a remembrance, a constant mindfulness. And always look at life with total acceptance. Then you can never be miserable. My wife has died; everyone has to die. Sooner or later I will die also, so death is a part of life. Once you are born you will die, so nothing untoward has happened – just a natural phenomenon, just a natural process.

"Secondly, my wife was ill, old, suffering; not only has my wife died, but also her oldness, her suffering has died. And this was worth that; this death was worth it. Now she is at ease. When I saw her face dead, it was the first time in my life I saw her blissful. She was never so blissful. So I am celebrating the event – at last, even my wife is blissful."

Interpretations... and moreover, Chuang Tzu is reported to have said, "This is the last time, the departure day. She was with me for so long. And she helped me and served me, and made my life in many many ways pleasant, happy, enjoyable. So what do you think? Should not I pay my gratitude, my respects, my thanks on the day of departure, the great departure? I am celebrating all the memories, all the pleasant memories that are associated with my wife. I am singing."

It depends. If you try to be blissful continuously, if you don't allow yourself to disturb yourself; if you remain centered in your being, undisturbed, unwavering – immediately the two others will happen. You will attain existence, and you will attain consciousness. These are the three paths.

To be blissful is one path; many have tried this.

To be conscious is another path, one of the most followed. Mahavira, Buddha... they all followed the path of being conscious.

To be existence – that too, the third path. These are the three basic paths, and they are basic paths because these three are the attributes of the ultimate reality.

Any attribute followed becomes a river.

You flow into it and move into the divine, into the supreme ocean. These three rivers fall there.

Really, it is just a symbol. In our mythology, we have been thinking of *Ganga, Jamuna, Saraswati* – these three rivers – as sacred rivers. These are the three rivers, the three paths. Ganga and Jamuna are visible, and the Saraswati has become invisible.

The path of bliss will be visible. Whosoever follows the path of bliss will be known everywhere, because his bliss will be coming out and flowing. His eyes, his movements, everything will be a blissful gesture. You cannot hide your bliss – that's impossible.

The man who follows the path of consciousness will also be visible, because his very effort to be conscious continuously, will give a very strange look to his features, to his movements, to his gestures. He will move consciously, his every step will be conscious. And you can see him – you can see a buddha walking; he walks differently. You can see a buddha speaking; he speaks differently. Every gesture is conscious. When every gesture is conscious, it gives a different quality to every movement. It cannot be invisible; it becomes visible. These are the Ganga and Jamuna.

And Saraswati is invisible – the path of existence. He simply goes on inside, remembering who is that which exists – he will not be known; you cannot feel him from outside. So those who have followed the path of existence are the unknown masters; they are not known ordinarily. Unless one goes in deep search of them, they are not known.

Sufis have been following the third path, Saraswati – the invisible, the river which no one can see. So if you ask any Sufi "Where is your master?" you may be sent to a cobbler or to a tailor, or to a sweeper. No one knows; even his neighborhood has never known that he is a master. He is just a cobbler, and even you cannot see how this man is a master. But you will have to live for two, three years, five years with him, in his vicinity, in his presence. And then, by and by, you will become aware that this man is different. But his difference has to be felt. It takes time; it is deep, invisible.

These are the three paths – and three only, because three are the attributes of the divine, of the absolute, or of existence.

Now, get ready for the meditation....

*The enquiry about the oneness of the soul and
the* brahman *to the great saying like* That Art
Thou *is known as the right listening.
And thinking in the right way on the meaning of
what has been listened to is known as right
contemplation.
And to harmonize and center one's mind with
the meaning, shorn of all doubts – that which is
derived from right listening and right contemplation
is what is known as meditation.
And finally when the meditator and meditation
are eliminated, and only you are fixed, meditating
upon the means, then the mind becomes unwavering and
settled like a flame in a place without air. And
that is called* samadhi.

This sutra uses four words as four steps – four steps towards the unknown. The first is *shravan*. Shravan means right listening – not just listening, but *right listening*.

We listen, everyone listens, but right listening is a rare achievement. So what is the difference between listening and right listening, shravan?

Right listening means not just a fragmentary listening. I am saying something, you are listening to it there. Your ears are being used; you may not be just behind your ears at all; you may have gone somewhere else. You may not be present there. If you are not present there in your totality, then it cannot be right listening.

Right listening means you have becomes just your ears – the whole being is listening. No thinking inside, no thoughts, no thought process, only listening. Try it sometimes; it is a deep meditation in itself. Some birds are singing – the crows – just become listening, forget everything – just be the ears. The wind is passing through the trees, the leaves are rustling; just become the ears, forget everything – no thought process, just listen. Become the ears. Then it is right listening, then your whole being is absorbed into it, then you are totally present.

And the *Upanishads* say that the esoteric, ultimate formulas of spiritual alchemy cannot be given to you unless you are in a moment of right listening. These spiritual formulas – ultimate, secret keys – cannot be handed over to you as you are: unconscious of yourself, fragmentary, partial, listening but not present there. These keys can be handed to you only when your total being has become receptive to take them in. They are seeds, and the seeds are powerful; they will explode in you. And they will begin to grow in you, but one has to become just a womb to receive them. If your ears have become just wombs to receive, and your total presence is there; if your whole body is listening – every fiber, every cell of the body is listening – only then these "great sentences" as they are called, *mahavakyas*, can be delivered to you.

So it has been a tradition in India, in the old India of ancient days, not to write down these mahavakyas, these great secret formulas – because if they are written, anyone can read them. He may not be ready. He may not be reading, he may not be listening, but he can become acquainted and that acquaintance becomes a barrier. When he begins to feel that he knows – and these secrets are not to be known through words, they can be known only through experience....

So the rishis, the writers of these *Upanishads* insisted for centuries not to write at all. These secrets were given from one individual to another, and not in an ordinary way – in a very extraordinary process. A teacher, a master would give these secrets to a disciple. And the disciple must wait, sometimes for years; just being near the master, forgetting himself completely; just becoming attention, just being attentive – whatsoever the master says, to listen; whatsoever he orders, to do. He had just to be obedient, serve, and remain there – constantly remaining in the presence of the master and waiting for the right moment. And the disciple cannot decide when the right moment is, so leaving it to the master, remaining in a let-go and waiting...and suddenly one day, any moment, the master will say it. When the master finds that now you can listen with your total being, that now you have become a womb, just receptivity, and now the secrets can be handed to you – then he will tell you.

And he will tell you very simple things; this sentence is very simple, the simplest, but the most difficult to realize: That Art Thou – *tat twamasi*.

We discussed last night that the *Upanishads* call the ultimate, *that*. So "that" is there; you are here. What is the relationship? What is the bridge between the two? This sentence says: *That Art Thou.*

"That" is not far away from you, it is just within you.

It is a within beyond.

402

It looks, it appears very far away because you have not recognized it; otherwise, it is just here and now within you.

You are that.

This is a very simple sentence; even a small child can understand it and learn it. But it takes lives and lives to realize it. *That Art Thou*, I am That. To realize this, that *my* being is one with the universal being, to realize that *my* being and the universal being are not two things, but one...how to realize it?

The first step is right listening – listen to the master in a right way. And the right way means, listen to the master with your total being, with your total receptivity. Become just ears; only then you can understand it.

The second step is right thinking. You can think in two ways: you can think negatively, then it is wrong; you can think positively, then it is right. Negative thinking starts with denial, negating. Negative thinking starts with a *no*, the no is the starting point. Observe within yourself whether you start with no. Whenever something is said, what is the first feeling arising in you? – no or yes? And you will find ninety-nine percent of the time a no arising in you. You may not have observed it. Even for futile things where no "no" is needed, "no" arises. A Child asking his mother, "Can I play outside?" Immediately – "No!" She may not even be aware why she is saying no.

No is our basic attitude. Why? – because with "no" you feel you are somebody. The mother feels she is somebody – she can say no. The child is negated, the child's ego is hurt and the mother's ego is fulfilled. "No" is ego-fulfilling; it is food for the ego, that's why we train ourselves in saying no.

Move anywhere in life and you will find no- sayers *everywhere*, because with no you feel authority – you are someone, you can say no. To say "yes sir" makes you feel inferior; you feel that you are someone's subordinate, nobody. Only then do you say "Yessir." Yes is positive and no is negative. Remember this: no is ego-fulfilling; yes is the method to discover the self. No is strengthening the ego; yes is destroying it.

Right thinking means yes-saying. First find out whether you can say yes

- if you cannot say yes, if it is impossible to say yes, only then say no. But our method is first to say no; if it is impossible to say no, only then, defeatedly, say yes. And wait for the moment when you can say no. No-oriented mind and yes-oriented mind....

In a religious search, no-saying is just undoing yourself because there, no-saying will not help. You are not there to strengthen your egos. Yes-saying...try it some day. Take it as a vow, that for twenty-four hours you will try in every situation to start with yes. And look what a deep relaxation it gives to you. Just ordinary things! – the child asking to go to the cinema...he will go; your no means nothing. On the contrary, your no becomes inviting, your no becomes attractive, because when you are strengthening your ego, the child is also trying to strengthen his. He will try to go against your no, and he knows ways to make your no a yes, he knows how to transform it. He knows it needs just a little effort, insistence, and your no becomes yes.

For twenty-four hours try in every way to start with yes. You will feel much difficulty, because then you will become aware: immediately, the no comes first! In anything, the no comes first – that has become the habit. Don't use it; use yes, and then see how the yes relaxed you. And particularly in the spiritual search, if you are working with a master, yes-saying saves much time, much energy. You become a total receptivity, and then in that total receptivity things begin to flower.

Right thinking means to start thinking with *yes*! It doesn't mean that you cannot use no; it only means to *start* with yes. Look with a yes-saying mind. And then if it is impossible, say no. You will not find many points to say no if you start with yes. If you start with no, you will not find many points to say yes. The starting means ninety percent is done – your start is ninety percent, done. Your start colors everything, even the end.

Right thinking means think, but think with a sympathetic mind. Think with a yes-saying mind. Use logic, use reason, but use reason and logic to find out how to say yes.

I will repeat: use reason, use logic, but use them as instruments to find out how to say yes. We go on using reason, logic, to find out how to say no. Our whole logic is just a structure to find no. It should be otherwise; then it is right thinking.

The third is right contemplation.

If you find something with right thinking to be true, then contemplate it, then meditate on it. Then try to find some harmony between you and it. Because a truth not lived is not a truth – sometimes it is even more dangerous than an untruth. A truth unlived is a burden. A truth unlived divides your mind. A truth unlived becomes a haunting – it is a nightmare. So it is good not to think about truth if you not going to transform yourself accordingly. Because if you are not going to transform yourself accordingly, the truth will haunt you, disturb your sleep. You will become more uneasy, you will have to suffer much unnecessarily.

So if you are ready to change yourself according to the truth, only then contemplate it; otherwise, it is dangerous. And don't play with dangers; it is playing with fire. It is better to be unaware of truths, because then you are blissfully ignorant. Ignorance has a certain bliss. The moment you begin to contemplate, that bliss will be destroyed. Uneasiness will come to you; you will feel nowhere, strange, an outsider. Now you cannot go back; there is no going back, there is no movement backwards. You cannot fall again into your blissful ignorance, you can only move forward.

And the third step is right meditation. Right listening, first; right thinking, second; right meditation, third. Now, whatsoever you have found – whatsoever you have encountered in right thinking – meditate on it. Try to create a bridge between you and it. Try to be like it yourself, transform yourself accordingly. Become a shadow to it, and follow it. Unless you do this, the truth will remain just intellectual. It will not become your bones, it will not become your blood, it will not become your heartbeats, it will not be your being. Contemplate, meditate, go on meditating. Remember this: that you become that upon which you meditate.

If you constantly meditate upon anything, by and by you will be transformed by your meditation; you will become like that. Meditation transforms you. Remember, the truth found in right thinking – meditate upon it. Create some harmony between you and the truth. Don't go on carrying it in your head; let it go deep – so deep that you begin to feel a certain one-ness with it. I say, "certain oneness." You cannot feel totally one with it at the third step, but a certain oneness, a similarity, a certain attunement – not total oneness, That total oneness comes at the fourth step.

That fourth is *samadhi*, right ecstasy. If the third step is attained and you have begun to feel a certain harmony, attunement, an opening, a bridge with the truth, now immerse yourself in it.

Samadhi means the remaining of only one. In meditation there are three points. Meditation is divided into three: the meditator, the meditated upon, and the relationship – meditation. So meditation has three things in it, three divisions: meditator, meditated upon, and the relationship – medi-tation. When these three dissolve, the meditator loses himself into medita-tion, and the meditation drops into the meditated upon. Anyway one re-mains, and the three are lost. What does it mean? Simple consciousness re-mains; simple knowing remains; simple awareness remains. You are not aware of anything, just aware. You are not aware; there is no you, just awareness – it is better to say, *only awareness remains*. Or, you can choose any point among the three – one remains.

There are different sets of seekers. One set says the object of medita-tion remains, another says the subject of meditation remains; another says object and subject both are lost; only meditation remains. But there is no conflict; this is just a difference in names.

Three are no more; three are lost into oneness.

This oneness is *That Art Thou.*

This oneness is to come to realize *I am That:*

Or That I am – *tat twamasi.*

Step by step, move into the unknown and become the unknown.

Now get ready for the meditation....

At the time of this samadhi, *the moods of the
mind take the form of the soul, and therefore they
are not apparent.
But after the meditator has come back from his
samadhi, those moods which had disappeared, are
inferred by memory.
In this world, which is without a beginning,
one accumulates millions of karmas conditioning from
actions. They are all destroyed in this samadhi, and
inner spontaneous qualities grow.
The great knowers of yoga describe this samadhi
as* dharmamegha, *because it showers like a raincloud
and inner spontaneity issues forth its thousand fruit.
Through this samadhi the whole crowd of desires
become extinct. And when the holds of karma known as*
punya *and* papa, *virtue and sin are uprooted, then
the great saying –* "tat twamasi," *That Art Thou –
becomes illumined.
First as indirect knowledge and then as a fruit
held in your palm, it becomes direct knowledge.*

In the morning we discussed four steps: right listening, right thinking, right meditation, and right *samadhi*.

This sutra goes beyond samadhi. This sutra says samadhi is the door into the unknown – not only the unknown, but the unknowable. it opens into the eternal, into the infinite.

The moment you enter samadhi you have to leave your mind behind. Your mind cannot enter samadhi; you can enter, but not your mind. Unless you can leave your mind behind, samadhi is not for you. Your luggage – thinking, memories, karmas, all your past lives, the whole luggage which is your mind – has to be left behind. When you have left your mind behind... and this is a basic condition: the mind cannot enter samadhi, only you can enter. Why? Because you are at the center; mind is just the periphery.

If you want to enter the center you have to leave the periphery. You cannot go with the periphery to the center. If you insist, "I will take my periphery, my circumference to the center," then you will remain on the circumference. Howsoever you endeavor, if you cling to the circumference you can never enter the center. Entering the center means leaving the periphery, leaving the circumference; mind is the circumference – this is a basic condition.

Samadhi means entering into yourself without the mind. But if you enter samadhi without the mind, you cannot *feel* samadhi – this is the essence of this sutra – you cannot feel, you cannot think. Really you cannot know what is happening, because the knower, the instrument of knowledge, is the mind.

It is as if you enter a garden. Your eyes are weak, and you cannot see without your specs. And this is the condition: you have to leave your specs at the gate. So you enter without specs. You enter the garden, but you cannot see because the very instrument of seeing is not with you.

Mind is the instrument to know, to feel, to recognize. Mind has been left behind. So a man who enters samadhi enters totally ignorant, just like a child. Jesus says, "Be like children; only then you can enter my kingdom of God. Be like small children." At the door of samadhi everyone is like a child – with no mind – just being, pure and simple and innocent. But then you cannot see what is happening, you cannot feel what is happening. The happening is there and you are too much in it; there is no distance.

Mind creates the distance between the known and the knower. If there is no mind, the known and the knower merge, they become liquid, they enter into each other and the distance cannot be maintained. And without distance, knowledge is impossible.

So in samadhi you know nothing. In samadhi, knowing, the knower, the known...they all cease and they become one ocean, just one unity, liquid, flowing. That doesn't mean that you are unconscious. You are conscious – fully conscious, for the first time – but the consciousness is so much, the consciousness is so unlimited, the consciousness is so infinite that it is impossible to make any differentiation between who is the knower and what is the known. You are immersed in it totally, as if a drop of water has become one with the ocean.

There is a beautiful story, and Ramakrishna used to repeat it many times. He used to say that there was a great gathering near the ocean once – some religious festival, and a great crowd gathered there. Two pundits, two great scholars also came, and they began to discuss whether the ocean is unfathomable or fathomable, whether the ocean can be measured or not. So they discussed around and around – discussions are always around and around, you go on beating around and around the bush. No discussion goes deep and direct, it cannot.

One simple man, just a villager, an innocent one, said, "I have been listening to your discussion, days have passed, and there seems to be no conclusion. And I think – I am an ignorant man – I suggest that unless you go deep into the ocean, how can you decide whether is is fathomable or not? You remain on the bank and you go on discussing; you go on arguing, quoting scriptures, and authorities. But I am asking a simple question: have you been to the ocean?"

Those two scholars said, "Don't interfere, you don't know scriptures." But the poor man said, "I know the ocean. I need not know your scriptures. You are talking about the ocean; what is the need for scriptures to be brought in? I suggest you take a jump, go to the bottom, and then come back and tell us."

So those two scholars jumped into the ocean, but they never came back.

Ramakrishna says, "They never came back because those two scholars were really men of salt, so as they went in, they began to melt. They were just salt; their bodies were made of salt."

In a way it is not inconceivable. Our bodies are made of ocean water, they are salty. Your body is seventy-five percent water – seventy-five percent! – and the water is just the same as the water which is found in oceans. The proportion of salt in your bodies is the same as it is in the ocean water, because man is just a developed form of fish and nothing else. So the story is not very absurd.

Man comes from the ocean, and is salty. Those two scholars were men of salt; their bodies were made of salt. They came out of the ocean – everyone has come out of the ocean. Now science says that man has come out of the ocean, just a developed form of fish – nothing else. And who can say whether he is developed or not? If you ask the fish they could not say that. They would say that some fish have gone astray – out of the ocean. They could not say those fish have developed – there would seem to be no reason. Only in man's reasoning it seems that man has developed; in a fish's reason it cannot seem so.

The two scholars never came back; the crowd waited and waited and waited. Ramakrishna used to say, "They cannot come back, because the deeper they went the more they melted, and when they reached the bottom, they were no more. So who can come back and who can say?"

When you leave the mind behind, you leave the bank; you take a jump into the ocean and you are part of the ocean – just the salt. When you enter into samadhi you take a jump into the ocean of consciousness – and you *are* consciousness. So when consciousness takes a jump into greater consciousness, infinite consciousness, it becomes one, the division is lost; you cannot experience anything. You experience the absolute, but you cannot say it is an experience. You cannot feel it as an experience.

This sutra says, when consciousness comes back to the mind again, and sees retrospectively from the specs of the mind what has happened, then it infers.

So all knowledge about God is inference. Those who have known …they too have to think it, to remember it, to live it again in memory, through the mind; then they can say what has happened: existence, consciousness, bliss – satchidananda. This is not the experience itself; it is mind looking at the experience – that's why the division. There was no division in the experience itself; mind divides it into three.

And remember, mind divides everything into three. Three is the basic division of the mind – it divides anything into three.

Look at the world, all the divisions, and you will find the basic division is always of three – always three; not only in religion, but in science also. Now they say – since the atom was split – now they say the basic unity of the atom is constituted of three elements: electron, neutron, proton. You may call them Brahma, Vishnu, Mahesh – *trimurti*, the three figures.

The basic division by the mind is three. Seen by the mind retrospectively, mind infers what has happened. Existence has happened, consciousness has happened, bliss has happened – but this is an inference.

This sutra says when you come back from that peak of ecstasy, back to the ground, you look again – now you remember. So all the scriptures, all that has been said about the ultimate truth is an inference of the mind, from memory. Remember it.

In samadhi, mind is not there; that's why you become spontaneous. Mind is the instrument which always destroys spontaneity. Mind always brings the past into the present, and that destroys spontaneity. This part of the sutra has also to be understood before we enter into meditation.

A spontaneous act is never from the mind. A spontaneous act always happens in the present. If it happens through the mind, then the past has come in. I say something to you; you react – the reaction is from the mind. You think about it, you bring your past memories, your knowledge, your experiences, and then you react accordingly. Then this act is not spontaneous; this act is dead, it is not alive. Reaction is dead, never alive; response is alive and spontaneous. I say something to you and you respond – *immediately*, without bringing the past in, without bringing the mind in – you respond.

For example, if you ask something to a buddha, to an enlightened one, you will get confused. If you ask the same question today and the same tomorrow and the day after tomorrow, you are not going to get the same answer. It is impossible for a buddha. He is not reacting. He is not a parrot; he responds. You ask the question and immediately his consciousness responds – responds to it. It is not a reaction of the mind; it is an encounter, direct, immediate. Every moment you go on asking the same question, but the same answer will not be coming.

Repetition is through the mind. Spontaneous consciousness is always new and fresh.

This sutra says that samadhi brings you back to your center of spontaneity. That spontaneity is known in the upanishadic terminology as *dharma*. Dharma means your natural, spontaneous, being, undistorted by the mind; your natural, spontaneous mirror, undistorted by anything, pure and innocent. Through samadhi you become spontaneous. Really, through samadhi you become religious. Before that, you can belong to a religion, but you are not religious. You can be a Christian, you can be a Hindu or a Mohammedan, but you are not religious.

You belong to a certain organization, a certain church, a certain sect. This belonging is mental. When you enter samadhi for the first time, you come into the world of dharma, of real religion. Now you become spontaneous, you become natural. Nothing is imposed from the mind, you act in totality, moment to moment. Your acts become atomic, always new and fresh and young. Whatsoever you do now is always fresh. This freshness of being is known as dharma. This is what a religious mind is. And unless you become a religious mind in this way, through samadhi, you cannot know what is meant by this *mahavakya - tat twamasi - That Art Thou.*

When you become spontaneous then you know you are *That.*

With the ultimate, now you are one.

Now your finite being is not finite.

Now the divine is not far away. Now you are divine, and the divine is you - the duality is lost. You become for the first time a knower that this sutra of tat twamasi - *That Art Thou* - is real, authentic. Now you can become a witness, now you can say, "This is so, because I have known it." And unless you can say, "I have know it," nothing is worthwhile.

Just a few days ago, a theologian came to me and he began to talk about God. I asked him again and again, "Please tell me, have you known? Have you seen?" But he began to quote *The Bible*; he began to quote scriptures. And he said, "This is written there, and that is written there."

I told him, "It may be written; I accept that it is written there, but that's not my question. I am asking whether *you* have know it?" But he would not answer the question. He would again repeat, "Jesus has said this in the New Testament." He opened the book - he had a book of the New Testament in his pocket. He opened the book and he began to read.

I told him again and again, "Don't read it! I have read it already, so I know what is written it it. Tell me directly, have you seen? Have you realized?" But there was no answer.

If someone asks you, "Have you seen the divine?" and you go on quoting the *Upanishads*, that's stupid. Say yes or no - and you cannot deceive, because there is no question of deceiving anyone. Say *to yourself* whether you have seen it, known it, realized it. If you have not, then start on a long journey - from right listening to right thinking; from right thinking to right meditation; from right meditation to right samadhi. Then only you will be able to know. And unless you know, the whole knowledge of the world is futile - unless *you know.*

Now be ready for our meditation.

*When desires do not arise even in the face of
the objects of enjoyment, know it as the state of
vairagya – non-attachment, desirelessness.
And when the ego ceases to rise, know it as the
highest state of knowledge.
When the moods that have become extinct do not
arise again, that state is known as one of the
indifference.
And the sage whose wisdom has become steady
attains eternal bliss. One whose mind has dissolved
into the supreme becomes innocent and inactive. And
the moods of the mind then dissolve in the unity of
the supreme self, and the purified individual self
remains choiceless and in a state of pure
consciousness.
This state is called wisdom, or pragya. And one
who has attained this wisdom throughout is called
jivanmukta – one free in life itself.
One who has no egoistic feeling in respect of
his body and the senses, and besides has ceased to
think in terms of "me" and "mine" in respect to
other objects, is called a jivanmukta.
When desires do not arise even in the face of
the objects of enjoyment, know it as the state
of vairagya – non-attachment, desirelessness.
And when the ego ceases to arise, know it as
the highest state of knowledge.*

Definitions about certain states of inner search, "in-search," are helpful, because when you enter yourself, you are alone. You will need certain definitions, certain criteria so that you can feel inside what is happening – where you are.

In the in-search one is always alone. One needs certain criteria to feel where one is. And the inner world is uncharted, no map exists which can be given to you. And even if some maps exist, they don't belong to you; they cannot be applicable to you. Buddha says something – that is about his own inner journey; that may not be your route at all. Really, it cannot be your route. Every individual enters into the inner world differently, uniquely, because every individual stands on a certain spot where no one else stands; every individual is unique. Buddha stands somewhere – you cannot stand on that spot. He starts his journey from there; every journey starts from where you are. So we have different routes to move on, no map can be helpful.

So this sutra is not going to give you a certain map, no. Just certain liquid definitions – you can feel your own path – and certain happenings inside, so that you know where you are, where you are moving, whether you are moving or not, whether you are nearing your goal or not.

First the definition of *vairagya* – because that is the entrance. Unless you are non-attached to the world you cannot enter inwards. Your back must be towards the world; only then your face is towards the inner center. So vairagya is the door – non-attachment to the world. What is the definition?

You can force yourself to be non-attached, you can force yourself in the about-turn. You can face the inner world forcibly, you can stand with your back to the world, but just your back to the world is not enough. Your mind may be still moving in the world.

It is not very difficult to go away, to leave, to renounce – it is not very difficult. You can escape to the Himalayas and the world is left far behind – but your mind will still be moving in the world.

Non-attachment, vairagya means: *when desires do not arise even in the face of the objects of enjoyment.*

You can close your eyes; you don't see anything. That is not vairagya, because with closed eyes you can continue desiring. Really, with closed eyes desires become stronger. With closed eyes the world is more charming than with open eyes. Really, if your eyes are open, sooner or later the world loses its charm. The more you penetrate it, the more you know it and see it, the attraction disappears. The attraction is in ignorance; with closed eyes it is more.

Non-attachment is authentic if your eyes are open and objects of enjoyment are there, and no desire arises in you. A naked, beautiful woman is before you and no desire arises. Tantra has used this sutra. Tantra is based on this sutra. Tantra says: Do not escape, because you cannot escape your mind. And the real problem is not the world of objects; the real problem is the mind. So wherever you go, *you* will be there, and *you* are the problem! How can you escape from yourself? Go anywhere, the mind will be there. You can escape from the world, but not from the mind, and mind is the real world. So tantra says, "Do not move away; rather go deep in the world, fully conscious, with open eyes, aware of the desires moving in you. Look at the world deeply." Tantra has developed its own techniques. The tantra technique is that if someone feels sexual desire, then just enforcing *brahmacharya*, celibacy, will not do. If you force celibacy on someone, if he takes a vow that now he will remain celibate, he will simply suppress sexuality and nothing else. And suppressed sex is dangerous – more dangerous than ordinary sex. Then the whole mind will become sexual. The suppressed energy will move inside; it cannot go out, so it moves more inside. It creates grooves, it becomes cerebral; the whole mind becomes sexual.

The sex center gathers more and more energy, and ultimately the whole body becomes a sex center.

Tantra says this is not the way to go beyond sex; this is stupid. Tantra has its own scientific techniques. Tantra says, "Okay, there is desire, there is sex – then move into sex, but move fully conscious." That is the only condition: If you want to touch a beautiful body, touch, but remain conscious, alert that you are touching the beautiful body. And then when you are touching, analyze your touch – what is happening? Observe your touch – what is happening? If you can observe your touch, the touch becomes futile, absurd, stupid; nothing is happening. *Nothing* is happening.

So tantra has techniques....Look at a beautiful naked body; observe it, and observe what is happening inside you. The desire arises: observe the desire, and observe the naked body. And really with a naked body, with a full alert mind, sex is neither suppressed nor indulged; it simply disappears. It may look contradictory – but bodies have become so important only because of clothes. Clothes are deeply sexual. They give the bodies a charm, a hidden charm, a secret attraction which is not there at all. Bodies are just bodies. You hide them and the very hiding creates a desire to look at them, to see. Humanity has become so body-conscious only because of clothes. The clothes create a secret desire to unclothe, to undress.

I was reading Oscar Wilde's *Memoirs*. He was a very sexual man, indulging rather too much. His whole life was just chasing after sex. He notes in his diary that "One woman will not do. I want to enjoy all the women of all the worlds – not only of this world, not only of this age. Unless I enjoy all the women of all the worlds, of all the ages, I cannot be satisfied."

Really, this is how the mind is – not only Oscar Wilde's, your also. And the same is applicable to women's minds also; they also want to enjoy – not this man, but man as such, all men. But Oscar Wilde relates a very strange incident. He was so mad in his sexual desire, that any woman passing on the street and he will become attracted. Then for the first time, he went to a prostitute. And the woman was really beautiful with a very proportionate body, alive, young, fresh. And the moment Oscar Wilde entered her room she immediately undressed – she was a prostitute. The very act of her undressing and Oscar Wilde says, "My desire disappeared – for the first time." And the woman was rare – not just ordinarily beautiful – and charming, a rare beauty. But the very act of her undressing immediately.. and Oscar Wilde notes, "My desire disappeared. Seeing her body naked – there was nothing hidden, and the attraction dissolved." Not only that, he couldn't love the woman, the erection would not come. He tried and tried, and the more he tried...he began to perspire. And he was young and healthy and strong. What happened? – the undressing killed the desire.

Any desire becomes futile if you observe it, if you know it in its totality. Tantra says do not escape; rather, be aware and move into the objects of enjoyment, and one day suddenly all the objects lose their charm.

This sutra says this is the definition of vairagya: *When desires do not arise even in the face of the objects of enjoyment, know it as the state of vairagya – non-attachment, desirelessnes.*

And when the ego ceases to arise, know it as the highest state of knowledge.

This is the criterion for knowledge, wisdom – when there is no ego, when ego doesn't arise.

Ego can arise in any situation. The ego is very subtle and its ways are very mysterious. On anything, ego can feed itself. You meditate and through your meditation your ego can be strengthened: "I am a meditator." And the whole point is lost, the whole meditation is lost. "I am a religious man. I go to church every Sunday, never miss." The ego has arisen. It has taken a religious shape, but the shape doesn't matter. "I fast," or "I take a certain food," or "I do this or that" – any ritual. "I do yoga" – whatsoever. If you feel that your "I" is strengthened, know that you are not on the path of knowing, you are falling down into ignorance.

Go on observing whatsoever you are doing. Do one thing continuously: go on observing whether your ego is strengthened by it. If you continuously observe, observation is a poison to the ego, it cannot arise. It arises only when you are not observing, when you are unconscious, unaware, unattentive. Go on observing, and wherever the ego arises just be a witness to it. Know well that the ego is arising: "I am meditating, certain experiences are happening, and the ego feels good." And the ego says, "Now you are on the path. Now you have known the inner light. Now the kundalini has arisen. Now you are extraordinary. Soon you are going to be a *siddha* – one who has achieved. The goal is now nearer." Know well: with this feeling of the goal being nearer, you are missing the goal. This ego feeling good is a fatal disease.

This sutra says, when the ego doesn't arise, it is the highest state of knowledge. When the feeling of "I" doesn't arise, you *are* but there is no "I."

We go on saying, "I am." The man of knowledge rarely feels only "am," not "I" – just "amness," existence, being, with no "I" attached to it. "Amness" is vast, infinite; "I" is finite. "Amness" is *brahma*.

When there is no "I," when there is only simple "amness," when the "I" is dead, this state is known as the state of a jivanmukta – one who has achieved freedom in lie, one who has achieved freedom while in the body, one who has known the infinite while alive.

You can also become a jivanmukta. The only problem is you. Throw it out, and you *are*. Nothing new is to be gained; the freedom is there hidden in you, but you are attached to the ego. That creates a boundary, a limitation. Look beyond the ego, and suddenly you enter another world. And it was always there, just to be seen, but our eyes have become fixed; we cannot move our eyes. We go on looking in one direction – the direction of the ego. The reverse is the dimension of the non-ego, and non-ego is the path.

One who has no egoistic feeling in respect of his body and the senses, and besides has ceased to think in terms of "me" and "mine" in respect to other objects, is called a jivanmukta. Egolessness is jivanmukti.

Egolessness is a great death. When you die only your body dies; when you attain *mukti*, freedom, your mind dies.

In the old scriptures the master, the guru, is known also as death: *acharyo mrityu*. The teacher is death, great death. He *is*, because through him your ego dies; he kills you.

In a way he is death, and in a way eternal life, because when the ego is

419

no more, for the first time you *are*.

Die to be reborn.

Jesus says, "Whosoever loses himself, attains, and whosoever clings to himself loses."

Now be ready to lose yourself in the meditation, so that you attain....

*One who does not ever discriminate through
intellect between the individual self and the
supreme self on the one hand, and between the
supreme and the universe on the other, is called a
jivanmukta.
One who treats equally both the noble person
who does him honor, and the ignoble who offends him,
is called a jivanmukta.*

The world does not remain the same as before for one who has known the supreme; therefore, if one sees the world as the same he should be taken for one who has not attained the knowledge, and who is still extrovert. So far as the experience of happiness, sorrow, et cetera, is concerned, it is assumed to be due to *prabdhakarma* – that is the predestined cause-effect chain – because every effect flows from the cause of action. There is no effect anyway without the cause. As upon waking, the effect of dreaming ends, so also upon the attainment of knowledge that "I am the supreme," the accumulated karmas, conditionings of millions of births, become extinct. One who does not ever discriminate through intellect between the individual self and the supreme self, and between the supreme and the universe, is called a *jivanmukta.*

Some more qualities of a *jivanmukta*; something more about the state of mind of a jivanmukta, of the state of consciousness....

The first: there is no division. He sees the whole world as an organic unity, there is no division. Things are not divided; the whole universe is one. He sees the unity. The diversity is there, but the diversity is just on the surface; a jivanmukta sees the unity behind it. Every diversity is just a hidden unity. Why? Why do we divide? – and a jivanmukta never divides.

It is because of the intellect, the medium of intellect. If you look through the intellect, everything is divided immediately. Intellect is the instrument to divide, to analyze. For example you see light, you see darkness, you see birth, you see death. Birth and death in existence are one; birth is death, two poles of one process. If you are born you are on the journey to die. The whole of your life is nothing but a gradual process of dying. But the mind divides; mind says birth is good, death is bad. Mind says life is good, death is bad. But death is part of life, life is part of death – they cannot be divided.

Have you ever seen anything alive which is not also dying simultaneously? A flower has come up, has opened its petals. This opening of the petals – can you see it as a process of death? The flower is alive, young, but it is dying already. The evening will come and the petals will wither away. And the withering of petals is really nothing but the conclusion; in the morning the process began, the petals opened. The very opening in the morning will become withering in the evening; the petals will wither away.

So where do you divide? Where is the line where you can say that the flower was alive, and then the flower started to die? Is there any distinction? Can we mark a boundary that up to this point the flower was alive, in the process of more and more life, and from this point the flower started to die? No, there is no possibility of division.

Birth and death is a continuous process. One pole is birth, another pole is death. But mind, intellect, thinking, divides. Mind says birth is good, celebrate it; death is bad, weep over it. And the same goes on; the whole of life becomes a division between things which are not divided. Because of this division we live in a false world, a mind-created world. You say this is love and this is hate, and this is religion and that is irreligion, and this is sin and that is virtue – all divisions, on all layers, on all planes, are through the mind.

Put aside the mind and look at life, and then everything is one: then life and death are one, then darkness and light are one, then love and hate are one.

A jivanmukta never divides because a jivanmukta looks at life without the mind coming in, interfering. Can you look without the mind, even for a single moment? Try it. It is one of the most arduous things, but if possible, the most beautiful. Look at a flower and don't allow the mind to come in between you and the flower. But the mind comes immediately – you have not even seen really, and the mind says, "This is a rose – beautiful, red," and the desire to possess it, to pluck it, arises. The mind starts functioning. The flower is there and the cloud of mind comes in, and you look through the mind. Don't allow this.

Look at the flower. Don't let your mind say, "This is a flower. This is a rose." Just look.

Stop the mind and just look.

Don't allow the mind. Don't move, and don't allow the mind any movement; just look. Become a stare. Let your whole consciousness flow from your eyes, and don't allow the mind to create any cloud between you and the flower. Then what happens? If you go on trying....

This is a meditation – a meditation based on non-verbalization. Don't verbalize, let the flower be there. Observe it, be a witness to it, but don't verbalize the experience. Don't translate it into language. The rose is there – red, alive. Feel it, see it, remain with it. But don't allow the mind to come in and say something – "This is beautiful," or something else. It is difficult in the beginning, but if you go on trying, sometimes for seconds there will be no language. The flower will be there in all its beauty, in all its aliveness, youngness, but with no name, with no linguistic concept attached to it. The rose has never known that it is a rose; it is you who have called it a rose.

A rose is a rose without ever being aware of being a rose. The name is given by your mind. The rose is simply a rose without knowing whether it is beautiful or ugly – you have called it so. If there is no mind in the world, the rose will be there but it will not be a rose, it will not be a beautiful flower; it will be just existence flowering with no name attached to it – no verbalization, no language, no valuation. It will flower. It will be just the same, simple existence. If you don't verbalize you will come to be acquainted with the flower as it is, without human interpretation. And when the mind is not there, for a single moment there is a breakthrough. The rose is there, you are here; and if the mind is not there to divide you, if the mind has dropped, suddenly you become one with the rose.

I don't mean that you become a rose. It will be very difficult then to become a human being again. I don't mean that you become a rose. You remain whatsoever you are, and the rose remains whatsoever the rose is –

424

but suddenly there is a communion, a meeting. Your consciousness moves directly, with no hindrance, and the rose also moves, comes nearer. You become close and intimate, and the flower enters you; the doors are open, and you enter the flower. The doors of the flower are always open, there is no mind to close them – but when your doors open, the flower moves in you, and you move in the flower, and there is a constant harmony. The flower contributes, you also contribute, and there is a meeting.

That meeting can become a glimpse into the cosmos, because a flower is not just a flower. It is the whole cosmos grown into a flower, the whole cosmos become a flower. You are also not just a human being – the whole cosmos has become consciousness in you; that too is a flowering. And when these two flowerings meet, that meeting is ecstatic, blissful. And through that meeting you for the first time become aware of a non-verbal existence.

Man has created verbalization, man has created language, man has created mental concepts. They all drop, and the whole of existence becomes a deep silence, a no-music.

The jivanmukta lives in this no-music. The jivanmukta lives in this silence. The jivanmukta lives without mind. It seems absurd – how can one live without mind? Then he will go mad....

So the last point to be remembered is never think that a madman has no mind. Really, a madman has a very fixed mind, solid. A madman has really more mind than you, that's why he has gone mad; too much mind has created the whole mess.

A madman and a jivanmukta are poles apart. The madman is too much mind; a jivanmukta is no mind, and we are in between somewhere. And we go on moving – sometimes we reach the madman, sometimes we have the glimpse of a jivanmukta. At any moment you can become mad. In anger you become temporarily mad, in sex you become temporarily mad – any moment you can become a madman, but fortunately you can come back. If you cannot come back, and become fixed in the extreme, you become mad.

So the madman is not without a mind; rather, he is with too much or with many minds – multi-minds. He is a crowd of minds. And a jivanmukta is just the opposite pole: no mind. That doesn't mean that he cannot think. Really, on the contrary, only a jivanmukta can think; you cannot think. What is the difference? Thoughts go on in you, thinking is an obsession with you. You are not the master. Thoughts go on and on, you cannot stop them. You cannot say, "Don't come," you cannot say, "Now I want to relax, no more thoughts." Whatsoever you say they are not going to listen to you; rather, if you disturb them they become more mad. If you say, "Don't come," they come more.

Try with a single thought: try to forget it, and you cannot forget it. Try to stop it, and it will haunt you. It will go on and on, and it will defeat you; you are not the master. You cannot think; just this mad crowd of thoughts, and you think that you think – you cannot think. Only a jivanmukta can think, because thoughts are not his masters. He uses thoughts just like you use your legs. When you want to walk, you use them; when you don't want to walk, the legs are relaxed, non- moving. But think of a man who says to his legs, "Please, now stop," and they go on moving! They say, "We cannot stop. Who are you to stop us?" Then we will say that the legs have gone mad. Your mind is like that. You say, "Stop" and it never stops. You say, "Think over this," and it goes on to think of something else. Try, and you will know your mind is not your slave.

So it is better to say that your mind thinks you, not that you think with your mind. Your mind possesses you, it is not you who are in possession of the mind. A jivanmukta uses his mind just like you use your legs: when he wants to, he thinks – and he thinks whatsoever he wants. If he never wants to think he remains quiet, silent; there is no mind inside.

When this mind is not there constantly, you come into contact with brahma, and then you know *tat twamasi* – *That Art Thou.* Without the mind there is no division; then the self inside becomes the supreme. When there is no division, the self and the supreme are one, one wave of existence.

Your self is nothing but the supreme come down to your body, resting in you – your body has been taken as an abode. Your body is just a host and the supreme has become a guest in you.

*The yogi, being alone and indifferent like the
sky, does not even in the least attach himself with
the future.
Even as the ether inside a wine jar remains
untouched by the smell of wine, so the self, even in
association with its covering, remains
uncontaminated by its nature.
As the arrow aimed at its target cannot but hit
it after it has left the bow, so the karmas
performed before the advent of knowledge will yield
its fruit, even after one has attained knowledge.
It implies that the fruits of karma done before
realization have to be lived out.
As the arrow shot at a tiger cannot be stopped
upon learning that it is a cow and not a tiger, but
rather goes forth and hits its object just as
forcefully.
So the action performed yields its fruits even
after knowledge has been attained.
One who knows his self as ever young and
deathless also remains so.
How could he even have an imagination of the
bondage due to past conditions? It means that there
is no relationship between the sage and the his
past conditionings.*

Some very significant and beautiful definitions about the ultimate experience....

The first thing to know about the ultimate experience is that it cannot be called an experience, because experience implies the experiencer and the experienced – the subject and the object. But the ultimate experience is absolutely undifferentiated, undivided. The experiencer is the experienced, the observer is the observed, the knower is the known, the lover is the beloved – there are not two; only one remains.

About this one who remains, this sutra says that one is like space, like sky – vacant, empty, yet full, fulfilled; yet whole.

Look at the sky: Sky is just emptiness, but everything exists in the sky. It cannot exist; otherwise, because to exist you need space, emptiness. So emptiness surrounds the whole existence. Existence comes out of this emptiness and again drops this emptiness – and this emptiness remains untouched, unaffected.

Observe the sky in the rainy days: Clouds come, the whole sky just disappears behind the clouds. You cannot even imagine where the sky has gone. It has gone nowhere; the clouds will rain and disappear, and the same sky will be there. It was always there; even when there were clouds the sky was there in its total emptiness. Clouds cannot disturb it, and clouds cannot affect it – they come and go and the sky remains the same.

It remains in its suchness, in its *tathata*.

This word "suchness" is to be understood deeply. What do I mean when I say the sky remains in its suchness? It remains in its nature, unchanged by anything that happens in it. It is just like a mirror: The mirror remains untouched in its suchness, in its mirroring – fresh, young, never old. Whatsoever happens before the mirror, whatsoever is reflected in the mirror, comes and goes; the mirror remains unscarred, the mirror remains eternally virgin. This is what is meant by sky. Sky is the eternal virgin. The virginity is never broken, the sky remains unmarried to anything, untouched. Everything happens in it and yet nothing happens to it.

The same sky is within you also. Without, there is space; within also, there is space. Space is everywhere. The space within is known as you self, and the space without is known as the supreme self. The body is just a material barrier – and it is porous, so the outer sky goes on coming in and the inner sky goes on coming out. There is a constant meeting. Your body is just like an earthen pot, porous. You have an earthen pot of the body, it divides, but it cannot divide totally; the space is not broken by it.

To know this inner space is the ultimate experience, because once you know this inner space you have know all; the quality of the inner space is the quality of the outer space. Inner and outer are not really two things; inner and outer are just two terms – because of this earthen pot, this body, we call it the inner space and the outer space. When the body drops, the inner becomes the outer and the outer becomes the inner; they become one.

In and out are false terms. You can put an earthen pot in the ocean; then the ocean is divided by the earthen pot – the ocean without, and the ocean within. But the earthen pot is porous, and some drops will escape from the within to the without, and some drops will go on coming in, from the without to the within. But then the earthen pot melts, and drops, and in and out become one.

When one comes to know this inner space as just an extension of the outer space – or vice versa: when one comes to know this outer space as just as an extension of the inner space, then inner and outer become meaningless. They are.

To know this while in the body is called the state of jivanmukta – while the body is there, the earthen pot is there, you have realized the inner space and the quality of space. Now there is no inner and outer. Of course the body is there, but now you know that the body never divides – the division is false. But the body will continue for a while......

The *Upanishads* say that even when you become a knower of the inner, a knower of the space – and you have come to realize that nothing can disturb you, nothing can scar you, nothing can touch you, your virginity is absolute – even then your past karmas will continue to have their effects. The body will continue; the body will continue to feel pleasure and pain, the body will become old, diseased, the body will die – this will continue.

Knowledge of the inner self is not the cessation of all karmas. The past karmas will drop only when they have reached their target. But now, no new karmas will be accumulated. When you attain to this knowing, past karmas will continue for a while, unless and until their momentum is finished – but new karmas will not be accumulated. And secondly, while these old karmas are going on in their continuity, you will know that they are not related to you. You will remain in your unrelatedness.

So a jivanmukta never says, "This is my body." He says, "This is my past karma's body." He never says, "I am ill and I am suffering." He only says, "This is a long procession of karmas and their effect; my past karmas reaching to their target – past reaching into the future. I am just a witness to it, unrelated." Because of this, because of this experience, observation, this realization that all the past karmas of all the past millions of lives have not affected my inner space – it has remained pure, crystal pure, innocent – this realization means cessation of the future.

Then you cannot long for happiness, you cannot long for success, you cannot long for riches, this or that. You cannot be for and against – this should be and this should not be – because now you know that nothing has ever happened to you, and nothing can happen to you. This knowing that the past has been absolutely futile to you – you have been just space, just like sky – like space, you have remained pure, simple, innocent...the future drops.

The future is just the past reflected again and again. Desiring something which was pleasant in the past, not desiring something which was unpleasant in the past, is the projection of the future. The future is just the past reflected again and again – modified, a little bit of change here and there, rearranged, re-structured, but all the elements belong to the past.

When the past appears unrelated to you, and you appear just like empty space…clouds have come and gone, lives have come and gone; birth, death, you were this and that – a beggar in one life, an emperor in another, unsuccessful in one, successful in another, educated, uneducated, good and bad, sometimes a thief and sometimes a saint – everything has come and gone, and the inner point has remained untouched. Nothing has happened to it; everything happened around it, near it, in the vicinity, but nothing has happened to *it* itself – knowing this, the whole future drops completely. Now you cannot project the whole nonsense that you were projecting in the past. Future drops. With future, time drops. With time, cessation of time – you enter the eternal.

But the past will have its fulfillment. Now you can watch the past moving into the future *without* you. You remain in the present; the past goes on moving into the future until the whole momentum gained in the past is finished.

A jivanmukta means one who has attained to the inner sky, inner space, but still he will have to live in the body. He will have to be a witness to all the past karmas and their consequences. When all the consequences are finished, and the past karmas have dropped, the body will drop. Then a jivanmukta becomes a mukta; then *moksha*, total freedom is attained.

A jivanmukta attains freedom from the past, freedom from the future – but he cannot attain freedom from the consequences of the past. They will have to be fulfilled…but he remains a witness.

One who knows his self as ever-young and deathless also remains so.

How could he even have an imagination of the bondage due to past conditions? It means that there is no relationship between the sage and his past conditionings.

The conditionings go on flowing but there is no relationship; you remain a witness.

If you can become a witness this very moment, you are severed from you past and from your future. Then the mechanism goes on moving, just like you are on a bicycle pedaling. You stop pedaling but the cycle will have some movement still, because of the movement of the past. You are not pedaling it, but it is not going to stop just now. It will move into the future without you pedaling it. It will go a little while and then it will drop.

The same happens with your body, your mind. It is just a cycle, just a mechanism. It will move, but without you it cannot move far. Unless it is fed continually, fueled continually, it cannot move very far; it will drop.

Buddha was dying. Ananda asked him, "Cannot you be with us a little more? Cannot we have you a little more? I have not yet attained and you are dying, and you are leaving us." Buddha had said that morning that he was going to die. "So if you have to ask anything," he had told his disciples, "you can ask. This is my last day. This evening will not come for me. This morning is the last; in the noontime I will drop. When the sun comes to its peak, I will drop."

So his disciples gathered and they began to weep and cry. And Ananda asked him, "Cannot you stay a little while more?" Buddha said, "That is impossible, because all the past karmas are finished. This is the last day, the last momentum; I feel it can last up to noon. The energy is gone, everything has ceased, and now the mechanism is just going to stop. And nothing can be done, because as far as I am concerned, I stopped pedaling long before – forty years.

Really, I have been dead for forty years as far as I am concerned. I have not been in the body for these forty years; it was only for you that it has appeared I have been in this body. For me, I have been beyond; I have gone out of it long before. But the body had to continue, and now this is impossible. The momentum is just in its last flicker, the flame is just about to go, the oil is completely finished. And I cannot pour more oil into it because the man who could pour is dead for forty years – who could pour more oil into it? So ask, don't wait. The noon is coming soon – if you have anything to ask, you can ask. The noon is coming very soon."

This happens – Buddha was a jivanmukta for forty years. A jivanmukta means one who is already dead – of course, the body is alive, and then moksha is attained and body also falls.

*Prarbdhakarma fulfills itself only
when one identifies the self with the body, but it
is no good identifying with the body. Who wants to
sever this identification and free him self of
prarbdhakarma, illusion of the body is the basis
for the projection of the prarbdhakarma.
But that which is projected or imagined by
illusion can never be real. And how can it arise or
manifest if it is not real? And how can it be
destroyed if it is not manifested? How can the
false, the unreal have the bondage of conditioning?
This body is the result of ignorance. And
knowledge destroys it fully. Ignorance then raises
doubt as to how this body exists even after
realization. To remove this doubt of the ignorant,
the scriptures have ordained the concept of
prarbdha externally.
In reality there is neither body nor prarbdha.*

This sutra is very strange, but very true. To understand this sutra is to understand many many things about scriptures, about teachers, about masters, methods, techniques, doctrines.

This sutra says that in reality there is no world, in reality there is no suffering; in reality whatsoever you feel and know is not – but in reality, remember. As far as you are concerned, it is real.

As far as *you* are concerned, it is real.

We should try to understand it through dream, because the Eastern mind has been very much fascinated by the reality of dream. And this sutra can be understood only through dream.

You are dreaming. While dreaming you can never doubt that the dream is a dream. While dreaming, the dream is true, real, as real as any reality – even more real. Why do I say even more real? I say this because when you get up in the morning, you can remember your dream – but when you go into sleep you cannot remember what has happened, what was happening when you were awake. This is a rare phenomenon.

You cannot remember that you are a doctor in the day while you are awake, or an engineer, or a minister. You cannot remember in your dream the facts of the day, when you were awake. The whole reality, the so-called reality of the day is completely washed away by the dream – it seems more powerful. But in the morning when you get up, when sleep has gone, you can remember your dream. It means the reality of your day is not strong enough to completely wash away the reality of the dream. In dream you forget your day completely, but in your day, in your waking state of mind, you can remember your dreams. Dreams appear to be more real –

that's why I say "even more real."

In dream you can never doubt that whatsoever you are seeing is unreal or real; it *is* real, it is felt to be authentically real. Why? Why does dream appear so real? – and this is not your first experience. You have been dreaming for your whole life, and every day in the morning you have come to know that the dream was unreal. Yet, when you go to sleep tonight and dream, you will not remember your whole life's experience, that dreams are unreal. Again you will fall into the illusion, and you will feel the dreams as real. In the morning again you will repeat that "it was just a dream, nothing real." What is happening? So much experience of dreaming, still the dream remains real. Why? – because really, anything becomes real if you are absent.

Your absence gives reality to false things.

In the dream you cannot remember yourself – so whatsoever passes in front of your eyes becomes real because you are not. You are so unreal that anything can be felt as real. If you can remember yourself in the dream, the dream will drop; it will cease immediately.

Gurdjieff used to give this technique to his disciples: to remember themselves continuously. In the day go on remembering "I am, I am." Do whatsoever you are doing but continuously make it a point to remember "I am" – not verbally, feel it – "I am." Eating, go on eating, and simultaneously feel "I am." Remember "I am." You are walking, go on walking; remember "I am." This Gurdjieff called "self-remembering." Buddha has called it "right remembering" – *samyak smriti*.

Go on remembering – "I am." If this feeling of "I am" goes deep, it will follow you in sleep also. And when there is a dream, you will remember – "I am." Suddenly the dream will stop: if you are, then there can be no dream.

This is just to explain to you a greater truth: in this life, the world *is* because we *are not*. This is the *Upanishad's* basic teaching. In this world, the world is, everything is – you are not. Only you are not; everything is.

That's why you cannot feel whether it is real or unreal. Remember yourself, be centered in yourself, be conscious, aware. And as you become

more intensely aware, you will feel simultaneously that the world is dropping its reality and is changing into a dream. When you become aware totally, the world becomes a dream. This means, if you are real, then whatsoever you experience is a dream – *whatsoever*, I say – if you are authentically
real, conscious, alert, then all your experiences are dreams.

If you are unaware of yourself, then your own reality is projected onto
the dreams, then your own reality is transferred to the dreams. Your own
existence is transferred to dreams and experiences and thoughts, and they
become real. They have a borrowed reality; your own reality has gone to
them. They are not real.

For example, look in a mirror. Your face is there in the mirror; it looks
real – it is not. It is just a borrowed reality, it is not real at all. You are real,
the mirror reflection is just a dream. Forget yourself completely – as it
happens particularly with women; they forget themselves completely –
and the mirror figure becomes more real. Look at a woman looking into
the mirror, observe her. What happens? She is no more – only the mirror
is, and the mirror-woman has become real. She has completely forgotten
herself. The mind is doing the same.

The world is just a mirror.

You have forgotten yourself, and the reflection has become real.

This is a borrowed reality.

Remember yourself!

Do it with a mirror and you will come to a deep realization. Do it with a
mirror: gaze constantly into the mirror, continuously, for thirty minutes,
forty minutes. Go on staring, and constantly go on remembering, "I am
real. This is a reflection. This which is mirrored is reflection. I am real, not
this reflection." Go on remembering inside, "I am, I am, I am," and go on
staring into the eyes of the reflected figure – your own figure. Suddenly –
any moment this can happen – the reflection will disappear. Suddenly the
mirror will be vacant. It is a very strange experience when suddenly you
are in front of the mirror, and the face has disappeared and the mirror is
vacant. Why does it happen? If you go on remembering "I am, I am," and
this remembering becomes authentic, then the borrowed reality comes

back to you and the mirror becomes vacant.

Even for a single moment if you can see the mirror as vacant – no face, nothing reflected – you will feel a sudden upsurge of reality in you. For the first time you may become aware that *you are.*

This same thing happens with the world when someone becomes a witnessing self. One day, this explosion comes to him – the whole world disappears, the whole world becomes just vacant; only I am, and the whole world has disappeared as if it was never there. This experience is the ultimate. Again the mirror will reflect your face, but now you know it is just a reflection. Again the world will come – for one moment you will see the world has disappeared, and again the world will be there – but now it will never be real again. It will be just a dream world, and all the figures will be dream figures. It will be a great drama.

But when you know it as a drama, a pseudo phenomenon, you are freed from it. Then there is no clinging, and then there is no slavery, no bondage.

Now get ready for the night meditation....

*The scriptures do not say that the body is real
for the knower, but they say so for the ignorant.
In reality, there is only the non-dual supreme,
which is one without a second, and nothing else
exists except it.
And the supreme is known as something without
beginning and without end – immeasurable, pure,
innocent, existential, conscious, eternal, blissful,
imperishable, all-pervading, non-dual, established
always in oneness.
With a face in every direction, one is unable
to renounce it or accept it, existing without any
foundation or support, attributeness, actionless,
subtle, artless, self-evident, pure, enlightened
and incomparable.
Thus you enjoy most blissfully the
undifferentiated self which you have known by your
own experience as indivisible; thus be a* siddha, *a
fulfilled one.
The scriptures do not say that the body is real
for the knower, but they say so for the ignorant.*

This has to be understood clearly. Particularly for the Western mind, this is very confusing. The Western mind has its own tradition. The Western mind is really the developed tradition of the Greek attitude, Socrates, Aristotle, Plato – they have built the foundations of the Western mind.

The Western mind insists on the fact, objective fact, objective proof, objective reality. Objective reality means it is not dependent on anyone. The objective statement of a fact is for all; it is not said for some, it is not true for some, it is universally true.

If I say that this tree is green, this is a factual statement. If I make certain conditions that this tree is green only for Hindus, and not green for Mohammedans... or if I say my statement is true only for Christians and not true for Buddhists, then the Western mind will say that this statement is subjective, not objective – imaginary, not real. If the statement is real that this tree is green, then it is true for everyone forever – it is unconditionally true, universally true.

Because of this insistence on objective truth, the West was able to develop a scientific mind. Objectivity must be determined; the individual, subjective knower must be put aside. The knowing must not get involved, the reality must be looked at with a neutral mind, and whatsoever you say must be true for all. Because of this Greek insistence the West could develop science. Science is the search for an objective reality.

The Eastern attitude is totally different. They say, "We are not concerned with facts." Really the Eastern mind says that there are no facts which are unaffected by the individual looking at those facts. Every fact is in a certain way affected. Every statement is an interpretation. Every knowledge is personal knowledge; no knowledge is impersonal.

Now in the West there is one thinker, Michael Polanyi, who has written one of the greatest books of this century – *Personal Knowledge*. Polanyi says that he is now the representative of the Eastern mind in the West. He says, "Every knowledge is personal." When you say something you are involved in it, you cannot say anything impersonal. Even a fact is just an interpretation. When I say this tree is green, What am I saying? I am saying only this, that when I look at this tree I feel greenness in me. My mind interprets this tree as green. A different mind – a mind from some other planet – may not see this tree as green, because green is not a fact but an interpretation. There is nothing as green in the tree. Rays reflected from the tree reach my eyes, then those rays penetrate, are translated, and my inside feels greenness. That greenness is not in the tree.

You may wonder – if we all close our eyes, then these trees are not green; they cannot be green without our eyes. They are green *through* our eyes; otherwise, they are not green.

When there is no light all colors disappear.

In your room you may have many colors. But when the light is put off there is no color, because color is just reflected rays. If there are no rays then there are no colors. But even if there are colors and there is no one to see in the room, there are no colors. This is now a scientific knowledge, scientific observation. When you move out of your room, all the colors move with you. The room becomes colorless, because color needs three things: rays, objects to be reflected upon, and eyes – three things. Then there are colors; otherwise, there is no color.

So when I say that this tree is green, it is a personal statement. And if it looks green to you also, that only shows that you just have eyes like me, nothing else. If the tree looks green to you also, it only means we have similar instruments, nothing else – and then too it is not really so. When I see the tree as green, my greenness and your greenness may not be the same. They cannot be really, because however similar are the eyes we have, they differ. So my greenness may have a different shade, your greenness may have a different shade, and there is no way to compare that my greenness is your greenness. I cannot put my greenness, my feeling of greenness out on a table. You cannot put your greenness out on a table so that we can compare what we have been calling green is the same thing – that's impossible. So it is just compromise, *just a compromise.*

There are certain persons – and many will be here – who are color blind. In ten persons, one person is somehow color blind. Bernard Shaw was color blind, he couldn't see the difference between yellow and green. Yellow and green both looked similar to him, and he did not recognize this fact until he was sixty. How could sixty years pass and he couldn't recognize the fact? And then on his birthday someone presented a suit, a green suit, to him. But the friend had forgotten to send a tie also; the tie was not there. So Bernard Shaw went to purchase a tie, and he purchased a yellow tie – just to match. Bernard Shaw's secretary said to him, "Why are you purchasing a yellow tie? The whole suit is green." Bernard said, "This is green. What! – is this yellow? What do you mean by yellow?" Then for the first time he became aware that he could see yellow. He had been always been seeing yellow and green as green; both were green for him. Blind spots in the eyes....

Whatsoever we know is a personal knowledge.

The Eastern attitude has always been this: that all knowledge is subjective. Not only that, but all statements are also personal. That means many things; the implication is very deep. It means that a statement made is always made to someone. It is not a pure statement made in the vacuum.

This sutra says that *shruti,* the scripture, the word for the knower has two planes of expression: one for the ignorant, and one for the non-ignorant. One for those who are deep in their ignorance, unaware of their inner center – the scripture speaks to them in a different language. To the knower the scripture speaks in a different language.

We have two words and two traditions of scripture. One is *Veda,* another is *Vedant.* The word "vedant" is very beautiful. This *Upanishad* belongs to vedant. Vedant means the end of the veda; vedant means beyond veda. Vedant is the statement for the knower; veda is the statement for the ignorant. Veda speaks the same truth, but for the ignorant; vedant speaks the same truth but for the knower. But then their statements become quite contrary.

For example, for a knower of oneself, one who has realized his own self, there is no body, there is no matter, there is no world, because then everything becomes just consciousness, manifestations of consciousness. Now, even physicists say there is no matter, only energy.

Just fifty years ago physics could not even conceive that there is only energy, no matter. Now there is no matter, because the more physicists penetrated into matter, the more they came nearer and nearer to energy. Now matter is completely non-existential. For science now there is no matter; science has penetrated into the immaterial energy. Now they say it is energy, and if you look and see matter, it is an illusion. It is just energy moving at such a great speed that the appearance of solidity is created. Your earth that you are sitting around, the trees all around it, the stones, the rocks – there is nothing like matter. The rock is not matter, but just electrons moving at a great speed. Because of their speed the rock appears to be solid. The speed is such, so great, that a solidity appears; it is not there. Just energy moving at fast speed creates matter, the appearance of matter.

Really, the language of modern physics is nearer vedant than anything. The modern physicists like Planck or Einstein or others are now talking in terms of vedant. Shankara says that the world is illusory, that it only appears to be. Now Einstein says that matter is illusory – it only appears to be. It only appears; it is false; it is in our eyes, not in reality there.

Vedant penetrated even more. Vedant says there is no energy even, only consciousness. These are the three layers: Matter is how things appear to be at first. Penetrate, go deep, and you enter a second layer which is energy; matter disappears into energy, vibrant energy, vibrations, but there is nothing material, nothing substantial in it. Enter more deeply, and you reach the third layer. Then energy also disappears, and only consciousness remains.

In your body also these are the three layers. The first layer is your physical body; the second layer, your mental body, which is energy; and the third layer is your self, which is consciousness.

Everywhere these are the three layers. But when you enter a deeper layer, the first layer disappears, because then it is nothing but a manifestation. Physics says matter is nothing but energy moving, dynamic energy. Vedant says energy in nothing but consciousness moving, dynamic consciousness. It is possible that *any* day now even science may drop from the energy layer and may come to encounter the consciousness layer. Fifty years ago, science couldn't conceive that matter is just an illusion. Fifty years on, it may be possible even for science to say that energy is nothing but pure consciousness condensed, moving fast.

If consciousness is reached, the whole world becomes just a manifestation of it. This is what is meant by the world being illusory, the body being illusory; everything is illusory except pure consciousness. That pure consciousness is known and named as brahman. That's the basic reality, but to the ignorant this cannot be said directly. The ignorant person believes in matter; he lives on the first layer. He doesn't know anything beyond it, and because he is unaware of anything beyond it, the language of the beyond will be meaningless, absurd.

So for the ignorant the scriptures speak in a different language. They say that the body is true, the body is real, the world is true, the world is real, but you are not the body. This is the way they detach you from the body, how they allow you to move away from the body, how they destroy your identification with the body. And when that identification is destroyed, suddenly you yourself will become aware that there is no body. It existed only in the attachment; it existed only through identification. When your identification is broken, you yourself will come to know there is no body.

There is a beautiful story about Rinzai. He used to say, "There has never been a Buddha. This Shakyamuni, Gautam Siddharth is just a false story." And he was a follower of Buddha, and he would worship in front of Buddha's statue every day in the morning, and would weep and dance. And after that, when he would speak; he would say, "There has been no

Buddha. This Shakyamuni, Gautam Siddharth is just a false story."

So one day someone said to Rinzai, "You go on worshiping Buddha, and you go on saying that this Gautam Buddha, Shakyamuni is just a false story. how do you reconcile these two contradictory things? You appear absurd, irrational."

So Rinzai said, "I believed in Shakyamuni – Shakyamuni, Gautam Buddha – I believed in him, that he was born; then he lived on this earth for eighty years, then he achieved realization, then he talked. I believed, but that belief was the belief of an ignorant one. Then by and by I followed this man who has never been here. By and by I began to love this man, and became a shadow of him. Then I came to realize that the body of Rinzai is just an illusion – my body is an illusion. Then the deeper I went, I realized my mind is an illusion. Then I came to know the innermost center of my being. The day I realized myself, my body, my mind – both became appearances. Now I know this Shakyamuni was never born, because now I know that this Rinzai was never born! Because how can a body be born which is not there – just an appearance. Now I realize that this mind of Rinzai was never born. So how can the mind of Gautam Buddha be born? This man has never been."

The unborn center once known, the undying center once known, the whole interpretation of existence changes. But the man insisted. The questioner said, "Then why go on worshiping? I have seen you this very morning in a prayerful mood before this statue of Buddha, and you say this man was never born. So how can you make a statue of a man who was never born? Why do you go on thanking him?"

Rinzai is reported to have said, "I go on thanking him, because following him I could realize this non-dying, this deathless, this unborn consciousness. I followed him, I became a shadow to him. Only then could I realize this fact, so I am grateful to him – to him who was never born, who has never been." But these are words for knowers.

If you say to someone that Buddha was never born, then he cannot conceive why to worship him, why to thank him. Then he cannot conceive, then everything becomes inconceivable for him, irrational.

So the *Upanishads* speak in two languages. They say the body is there, the world is there, you are in it, so find out who you are in your body. When you have found it, the body will disappear, then the world will disappear. That doesn't mean that these rocks will not be there. They will be there, but then you will not see any solidity in them. That doesn't mean that those rocks will not be there, but that you will not be able to see that those rocks are dead. They will become alive; not only alive, you will feel those rocks have a consciousness of their own. Then this whole world becomes a manifestation of consciousness, a manifestation of brahma. The world disappears as it is, but a new world arises, the world of consciousness. The world of matter becomes illusory; the world of consciousness becomes real. Why?

When you are attached to your body, you feel the world as material. When you move away from your body, centered in your consciousness, the whole world becomes consciousness. What you know about your world is really your knowledge about yourself, it is just a subjective reflection. If you think that you are a body, the world is material. If you know you are not a body, just consciousness, the world becomes consciousness.

The world is just an interpretation of your own state of mind.

Move in, and the outer layers disappear. Be rooted in your being, and this sutra says you become a *siddha*. A siddha means that they function as one. *Thus you enjoy most blissfully the undifferentiated self which you have known by your own experience as indivisible; thus be a siddha,* a fulfilled one.

Move in, reach the third layer of consciousness. Move away from body-matter, move away from energy-mind. Go deep to the ultimate core, to the last point of your existence, the center, consciousness. You are a siddha. Why? Why a fulfilled one? – because then no desire arises, because then no suffering is possible, because then you are constantly merged into bliss, because then nothing is to be achieved.

You have achieved all that without which there is desire. You have achieved that one through which everything is achieved. One becomes fulfilled, one becomes a siddha.

By listening to these above teachings the
disciple attained knowledge and he exclaimed,
"Whither has that world gone? Whither has gone that
world I have just seen? Who did it take away? And in
what way has it dissolved? Is it not immensely
astonishing that it is not?
What have I now to renounce in this great
oceanlike brahma, which is whole and full of a
nectar of bliss? What is the other? What is more unique?
Here, I do not even see anything. I do not even
hear anything, and I do not even know anything,
because I am the ever-blissful self. I am unique. I
can be compared to none. I can be compared only to myself.
I am absolutely alone, without body.
I cannot be indicated. No symbol can represent me.
I am the supreme God Hari. I am immeasurably silent.
I am the infinite, absolute, and the most ancient.
I am not the doer.
I am not the one who indulges.
I am without growth. I am the imperishable.
I am already pure and knowledge itself.
I am the Sadashiv, the eternally good."
This knowledge was transmitted by the guru to
his disciple, Apantaram, who in his turn
transmitted it to Brahma. Brahma gave it
to Ghora Angirasa, and the latter to Raikwa.
Raikwa gave it to Rama, and Rama gave it
to all of humanity.
This is the teaching of Nirvana, of knowledge,
Veda. It is ordained by the Veda itself.
Here ends this Upanishad.

This is a very unique happening. The teacher was saying that this world is just a dream, and unless this dream ceases, the world of reality, the world of truth cannot be attained. "Cease dreaming and enter the world of reality," he was teaching. And he would never have imagined that just by listening to this, the disciple attained to knowledge. How can it happen? It is not happening to us. We have heard it also; it has not happened to us. Why? And why could this happen to that disciple? What is the difference? You are listening, but that listening is not of the heart.

You are listening, but that listening is not total.

You are listening, but you go on standing outside.

Only the mechanical part of your ears hears it. Or at the most, the mechanical part of your mind thinks about it, but the heart remains untouched. You go on protecting your heart from the teaching. You are afraid that if this teaching goes deep into your heart, you will not be the same again. And then you will be thrown into insecurity; you will be thrown into the unknown – and everyone is afraid of the unknown. That fear becomes a barrier.

Unless you are ready to go into the unknown, to move into the unchartered, to move in a world where you do not know anything...insecurity will be there, you will be vulnerable; danger will be there, even death. Unless you are ready to take a jump into the unknown, this teaching cannot become a deep happening for you.

But to this disciple it happened. He heard it; he must have heard it through his heart. He must have heard it through his total being; he must have become one while the teaching was being delivered. The teacher and the taught must have felt a deep communion. The teacher must have gone deep into the disciple's heart through his teaching.

The disciple was ready and receptive. He never doubted; he simply believed – there was no question.

The whole *Upanishad* is without a question, there is no question, no questioning at all. The disciple remains completely silent through the whole discourse. Only in the end do we suddenly become aware that there has been a disciple present. The teacher was talking, the teacher was giving his message, but we were never aware that a disciple was there. Suddenly we become aware in this last part of the *Upanishad,* when the disciple says, *Whither has gone that world I have just seen?* Where is that world? When I came to you, there was a world around me. Now I look and there is no world to be found. Where has it gone? It is immensely astonishing. You were teaching me that the world is not, and now I see that it is not!

What has happened to the disciple? Now he is looking from a new standpoint; now he is looking from a deeper center. Now he is looking really, from his being. When you look from your being, the world of becoming disappears like a dream.

That's how I started this commentary on the *Upanishad.* When we live on the circumference, then the world is real. When we move towards the center, the world becomes more and more unreal. When you stand at your center, when you are centered in yourself, the world completely disappears. *What have I now to renounce in this great oceanlike brahma, which is whole and full of a nectar of bliss? What is the other? What is more unique?*

The disciple is just shocked – what has happened to the world? When for the first time one explodes into that realm of the divine, the first thing is a shock – the world disappears.

And when the world disappears suddenly, you cannot face, you cannot see the other world that arises. The curtain falls, the barriers fall, but your mind has been always attuned to this world of ignorance, of dream. When this dissolves suddenly, you cannot become aware of the other world that is now before you.

Your eyes will need a new attunement; your consciousness will need a new way of looking. Now you will need a new dimension, a new opening in you. Only then you will feel that although the world has disappeared, a new existence has come up and has appeared: *Here, I do not even see anything. I do not even hear anything, and I do not even know anything....*

All old knowledge has become futile. All old ways have become futile. All the senses have become futile, because they were meaningful only when the world was there – but the world of senses has disappeared, senses have become useless: "I cannot see, I cannot hear, I do not know; because all my knowledge was concerned with the world."

Whatsoever you know is concerned with the world If the world disappears, what will be the difference between a learned man and one who is ignorant? What will be the difference? No difference – if the world disappears, then the learned will be just like any ignorant man, because all your learning is concerned with the world. So the disciple says: *I do not even know anything...* only this much I know: *I am the ever-blissful self... unique. I can be compared to none. I can be compared only to myself...I am like myself;* only this much I know.

The knowledge of a Mahavira, the knowledge of a Buddha, or a Jesus, or a Krishna, is not the knowledge of a learned man. They do not know anything about the world; they know only about their own selves.

Mahavira has said that if you can know your own self, you have known all; and if you know everything except yourself, you know nothing.

They know about their own central force, energy, life. They know about their own inner being, and they do not know anything about the world, because the whole world has disappeared. They know only one thing, that *I am the ever-blissful self.*

When you know about the world, you know many, many anxieties, you know anguish, you know tensions, you know misery. When you know many things about the world, the misery goes on growing with your knowledge. The more you know, the more miserable you are. We can observe this all over the world. Now, for the first time, we have gathered great knowledge – not only have we gathered, we have dispersed it to everyone through universal teaching, education. And now every man is miserable, and the misery keeps growing. On the one hand, knowledge grows, on the other hand, misery grows.

What is happening? This seems quite inconceivable, because if with knowledge misery grows, then for what is this knowledge? Knowledge of the without goes deeper and deeper, but then misery also goes deeper and deeper.

There is another knowledge also, that this *Upanishad* is talking about – the knowledge of the inner self. With the knowledge of the inner self, blissfulness grows. So this is just an indication: if you are becoming more and more blissful, know that you are growing in inner knowledge. If you are becoming more and more miserable, know that you are growing in outer knowledge.

The biblical story is beautiful:

Adam was expelled from Eden because he disobeyed God. And what was the disobedience? The disobedience was this: God has forbidden Adam and Eve...he has said to them that they are not to eat the fruit of the tree of knowledge. In the Garden of Eden in heaven, there was a tree, the tree of knowledge, and God has forbidden Adam and Eve to touch that tree, to eat the fruit of that tree. But because of this, Adam and Eve must have become attracted to the tree.

The garden was big and there was only one tree of knowledge. But because of this order, they rebelled. And when they ate the fruit of the tree of knowledge they were expelled from Eden.

This story is beautiful. They were expelled because of knowledge, and man is continuously being expelled from Eden because of knowledge. The more you know, the more heaven becomes just impossible, and hell the only possibility. But there is another tree also in the Garden of Eden. It is not mentioned in *The Bible*, but I will tell you about it. That tree is the tree of inner knowledge, and unless you eat the fruit of that tree you can never enter again into heaven.

There are two types of knowledge: knowledge of things and knowledge of self. The devil tempted Adam and Eve to eat the fruit of the forbidden tree of knowledge – and the *Upanishads* tempt you to eat the fruit of the other tree of knowledge. Unless you enter yourself, and eat the fruit of inner knowledge, you cannot be redeemed; you cannot be liberated, you cannot become free. And you can never be blissful.

I am absolutely alone, without body.
I cannot be indicated. No symbol can represent me.
I am the supreme God, Hari.
I am immeasurably silent.
I am the infinite, absolute, and the most ancient.
I am not the doer, I am not the one who indulges.
I am without growth. I am imperishable.
I am already pure and knowledge itself.
I am the Sadashiv, the eternally good.

The disciple tells his teacher his own experience now. The teacher was telling the disciple his experience; the disciple is not saying, "I am convinced now that whatsoever you say is true," or "I am convinced a little bit, and later on I will think more about it"; nor "Whatsoever you say must be true, because you are a reliable man." No, he simply tells his own experience. He has not even mentioned it, that "Whatsoever you have taught me is true." No reference is made to the teaching at all. He simply says, "Now this is my experience: I am the divine, I am Hari. I am immeasurably silent. I am absolute, infinite." He has attained to experience. This is not a conversion, intellectual; it is a transformation.

This knowledge was transmitted by the guru to
his disciple, Apantaram, who in his turn
transmitted it to Brahma. Brahma gave it to
Ghora Angirasa, and the latter to Raikwa. Raikwa
gave it to Rama, and Rama gave it to all of humanity.
This is the teaching of nirvan, of knowledge,
of the *Veda*. It is ordained by the *Veda* itself.
 Here ends this *Upanishad.*

This last paragraph, last sutra, has to be understood:

Knowledge of the absolute is eternal.
It is never new, never old.
It is not a growing body of knowledge.
Science grows; religion is eternal.
Science goes on growing, increasing. No scientific truth is absolute; it is relative. And no scientific truth can be called really a truth, because it is always more or less approximate. Time will change it, time always changes it. Whatsoever Newton said is no longer said; even what Einstein said is now doubtful.

Time changes science, but time never changes religion. Why? – because the religious experience is attained only when you enter a timeless moment. When you enter in yourself and time stops completely – no flow of time is there...no past, no present, no future; time stops completely – you are here and now. Only this moment remains, and this moment becomes eternal. In timelessness, religious experience is attained; that's why time never alters it.

This sutra says that whatsoever is taught in this *Upanishad* is not something new, it is not original. Our modern world is too obsessed with originality. People go on saying, and trying, and proving that whatsoever is said is original. Particularly in the West, every thinker tries to prove that he is original, that whatsoever he is saying, no one has ever said before. Unless a theory can be proved original it is never appreciated in the West. If someone else has already said it then what is the use? Then what are you doing wasting your time? So everyone tries to be original.

But originality is impossible as far as religion is concerned. As far as science is concerned, originality is possible. In science there are old truths dying, new truths being born. Science is relative, growing. But in religion there can be nothing original. In religion everything is eternal. Whatsoever a buddha says will be said always by anyone who becomes enlightened, who becomes a buddha. Language may differ, terminology may be different, but the experience can never be different.

So in the old India, in the East, it was a tradition always: whenever someone would say something, he would say, "I am not the originator of it. I have also attained to it, but before me it was given by A to B, by B to C, by C to D – it is an eternal message." When one thinks and says, "I am original," this is an egoistic standpoint. The ego always tries to be original; only then it feels strengthened. But these teachings are not ego teachings, ego oriented; they are egoless teachings. Those who had attained to egolessness have said them. That's why this sutra:

This knowledge was transmitted by the guru
to his disciple, Apantaram, who in his turn
transmitted it to Brahma. Brahma gave it
to Ghora Angirasa, and the latter to Raikwa.
Raikwa gave it to Rama, and Rama, gave it to all of humanity.
Here ends this Upanishad.

The scripture ends here but not the journey.
For you, really, now begins the journey.
The *Upanishad* ends, your journey begins.

BOOKS BY
BHAGWAN SHREE RAJNEESH

ENGLISH LANGUAGE EDITIONS

Neo-Sannyas International

Recent Releases

Sermons in Stones
The Rebellious Spirit
The Messiah *(Volumes 1&2) Commentaries on Kahlil Gibran's The Prophet*
The Rajneesh Bible *(Volumes 1-4)*
Bhagwan Shree Rajneesh
    On Basic Human Rights
The Last Testament *(Volume 1) Interviews with the World Press*
The Rajneesh Upanishad
Beyond Enlightenment
The Book: *An Introduction to the Teachings of Bhagwan Shree Rajneesh*
    Series I from A - H
    Series II from I - O
    Series III from R - Z

BIOGRAPHIES

Books I have Loved
Glimpses of a Golden Childhood
Notes of a Madman

Autobiographies

The Sound of Running Water
    Bhagwan Shree Rajneesh and His Work 1974-1978
This Very Place The Lotus Paradise
    Bhagwan Shree Rajneesh and His Work 1978-1984

The Bauls

The Beloved *(Volumes 1&2)*

Buddha

The Book of the Books *(Volumes 1-4)*
    The Dhammapada
The Diamond Sutra
    Vajrachchedika Prajnaparamita Sutra
The Discipline of Transcendence
    (Volumes 1-4) Sutra of 42 Chapters

The Heart Sutra
Prajnaparamita Hridayam Sutra

Buddhist Masters
The Book of Wisdom *(Volumes 1&2)*
Atisha's Seven Points of Mind Training
The White Lotus
Sayings of Bodhidharma

Early Discourses and Writings
A Cup of Tea *(Letters to Disciples)*
From Sex to Superconsciousness
And Now, and Here *(Volumes 1&2)*
Beware of Socialism
Krishna: The Man and His Philosphy
The Long and the Short and the All
The Perfect Way
In Search of the Miraculous *(Volume 1)*

Hassidism
The Art of Dying
The True Sage

Jesus
Come Follow Me *(Volumes 1-4)*
Sayings of Jesus
I Say Unto You *(Volumes 1&2)*
Sayings Of Jesus
The Mustard Seed
The Gospel of Thomas

Kabir
The Divine Melody
Ecstasy: The Forgotten Language
The Fish in the Sea is Not Thirsty
The Guest
The Path of Love
The Revolution

Meditation
The Orange Book
Meditation Techniques
of Bhagwan Shree Rajneesh

Responses to Questions
Be Still and Know
The Goose is Out
My Way: The Way of the White Clouds
Walk Without Feet, Fly Without Wings
and Think Without Mind
The Wild Geese and the Water
Zen: Zest, Zip, Zap and Zing

Sufism
Just Like That
The Perfect Master *(Volumes 1&2)*
The Secret
Sufis: The People of the Path
(Volumes 1&2)
Unio Mystica *(Volumes 1&2)*
The Hadiqa of Hakim Sanai)
Until You Die
The Wisdom of the Sands *(Volumes 1&2)*

Tantra
The Book of the Secrets *(Volumes 4&5)*
Vigyana Bhairava Tantra
Tantra, Spirituality and Sex
Excerpts from The Book of the Secrets
Tantra: The Supreme Understanding
Tilopa's Song of Mahamudra
The Tantra Vision *(Volumes 1&2)*
The Royal Song of Saraha

Tao
The Empty Boat
the Stories of Chuang Tzu

The Secret of Secrets *(Volumes 1&2)*
   The Secret of the Golden Flower
Tao: The Golden Gate *(Volumes 1&2)*
Tao: The Pathless Path
   Stories of Lieh Tzu
Tao: The Three Treasures *(Volumes 1-4)*
   The Tao Te Ching of Lao Tzu
When the Shoe Fits
   Stories of Chuang Tzu

The Upanishads

I Am That
   Isa Upanishad
The Ultimate Alchemy *(Volumes 1&2)*
   Atma Pooja Upanishad
Vedanta: Seven Steps to Samadhi
   Akshya Upanishad
Philosophia Ultima
   Mandukya Upanishad

Western Mystics

The Hidden Harmony
   Fragments of Heraclitus
The New Alchemy: To Turn You on
   Mabel Collins' Light on the Path
Philosophia Perennis *(Volumes 1&2)*
   The Golden Verses of Pythagoras
Guida Spirituale
   The Desiderata
Theologia Mystica
   The Treatise of St. Dionysius

Yoga

Yoga: The Alpha and the Omega
   (Volumes 1-10) Yoga Sutras of Patanjali
Yoga: The Science of the Soul
   (Volumes 1-3)
   Originally titled Yoga: The Alpha and the Omega

Zen

Ah, This!
Ancient Music in the Pines
And the Flowers Showered
Dang Dang Doko Dang
The First Principle
The Grass Grows By Itself
Nirvana: The Last Nightmare
No Water, No Moon
Returning to the Source
A Sudden Clash of Thunder
The Sun Rises in the Evening
Zen: The Path of Paradox *(Volumes 1-3)*
Zen: The Special Transmission

Zen Masters

Hsin Hsin Ming: The Book of Nothing
   Discourses on the Faith-Mind of Sosan
The Search - *The Ten Bulls of Zen*
Take It Easy *(Volumes 1&2) Poems of Ikkyu*
This Very Body the Buddha
   Hakuin's Song of Meditation

Darshan Diaries

Hammer on the Rock
   (December 10, 1975 - January 15, 1976)
Above All Don't Wobble
   (January 16 - February 12, 1976)
Nothing to Lose But Your Head
   (February 13 - March 12, 1976)
Be Realistic: Plan For a Miracle
   (March 13 - April 6, 1976)
Get Out of Your Own Way
   (April 7 - May 2, 1976)
Beloved of My Heart
   (May 3 - 28, 1976)

The Cypress in the Courtyard
  (May 29 - June 27, 1976)
A Rose is a Rose is a Rose
  (June 28 - July 27, 1976)
Dance Your Way to God
  (July 28 - August 20, 1976)
The Passion for the Impossible
  (August 21 - September 18, 1976)
The Great Nothing
  (September 19 - October 11, 1976)
God is Not for Sale
  (October 12 - November 7, 1976)
The Shadow of the Whip
  (November 8 - December 3, 1976)
Blessed are the Ignorant
  (December 4 - 31, 1976)
The Buddha Disease *(January 1977)*
What Is, Is, What Ain't, Ain't
  (February 1977)
The Zero Experience *(March 1977)*
For Madmen Only (Price of Admission:
  Your Mind) *(April 1977)*
This is It *(May 1977)*
The Further Shore *(June 1977)*
Far Beyond the Stars *(July 1977)*
The No Book (No Buddha, No Teaching,
  No Discipline) *(August 1977)*
Don't Just Do Something, Sit There
  (September 1977)
Only Losers Can Win in this Game
  (October 1977)
The Open Secret *(November 1977)*
The Open Door *(December 1977)*
The Sun Behind the Sun Behind the Sun
  (January 1978)
Believing the Impossible Before Breakfast
  (February 1978)

Don't Bite My Finger, Look Where I'm
  Pointing *(March 1978)*
Let Go! *(April 1978)*
The 99 Names of Nothingness *(May 1978)*
The Madman's Guide to Enlightenment
  (June 1978)
Don't Look Before You Leap *(July 1978)*
Hallelujah! *(August 1978)*
God's Got a Thing About You
  (September 1978)
The Tongue-Tip Taste of Tao
  (October 1978)
The Sacred Yes *(November 1978)*
Turn On, Tune In, and Drop the Lot
  (December 1978)
Zorba the Buddha *(January 1979)*
Won't You Join the Dance?
  (February 1979)
You Ain't Seen Nothin' Yet *(March 1979)*
The Shadow of the Bamboo *(April 1979)*
Just Around the Corner *(May 1979)*
Snap Your Fingers, Slap Your Face &
Wake Up! *(June 1979)*
The Rainbow Bridge *(July 1979)*
Don't Let Yourself Be Upset by the Sutra,
Rather Upset the Sutra Yourself
  (August/September 1979)
The Sound of One Hand Clapping
  (March 1981)

Books on
Bhagwan Shree Rajneesh
The Most Dangerous Man Since Jesus
Christ *by Sue Appleton*

Other Publishers

UNITED KINGDOM

The Book of the Secrets *(Volume 1,
    Thames & Hudson)*
Roots and Wings *(Routledge & Kegan Paul)*
The Supreme Doctrine
    (Routledge & Kegan Paul)
Tao: The Three Treasures
    (Volume 1, Wildwood House)

Books on
Bhagwan Shree Rajneesh

The Way of the Heart: the Rajneesh
Movement
    *by Judith Thompson and Paul Heelas,
    Department of Religious Studies,
    University of Lancaster
    (Aquarian Press)*

UNITED STATES
OF AMERICA

The Book of the Secrets
    (Volumes 1-3, Harper & Row)
The Great Challenge *(Grove Press)*
Hammer on the Rock *(Grove Press)*
I Am the Gate *(Harper & Row)*
Journey Toward the Heart
    *(Original title: Until You Die,
    Harper & Row)*
Meditation: The Art of Ecstasy
    (Harper & Row)
The Mustard Seed *(Harper & Row)*
My Way: The Way of the White Clouds
    (Grove Press)

The Psychology of the Esoteric
    (Harper & Row)
Roots and Wings *(Routledge & Kegan Paul)*
The Supreme Doctrine
    (Routledge & Kegan Paul)
Words Like Fire *(Original title:
    Come Follow Me, Volume 1)
    (Harper & Row)*

Books on
Bhagwan Shree Rajneesh

The Awakened One:
The Life and Work of
Bhagwan Shree Rajneesh
    *by Swami Satya Vedant
    (Harper & Row)*
The Rajneesh Story:
The Bhagwan's Garden
    *by Dell Murphy (Linwood Press,
    Oregon)*

FOREIGN LANGUAGE EDITIONS

Chinese
I Am the Gate (Woolin)

Danish
Hu-Meditation and Cosmic Orgasm
(Borgens)
(Hu-Meditation Og Kosmik
Orgasme)
The Book of the Secrets (Volume 1,
Borgens)
(Hemmelighedernes Bog)

Dutch
Bhagwan Shree Rajneesh
On Basic Human Rights
(Stichting Rajneesh Verlag)
(Bhagwan Shree Rajneesh Over de
Rechten van de Mens)
Come Follow Me
(Volume 1, Ankh-Hermes)
(Volg Mij)
Come Follow Me
(Volume 2, Ankh-Hermes)
(Gezaaid in Goede Aarde)
Come Follow Me
(Volume 3, Ankh-Hermes)
(Drink Mij)
Come Follow Me
(Volume 4, Ankh-Hermes)
(Ik Ben de Zee Die Je Zoekt)
I Am the Gate (Ankh-Hermes)
(Ik Ben de Poort)
Just Like That (Mirananda)
(Heel Eenvoudig)
Meditation, the Art of Inner Ecstasy
(Mirananda)
(Meditatie:
De Kunst van Innerlijke Extase)
My Way: The Way of the White Clouds
(Arcanum)
(Mijn Weg,
De Weg van de Witte Wolk)
No Water, No Moon
(Volumes 1 & 2, Mirananda)
(Geen Water, Geen Maan)
Tantra, Spirituality & Sex (Ankh-Hermes)
(Tantra, Spiritualiteit en Seks)
Tantra, The Supreme Understanding
(Ankh-Hermes)
(Tantra: Het Allerhoogste Inzicht)
Tao: The Three Treasures (Volume 1,
Ankh-Hermes)
(Tau)
The Book of Secrets
(Volumes 1-5, Mirananda)
(Het Boek der Geheimen)
The Hidden Harmony (Mirananda)
(De Verborgen Harmonie)
The Mustard Seed
(Volumes 1 & 2, Mirananda)
(Het Mosterdzaad)
The New Man
(Volumes 1 & 2, Zorn/Altamia)
(Excerpts from The Last Testament,
Volume 1)
(De Nieuwe Mens)
The Orange Book (Ankh-Hermes)
(Het Oranje Meditatieboek)
The Psychology of the Esoteric
(Ankh-Hermes)
(Psychologie en Evolutie)
The Tantra Vision
(Volumes 1 & 2, Arcanum)

(De Tantra Visie)
10 Zen Stories (Ankh-Hermes)
(Zoeken naar de Stier)
Until You Die (Ankh-Hermes)
(Totdat Je Sterft)

French

I am the Gate (EPI)
(Je Suis la Porte)
Meditation, The Art of Inner Ecstasy
(Dangles)
(La Meditation Dynamique)
The Psychology of the Esoteric (Dangles)
(L'eveil a la Conscience Cosmique)
The Book of Secrets
(Volume 1, Soleil Orange)
(Le Livre des Secrets)

German

Above All Don't Wobble
(Fachbuchhandlung fuer Psychologie)
(Und vor Allem: Nicht Wackeln)
A Cup of Tea (Sannyas)
(Der Freund)
Beware of Socialism (Rajneesh Verlag)
(Vorsicht Sozialismus)
Bhagwan Shree Rajneesh
On Basic Human Rights
(Rajneesh Verlags GmbH)
(Bhagwan Shree Rajneesh
über die Grundrechte des Menschen)
Come Follow Me
(Volume 1, Sannyas/Droemer Knaur)
(Komm und folge mir)
Come Follow Me (Volume 2, Sannyas)
(Jesus aber schwieg)
Come Follow Me (Volume 3, Sannyas)
(Jesus - der Menschensohn)

Dimensions Beyond the Known (Sannyas)
(Sprung ins Unbekannte)
Ecstasy: The Forgotten Language
(Herzschlag)
(Ekstase: Die vergessenen Sprache)

From Sex to Superconsciousness
(New Age/Thomas Martin)
(Vom Sex zum
kosmischen Bewusstsein)
Glimpses of a Golden Childhood
(Goldmann)
(Goldene Augenblicke:
Portrait einer Jugend in Indien)

Hammer on the Rock (Fischer)
(Sprengt den Fels der Unbewusstheit)
I Am the Gate (Sannyas)
(Ich bin der Weg)
Intelligence of the Heart
(Compilation only in German,
Herzschlag)
(Intelligenz des Herzens)
Meditation: The Art of Inner Ecstasy
(Heyne)
(Meditation: Die Kunst,
zu sich selbst zu finden)

My Way: The Way of the White Clouds
(Herzschlag)
(Mein Weg:
Der Weg der weissen Wolke)
Nirvana: The Last Nightmare
(Rajneesh Verlag/RFE)
(Nirvana:
Die letzte Huerde auf dem Weg)
No Water, No Moon (Herzschlag)
(Kein Wasser, Kein Mond)
Roots and Wings
(Volume 1, Edition Lotus)
(Mit Wurzeln und Fluegeln)

Roots and Wings
    (Volume 2, Edition Lotus)
    (Die Schuhe auf dem Kopf)
Spiritual Development & Sexuality
    (Fischer)
    (Spirituelle Entwicklung
    und Sexualitaet)
Tantra, Spirituality & Sex
    (Rajneesh Verlag)
    (Tantra, Spiritualitaet und Sex)
Tantra, Spirituality & Sex (Sannyas)
    (Tantrische Liebeskunst)
Tantra, The Supreme Understanding
    (Sannyas)
    (Tantra: Die hoechste Einsicht)
The Book of the Secrets
    (Volume 1, Heyne)
    (Das Buch der Geheimnisse)
The Goose Is Out! (Rajneesh Verlag)
    (Die Gans ist raus!)
The Great Challenge (Sannyas)
    (Rebellion der Seele)
The Hidden Harmony (Sannyas)
    (Die verborgene Harmonie)
The Mustard Seed
    (Rajneesh Verlag/Heyne)
    (Die verbotene Wahrheit)
The Orange Book (Rajneesh Verlag/RFE)
    (Das Orangene Buch)
The Psychology of the Esoteric (Sannyas)
    (Esoterische Psychologie)
The Search (Sambuddha)
    (Auf der Suche)
The Sound of One Hand Clapping
    (Edition Gyandip)
    (Das Klatschen der einen Hand)
The Tantra Vision (Volume 1, Heyne)
    (Tantrische Vision)

The True Sage (Edition Lotus)
    (Alchemie der Verwandlung
Until You Die (Edition Gyandip)
    (Nicht bevor du stirbst)
What is Meditation
    (Compilation, Sannyas)
    (Was ist Meditation?)
Yoga: The Alpha and the Omega
    (Volume 1, Edition Gyandip)
    (Yoga: Alpha und Omega)
Intelligenz des Herzens
    (Excerpts, only in German,
    Herzschlag)
Sexualitaet und Aids
    (Excerpts, only in German,
    Rajneesh Verlag)
Der Hoehepunkt des Lebens
    (Excerpts, only in German,
    Rajneesh Verlag)
Kunst kommt nicht vom Koennen
    (Excerpts, only in German,
    Rajneesh Verlag)
Liebe beginnt nach den Flitterwochen
    (Excerpts, only in German,
    Rajneesh Verlag)

Greek

Bhagwan Shree Rajneesh on
    Basic Human Rights
    (Swami Anand Ram)
    (Bhagwan Shree Rajneesh Gia
    Ta Vasika Anthropina Dikeomata)
The Hidden Harmony (PIGI/Rassoulis)
    (I Krifi Armonia)

Hebrew

Tantra: The Supreme Understanding
    (Massada)
    (Tantra: Ha'havana Ha'eelaeet)

Italian

Bhagwan Shree Rajneesh
  On Basic Human Rights
  (Rajneesh Services Corporation)
  (Bhagwan Shree Rajneesh Parla
  Sui Diritti Dell'Uomo)
Dimensions Beyond the Known
  (Mediterranee/Re Nudo)
  (Dimensioni Oltre il Conosciuto)
Ecstasy: The Forgotten Language
  (Riza Libri)
  (Estasi: Il Linguaggio Dimenticato)
From Sex to Superconsciousness (Basaia)
  (Dal Sesso all'Eros Cosmico)
Guida Spirituale (Mondadori)
  (La Guida Spirituale)
I am the Gate (Meditarranee)
  (Io Sono La Soglia)
Meditation: The Art of Inner Ecstasy
  (Mediterranee)
  (Meditazione Dinamica:
  L'Arte dell'Estasi Interiore)
My Way: The Way of the White Clouds
  (Mediterranee)
  (La Mia Via:
  La Via delle Nuvole Bianche)
Nirvana: The Last Nightmare (Basaia)
  (Nirvana: L'Ultimo Incubo)
No Water, No Moon (Mediterranee)
  (Dieci Storie Zen di Bhagwan Shree
  Rajneesh: Ne Acqua, Ne Luna)
Philosphia Perennis (ECIG)
  (Philosofia Perennis)
Seeds of Revolution (Sugarco)
  (Semi di Sagezza)
Tantra, Spirituality & Sex
  (Rajneesh Foundation Italy)
  (Tantra Spiritualita e Sesso)

Tantra, The Supreme Understanding
  (Bompiani)
  (Tantra: La Comprensione Suprema)
Tao: The Three Treasures
  (Volumes 1-3, Re Nudo)
  (Tao: I Tre Tesori)
Techniques of Liberation (La Salamandra)
  (Tecniche di Liberazione)
The Book of The Secrets
  (Volume 1, Bompiani)
  (Il Libro dei Segreti)
The Hidden Harmony
  (Volumes 1 & 2, Re Nudo/ECIG)
  (L'Armonia Nascosta)
The Mustard Seed (Volumes 1-3,
  Rajneesh Foundation Italy)
  (Il Seme della Ribellione)
The New Alchemy To Turn You On
  (Vol. 1&2,Psiche)
  (La Nuova Alchimia)
The Orange Book (Bompiani)
  (Il Libro Arancione)
The Psychology of the Esoteric
  (Mediterranee)
  (La Rivoluzione Interiore)
The Rajneesh Bible (Volume 1, Bompiani)
  (La Bibbia di Rajneesh)
The Search (La Salamandra)
  (La Ricerca)
The Supreme Doctrine (Rizzoli)
  (La Dottrina Suprema)
The Tantra Vision (Riza)
  (La Visione Tantrica)

Japanese

Bhagwan Shree Rajneesh
  On Basic Human Rights
  (Meisosha Ltd.)

Dance Your Way to God
 (Rajneesh Publications)
From Sex to Superconsciousness
 (Rajneesh Publications)
Meditation: The Art of Ecstasy (Merkmal)
My Way: The Way of the White Clouds
 (Rajneesh Publications)
Tantra: The Supreme Understanding
 (Merkmal)
Tao: The Three Treasures
 (Volumes 1-4, Merkmal)
The Beloved (Volumes 1 & 2, Merkmal)
The Diamond Sutra
 (Meisosha Ltd./LAF Mitsuya)
The Empty Boat (Volumes 1 & 2,
 Rajneesh Publications)
The Grass Grows by Itself (Fumikura)
The Heart Sutra (Merkmal)
The Mustard Seed
 (Volumes 1 & 2, Merkmal)
The Orange Book
 (Wholistic Therapy Institute)
The Search (Merkmal)
Until You Die (Fumikura)

Korean
Tao: The Pathless Path (Chung Ha)
 (Vol 1&2 The Pathless Path,
 Vol 3&4 Theory of Happiness)
The Art of Dying (Chung Ha)
The Divine Melody (Chung Ha)
The Empty Boat (Chung Ha)
The Grass Grows by itself (Chung Ha)

Portuguese
Come Follow Me
 (Volume 1, Global/Ground)
 (Palavras De Fogo)

Dimensions Beyond the Known (Cultrix)
 (Dimensoes Alem do Conhecido)
Ecstasy, The Forgotten Language (Global)
 (Extase: A Linguagem Esquecida)
From Sex to Superconsciousness (Cultrix)
 (Do Sexo A Supersconsciencia)
I am the Gate (Pensamento)
 (Eu Sou A Porta)
Meditation: The Art of Inner Ecstasy
 (Cultrix)
 (Meditacao: A Arte Do Extase)
My Way: The Way of the White Clouds
 (Tao Livraria & Editora)
 (Meu Caminho:
 O Cominho Das Nuvens Brancas)
No Water, No Moon (Pensamento)
 (Nem Agua , Nem Lua)
Notes of a Madman (NAIM)
 (Notas De Um Homem Louco)
Roots and Wings (Cultrix)
 (Raizes E Asas)
Sufis: The People of the Path
 (Maha Lakshmi Editora)
 (Sufis: O Povo do Caminho)
Tantra, Spirituality & Sex (Agora)
 (Tantra: Sexo E Espiritualidade)
Tantra, The Supreme Understanding
 (Cultrix)
 (Tantra: A Suprema Comprensao)
The Art of Dying (Global)
 (Arte de Morrer)
The Book of the Secrets
 (Volumes 1 & 2,
 Maha Lakshmi Editora)
 (O Livro Dos Segredos)
The Cypress in the Courtyard (Cultrix)
 (O Cipreste No Jardim)
The Divine Melody (Cultrix)
 (A Divina Melodia)

The Hidden Harmony (Pensamento)
  (A Harmonia Oculta)
The Mustard Seed (Volumes 1 & 2,
  Tao Livraria & Editora)
  (A Semente De Mostarda)
The New Alchemy To Turn You On
  (Cultrix)
  (A Nova Alquimia)
The Orange Book (Pensamento)
  (O Livro Orange)
The Psychology of the Esoteric
  (Tao Livaria & Editora)
  (A Psicologia Do Esoterico)
Unio Mystica (Maha Lakshmi)
  (Unio Mystica)

Russian
Bhagwan Shree Rajneesh
  On Basic Human Rights
  (Rajneesh Foundation Europe)

Serbo-Croat
Bhagwan Shree Rajneesh (Compilation of
  various quotations, Swami Mahavira)

Spanish
Come Follow Me
  (Volume 1, Sagaro, Chile)
  (Ven, Sigueme)
I am The Gate (Editorial Diana, Mexico)
  (Yo Soy La Puerta)
Meditation, The Art of Inner Ecstasy
  (Rosello Impresiones)
  (Meditacion: El Arte del Extasis)
My Way: The Way of the White Clouds
  (Editorial Cuatro Vientos)
  (El Camino de las Nubes Blancas)

Only One Sky (Collection Tantra)
  (Solo Un Cielo)
Tantra: The Supreme Understanding
  (Volumes 1 & 2, Rosello Impresiones)
  (Introduccion al Mundo del Tantra)
Tao: The Three Treasures
  (Editorial Sirio, Spain)
  (Tao: Los Tres Tesoros)
The Heart Sutra (Sarvogeet, Spain)
  (El Sutra del Corazon)
The Psychology of the Esoteric
  (Editorial Cuatro Vientos, Chile)
  (Psicologia de lo Esoterico:
  La Nueva Evolucion del Hombre)
The Ultimate Risk
  (Editorial Martinez Roca, Spain)
  (El Riesgo Supremo)
What Is Meditation?
  (Koan/Rosello
  Impresiones/Pastanaga)
  (Que Es Meditacion?)

Swedish
The Great Challenge (Livskraft)
  (Den Vaeldiga Utmaningen)

RAJNEESH MEDITATION CENTERS, ASHRAMS AND COMMUNES

ARGENTINA
Niketana Rajneesh Meditation Center
Combate de los Pozos 764
1222 Buenos Aires
Argentina

AUSTRIA
Deepa Rajneesh Meditation Center
Kripstrasse 31
6060 Absam
Austria

AUSTRALIA
Prabhakar Rajneesh Meditation Center
c/o Post Office
Innot Hot Springs
North Queensland 4872
Australia

Rajneeshgrad Neo-Sannyas Commune
P.O. Box 1097
160 High Street
Fremantle WA 6160
Australia

Kalika Rajneesh Meditation Center
25 Martin Street
Cairns 4870
Australia

BELGIUM
Suryodaya Rajneesh Meditation Center
Rue de Drapieres 12
B-1050 Bruxelles
Belgium

BRAZIL
Sudhakar Rajneesh Meditation Center
Rua Getulio Vargas 80
Cabos Rio
Rio de Janeiro 28900
Brazil

Abhudaya Rajneesh Meditation Center
Caixa Postal 2651
Porto Allegre 90000 R/S
Brazil

Amaraloka Rajneesh Meditation Center
Rua Noel Torezin No. 83
Campo Belo
Sao Paulo SP 04615
Brazil

Purnam Rajneesh Meditation Center
Caixa Postal 1946
Rio Grande do Sul
Porto Allegre 90000
Brazil

Anurag Rajneesh Meditation Center
Avenida Recife 4282
Modulo 4, Ap.to 314 ES
Tancia-Recife 50000
Brazil

Jwala Rajneesh Meditation Center
Avenida Nico Pecanta 50
Sala 2315, Edificio Rodoefo
De Padi Centro
Rio de Janeiro
Brazil

Premadhara Rajneesh Meditation Center
Av. Dep. Paulino Rocha 1001
Ap.to 402, Sqn. Bloco H
Castelao
Fortaneza-Ceara 60000
Brazil

CANADA
Samaroha Rajneesh Meditation Center
1774 Tolmie Street
Vancouver B.C. V6R 4B8
Canada

CHILE
Pramada Rajneesh Meditation Center
Genaro Prieto 2363
Providencia
Santiago
Chile

COLOMBIA
Padma Rajneesh Meditation Center
Apartado Aereo 4128
Medellin
Colombia

DENMARK
Sahajo Rajneesh Meditation Center
Sudergade 26 1
3000 Helsinger
Denmark

Rajneesh Institute for Spiritual Creativity
Bogballevey 3
Tonning
8740 Braeostrup
Denmark

Khalaas Rajneesh Meditation Center
Museumsstien 8
9990 Skagen
Denmark

Anwar Rajneesh Meditation Center
Thorsgade 74, 4TV
2200 Copenhagen N
Denmark

ECUADOR

Moulik Rajneesh Meditation Center
Eustorgio Salgado 197, piso 3
Miraflores Quito
Ecuador

FINLAND

Leela Rajneesh Meditation Center
Merimiehenkatu 16B 24
00150 Helsinki 15
Finland

FRANCE

Rajneesh Meditation Center
60 Ave. Charles de Gaulle
92200 Neuilly
France

GREECE

Darshan Rajneesh Meditation Center
20 Aribou Street
11633 Athens
Greece

Surya Rajneesh Meditation Center
Oia-Santorini
Greece

Mallika Rajneesh Meditation Center
Nikiforou Ouranour 25-A
11499 Athens
Greece

INDIA

Rajyoga Rajneesh Meditation Center
C5/44 Safdarjang Development Area
Opposite ITT, Palam Road
110016 New Delhi
India

Rajneeshdham Rajneesh Neo-Sannyas
Commune
17 Koregaon Park
411001 Poona
India

Shanti Rajneesh Meditation Center
236 Guru Teg Bahadur Nagar
Jalandar City
Punjab
India

ITALY

Divyananda Rajneesh Meditation Center
Pensione Tambo
Alpe Motta
Italy

Vishad Rajneesh Meditation Center
Castelvecchio di Compito
55062 Lucca
Italy

Devamani Rajneesh Meditation Center
Via Basilica 5
10122 Torino
Italy

Miasto Rajneesh Neo-Sannyas Commune
Podere San Giorgio
Cotorniano
53010 Frosini (SI)
Italy

JAPAN
Eer Rajneesh Neo-Sannyas Commune
Mimura Building 6-21-34 Kikuna
Kohoku-ku
Yokohama 222
Japan

Mahamani Rajneesh Meditation Center
105 Country Heights
635 Shimabukuro
Kitanakagusuku-son
Okinawa 901-23
Japan

Sitara Rajneesh Meditation Center
498-218, Teine-miyanosawa
Nishi-ku
Sapporo-shi
Hokkaido
Japan

Svagat Rajneesh Meditation Center
1-22-46 Nishi-Nakada
Sendai-Shi Miyagi-Pref. 981-11
Japan

KENYA
Archana Rajneesh Meditation Center
P.O. Box 82501
Mombasa
Kenya

Preetam Rajneesh Meditation Center
P.O. Box 10256
Nairobi
Kenya

MEXICO
Madhu Rajneesh Meditation Center
Rancho Cutzi Minzicuri
San Juan de Vina
Tacambaro
Michoacan
Mexico

NEPAL
Asheesh Rajneesh Meditation Center
P.O. Box 278
Pulchowk
Kathmandu
Nepal

Rajneesh Teerth Neo-Sannyas Commune
Masina Patan
P.O. Box 91
Pokhara
Nepal

Satmarga Rajneesh Meditation Center
Mahendra Pul
Pokhara
Nepal

NETHERLANDS
Arvind Rajneesh Meditation Center
Hoge Larenseweg 168
1221 AV Hilversum
Netherlands

Amaltas Rajneesh Meditation Center
Staalwijklaan 4
3763 LG Soest
Netherlands

Mudita Rajneesh Meditation Center
Veldhuizenstraat 2 Gein
1072 Amsterdam
Netherlands

De Nieuwe Mens
Enschedesestraat 305
7552 CV Hengelo (O)
Netherlands

Rajneesh Humaniversity Foundation
Dr Wiardi Beckmanlaan 4
1931 BW Engmond aan Zee
Netherlands

Wajid Rajneesh Meditation Center
Prins Hendrikplein 1
2518 JA Den Haag
Netherlands

Prakash Rajneesh Meditation Center
Dykhuizenweg 70
9903 AE Appingedam
Netherlands

De Stad Rajneesh Mystery School
Cornelis Troostplein 23
1072 J Amsterdam
Netherlands

Padam Rajneesh Meditation Center
Koningsoord 10
9984 XH Oudeschip
Netherlands

NEW ZEALAND
Shunyadeep Rajneesh Meditation Center
42 Park Road
Mirimar
Wellington
New Zealand

Rajneesh Meditation Center
P.O. Box 29132
Greenwoods Center
Epsom
Auckland 3
New Zealand

NORWAY
Devananda Rajneesh Meditation Center
Post Box 177
Vinderen
N-0319 Oslo 3
Norway

PERU
Adityo Rajneesh Meditation Center
Paseo de la Republica 4670 Depto E
Miraflores
Lima 18
Peru

PORTUGAL
Karam Rajneesh Meditation Center
Rua Conselhevio Fernando de Mello
3360 Penacova (Coimbra)
Portugal

SPAIN

Kamli Rajneesh Meditation Center
Apartado de Correos 607
Ibiza
Spain

La Gomera
Argayall
Valle Gran Rey
Canary Islands
Spain

Krisana Rajneesh Meditation Center
Futonia S.A.
c/ Juan de Urbieta 61
28007 Madrid
Spain

SWEDEN

Madhur Rajneesh Meditation Center
Foervattarvagen 40
S-16142 Bromma
Sweden

SWITZERLAND

Almasta Rajneesh Meditation Center
9 Av. des Arpilleres
1224 Chene-Bougerie
Geneva
Switzerland

Mingus Rajneesh Meditation Center
Asylstrasse 11
8032 Zurich
Switzerland

Nisargam Rajneesh Meditation Center
16 Rue Etienne Dumont
1204 Geneva
Switzerland

USA

Bhagwatam Rajneesh Meditation Center
P.O. Box 2886 (Altos)
Old San Juan, PR 00905
U.S.A.

Devadeep Rajneesh Meditation Center
Dicob Road
P.O. Box 1
Lowville, NY 13367
U.S.A.

Devadeep Rajneesh Meditation Center
1430 Longfellow St. NW.
Washington, DC 20011
U.S.A.

Devatara Rajneesh Meditation Center
155 Spencer Ave.
Lynbrook, L.I., NY 11563
U.S.A.

Dharmadeep Rajneesh Meditation Center
2455 6th Avenue N.
St. Petersburg, FL 33713
U.S.A.

Fulwari Rajneesh Meditation Center
1726 Hillmont Drive
Nashville, TN 37215
U.S.A.

Mahima Rajneesh Meditation Center
P.O. Box 1863
Makawao, HI 96768
U.S.A.

Nanda Rajneesh Meditation Center
31486 West St.
South Laguna, CA 92677
U.S.A.

Neeraj Rajneesh Meditation Center
2493 McGovern Drive
Schenectady, NY 12309
U.S.A.

Premsindhu Rajneesh Meditation Center
214 Beryl Street
Mill Valley, CA 94941
U.S.A.

Rajneesh Institute for Meditation
and Therapy
P.O. Box 13515
Boulder, CO 80308
U.S.A.

Rajneesh Institute for Tao
201 North Ave.
Weston, MA 02193
U.S.A.

Rakesh Rajneesh Meditation Center
P.O. Box 1554
Kapas, HI 96746
U.S.A.

Sangit Rajneesh Meditation Center
2920 Healy Ave.
Far Rockaway, NY 11691
U.S.A.

Sudhakar Rajneesh Meditation Center
1511 7th Street
Wausau, WI 54401
U.S.A.

Sukhdhama Rajneesh Meditation Center
1546 28th Street No. 412
Boulder, CO 80303
U.S.A.

Suranga Rajneesh Meditation Center
5852 Dewey Blvd.
Sacramento, CA 95824
U.S.A.

Suravi Rajneesh Meditation Center
P.O. Box 20026
Seattle, WA 98102
U.S.A.

Surdham Rajneesh Meditation Center
The Nest, 75-111
Indian Wells, CA 92210
U.S.A.

Tara Rajneesh Meditation Center
2240 S. Patterson Blvd. 4
Dayton, OH 45409
U.S.A.

Vibhakara Rajneesh Meditation Center
P.O. Box 5161
Woodland Park, CO 80866
U.S.A.

Yakaru Rajneesh Meditation Center
P.O. Box 130
Laytonville, CA 95454
U.S.A.

VENEZUELA

Dana Rajneesh Meditation Center
Edif. La Vera Piso 7 Apto 74
Resid. Sans-Souci
Chacaito
Caracas
Venezuela

WEST GERMANY

Prasuna Rajneesh Meditation Center
Denekinger Weg 60
5880 Luedenscheid
West Germany

Nishant Rajneesh Meditation Center
c/o Tassy Family
Hoer Rain 6 Weichendorf
8608 Memmelsdorf
West Germany

Pradip Rajneesh Meditation Center
and Art Center
Hardtstrasse 7
5000 Cologne 41
West Germany

Darpan Rajneesh Meditation Center
Suedendstrasse 36
7500 Karlsruhe 1
West Germany

Mukto Rajneesh Meditation Center
Roonstrasse 79
2800 Bremen
West Germany

Rakesh Rajneesh Meditation Center
Am Hang 1
8063 Oberumbach
West Germany

Digant Rajneesh Meditation Center
Philippinenhoeferweg 75
3500 Kassel
West Germany

Sirat Rajneesh Meditation Center
Hohbuchstrasse 50
7410 Reutlingen
West Germany

Sampat Rajneesh Meditation Center
Mendelweg 5
7900 Ulm/Lehr
West Germany

Geha Rajneesh Meditation Center
Winterstetten 44
7970 Leutkirch
West Germany

Prabha Rajneesh Meditation Center
Husarenstrasse 38
3300 Braunschweig
West Germany

Ansumala Rajneesh Meditation Center
Kaps 1
8219 Rimsting
West Germany

Dharmadeep Rajneesh Institute
for Meditation and Spiritual Growth
Karolinenstrasse 7-9
2000 Hamburg 6
West Germany

Doerfchen Rajneesh Institute for Spiritual
Therapy and Meditation
Dahlmannstrasse 9
1000 Berlin 12
West Germany

Mani Rajneesh Meditation Center
Johannes-Buell Weg 13 II
2000 Hamburg 65
West Germany

Nityam Rajneesh Meditation Center
Villa Roedelstein
6551 Altenbamberg
West Germany

Premapara Rajneesh Meditation Center
Asternweg 4
8900 Augsburg 1
West Germany

Purnam Rajneesh Neo-Sannyas
Commune
Graf-Adolf Strasse 87
4000 Duesseldorf 1
West Germany

Rajneesh Academy for Harmonious
Integration
and Meditation (RAHIM)
Rahim/Rast e.V.
Merianstrasse 12
7800 Freiburg
West Germany

Rajneesh-Stadt
Strickhauserstrasse 39
2882 Ovelgoenne
West Germany

Tao Rajneesh Zentrum
Klenzestrasse 41
8000 Muenchen 5
West Germany

Uta Rajneesh Institute fuer Spirituelle
Therapie und Meditation
Venloerstrasse 5-7
5000 Koeln 1
West Germany